IN PRAISE OF ENGLISH

IN PRAISE OF
ENGLISH

THE
GROWTH & USE
OF LANGUAGE

JOSEPH T. SHIPLEY

Times
BOOKS

Grateful acknowledgment is made for use of the
following material: from *Man and Superman*, to the
Society of Authors on behalf of the Bernard Shaw
Estate; four clerihews of E. C. Bentley, to Nicolas
Bentley; verses from *Poems* by C. S. Lewis, to Wil-
liam Collins Sons and Co., Ltd.

Designed by Beth Tondreau

Library of Congress Cataloging in Publication Data

Shipley, Joseph Twadell, 1893–
Word ways in English.

Bibliography: p.
Includes index.
1. English language. I. Title.
PE1072.S54   420   77–4956
ISBN 0–8129–0696–9

CONTENTS

PREFACE

UNTOLD NUMBERS OF SPECIALIZED BOOKS have been written on the various forms and functions of words—words growing into language, words expressing ideas, words shaped for practical uses, words fashioned into entertainment and art. And it occurred to me that perhaps I could weave the many threads into a new design, with thoughts of my own, within the compass of a single volume. This has been my endeavor.

The book begins, then, with the speculations as to the way prehistoric man acquired the faculty of speech, on his gradual climb toward humanity—the ability to make not merely sounds but words. It then journeys along the three thousand or more years from the great migrations of the Indo-European tribes—which, as it indicates, fortified male dominance—up the long road to modern English; with a further view of the trips across the Atlantic and the shaping of the language in the United States.

The book then turns to words in themselves, and in their relations to other words. It examines the basic democratic process in word formation; how the lower levels of society are indeed more influential in the constant change of language than the "upper crust"—as most of our English words from Latin through French came not from the polished prose of Cicero, but from the "vulgar" speech, the talk of the rough Roman soldier and the itinerant trader.

The various ways of word growth are thus examined. We see how grammar spreads into linguistics, how synonyms and antonyms add complexity and discrimination to our tongue. We note the accident of homonyms—words that are alike in sound or form —leading on the one hand to wordplay, to puns, and on the other hand to confusion, to boners and similar blunders. We observe the problems of jargon, and the prevalence of slang, bringing quick color to the current speech. The ways of words may be weird.

Then the book faces the questions raised by recorded language. Since for centuries words were never set down, since even today all over the world great numbers are illiterate, we must ask how essential, really, is the ability to read and write. We note that there are many different forms of writing—English, Hebrew, Arabic, Greek, Russian, Chinese, and more—so that to those unfamiliar with a particular script (as most of us are, with written forms other than our own), the characters set down might as well be hieroglyphics. And even in any one language, as in English, on the surface level we observe different problems, such as pronunciation in speech, and punctuation in writing.

The book, turning to communication, observes the various ways in which men have railed at one another, the vitupery of swearing. We note that there have even been formal varieties of verbal abuse, as when the bard preceded the ancient army onto the battlefield, hurling insults like so many darts at the advancing foe; as in the early English rhymed scurrilous flytings; as in the more recent (Black) dozens.

More often, we note, men have sought to avoid disagreeable subjects; euphemism, a pleasant way of referring to an unpleasant matter, is well-nigh universal. And here, *for the first time,* is a survey, with illustrative quotations, of the changing attitudes toward the sexual "taboo" words, the socially "forbidden" four-letter words, from the time of Chaucer to our own day.

Noting that words exist to convey (or conceal) ideas, we are drawn to the field of logic. The book considers the various types of reasoning, different for questions of fact and questions of policy. "Lies, damn lies, and statistics." The four meanings of *average.*

The book notes how psychology and advertising look at the same things from different points of view, pointing out how the promotion of cosmetics—even of habit-forming drugs—is bound up with words.

But, as words are also used to express our feelings, scientific language must be distinguished from emotive. We observe that belief itself is partly a matter of words: given a name, like flying saucers or the Loch Ness monster, one tends to assume that it stands for something real.

The emotive use of words leads us to the wide field of art. The book first examines, here, the distinction between poetry and prose. This is a prelude to the examination of what we embrace in the word *beauty*.

This is followed by a consideration of the other literary forms, drama, novel, and essay. No history of these is attempted, but rather an examination of their fundamental qualities and forms. The "geography" of the novel. The four degrees of likelihood in fiction. Originality. Satire, with its various aids, such as irony. This brings us to look at recent emphases: black humor, the angry, the absurd. The book takes a special look at criticism, and the critic.

The book then turns to the chief weapons of emotive language, in both art and life (as in slang): metaphor, and symbolism. It shows how the new ways of handling metaphor are the source of much of the difficulty in interpreting modern poetry. And it traces a potent application of symbols in the age-long influence of astrology, which is little checked by religion.

A special chapter on word games (riddles, anagrams, crosswords, and more) indicates how patterns that had serious beginnings, in ancient Greece, in the Bible, and in folklore, have lapsed into play—and may soar into beauty.

Finally, the problems of confused or misused language are faced, and the emphases of thought versus feeling. Examples are given of obfuscation, which blurs the distinction between the pretended and the profound. Man's future depends upon the proper use of words.

At appropriate points throughout the volume, there are observations on other aspects of words: long words, hard words, abandoned words, ghost words, words that mean their own opposite, nymble words, words of play, words of taunting, words of wisdom.

In other words, where in life do we get along without words? Such areas are not within this book's ranging and arranging.

And I hope you will enjoy the journeying as much as I enjoyed the tracing of the itinerary.

JOSEPH T. SHIPLEY
New York and London
1977

IN PRAISE OF ENGLISH

1.

THE START

THE BASIC UNANSWERED QUESTION about language is how it came to be. A simple response is to state that on a Friday in October 4004 B.C. (as calculated in the seventeenth century by Bishop Ussher) God, who in the beginning was the Word, created Adam, then Eve, and gave them the gift of the Word. And God led all the animals—well, a goodly variety of them—before Adam, and what Adam called each of them, that was its name.

The problem is more complex for those that believe God, or nature, or a Big Bang—or, more precisely, a Big Squeeze—perhaps twenty billion years ago started radiation and whirling atoms in a not wholly understood process of evolution, which worked its way tortuously to what biologists call *homo sapiens*, but we may call *homo loquens*, talking man. That the organs of speech were ready in anticipation of their use we may call teleology, but to label is not to explain.

In the absence of knowledge, various guesses as to how speech began, labeled hypotheses, have been advanced. Each of these has many scornful dissenters, and the methods have been given names by the mockers. In this century, these have become the usual terms.

1. The bow-wow notion suggests that human speech arose in imitation of animal cries. This is perhaps the weakest of the suggestions, for, while animals can roar, growl, whimper, purr, and whine, incipient men could no doubt make similar emotional sounds, and there seems no good reason to suppose that they learned speech from creatures with smaller and less convoluted brains. As Bertrand Russell phrased the objection, no matter how eloquently a dog may bark, he cannot tell you that his parents were poor but honest.

3

2. The ding-dong notion has the largest number of actual words in its support, for it suggests that speech arose in imitation of the sounds of nature. There are indeed many echoic (onomatopoetic) words, such as *crack, buzz, click, snap, splash,* with more intricate approximations of nature such as Tennyson's lines in *The Princess:*

> Sweeter thy voice, but every sound is sweet;
> Myriads of rivulets hurrying thro' the lawn,
> The moan of doves in immemorial elms
> And murmuring of innumerable bees.

Other people hear other sounds. A Chinese scholar has protested to me that his ears are alerted to quite different noises when a hen clucks, a bee buzzes, a stick cracks, a gun fires. This, however, in no way challenges the theory, as each language may form words from the sounds its users hear. This is true even within one language family; English *cockadoodledoo* is French *coquerico.* (And next time you are in the barnyard, try to hear that initial *k* sound!) A cat in France purrs *ron-ron;* in Germany it purrs *schnurr.*

It remains difficult, however, to discern an echoic origin for most of our words, such as *make, steal, happen,* not to mention *beauty, science, machine, hypothesis.*

3. The ha-ha notion claims that speech evolved from the bubbling spontaneous laughter of the happy babe, whose meaningless joyful prattle gradually assumed significance. This idea is strengthened, is complemented rather than replaced, by the next.

4. The ba-ba notion lays greater stress on the crying of the hungry or uncomfortable infant. At first its cries are automatic; then it discovers that the noise activates a parental response, whereupon the crying becomes deliberate, directed toward a goal: the proffer of breast or bottle, or dry diaper. And with that purposeful utterance, says philosopher R. G. Collingwood, "language is born; its articulation into fully developed speech in English or French or some other vernacular is only a matter of detail." This assumes, however, that the adults are already speaking a vernacular, have already acquired the true (not the "ecstatic") gift of tongues. These two processes may thus more accurately describe the manner in which each newborn child in every generation learns to talk, than the way in which speech originally came into being. The next few suggestions therefore turn to aspects of more adult learning.

5. The sing-song notion suggests that man's first speech was

song. Looking down a hillside to a lush valley watered by a limpid stream, all graced by the warming sun, man in exuberant spirits burst into exultant or thankful sound. A sort of primitive yodeling soon became a signal to fellow-tribesman or mate on the opposite hill. The Greeks accepted this idea of the origin of speech; it had weight also with Darwin, and the astute linguist Jespersen.

6. The pooh-pooh notion turns upon other spontaneous utterances, emotional cries of anger, triumph, pain. Expressive gestures are naturally accompanied by appropriate sounds. And gradually the symptom becomes the symbol.

7. The yo-he-ho notion is allied to this, in the thought that speech arose from the grunts and calls and signals of cooperative labor. Men surrounding a bear at bay, men hauling a great log to hew out a boat, called together, often rhythmically, to guide their movements, and evolved a primitive speech.

8. Abandoning these approaches, the ma-ma notion claims that the speech faculty is given, not derived; it is innate. In India, the god Indra is credited with inventing speech, and myths around the world make similar attributions. Socrates declared that the gods named things in the proper way. Words were thus holy; from this sprang the relation of *nomen et omen:* knowledge of the name gave power over the thing named. Even today, the Jews do not use the hidden name of their God. As William James remarked: "Solomon knew the names of all the spirits and, knowing their names, he held them subject to his will." Words may have magic power. Ali Baba said "Open sesame" and the treasure cave of the Forty Thieves unshut its hermetic door.

Those accepting the idea of an innate capacity for speech without attributing its existence to a god, assume a natural development, such as the pursing lips of the suckling babe, which seem to form an *m-m-m.* We return to this sound when we call something 'yum-yum,' and of course it comes close to us in *mamma—mother, Mutter, mater, mère,* and all the suckling *mammals.* Greek *mamme* meant 'grandmother'; Ben Jonson coined *mammethrept* to mean 'spoiled child'.

9. Finally, the pa-pa notion relies on the simple method of trial and error. There was a need to communicate—and language emerged. Difficult or inappropriate sounds were sloughed; communication struggled through. This idea has at least the added attraction that it is the second step in all the other hypotheses. However language may have started, this is how it grew, and still is growing.

While a germ of truth may lie within each of these notions, there is no carbon test or other device to probe prehistory and establish when or how the first speakers achieved meaningful word forms. To check unending argument, in 1866 the Linguistic Society of Paris ruled that its members indulge in no further speculation as to the origin of language. It may be well, now, to obey that rule.

Language, of course, depends mainly upon sound. There seem to be, in all human speech, some ninety phonemes, units of sound. English uses forty-five sound devices, lacking, among others, the rolled r of the French, the *ch* of the German, and the clicks of the Hottentot and the Xhosa. It employs twenty-one consonants, nine vowels, three semivowels (r,w,y). In addition, as a paralanguage, there are four stresses, four pitches, three terminal contours (as the voice rises, falls, or stays level), and one juncture.

Stresses, accents—the loudness or softness, the volume of sound put into a syllable—may in English indicate a difference in use, as con'duct for the noun, conduct' for the verb; or a difference in meaning, as with en'trance and entrance'. In ancient Greece, a courtesan's fate might depend upon a judge's emphasis. The sentence *Hetaira khrysia ei phoroie, demosia esto,* if stressed *demo'sia,* means "If a courtesan wears gold ornaments, they are to become public property"; if stressed *demosi'a:* "*she* is to become public property."

Pitch—the degree of highness or acuteness, lowness or graveness, of a sound, determined by the rapidity of the vibrations by which it is produced—may indicate a question, or a mood such as surprise, indignation, depression, remorse. In other tongues—some Chinese languages have as many as nine pitches—it may mark a change of meaning. In Northern Chinese, for instance, *ma* in a level tone signifies 'mother'; a rising tone, 'hemp'; a falling tone, 'curse'.

Juncture is the linking of sounds to form words, and their separation, to distinguish one word from another. The placing of an almost imperceptible but significant pause distinguishes *that stuff* from *that's tough.* "It's mother love" may easily become "smother love." The household poetess Ella Wheeler Wilcox no doubt felt it a stroke of genius when she wrote "My soul is a lighthouse keeper." She was less overjoyed when she saw in proof: "My soul is a light housekeeper." Improper juncture is slovenly, and may lead to misunderstanding; but even children may be, crudely, aware of juncture, as when a boy writes, and asks his friend to pronounce, "Iced ink."

In colloquial speech, English may take on a faulty assimilation: "I'm going gout. Goobye. I'll be back in teminutes." In French, it is not an error but a standard binding liaison, when a usually unpronounced final letter (s, t, z) is sounded, attached to the vowel that begins the following word. Such improper juncture, in English, has changed some words: *an ekename* ('extra name') is now *a nickname; a nauger* is now *an auger*.

The juncture pause, always essential, may be extended and acquire special significance. Silence, says psychiatrist Joost A. M. Meerloo, is a neglected aspect of the study of communication. An orator, and a comedian, should have a good sense of timing, knowing when, and how long, to pause. A good dramatist makes constant use of this aspect of speech, with keen awareness of its values. "The most precious things in speech," said actor Sir Ralph Richardson, "are pauses." Talking, said the Autocrat of the Breakfast Table, "is like playing on the harp: there is as much in laying the hands on the strings to stop their vibrations as in twanging on them to bring out their music." Without juncture, speech would be a confusing continuum of sound.

In addition to these more formal devices of sound, and silence between sounds, there are the accompanying indications of the body, in posture, gesture, and facial expression, which help to establish the speaker's intent, be it pleasant or provocative, ingratiating or ironic. Some utterances impel the persons addressed to demand: "Say that with a smile!" A specific motion, posture, or facial expression is called a *kinè*, from *kinesics*, the study of nonverbal communication.

Paralanguage may be in part determined by one's profession. The minister, the teacher, the disc jockey, may develop patterns of address that carry their professional manner into their everyday conversation. A successful trial lawyer may talk in private company as though he were addressing a jury.

Talk over the phone is more prone to misunderstanding than conversation face to face. Writing, to be read in lone silence, makes still more difficult demands. One's whole personality irradiates one's speech.

Human sound combinations and associated devices have been built, in various times and regions, into almost six thousand separate languages. These are subdivided into countless dialects, and here and there blurred and blended into pidgin.

A *dialect,* a variation of a language as spoken in a particular locality within that language realm, may vary by peculiarities of pronunciation, vocabulary, and grammatical form, sometimes so divergent as to be almost unintelligible to those speaking the same language in another locality. In one of his novels, J. B. Priestley has the English narrator refer to his great-aunts "with accents so broad, with so many dialect words, they might have been talking a foreign language." Both in Britain and in the United States, there are extensive dialect dictionaries and continuing studies.

Pidgin (the word a nineteenth-century Chinese corruption of *business*) is a speech sprung from the effort of a people to make itself understood by the soldiers, missionaries, and traders who have descended upon it from more powerful nations. There are several pidgins in different parts of the world; dictionaries of them were made for American soldiers in World War II.

The many languages humans have spoken or speak may be classified in three main types: isolating or analytic; agglutinative or synthetic; and inflectional.

Words in the *analytic* languages, like Chinese, are monosyllabic, and invariable. Word order is important. As verbs have but one form, the person and time of action must be indicated by separate words: "He go yesterday."

In the *synthetic* languages, like Turkish, there is free combination of elements into single words. In Eskimo, one word may include subject, verb, direct and indirect object. One Japanese word, for instance, combines *jin* ('man'), *riki* ('power') and *sha* ('vehicle'). German is to some degree synthetic, but like most Indo-European languages it is mainly of the third type, the inflectional.

Words of the *inflectional* languages have many endings, to indicate various relationships or functions. Singular and plural of nouns and verbs, the time of an action, the subject or the object, may be indicated by the variant ending of the same word. Hence, as in Latin, words may be arranged in an order that will lend emphasis to a particular aspect of the idea, as the endings show which words belong together in the meaning of the passage.

English is in the happy position of sharing elements of all three types of language. As with the isolating tongues, word order may be important. "The bull threw the cowboy" must not be confused with "The cowboy threw the bull." There is a difference between a green deep and a deep green, a garden flower and a flower garden. On the other hand, many English words are synthetic.

Friend/li/ness combines three elements; *philosophy* binds two Greek words, meaning love of wisdom. Most scientific words are combinations of two or more stems; *hydrogen*, for instance, is 'water-maker'. A root, such as *gen*, may be used in many combinations, as *oxygen* ('acid-maker'), *generation*, *general*, and more. Finally, English has a heritage of inflections: *he, his, him; she, hers, her; they, their, theirs, them.*

English is, however, decreasing the number of inflected forms, growing toward a greater simplicity. Thus the Old English *ridan* had thirteen forms. Modern German *reiten* retains sixteen forms; Modern French has thirty-eight verbal forms; Modern English— *ride, rides, rode, riding, ridden*—has only five.

As a consequence of this amalgamation of language types, English has a greater flexibility of function. A verb, as *ride*, may also be a noun. There is an increased use of adverbs and prepositions: one can make *out*, make *for*, make *off*, make *after*, make *up* (the face, a story, for lost time, after a quarrel). This is especially valuable, as verbs are the most frequently used terms. In Schmidt's *Shakespeare Lexicon*, for instance, among words taking more than a page each (thirty-two lines), 47 percent are verbs, 18 percent nouns, 10 percent adjectives.

English is a comparatively recent language of the Indo-European family, one of about a hundred families that have been distinguished, in each of which the languages are linked by vocabulary and grammatical forms that suggest a common origin. Here are eight important families:

1. Hamito-Semitic (from the Biblical Ham and Shem). This family includes Hebrew, Arabic, Aramaic, and some thirty Caucasian tongues. In Africa it includes Coptic (Egyptian), Berber, Ethiopian (Amharic), Chad, Hausa, and over sixty more—Bana, Sokoro, Data, Hina, etc. Hausa is widely used for commerce, in Niger, Nigeria, and Cameroon.

The earliest recorded Semitic language is Eblan, spoken around 2400 B.C. in Ebla in northern Canaan. It came to light in 1975, with the discovery of some 15,600 clay tablets in a palace long under ground, thirty-four miles south of Aleppo. The palace was destroyed by fire about 2250 B.C. by Naram-Sin, grandson of King Sargon of Babylon, founder of the Semitic dynasty of Akkad; the conflagration hardened and thus preserved the clay tablets.

2. African. There are well over eight hundred other languages in Africa, grouped in several families. Chief are: (a) The Niger-Kordofanian family, spoken in Niger and along the Congo. Its main subdivision is Mande (Mandingo), the tongue of the

greatest African empire, Mali, which flourished from the seventh century until 1513, and is memorialized in the Republic of Mali, formed from the French Sudan in 1958. Over 1,200,000 there speak Mandingo dialects, also spoken on the Ivory Coast, in Senegal, and Gambia. This family also includes the Bantu group. Ngala, or Lingala, is spoken by the Bangala in the Mangala area of Zaire. Bantu tongues are like that. Try Uganda: to those living there, *Baganda* is the country; a *Muganda* is a native; natives—plural—are *Baganda;* and the language is *Luganda.* Near the Equator, within the northern bend of the Congo, dwell the Mongo, or Lomongo, the Bakongo, and the Basongo. (b) The Nilo-Saharan family, which has three main branches: Chari-Nile; Central Sudanic; Eastern Sudanic (Nilotic and Nubian); also Songhai, spoken in Timbuktu. (c) The Khoisan family, which includes Bushman and Hottentot. (d) The Banta-Sudanese family, which includes Swahili, spoken in East Africa and Malagasy (Madagascar).

3. Sino-Tibetan, embracing the various Chinese tongues, which are difficult even for the natives to set down. Of the two thousand most common Mandarin characters, only some six hundred are written with fewer than eight strokes; some require up to twenty-seven. The Communists are making tremendous efforts to increase the number that can read, it being a mark of distinction and pride to peruse the little red book of the late Chairman Mao.

4. Dravidian. This was the family spoken by the aborigines of India, driven southward by the Aryan invasion. It includes Tamil, Telugu, and Malayalam.

5. Austro-Asiatic. Papua-New Guinea, recently freed from Australia, contains nine hundred ninety-eight tribes (including head-hunters and cannibals), who speak some seven hundred languages. Khmer, a monosyllabic language, flourished for thirteen centuries, until the kingdom was destroyed by the Siamese in 1432.

6. Ural-Altaic. This family includes Hungarian and Turkish and, with a leap across Europe, Finno-Ugric (Suomi) and Lapp.

7. American Indian. Columbus little knew that in 1492 some 2,200 languages were spoken in the Americas. We have deciphered 27,000 words of the Aztecs; the King James English Bible uses but 7,000. Many of the Indian tongues are extinct or dying; some are still spoken by no more than a dozen old folk. About six million, however, still speak Quiché, a Mayan language of Guatemala; some four million on the Andean plateaus speak

the tongue of the Incas, Quechua; and a million in Mexico speak Nahua.

8. The most widespread of the language families is the Indo-European. In the Indic branch are Sanskrit, Sumerian, Hindi, and Persian. Urdu, the language of Pakistan, is a mixture of Sanskrit and Persian; the invading Parsi are perpetuated in the name: *urdu* is the Persian word for 'army'; it has come into English as *horde*. Near the mountains that separate North India from Pakistan, in "the paradise land of Hunza," vividly described by the Hyderabad poet Mehdi Ali Seljouk, the people with the reputedly longest lives on earth speak Waggi, Shina, or (mainly) the unrelated Burushashki, none of which has been set down in writing.

In the more northerly branch of Indo-European are Greek, Latin, the Romance tongues; also Germanic, Slavic, Celtic, and Baltic. Dead languages in this family include Minoan, Oscan, Gothic, Vandal, Cornish and, but recently, Manx. English, with much admixture, is an outgrowth of the Germanic line.

A few surviving languages have no recognized affinities with any of the families. Among these are Eskimo; Ainu, spoken on the northern island of Japan; and Basque, whose speakers are even now seeking autonomy in Spain.

It has been an idle speculation of otherwise better employed persons, as to which was the first language. Herodotus (ca. 430 B.C.) tells us that King Psammetichus of Egypt kept an infant from hearing any human sound. When bread was brought to the growing child, it exclaimed "Bekos!" Since *bekos* means 'bread' in Phrygian, the King felt that he had discovered the primeval tongue.

Until early in the nineteenth century, many Christians and Jews assumed that Hebrew was the first language, that in which God spoke with Adam. Jonathan Swift, among his satiric works, set out to prove that English was older than Greek. As one of his arguments he pointed to the word *kill-joy*. Similarly, he declared, there was a testy warrior among the Greeks whose presence made everybody nervous; naturally, they called him *a kill-ease*, Achilles. Q.E.D.

There are today 149 languages each spoken by over a million persons. And there are the Big Ten, each the native tongue of more than a hundred million. Here they are, with the approximate number of native speakers. You will note, as they are italicized, that seven of the ten are Indo-European. Mandarin Chinese (which the Communists prefer to call by the less aristocratic name *p'u-t'ung hua*, 'the generally understood language', or *kuo y ü*, 'the national speech'), 650 million; *English*, 350 million; *Great Russian*, 210m; *Spanish*, 195m; *Hindi*, 195m; *German*, 120m; Arabic, 119m; *Bengali*, 110m; *Portuguese*, 110m; Japanese, 110m. You should also note the absence of five languages that have played major roles in the culture of the western world: ancient Greek and Latin; the recently resuscitated Hebrew; and modern Italian and French. Their attainments, rather than the number of their speakers, warrant their special mention. And they have all offered golden building blocks to modern English.

2.
THE MOVEMENT
TO ENGLISH

OVER FIVE THOUSAND YEARS AGO, a family dwelled in the fields and forests of southwest Asia. This is the fertile region of the steppes, with plentiful food from fishing, and easy venturing beyond. It shores upon the Black Sea, into which flows the Danube, with its three hundred tributaries, the second longest river in Europe. The longest, the Volga, the third longest, the Dnieper, as well as the Bug, and the Donetz which is tributary to the quiet Don, also lave this region with their waters. And through a dozen centuries the family grew into a tribe, and the tribe became a race, which we call *Aryan*, the noble race (Sanskrit *arya*, 'noble').

About 3000 B.C. these people began to migrate—moved by we know not what climatic changes, pressure of other westering tribes, need of wider territory, or some vague wanderlust: the untrod grass is greener. And their descendants have never ceased the movement, in more recent years coming in surges to the Americas, to South Africa and Australia, to form Dutch and English colonies in the Asian seas, to settle in eastern mainland spots like Hong Kong, Singapore, Macao. And, as one of their sons sighed that there were no more worlds to conquer, so their scions today look forward to moon colonies, to future possible habitations on the "wandering stars" (Greek *planetes*, 'wanderers').

The words these distant ancestors of ours spoke are unknown to us, but certain basic ideas held root in forms that are alike, cognate, in the languages that arose in their later wide spreading. Thus from Sanskrit *bhratar*, Old Slavic *brata*, to Irish *brothair*, the words for 'brother' are too alike for coincidence. The sister

was less regarded; but there is a widespread basic term for
'daughter-in-law', which also meant 'bride'; in those early days,
when a woman married, she moved to her husband's father's
home.

In most of the family languages *mer* (which appears in English
maritime and, as we shall see, in the Irish name *Murphy*) remains;
it meant not the ocean but an inland sea. *Snow; bee;* the numerals
two to *ten; sen* for 'old'; *newo,* 'new'; *eu* (*su*), 'good'; *dys,* 'bad':
these are some of the basic word roots that the race took along
on its migrations.

The journeyers also bore with them a sense of the dominance
of the male. This may have been an essential aspect of a people
on the march, for it is manifest in the other great migration of
early times, that of the Semites. The orthodox Jew even now, in
his daily prayer, thanks the Lord that he was not born a woman.
It may seem compensation for this morning thankfulness that at
the Sabbath evening service the husband recites the Psalmist's
words (*Proverbs* 31, verses 10–31, an alphabetical acrostic) in
praise of the virtuous wife. This, however, provides a weekly
reminder to the woman of the household as to how she had better
behave to earn such approval.

Women in the Arab world are but beginning to struggle out
of the all-enclosing harem and the all-curtaining system of purdah.
I have lectured in Pakistan where such a curtain, down the center
of the room, protected the women students from the glances of
the men. And even in the streets of London today, there walk
women from the Near East covered from crown to toe in a great
hooded black burnoose, with a yashmak or half-mask hiding the
face—the nose now sheltered by a strange black plastic peak.
The University of Cairo in 1976 ordered its faculty to wear not
western but native garments. A formal address to a woman of
rank in the Arab world was "O veiled and virtuous!"

In even greater depreciation of women, the Greek Plato stated
that if a man lived an evil life, his soul would return in the body
of a woman; if the evil persisted, in its next cycle the soul would
be embodied in an appropriate beast.

Among the gods, as they moved northward, the male still
reigned supreme. The females are pictured as having wrought
mischief in the world, like Eris, goddess of Discord, whose tossed
apple brought on the Trojan War. The temptress Eve is Semitic,
but her tale is in the Bible of the whole western world. And in
the western myths and legends, the feminine evil runs on. Lady
Macbeth spurred her husband. Hamlet's mother spread bait for

his uncle's crimes. Goneril and Regan double the odds on Lear's Cordelia, who herself was too rigid for her own good. "Three things there are that are insatiable, yea, four things say not, it is enough. The grave, and the barren womb; the earth that is not filled with water; and the fire that saith not, It is enough." The only insatiate human desire is the lust of the unfulfilled woman.

Attempting today to impose the use of such terms as *chairperson* seems, however, a clumsy way of redressing the linguistic imbalance. A caustic critic of such efforts has pointed out, twisting the *menses*, the feminine monthly flow, that the most flagrant instance of male dominance is in the word *menstruation;* it should, of course, be *womenstruation!* Such are the bywords of early women's lib. The male sense of superiority, none the less, has continued in verbal channels. Look at two definitions in the *Oxford English Dictionary* (O.E.D.), reprinted in the *Shorter Oxford* of 1973: "*Satiriasis*, excessively great sexual desire in the male." "*Nymphomania*, a feminine disease caused by morbid and uncontrollable sexual desire." Here lies legitimate ground for feminine ploughing.

Two words, at least, have been sexturned to separate senses. Virtue, for several centuries, meant, in the male, 'manliness', courage; in the female, chastity. And up to the end of the nineteenth century, purity was the feminine, truth the masculine, of honour. Note, however, that the *domination of women* is an ambiguous term: one needs further discussion to discover whether the *of* stands for *over* or *by*.

(The 1976 Supplement to the O.E.D. boasts on the jacket: "The Loch Ness monster appears in the present volume, if nowhere else, along with ... male chauvinist pig, napalm, nitty-gritty ..." It does not correct the prudish maldefinition of *monocordise*, nor modify the "male chauvinist" definition of *nymphomania*.)

About 3000 B.C., then, our hardy male ancestors led their womenfolk on the great migration. It took two main directions. One branch moved southward into Persia and India. The other moved west and northwest, but by two divergent routes. The first traversed the anfractuous shorelines and the island-blessed waters of the Mediterranean ("Middle of the Earth") Sea, to Greece, Italy, France, Spain. The second went by land into the heart of Europe, following the course of the streams into the inviting northern lands, or through the wooded valleys, with their many lakes, of Middle Europe. Daring the mountain passes between the peaks of perpetual snow, they reached the Rhine, and moving on went north into the Scandinavian countries, and west across the Channel—these were the Celts (Picts, Irish, Scots, Welsh, Manx)—to settle on the British Isles. And through the centuries, although their tongues took on many variations, they spoke with forms and words linked in the large Indo-European family of languages.

The early wanderers may have been attended by a few dogs, or small flocks of sheep; but domestication of animals, like agriculture, demanded a more stable society. The word for horse, coming after the dispersion, varies greatly in the different tongues: Russian *loshad;* German *Pferd.* Greek *hippos,* horse, comes to English in the name *Philip,* 'lover of horses'; in *hippopotamus,* 'river horse'; and in *hippodrome,* a place for running horses, as in the exciting chariot races. (These, incidentally, stirred more eager betting and roused even greater riots than football in Europe and South America today.) The Latin *equus*—which gives English *equestrian,* opposed to *pedestrian*—is the title of a very successful play in the mid-seventies in London and New York. The Romance terms for horse, Italian *cavallo,* Spanish *caballo,* French *cheval*—English *cavalry* and the mounted knights of medieval *chivalry*—grew from a Late Latin colloquial word for a work-horse. The foot-soldiers were drawn from the proletariat, the common citizens reared to proliferate (Latin *proles,* 'offspring', whence also *prolific*), to bear offspring to serve in the army and carry on the onerous and distasteful tasks of the state. They were, none the less, citizens and thus had freedoms denied their captives, who became slaves. The better equipped and trained armies of the Romans—until the surging tribes of the fifth century broke through the walls of Rome—overpowered their neighbors to the north, so that the word *Slav,* which to the natives meant 'glory', became the Roman *slave.* The German tribes, too, had been enslaving their eastern neighbors. The word was new, but not the system.

Before the Romans marched northward, earlier tribes had established more permanent settlements in Gaul and Britain. Forests were generous with fruits and timber; and the settlers named trees new to them: elm, hazel, oak. *Acorn* originally meant any fruit of the field; it is allied to the word *acre,* from Latin *ager,* from the verb *agere,* 'to drive', as cattle to pasture or oxen to plough. Pasture land was cleared for grazing, then for agriculture. Hence also the *pastor* (Latin *pascere, pastum,* 'to feed'), who tended his flock. With planting, the new word *weed* came with its nuisance meaning. The settlements were by choice on a hilltop, for defense; the word for 'high', *bherg* (German *Berg*, 'mountain') became associated with the town, the *burg*, and *borough*. A borough was first a fortified place, then a castle, then the town that grew in the shelter of the castle walls; it is entangled with the Old English *beorgen*, 'to protect'.

Thus new words came with the new conditions. As the Arabs, in their hot and sandy regions, made twelve words for the useful camel, so the colder climate produced a baker's dozen words for frozen water: *ice, snow, sleet, hail, hailstone, icicle, iceberg, iciclet, glacier, frost, slush,* and the now obsolete *posh* and *brash*.

On the British Isles, the growth of an ordered civilization brought such new words as *king, earl, churl*. A permanent hearth for the home fire could be set up; the word *stove* came, with *broth* and *brew*. As the Celts were driven from the main centers by later invasions, however, they left few words in the language. The word *avon* meant 'river'; *bryn* meant 'hill'; *combe*, 'valley'; these are retained in place names. A *down* was a highland, as still the *dunes* and the English *downs; adown*, 'off the down', lost the prefix and kept the current meaning of 'down'. *Dun* meant 'town'; Dunbarton thus has a town at both ends. *Town* (*ton, tun, tune*) first meant 'fence' or 'hedge', then 'an enclosed garden or farmyard'; the current sense of 'a community larger than a village' did not come until after the Norman Conquest, being first recorded in 1154.

In 55 B.C. the Romans under Caesar sailed to Britain, from which land they had been getting slaves and tin. Under Claudius in 43 A.D. they established some settlements, and remained for four hundred years; but they lingered rather as conquerors than as colonists, and when they departed left little for today beyond some well-constructed roads, the remnants of walls, and the ruins of baths, as at Chester on the border of Wales. They also left a few names in the language. Latin *colonia*, 'colony', survives in *Lincoln*. Latin *vicus*, 'village', remains in *Warwick* and *Greenwich* (Latin *v* was pronounced like our *w*). The Roman camp, *castra*, was more widespread, and took different sounds in different parts of the country. It thus abides in *Lancaster*, in *Westchester*, and in *Worcester*. The last of these, a Celtic place name plus the Roman camp, with the added Saxon word for 'county', *shire*, has come into our current vocabulary as the name of a sauce.

When the Romans withdrew from Britain, drawn home by domestic disaster about 450 A.D., the Celts—as is frequent in families—renewed their strife. The King of Kent, Wytgoern, in-

vited the Saxons from the Continent, to aid him in battle against
the Picts and Scots. The Saxons, Angles, Jutes, and Frisians
eagerly responded; and by the sixth century they had imposed
their rule and their language upon the land. The newcomers, who
gave England its name, 'Angleland', gave the language not only
their vocabulary but the framework. Most of our prepositions,
pronouns, conjunctions—the workhorses of speech—are from the
Low German these people brought. And although in our current
English dictionaries some three-fifths of the words are of Greek,
Latin, and Romance origin, in our actual speech more than half
the words we use are from the Old English.

(Our speech is commonly divided into three periods: Old
English or Anglo-Saxon, to 1100; Middle English, to 1500; and
Modern English. Nearest of the still-spoken Germanic tongues
to Modern English is Frisian.)

The Germanic practice of compounding, brought over by the
Saxons, has somewhat lapsed in English. We still say *withhold,
withstand, withdraw;* but we have dropped *withchoose* ('reject'),
withspeak ('contradict'), and almost fifty more with that prefix.
Leechcraft has become *medicine;* the *earthstepper* is now a
wanderer. And there were once a hundred words like *behead,
besmirch, bewitch.* An early English book is entitled *Againbite of
Inwit,* meaning 'Remorse of Conscience'. (*Remorse* means 'back-
bite'; a 'small bite' is a *morsel.*)

Some Saxon words had already, on the Continent, been borrowed from Roman soldiers and traders: *inch, mile, pound, street,
wall, table, mule, chest, pillow, wine.* But the words nearest our
hearth and heart—*love, come, live, eat, speak*—are native Saxon.

In the sixth century a young priest, Gregory, was impressed by
the spectacle of fair-haired and fair-skinned slaves in the Roman
Forum. Told who they were, he demurred: "They are not Angles
but angels." In 597, now Pope Gregory, he sent forty missionaries
to Britain, led by (Saint) Augustine. They found the Frankish
Queen Bertha, wife of King Æthelbert of Kent, already Christian,
and happy to welcome them. Within a century, England was a
Christian land.

Christianity by this time had become a widely potent force,
and added many terms to the language. Since 332 B.C., when
Alexander had sacked Sidon and Tyre, Greeks and Hebrews had
lived side by side. In the second century B.C. the Bible was
translated into Greek; the version, probably prepared by a committee of seventy, is therefore called the Septuagint. A little later
the Romans conquered Syria, which included Nazareth, where

Jesus was born. In the fourth century A.D., Christianity became the official religion of the Roman Empire; the canons of orthodoxy and the apocrypha were established, and the Vulgate became the Bible of the western church for over a thousand years. (The Vulgate translation into Latin by Jerome, is thus called for the *vulgar,* the 'common people'.) It is the most influential of all versions, the one from which translations into English—into some fourteen hundred world's languages—were subsequently made. From the Latin, or from the Greek through Latin, now came into English such words as *candle, clerk, creed, hymn, psalm, martyr, bishop, devil, priest.* Some old Germanic terms changed their meaning: *heaven* had formerly meant a 'canopy'; to *bless* was originally to 'consecrate with blood'. *Mercy,* from the Latin *merces,* 'reward', came to be applied to a reward in heaven for deeds on earth; the original sense is retained in *mercenary,* and developed in *mercantile, merchant, market,* and *Mercer Street,* the 'street of traders', both in the center of London and a block west of Broadway in downtown New York. *Mercury* was the Roman god of both merchants and thieves.

To some degree the Latin words dealt with the material world; the Greek words, with the world of thoughts and feelings. Later, this difference was more marked; words from the Latin were more practical, as in the code of law; those from the Greek, more speculative, as in the terms of philosophy and art.

The English welcomed the Christian faith, and flourished through peaceful years. In the seventh and eighth centuries, with scholars such as the Venerable Bede, and poets such as Caedmon and Cynewulf, the English people were at the force of western civilization. The best extant manuscript of the Vulgate Bible, the Amiatinus Codex, was written in the early eighth century in England. When the ambitious Charlemagne (742–814) sought to spread learning in France, he invited Alcuin of York to direct the palace school, to bring over the studies and the discipline of the Anglo-Saxon churchmen. Among Alcuin's achievements was the development of the Carolingian minuscule, a simpler and more legible style of writing, which became the literary hand of all Western Europe.

Devastation struck the eastern coast of England in 865, in the form of 350 Viking ships; the subjected East Anglia became a Danish colony. The Vikings, as they settled in the land, established new words as well: *husband* (the 'house dweller'); *law* (that which is 'laid' down) vs. the older word *order; lord* vs. *master; ways* vs. *means; help* vs. *succor*—thus creating many synonyms to enrich the language. The possessive apostrophe, as *John his hoe* became *John's hoe,* came as a welcome simplification.

There was a temporary revival of the English culture in the late ninth century, under King Alfred. He encouraged translations, in which many of the foreign terms were Anglicized. Thus *exodus* was rendered as *outfaring, discipulus* became *learning-boy.* Alfred established the Anglo-Saxon Chronicle, which was continued until 1154.

In 1016 the Danish King Knut (Canute) came to power. He was a temperate monarch, who rebuked the folly of his over-adulant courtiers by demonstrating that the tide would not turn at his bidding. (An earlier, less moderate, monarch, the Persian Xerxes, had ordered his soldiers to whip the waters when they foiled him with overwhelming waves.) In Knut's time, more Teutonic words took hold upon the English tongue. Preserved at the end of place names are *thorpe,* meaning 'village'; *ness,* meaning 'promontory'; and *by,* meaning 'farm' or 'hamlet'. Derby and Rugby are two of the six hundred current place names ending with the Scandinavian *by.*

The pressure of Saxons and Scandinavians had meanwhile driven the Celtic people farther west, to Cornwall, to Ireland; some of them (the Britons, who gave Britain its name) returned to the Continent and settled in Brittany. Thus in Cornwall, on the southwest tip of the island, some 80 percent of the place names are Celtic, compared to 2 percent in Suffolk, on the eastern coast. The Celts left but few words in the language, among them *glen, bog, banshee, galore. Car,* in reverse journey, went from Celtic into Latin, on its return giving up *chariot.* But all these racial radiations paled in the face of a new invasion in 1066.

After the Battle of Hastings, in 1066, William the Conqueror imposed Norman rule upon England. He was of Viking ancestry, but his fathers had spent 150 years in Normandy, and their language was Vulgar Latin, the speech of the Roman soldiers and traders, corrupted into Norman French. William wiped out the Saxon nobility, supplanting them with his own followers, whose names are recorded in his census, the Domesday Book.

The ascendancy of the French-speaking Normans over the English-speaking Saxons thrust two languages into opposition in the land. The servants, adjusting themselves as best they could, sloughed many of the endings of the new Norman words. Thus, in the course of the next centuries, the fusing language lost most of the inflections. The practice, still marking French and German today, of giving every noun a gender—masculine, feminine, neuter—with which any modifiers must agree, died out in these days in England. The final *e*, even now pronounced in German, and in French poetry, gradually lapsed into silence in English. It was still used to a large extent by Chaucer, who died in 1400; but by 1500 the very memory that it had been sounded was lost, so that the Elizabethan critics spoke of Chaucer's broken or rough lines—until Thomas Tyrwhitt in 1775 brought it back to critical attention. Meanwhile the final *e* in English came to indicate a lengthened preceding vowel, as *mat* changes sound to *mate*.

Since the household servants, including the nurses of the nobles' children, were Saxon, their speech affected that of the growing generations; thus the homey words, the basic emotional words, on our tongues today are Saxon. As the child grew older, more intellectual words might come from French, which means ultimately Latin and Greek, sources. Thus *friendship* might later be spoken of as *amity*. The natural *freedom* becomes a sought-for *liberty;* blunt *hatred* loses direct bite in *enmity*. The *brotherhood* of man is a feelingful ideal; its twin *fraternity* (natural to the French in *fraternité*) in English suggests a college society. *Motherhood* makes a direct appeal to our emotions; *maternity* brings to mind a hospital ward.

Another opposition of Saxon and Norman terms is pointed out by Wamba the jester, in the first chapter of Scott's *Ivanhoe*. He calls the attention of the swineherd Gurth to the fact that, while the domestic animals are alive and must be cared for in the *fold, sty,* and *stall*, they are serf Saxon *sheep, hog, bull, calf;* when they are cooked and served at the noble's table, they become proud Norman *mutton, pork, beef, veal.*

For almost four hundred years, French was the language of the rulers, at the royal court; not until 1362 was English made the language of the law courts. In church, and at Oxford University, one used either Latin or French. In these centuries, almost three-quarters of the Saxon words died; but enough remained to keep the basic form, the "feel" of the language, Saxon, while enriching it with the new host of Norman terms.

The many enforced mixtures, from Celtic times on, also made the language amenable to borrowing. While the French, for example, even today resent the intrusion of foreign terms, and strive to keep their language "pure," free from "contamination" by what they scornfully call *Franglais*, English continuously welcomes new terms from other tongues, and even builds upon them. Thus English has, more than any other tongue, enriched itself with words from all the world. It has the largest vocabulary of any language, and is capable not only of infinite variety but of finest shades of discrimination.

While the Norman conquest was thus directly affecting English speech, events in other regions of the world were also to make their mark upon the language. In the same century, the Crusades began. Intended to free the Holy Land from the infidel, they brought the European Christian into contact with the Arab Muslim world. It was in that world, fortunately, that the treasures of pagan Europe, discarded when not destroyed by the early Christians, had been preserved. The works of Aristotle, Greek scientific speculation, Greek medicine, were reintroduced into Europe. With them of course came their vocabulary: *zenith, astronomy, artery, vein, asthma, gout, demon, goblin. Alchemist* and *algebra* show *al*, the Arab prefix for 'the'; it occurs also in *alcohol* ('the kohl'), and *albatross* (the first part a folk change because of the bird's color— Latin *alba*, 'white') from Portuguese *alcatraz*, from Arabic *al qadus*. Of tremendous importance was the introduction of the Arabic numerals. Imagine (without computers) the difficulty of multiplying, in Roman figures, XXXIV by XLVIII. And from the Arabs came the even greater simplification provided by their cipher, zero, 0— which radically altered methods of calculation, and made manifest the advantages of the decimal system.

In England, the people were learning how to live together. In 1215, the barons extracted the Magna Carta from a reluctant King John at Runnymede, taking the first step from the divine right of kings toward democracy. It is interesting to note that, although John is the most common male Christian name, no other English king has been given the name of the humiliated signer of that fateful document. There are eighty-four Saints John.

The Hundred Years' War, which troubled the years from 1337 to 1453, brought a resentment against the French people and their language, which helped to give English the ascendancy. The East Midland dialect was becoming the dominant, standard English tongue. It was the speech of London, which, with a population of forty thousand, was the largest city in England.

In 1349 the Black Death wiped out one-third of the population in a few months. Economic conditions were oppressive, and in 1381 there erupted the Peasants' Revolt against the heavy taxes. But with recovery came the rise of the middle class, the successful businessmen and traders, the skilled craftsmen in their powerful guilds; and also a measure of leisure. Some new terms were borrowed from sports in which the people now indulged: *to bowl over; crestfallen*, from the cockpit; *to worry*, from the dogs turned loose upon the badger or bear.

Despite the hostility between the English and the French, the two languages persisted side by side. In the last quarter of the fourteenth century the poet Gower, with his eyes on the future, wrote three long poems: one, *Vox Clamantis*, in Latin; one, *Speculum Meditantis*, in French; and one, *Confessio Amantis*, in English. His greater contemporary, Geoffrey Chaucer, although he knew other tongues—he traveled much on the Continent on errands for the King—perhaps indeed because he there became acquainted with the Italian vernacular works of Dante and Boccaccio, chose to write in his own native English, and that "well of English undefiled" gave us in full freshness the first great treasure of English literature. "There sprang the violet all new." The Prologue to *The Canterbury Tales* begins:

> When that Aprille with his shoures sote
> The droghte of Marche hath perced to the rote,
> And bathed every veyne in swich licour,
> Of which vertu engendred is the flour;
> When Zephirus eek with his swete breeth
> Inspired hath in every holt and heeth
> The tendre croppes, and the yonge sonne
> Hath in the Ram his halfe cours y-ronne,
> And smale fowles maken melodye,
> That slepen al the night with open yë,
> (So pricketh hem nature in hir corages):
> Then longen folk to goon on pilgrimages

—and there is little that will trouble the twentieth century reader.

The following years marked a period of consolidation. Poetry was still striving to find appropriate forms, but in its native patterns was not yet smooth. As John Skelton, tutor to Prince Henry (later Henry VIII) put it:

> For though my ryme be ragged,
> Tattered and jagged,
> Rudely rain beaten,
> Rusty and moth eaten,
> If ye take well therwith
> It hath in it some pith.

In 1476 William Caxton established the first English printing press, at Westminster; by 1500, some 25,000 books had been printed. By 1550 the Renaissance had come to England, and the language acquired the forms, the variety and the flexibility, of which we can take advantage today. The sonnet form (by Wyatt) and blank verse (by Surrey) were introduced into England, and soon became most popular. There were many sonnet sequences (Shakespeare's was printed rather late); while blank verse, through Christopher Marlowe, became richly attuned to drama, and its frequent form.

The surge of activity under Henry VIII, continuing under the great Elizabeth, which we know as the English Renaissance, was of course as manifest in the lives of the Englishmen as in their language. The English gentleman completed his education by taking the Grand Tour, which might mean spending as much as two years in France and Italy—where he gave impetus to the saying *Inglese Italiano è un diavolo incarnato*. Many such a gentleman came back aping the costumes and manners of the Continentals, rolling foreign phrases on his tongue, becoming in full regard the Italianate Englishman. Rosalind, in *As You Like It*, says to Jacques:

> Farewell, Monsieur Traveller: look you lisp and wear strange suits, disable all the benefits of your own country, be out of love with your nativity, and almost chide God for making you that countenance you are, or I will scarce think you have swam in a gondola.

Many such travelers affectedly added scraps of Latin or Italian to their English speech, a practice that Puttenham called the mingle mangle. Queen Elizabeth, when a mere lass of twelve, translated a collection of Prayers and Meditations into Italian; her royal signature, Elizabeth R, is in Italian script; and once she remarked: "I am half Italian myself."

Nor did this attraction soon die. A century later Samuel Johnson, whose journeying took him only to the north of Britain, declared: "A man who has not been to Italy is always conscious of an inferiority." The Italianate Englishman of the eighteenth century was derisively called a *macaroni*, as in the song with which the Redcoats laughed at the Colonials, but which the Americans blandly adopted as their own:

> Yankee Doodle came to town,
> Riding on a pony,
> Stuck a feather in his cap
> And called it Macaroni.

And still in the nineteenth century the lure was strong, on Byron who died in Greece, on Shelley who died in Italy. Elizabeth Barrett Browning also died in Italy; not only for this reason did her husband Robert write:

> Open my heart and you will see
> Graved inside of it "Italy."

The Elizabethan tradesman, similarly extending his horizon, engaged in worldwide commerce, his ships circumnavigating the globe in his search for gold, jewels, and exotic fashions and foods. They naturally brought back new terms for the new goods from many lands. The scholar, aided by the new printing press and the wider dissemination of knowledge, brought into English literature not only the translated Greek and Latin classics, and the terms of classical grammar and criticism, but also the plots of the Italian and French storytellers. The writers, too, enriched the language, often fruitfully, but sometimes with the results of their elucubrations in "inkhorn terms" too cumbersome for keeping.

The eighteenth-century French Voltaire hoped that his time would leave "vocabular ghosts undisturbed in their lexicon-limbo"; but nineteenth-century Isaac D'Israeli, father of Queen Victoria's Empire-builder, lamented the loss of "words wise Bacon or brave Rawleigh spake":

> If we acknowledge that the creation of some neologisms may sometimes produce the beautiful, the revival of the dead is the more authentic miracle; for a new word must long remain doubtful, but an ancient word happily recovered rests on a basis of permanent strength; it has both novelty and authority. A collection of picturesque words, found among our ancient writers, would constitute a precious supplement to the history of our language. Far more expressive than our own term of *executioner* is their solemn one of the deathsman; than our *vagabond*, their *scatterling*; than our *idiot* or *lunatic*, their *moonling*.

The call of the grasshopper grows vivid as *pittering*; the atmosphere is softened if we see the threat of storm *dusking* the pasture.

A few other forgotten words, indeed, might pleasantly be revived. *Ochlochracy* sounds sufficiently cacophonous to fit its meaning: 'mob rule'. *Emacity* describes many a housewife's affliction: 'an itch to be buying.' "That's *phthiriatic!*" (thi' ree atic) may be a seemingly approving way of saying "That's lousy!"—especially as the pronunciation gives the hearer no cue as to where to turn in an unabridged dictionary.

The officers of the new Church of England, as well as the Puritans and the other dissenters, were quick with pamphlets advocating their special brand of faith, excoriating the unbelievers, joining in the general attack upon those that still acknowledged the spiritual authority of the Pope. Religious and racial antagonisms combined to keep the national temper at a high pitch, with new religious phrases springing from each faction, and more piling invectives fashioned by them all.

The Elizabethan author was fully conscious of the golden opportunity his age afforded him, in the use, nay the invention, of new words. He not only took full advantage of the freedom to coin words; he proudly displayed his own creations and loudly attacked those of his fellows. Thus Puttenham in 1589 boasted of having formed the words *scientific, idiom, methodical, savage, audacious, numerosity, implete, politien*—the last three of which did not linger on English tongues. Thomas Nashe, who vainly suggested *carminist* for 'songwriter', in 1592 rebuked Gabriel Harvey for inventing *conscious, jovial, rascality, notoriety, extensively*—all of which have prevailed. The playwright (in prose) and poet John Lyly laughed at the new expression *to make love*, stating: "When I hear of what fashion it is made, if I like the pattern, you shall cut me a partlet." The *logomachy*, the battle of words, entered the drama. In *The Poetaster* (1601) Ben Jonson makes John Marston spew out the words *retrograde, damp, strenuous, spurious, defunct, clumsy, prorump, obstupefact, ventositous*—again the last three have remained in the discard.

Not only the words were attacked, but also their creators. Thus Nashe characterized Harvey:

> Cowbaby, Gorboduck, Huddle-duddle, Gogmagog, Jewish Talmud of absurdities, coarse himpenhempen Slampant, stale Applesquire Cockledemoy—creator of rascally hedge raked-up terms, familiar to roguish morts and doxies, ridiculous senseless sentences, finical flaunting phrases, and termagant inkhorn terms... hermaphrodite phrases, half Latin, half English.

Shakespeare seems to have written nothing but poems and plays; his criticism is incidental; but the intricately wrought style of Lyly's *Euphues* (1580)—which was widely influential, and which gave its name, *euphuistic*, to its flowery fashion of antitheses in balanced sentences, with alliterative decoration and illustrations from "unnatural Natural History"—is both utilized and

gently mocked in *Love's Labor's Lost* (1595). Many of the play's
scenes show Shakespeare's awareness of words. Thus, holding up
to ridicule the fantastical Spaniard Armado—an appropriately
named target, after the recent defeat of the Spanish "invincible"
Armada—the schoolmaster protests against his saying *dout* instead
of *doubt, det* instead of *debt, abominable* instead of *abhominable*:
all these insertions are due to imitation of the classics, although
in the third instance the pedantical schoolmaster is on the wrong
side, as though the word meant 'away from man', *hominem*,
instead of 'with bad augury', *ominem*.

The hero of the play, Berowne, celebrating women (whose
charms the men have forsworn, to devote themselves to study)
roundly protests:

> Fie, painted rhetoric! O, she needs it not! . . .
> From women's eyes this doctrine I derive:
> They sparkle still the right Promethean fire;
> They are the books, the arts, the academes
> That show, contain, and nourish all the world.

And the idea has sparked Berowne to one of Shakespeare's longest
speeches, seventy-six lines of the ornately figurative "painted
rhetoric" he began by dismissing. At the end of the play, when
Rosaline has seen through his masquerade, Berowne recants:

> Taffeta phrases, silken terms precise,
> Three-pil'd hyperboles, spruce affectation,
> Figures pedantical—these summer flies
> Have blown me full of maggot ostentation,
> I do forswear them; and I here protest . . .
> Henceforth my wooing mind shall be expressed
> In russet Yeas, and honest kersey Noes.

The dandified Armado "that hath a mint of phrases in his brain,"
writes a letter to "a child of our grandmother Eve, a female; or,
for thy more sweet understanding, a woman." He will go, he avers,
in "the posteriors of this day, which the rude multitude call the
afternoon."

Costard, the clown, and Moth, Armado's page, discuss the talk
of the Spaniard, the schoolmaster, and the pedant priest:

MOTH: They have been at a great feast of language, and stolen
the scraps.
COSTARD: O! They have lived long on the alms-basket of
words. I marvel thy master hath not eaten thee for a word, for

thou art not so long by the head as honorificabilitudinitatibus; thou art easier swallowed than a flapdragon.

"Moth" being the listener, one today might imagine that a flapdragon is also an insect. The Elizabethan knew that a flapdragon was a raisin soaked in flaming brandy, which the gourmet gallant was to pluck and swallow, extinguishing the fire by closing his lips. But what of that 27-letter Brobdingnagian word, with its alternating consonants and vowels: how did Shakespeare come to concoct this particular nonce-word? Those that plump for Bacon as the author of the "Shakespeare" plays have their answer: turn these letters about and they form the Latin sentence *Hi ludi F. Baconis nati tuiti orbi,* 'These plays, born of F. Bacon, are preserved for the world'. Words make good balls for intellectual juggling.

[The suggestion that William Shakespeare of Stratford-upon-Avon, who spelled his name some thirteen ways, is not the author of the plays, is not a mere exercise of iconoclastic triflers. Upon the Bard of Avon hangs the claim of spontaneous genius, as opposed to the skills of the bred and trained artist. As Pope puts the opposition:

> True ease in writing comes from art, not chance,
> As those move easiest who have learned to dance.

If a butcher boy from a country town could come to London, and display not only such command of language, but such knowledge of music, medicine, law, and courtly ways, the "hobohemian" finds justification for his heedless ways: genius is all. Each of the proposed authors of the Shakespeare plays—Bacon, Derby, Oxford—was a scholar or well-trained noble, with a background seemingly more attuned to the creation of the plays. It might analogously be noted, in science, that the reported "accidents" that have led to important discoveries all happened to men so trained as to recognize their significance. Newton was not the first to feel an apple fall. One must do more than shake a spear to be an accomplished soldier.]

At the end of the scene in *Love's Labor's Lost,* the schoolmaster remarks to the Constable: "Via, good man Dull! Thou hast spoken no word all the while." He retorts: "Nor understood none, neither."

Shakespeare, as might be expected, was the greatest word-maker of them all. Of the 17,677 words Shakespeare employs in his plays and poems, his is the first known use of well over 1700: one new word in every ten. Here is just a representative gleaning:

aerial, auspicious, assassination, barefaced, bump, castigate, changeful, clangor, critic, critical, compunctious, conflux, countless, what the dickens, eventful, laughable, leapfrog, misplaced, monumental, road, seamy, lapse, hurry, perusal, sportive, impartial.

Not all his inventions were equally happy. In *Othello* we find "traitors ensteeped to enclog the guiltless keel." He also tried *enfreedom*, and *ensky*. *Gloomy* is a welcome word, but he also ventured *barky, barry, brisky, sphery*. Among the playwright's many gifts, however, was a genius for verbal felicities; by far the most of his new words remain in our vocabulary; without them, our language would be immeasurably less rich. As Pater exclaimed: "What a garden of words!"

The extent of Shakespeare's concern with words may be judged by the fact that, in *Stevenson's Book of Shakespearean Quotations*, the sections of Word, Speech and associated terms fill seventy-four columns; the next largest entry, Love, takes fifty-seven.

In the midst of our own economic and social troubles, we may hope, with Shakespeare's indomitably optimistic but not wholly literate Costard on his way to jail, that "affliction will some day smile again."

Out of this welter of words, many doublets came into the language, words from a single source arriving by different pathways and often acquiring different meanings. Thus from Norman French came *canal;* now in the direct contact with Paris French came *channel;* similarly *catch* and *chase, reward* and *regard, warranty* and *guarantee, wage* and *gage*. More than two words, a veritable delta of terms, may reach the language sea: the Latin *discus* came directly into English, but by different paths gave us also *disc, dish, dais,* and *desk*. Many word-books, including my own *Dictionary of Word Origins*, give long lists of doublets.

There are also sets of three, as Anglo-Saxon words survive along with their French and Latin fellows. One may be *weak*, or *frail*, or *fragile;* one's reception may be *kingly*, or *royal*, or *regal*. One may have *faith*, own *fealty*, or manifest *fidelity*. One may reach even farther ranges, of increasing intensity, as the Old English *fire*, French *flame*, spreads to Latin *conflagration*, Greek *holocaust* ('complete burning').

There was, however, a conflict lurking in this rank growth of verbiage. There are always those that enjoy the rich panoply of verbal ornamentation, who seek to adorn their sentences with elaborate jewels of words, achieving perhaps in the midst of ordinary phrasings what the Roman Horace called a purple patch. And there are those that desire a stark simplicity, a direct and brief expression of the thought. After Elizabeth, the church and the court came soon to divide them, as strict Roundhead and lively Cavalier. The conscious warriors enlisted the current jingoïsm in their fight. "The more monosyllables you use," declared George Gascoigne in the first English critical essay (1575), "the truer Englishman you shall seem, and the less you shall smell of the inkhorn." Subtle mockery of this attitude peers through the later phrasing of the counsel: "Avoid Latin derivatives; use brief, terse, Anglo-Saxon monosyllables"—in which neat bit of advice the only Anglo-Saxon word is "Anglo-Saxon." The admonition was given seriously again in this century, on the opening page of the Fowlers' guide to *The King's English:* "Prefer the familiar to the far-fetched, the concrete word to the abstract, the single word to the circumlocution, the short word to the long, the Saxon word to the Romance."

Periodic attempts to return to the "pristine purity" of Anglo-Saxon perhaps reached their final phase in Edna St. Vincent Millay's play *The King's Henchman* (1927), set in the hall of King Edgar in tenth-century England, which sought to use no word that came into the language after the Norman Conquest. The play begins, bewailing the death of King Cynewulf:

> Wild as the white waves
> Rushing and roaring, Heaving the wrack
> High up the headland; Hoarse with the howling
> Winds of the winter   When the lean wolves
> Harry the hindmost. . . .

The opposition of the churchmen and the courtiers came to a head when Charles I was beheaded in 1649; but 1611 is a more significant date in the battle of words. In that year, Thomas Middleton wrote a melodrama called *The Roaring Girl,* based on the career of Mary Frith, better known as the highwaywoman Moll Cutpurse. He followed this with *A Fair Quarrel,* in which he presents a more detailed picture of the roarers. A roarer was one of the young bloods who roamed the London streets, less violently than the Mohocks to come in the eighteenth century, but with more verbal effrontery imposing themselves upon the sedate and busy citizens.

In Middleton's play, Chough and his man Trimtram have paid £20 to learn the art of roaring. They set out to test their skill on an approaching Captain and his two wantons, Priss and Meg. "Offer the jostle, Trim," says his master.

CAPT.　Ha! What meanest thou by that?
TR.　I mean to confront thee, Cyclops.
CH.　I'll tell thee what 'a means—is this thy sister?
CAPT.　How then, Sir?
CH.　Why then, I say, she is a bronstrops; and this is a fucus.
PRISS.　No indeed, Sir; we are both fucusses.
CAPT.　Art thou military?—art thou a soldier?
CH.　I scorn to be so poor. I am a roarer.
CAPT.　A roarer?
TR.　Ay, Sir, two roarers.
CH.　Deliver up thy pandragon to me.
TR.　And give me thy sindicus.
CAPT.　Deliver?
MEG.　I pray you, Captain, be contented; the gentlemen seem to give us very good words.
CH.　Good words? Ay, if you could understand 'em; the words cost us twenty pounds.
MEG.　What is your pleasure, gentlemen?
CH.　I would enucleate your fructifier.

At Chough's request Meg sings for them, whereafter he and Trimtram alternate alliterative praises:

Melodious minotaur! Harmonious hippocrene! Sweet-breasted bronstrops! Most tunable tweak! Delicious duplar! Putrefactious panagron! [They begin to go awry.] Calumnious calicut! And most singular sindicus!

The prostitutes go off with the roarers; the Captain resolves that he too will learn to roar. In James Shirley's *The Gamester* (1633) Young Bernardo also aspires to be a roarer. Young blades in London continued to roar for a hundred years.

"The Lord is my shepherd, I shall not want. He maketh me to lie down in green pastures: He leadeth me beside the still waters. He restoreth my soul." The year 1611 is also the year of the Authorized Bible.

The version produced by King James' Committee was not the first translation into English. But the two unfinished attempts of Wycliffe around 1380 left little impression, as he was quickly charged with heresy. And the full Scripture for the English people, of Tyndale by 1535, too "plainly laid before their eyes in their mother tongue," did not outlast its day. He translated "Use not vain repetitions," for instance, as "Babble not much."

The shifted meaning of *charity* for our day makes more appropriate Tyndale's trinity of "faith, hope, and love," but later versions returned to the more literal translation of *caritas*. The rhythms of Tyndale, however, and his tone as of spoken word, were sustained in the later translation. The seven thousand words of the King James Bible have not been excelled in simple majesty, in quiet beauty, or in vehement malediction, nor in their influence upon the diction (as on the lives) of the generations that have used the book as their constant and holy guide, in England, and in the American colonies and early states.

How direct the English language is, how concise and succinct, may be indicated by a simple check, which has been made, of the number of syllables in various translations of the Gospel according to Mark:

Teutonic languages (average)	32,650
French	36,500
Slavic languages (average)	36,500
Romance languages (average)	40,200
Indo-Iranian languages (average)	43,100
English	29,000

The King James Bible sets a standard no work has since surpassed.

The year 1611, a literary *annus mirabilis*, also saw the publication of Chapman's translation of Homer's *Iliad*, which opened a rich vein of classical lore, evoked one of Keats' great sonnets, and was influential for over three centuries.

In the seventeenth century, science was waging one of its major attacks on superstition, but there was also in these years a cultural effort to reconcile the opposing attitudes. Francis Bacon, with his emphasis on direct experimentation, yet held a lingering belief in such unscientific activities as foreseeing the future. Ingeniously, he explained the truth of a "trivial prophecy" he had heard in his boyhood, when Elizabeth was in "the flower of her years": "When hempe is spun, England's done." *Hempe*, he pointed out, is an acrostic of England's rulers: Henry, Edward, Mary with Philip, and Elizabeth. Many, therefore, expected that England would thereafter come to "utter confusion." Behold, when Elizabeth died, in 1603, James who peacefully succeeded her was the ruler not of England but of Great Britain!

Bacon wrote his serious works in Latin, his—to him—more trivial essays, in English. (It is the essays that survive.) He was concerned with knowledgeable men, whom he sorted into three classes: Men of experiment, who, like the ant, merely collect and use. Reasoners, who resemble the spider, which spins a web from its own bowels. And philosophers, who, like the bee, draw their material from the world around but digest and recreate it with a power of their own. The bee, as Matthew Arnold after him observed, gives us honey and wax, sources of sweetness and light, great gifts too of art's bestowing.

Following Bacon, Galileo in Italy in 1633 declared—though he officially recanted—that the earth revolves around the sun. Man was no longer the center of the universe. Four years later, Descartes in France announced his views with the noted *Cogito, ergo sum*—"I think, therefore I am"—and formally ushered in the age of reason. The word consciousness had just come into the English language; man recognized that his own resources must be tried.

The old attitude, and the new, may be simply distinguished. Aristotle in the fourth century B.C. stated that, obviously, a heavy stone falls more rapidly than a light stone. And all the western world accepted this as fact—until on a calm day some eleven hundred years later Galileo Galilei dropped two unequal stones from the Leaning Tower of Pisa, and demonstrated that they reached the ground together. The experimental method proved its worth.

In England there were still upheaving changes. The pious regicides set up the Lord Protector, Oliver Cromwell, whose weak son ruled for a year before the Restoration brought back the astute but licentious Charles II, with his free-loving, free-living courtiers from France. In the midst of their effervescence, their heedless gaiety, their mistresses often chosen from the theater, where women now first acted in public on the English stage (like Charles's own Nell Gwyn, who—when the royal coach was being stoned because the people thought Charles' French mistress, the French King's spy, was riding—thrust out her head and called: "No! No! I am the English whore!"), in the midst of this frivolity, heedlessness, and hedonism, there came from prison the manuscript of *The Pilgrim's Progress* (1678), picturing the ascent of an honest and resolute soul through earthly trials to heaven. Its author, John Bunyan, said "I was never out of the Bible, either by reading or meditation," and his book is a model of direct simplicity, of clear and powerful presentation. It was immediately popular, and has been translated into over a hundred languages. The Bible and *The Pilgrim's Progress* constituted the entire library of many an early New England home. Three hundred years later, in *The New York Times* of October 10, 1976, John Steinbeck was quoted: *"Pilgrim's Progress* was mixed with my mother's milk."

Comparison of the opening of *The Pilgrim's Progress* with that of a recent book may indicate how styles have changed. Bunyan begins: "As I walked through the wilderness of this world, I lighted on a certain place where there was a den, and I laid me down in that place to sleep; and as I slept, I dreamed a dream." *Brave New World,* by Aldous Huxley (1952), a parable like Bunyan's book, begins: "A squat gray building of only 34 storeys. Over the main entrance the words Central London Hatchery and Conditioning Center, and, in a shield, the World State's motto, Community, Identity, Stability." The earlier passage has six finite verbs, one infinitive of purpose, six nouns, and one adjective. The recent one has eleven nouns, eight adjectival terms, and not a single verb. Bunyan has unquestionably the livelier narrative style.

In 1662 there was established the Royal Society. Prominent among its members was Isaac Newton, who built the discoveries of Copernicus, Kepler, and Galileo into a single system. The Society was second after the 1603 Accademia of Rome. The Académie Française was established in 1666; that of Germany in 1700; of Sweden in 1739, which was dominated by Carl Linnaeus, who systematized the classification and naming of plants. In 1743 came the American Philosophical Society, whose leading spirit was the inventor, author, and statesman Benjamin Franklin. Although Swift and Dryden sought to have the Royal Society regulate the English language, they never succeeded, as did the forty "immortals" in France, who even today determine the "official" language of the land; and English was left to move on its own untrammeled courses.

Just a few words as used by Milton will indicate that words have not been standing still. To Milton, *amuse* meant 'bewilder'; *defend* meant 'forbid'; *fond* was 'foolish'; *virtuous* was 'powerful'; and a *toil* was a 'snare'. If you took someone's *pulse,* it was beans or peas you got.

Among the new words of the seventeenth century were some from the Dutch, who were then the chief maritime rivals of the English, and had settled in New Amsterdam plumb in the middle of the English colonies on the Atlantic coast. Such words include *skipper, cruiser, freight, buoy, avast, belay, dock, rover.* After the Dutch Admiral Van Tromp nailed a broom to his masthead, as a sign that his navy swept the seas, the English added the word *Dutch* to a score of terms, in scorn. These include *Dutch courage,* the impudence brought on by drink. A *Dutch wife* is a pillow between the legs—actually used, in the world's hot climes, to absorb perspiration. To be *in Dutch* is usually unpleasant. And a *Dutch treat,* "going Dutch," of course, means that everyone pays for himself.

That rivalry came to an end when New Amsterdam, in 1664, became New York, and when William of Orange, with Mary, in 1689 ascended the English throne. A spell of peace followed, during which the country moved toward prosperity and the culture moved toward balance. There had come into men's minds the idea of infinite progress, checked only by their own errors, as opposed to the notion of man's degeneration after the Garden of Eden. It also became recognized that language was not a gift but a growth, neither fixed nor permanent; that words were capable, like their speakers, of being born and of dying. Pope wrote, in 1729:

> Think we that modern words eternal are?
> Toupet and tompion, cosins, and colmar
> Hereafter will be called by some plain man
> A wig, a watch, a pair of stays, a fan.

He was wrong on only two counts: *toupet* has been recently revived as a euphemism for 'wig'; *stays* went out with the whalebone corset.

But scientific terms increased, and new expressions arose in philosophy. Modern styles of writing were developed: the familiar essay as in the *Spectator* papers, especially those of Addison; the epistolary style—the first great novel, Richardson's *Pamela* (1740) was begun as a guide to letter-writers—and the new fashions of the novel, which quickly reached its heights in Fielding's *Tom Jones* (1749). At the same time, with the increasing literacy and power of the upper middle class, there was an increasing concern with words, as well as a greater chance of a livelihood from writing, with patrons on both political sides engaging pamphleteers. Samuel Johnson's *Dictionary* in 1755 was a sign of this emphasis on expression, while its Preface was a resounding challenge to the system of literary patronage. Robert Lowth's *Grammar,* in 1761, for the first time dealt with English rather than Latin.

Johnson's was the first full dictionary of the English language. Earlier works were glossaries of "hard" words, or Latin-English helps. [One exception was John Florio's *A Worlde of Wordes* (1598), an Italian-to-English dictionary. Florio is perhaps ridiculed as Holofernes in *Love's Labour's Lost.* Gonzago's description of an ideal state in *The Tempest* was taken from Florio's influential translation of Montaigne's *Essays.* Both Florio and Shakespeare dedicated works to the Earl of Southampton. A probable signature of Shakespeare, and an authenticated one of Ben Jonson, are in copies of Florio's *Montaigne*. Florio's dictionary was reissued in the potent year of 1611, dedicated to Queen Anne. Its Preface contains a modest but shrewd observation: "To be a Reader, requires understanding; to be a Critike, judgement. A Dictionarie gives arms to that, and takes no harme of this, if it mistake not."] English lexicography began with Samuel Johnson.

Johnson's *Dictionary* was the work of a single industrious man, collecting material through a half-dozen difficult years, with no encouragement from his supposed patron, Lord Chesterfield. To this gentleman's tardy recognition when the book was being printed, Johnson responded with a courageous and famous letter, ending:

> Is not a patron, my Lord, one who looks with unconcern on a man struggling for life in the water, and, when he has reached ground, encumbers him with help? The notice which you have been pleased to take of my labours, had it been early, had been kind; but it has been delayed until I am indifferent, and cannot enjoy it; till I am solitary, and cannot impart it; till I am known, and do not want it.

With a neat turn the proud Johnson brought the letter to its close:

> I have been long wakened from that Dream of hope, in which
> I once boasted myself with so much exultation,
>> my Lord,
>> Your Lordship's most humble and
>> Obedient Servant,
>> S.J.

The ever blunt Johnson later wrote, of Lord Chesterfield's *Letters* to his (bastard) son: "They teach the morals of a whore, and the manners of a dancing master."

Johnson's intention, as expressed in the 1747 Plan of the *Dictionary*, was to establish a work by which the purity of the language "may be preserved, its use ascertained, and its duration lengthened." (This was an echo of Swift's proposal, thirty-five years before, "for correcting, improving and ascertaining the English tongue"—the only work to which Swift ever signed his own name.) To this end, Johnson collected words as far back as Sidney (1580). Johnson's idiosyncrasies glint throughout the work. He defines *lexicographer*: 'a writer of dictionaries, a harmless drudge'. (A book review in the *New York Times* of November 26,

1972, amended: "*Homo lexicographicus* is a chalcenterous species of mankind." The word of Greek origin means 'with bowels of brass'.) Johnson's often expressed hatred of the Whigs finds print: "*Tory:* One who adheres to the ancient constitution of the state, and the apostolical hierarchy of the Church of England—opposed to a Whig." "*Whig:* the name of a faction." His scorn of the Scots finds vent in his definition of *oats:* "A grain, which in England is generally given to horses, but in Scotland supports the people"— to which a Scot retorted: "That's perhaps why the English are proud of their horses, and the Scots are proud of their men." With a humor as heavy as his person, Johnson defined *net:* 'Any thing reticulated or decussated at equal distances, with interstices between the intersections'. When a lady, who had probably ridden to hounds, asked him why he had defined *pastern* as 'the knee of a horse', he replied "Ignorance, Madam, pure ignorance!" He also, of several words, admitted ignorance in the dictionary itself, as with *etch:* 'A country word of which I know not the meaning'. Do not smile loftily, you with etchings on your walls; the example the Doctor gives is: "Lay dung upon the etch, and sow it with barley." (It is a "country word" for loosened soil, in which to plant a second crop.)

Johnson set the example of giving passages from various authors to illustrate the meanings, followed in the great *Oxford English Dictionary* with its almost two million quotations.

In and out of his dictionary, Johnson maintained his attitude toward women. He defined *to walk:* "To be in motion; applied to a clamorous or abusive female tongue". And he remarked in conversation: "Sir, a woman preaching is like a dog's walking on his hinder legs. It is not done well; but you are surprised to find it done at all."

Johnson built his reputation on his uninhibited but sesquipedalian speech, which he found effective on all occasions. On the street one day, a sweeping-woman was raising a cloud of dust as he approached. He cried: "Woman, thou art a parallelogram!" and as the startled sweeper gawked, walked cleanly by. He remarked of the Duke of Buckingham's play *The Rehearsal:* "It has not wit enough to keep it sweet"—then hemmed, and spoke again: "It has not vitality enough to preserve it from putrefaction." Perhaps the one occasion he was surprised into monosyllables was when he was told that someone had called Johnson's own tragedy *Irene* a masterpiece. Johnson growled: "If the man said that, the man lied." Even the pundit's rare moments of sexual temptation were expressed in grandiloquent terms, as when he confessed to his early pupil and lasting friend, the actor Garrick: "I'll come no more behind your scenes, David, for the silk stockings and white bosoms of your actresses arouse my amorous propensities."

In his literary evaluations, none the less, the critic did not suffer his personal mannerisms to overcome his judgment. "Whoever wishes to attain an English style," he declared, "familiar but not coarse, and elegant but not ostentatious, must give his days and nights to the volumes of Addison." Addison's essays are indeed far from Johnsonese—though in the lexicographer's milder moments his style is referred to as Johnsonian. What "Johnsonese" is like may be inferred from Edmund Burke's protest when Boswell suggested that Herbert Croft's *Life of Dr. Young* was a good imitation of Johnson's style. "No, no," the meticulous Burke protested:

> It is not a good imitation of Johnson; it has all his pomp, without his force; it has all the nodosities of the oak without its strength; it has all the contortions of a Sibyl without the inspiration.

Croft's forgotten biography evinces, as does many a scholarly dissertation since, the petrifactions of a plodding pate.

Styles and words have come and gone since Johnson's day, but no more major invasions of the land are likely to bring tremendous changes in diction and form. The three unresting voyagers, the soldier, the trader, and the priest, still go on their missions around the world, and bring back foreign phrases. Internal alteration never stops; Byron described the process a century after Pope:

> As forests shed their foliage by degrees,
> So fare expressions that no longer please.

Burier, then (Hamlet's) *grave-digger,* became, literally, *undertaker,* then *funeral director,* not yet entirely supplanted by *mortician.* Slang constantly comes and usually goes. New inventions require new names, sometimes superseding the older, as *nickelodeon* gave way to the *cinema* and the *motion-picture house.* Processes of word formation, which we shall consider soon, are ever at work.

Before we follow the language westward across the ocean, let us look at a few samplings of words brought back to England from other lands:

African: (Bantu) zebra; (Bechuana) tsetse; (Dahomey) voodoo; (Kongo) goober; (Mandingo) mumbo jumbo; (Mbuba) okapi; (Sudanese) chimpanzee

Australian: kangaroo, boomerang
Arabic (some via Spain): coffee, café, tariff
Basque: bizarre
Chinese: sampan; (Amoy) tea, (Cantonese) typhoon (*tai fung*, 'supreme wind')
Czech: robot
Egyptian (Coptic): ebony, oasis
Finnish: sauna
Hawaiian: poi, ukelele
Hindi: nabob, pundit, punch, juggernaut, polo, guru
Hungarian: goulash, paprika, coach
Italian: (direct) incognito, broccoli, ghetto; (via French) burlesque; (Anglicized) sonnet, balcony; (military) canteen, barracks, squadron, sentinel; (music, three-quarters of our terms) pianoforte, aria, mandolin, violin (from the Latin) opera, (from the Greek) orchestra; (art) sketch, model, medal, bust, fiasco, fresco
Japanese: kimono, tycoon, karate
Lapp: lemming, tundra
Malagasi: bantam, kapok
Malay: ketchup, bamboo, orangutan
Malayalam: atoll, teak
Persian: scarlet, lilac, bazaar, khaki, chess
Polish: mazurka
Portuguese (some through Spanish): apricot, marmalade, molasses, verandah; (from Javanese) junk; (from Tamil) mango, fetish, caste
Quechua: llama, puma
Russian: pogrom, astrakhan, sputnik (1957; originally Greek *syn*, 'together', plus Indo-European *put*, 'way', plus *nik*, a personal ending, borrowed for beatnik, nudnik)
Sanskrit: zen
Siberian: mammoth
Slavic: vampire, sable
Tahitian: tattoo
Tamil: pariah, curry, anaconda, catamaran, mulligatawny
Tibetan: lama, yak
Turkish: turban, tulip, caviar, yogurt
Tongan: taboo

This, of course, but skims the surface of our foreign borrowings. And doubtless, if our descendants make contact with thinking beings on planets of other stars, new words from outer space—instead of science-fiction inventions—will join the vocabulary of the greatest language on earth.

3.
ENGLISH CROSSES
THE ATLANTIC

THE SETTLEMENT OF NORTH AMERICA by the English had scarcely begun when Samuel Daniel, in 1599, in the full glory of Elizabeth's reign, boasted of the language, and prophesied better than he knew of its later spread. He begins with a still pertinent warning:

> Or should we, carelesse, come behinde the rest
> In power of words, that go before in worth,
> Whenas our accents equall to the best
> Are able greater wonders to bring forth:
> When all that ever hotter spirits exprest
> Comes bettered by the patience of the north.
> And who, in time, knows whither we may vent
> The treasure of our tongue, to what strange shores
> This gaine of our best glory shall be sent
> T'inrich unknowing Nations with our stores?

The early English colonists on the strange American shores, as they secured their hold upon the Atlantic coast, perforce grew acquainted with Indian habits and word ways, as they frequently buried the hatchet and smoked the pipe of peace before renewed hostilities. *Lacrosse* is a French word for the Indian *baggataway* game, which gets the name we use from the stick's resemblance to a bishop's crozier; but the name was written into American history. On June 4, 1763, when the Ojibway and the Sac Indians, "to celebrate the birthday of George III," staged a lacrosse game in the clear space outside Fort Michillimackinac, the ball flew over the fort wall; the Indians, rushing in to retrieve it, snatched weapons hidden by their watching squaws, and massacred the garrison.

As the contacts widened westward, more and more Indian words filtered into the language, up to the start of the twentieth century. Here are samples of Indian words that, through the years, have become part of our vocabulary:

From the Algonquian: *tomahawk, pecan, skunk, moccasin.* Cree: *woodchuck.* Narragansett: *moose, sachem.* Natick: *mugwump* (defined as a man with his mug on one side of the fence and his wump on the other). Ojibway: *makinaw, totem, wigwam.* Penobscot: *sagamore.* Powhatan: *raccoon.* Sioux: *tepee.* Wolf: *tuxedo* (from the Algonquian word for 'round foot' applied in scorn to the Wolf tribe in mid–New York State. The land there, Tuxedo Park, was acquired by the Griswold family in payment of a debt; they opened an exclusive club, at which young Griswold Lorillard in the 1880s wore the first dinner jacket without tails. The wearer of a tuxedo may again be called a wolf.) New York's *Tammany* was the name of a Delaware Indian; it means 'affable'.

From farther south came other words. Carib: *canoe, hammock, hurricane, tobacco, iguana.* Taino: *key* (meaning 'reef' or 'islet'), *potato.* Tupi: *mahogany, jaguar, buccaneer.* Arawak: *barbecue.* Quechua: *quinine, alpaca, vicuña.* Nahuatl: *chocolate, tomato, tapioca, banana.* And from the far north Eskimo: *kayak, igloo, anorak.*

The English colonists' first major contact with other Europeans in America was with the Dutch, when the settlers of New Amsterdam were so dissatisfied with Governor Peter Stuyvesant's dictatorial ways that in 1664 they surrendered without a struggle to the soldiers of the Duke of York. Many of the Dutch place names were Anglicized: *Flatbush, Flushing, Van Cortland Park,* the *Bronx. Gramercy Park* is named not for French *grand merci,* 'many thanks', but from Dutch *Krum Marisje,* 'crooked little marsh': the waters of the East River then spread that far inland. And the northern creek that made Manhattan an island, through which the tides poured swiftly, was called *Spuyten Duyvil,* 'despite the Devil'. Dutch words that were turned into English include *boss, sleigh, cooky, cruller, coleslaw, scow.*

Names, indeed, have gone through curious alterations on both sides of the Atlantic. In old England, the tavern with the Norse name *Piga Waes Hael,* 'Hail to the Virgin', was made easier on thirsty English tongues as the *Pig and Whistle.* The pious pub (public house) *God Encompasses Us* became the more diverting

Goat and Compasses. The reveling *Bacchanals* was attuned to its frequenters as *Bag o' Nails.* A tavern named for the Spanish Crown Princess, *La Infanta de Castilla,* when Spain became an enemy turned into the *Elephant and Castle.* Along the way, the King's Road (*La Route du Roi*) was cockneyfied into *Rotten Row;* and by the farmers of England *Le Pied Poudreux* ('Dusty Foot'), the summary court for disposing of vagabonds at the county fair, was called the *Pie Powder* Court.

In the New World, many hundreds of our place names, from *Manhattan* in New York to *Puyallup* in Washington, are adaptations of the Indian names, which were transmogrified even more than the Dutch. There are 131 spellings recorded for what finally became *Winnipesaukee.* Many variations, including *Minnay Sota* ('Muddy Water') were used before the settlers settled on *Minnesota.* Other Indian names finally became *Neversink, Chattahoochee, Okefenokee, Okeechobee, Tippecanoe.*

French in its turn was twisted on pioneer tongues. *Du Chemin* became *Dishmaugh. Des Ruisseaux* is now *Dairysaw; Ile aux Galets, Skilligalee. L'Eau Froide* ('Cold Water') froze into *Low Freight. Chemin Couvert* ('Covered Way') came out as *Smackover.* The *Purgatoire* River in Texas flows on as *Picketwire.*

Even Latin became involved in American place names. When two explorers found the lake from which the Mississippi takes its course, one of them suggested calling it the Latin for 'true source,' *Veritas Caput,* as he put it; his less learned but more practical comrade sliced the words in half, giving its name to Lake *Itasca.* Of course, hundreds of American places just borrowed names from earlier cities abroad: *Syracuse, Ithaca, New London, Troy.*

By the steadfast stay-at-home English, the language divagations of the colonists were regarded with scorn. In 1735 Francis Moore wrote home of Savannah, Georgia: "It stands upon the flat of a hill; the bank of the river (which they in barbarous English call a bluff) is steep." With the Revolution, English scorn of the language spread to the culture. In 1778 Samuel Johnson bombasticated: "I am willing to love all mankind, except an American." At the opening of the War of 1812, Robert Southey wrote to Walter Savage Landor: "See what it is to have a nation take its place among civilized states before it has either gentlemen or scholars!" and in 1820 Sydney Smith exclaimed: "Who reads an American book!" How wrong he was!

In that very year appeared Washington Irving's *Sketch Book.*

In this, the essay on Westminster Abbey was, and remains, the best description and appreciation that monument to English history and culture has received. And the essay on the Alhambra influenced the Spanish authorities to rescue that great palace and estate from the despoiling gypsies and establish it as a free landmark for the people. In 1821 James Fenimore Cooper's *The Spy* won readers in many parts of Europe. And Benjamin Franklin was already a "best seller" on two continents. As the century advanced, the works of Hawthorne, Longfellow, Emerson, and Poe became known abroad. The great French poet Mallarmé learned English to read Poe in the original; the greater Baudelaire translated some of the American's works.

The Americans themselves were aware of their changing speech ways. In 1780 John Adams called (in vain) for an "academy for refining, improving, and ascertaining the English language." The next year Dr. John Witherspoon, President of the College of New Jersey (now known as Princeton) coined the word *Americanism*, in a series of essays "upon the general state of the English language in America, and to attempt a collection of the chief improprieties." Among these he listed *mad* (for *angry*); *clever*; and *fellow-countrymen*, calling the first part of this word redundant: does not Shakespeare have Antony say merely "Friends, Romans, Countrymen"? In 1789 a backwoods schoolteacher, Noah Webster, wrote the first of three volumes—a grammar, a speller, and a reader—that were the major American language textbooks for a century. In the prolegomenon to his Dictionary, a "Dissertation on the English Language," Webster advocated separate standards for American speech, and prophesied that in a hundred years the new language would differ as much from English as Danish from German. He dedicated his work to Benjamin Franklin, who was cool to Webster's enthusiasm for a separate American speech.

Of necessity, the new American was a political animal, and many of his new terms arose from his new form of government. *Electioneering* included *campaigning* for one's candidate. *Logrolling* was taken over from the woodsman. *Stump* speeches were made from the bottoms of felled trees still rooted in the village green. *Lobbying* was practiced as early as 1808. *Gerrymander* (1812) sprang from the curious salamander shape into which Governor Gerry of Massachusetts fashioned an election district so that his party could retain control. The odd shape of various cities' election districts shows that the practice has not been abandoned. A *maverick*, who acknowledges no party label, perpetuates the name of a man who did not brand his cattle, letting them roam without sign of an owner. The political parties took names from the new form of government: Federalist, Republican, Democratic. *Muckraker,* however, was first used by Teddy Roosevelt in 1906.

Free from European threats after 1812, the Americans moved westward across their widespread land. From Canada down the Mississippi to New Orleans they encountered the French, from whom they took, along with the land, a number of words: *chowder, rapids, pioneer, prairie.* The last of these widened in well over a hundred combinations, such as *prairie grass;* the *open prairie; prairie schooner,* for the covered wagon of the pioneers. *Prairie coal* was dried buffalo chips, used as fuel. A *Prairie oyster,* or *prairie cocktail,* was a raw egg in whiskey. *Cocktail* itself is of disputed origin; but the drink was at once popular—and politicized, in the Republican remark that cocktails were good for campaigning Democrats to proffer, because after a man had swallowed a cocktail, he was ready to swallow anything.

America was on the march. The pioneer was rough and ready, hail-fellow-well-met, hospitable, exuberant. He would offer a passer-through the continent, and serve him a tin cup of moonshine. On his surging course, and in his newly cleared towns, he coined many colorful words: *scoot, skidoo, high-falutin, scrumptious, hunkydory, spondulix, bullfrog, scalawag;* but also more sweet-sounding compounds like *morning-glory, honeysuckle, whippoorwill.* Journalists for a time were amused to refer to *hatches, matches, and dispatches:* items for the birth, marriage, and obituary columns. As Lowell astutely remarked, vulgarisms are poetry in the egg.

Words from various activities moved back eastward into the nation's word ways. From the woodsman, from the miner, as well as the cowboy, they returned along the railroad, with the *cowcatcher* in front and the *caboose* behind—caboose soon becoming slang for a person's rear end. With steam along the riverways, the sidewheel propelled ships up the Hudson to Albany; more colorful was the journey from Cincinnati down the Ohio River and the Mississippi to New Orleans, with stern paddlewheel and a lineman prober at the prow, with his plumb line, for shifting shoals. This watcher would call out the marks that told the depth—one of his measures grew famous as the pseudonym of Samuel Langhorne Clemens: Mark Twain. There was also the showboat, with its calliope (pronounced Kallyope), which also made music for the circus parade when the animals, clowns, and acrobats came to town. The riverboats still ply the waters; in August 1976 the *Mississippi Queen* made its maiden voyage from Cincinnati to New Orleans, a luxury ship that took seven days, at fifteen miles an hour, for a trip now made by plane in two hours.

Speaking of Cincinnati brings to mind that in that inland city, *Cincinnati oysters* were pigs' feet. Another term, from the Civil War General Ambrose Everett Burnside, is *sideburns,* for his moustache with mutton chops, the chin shaven. Other phrases that rose into general use are *the whole caboodle,* and *in cahoots with.* Terms of scorn, of course, were common: *nickel-nurser* for a *pinch-penny;* a little later, *flat tire* for one by no means the life of the party.

Southward, and ultimately in the Far West, the expanding nation fell upon the Spaniards. From Florida, and along the Mexican border, more words came onto the tongues of the settlers and the cowboys: *fiesta, parade, siesta, sombrero, bonanza, mustang, lasso.* A *ranch* was at first a hut for the far-ranging herdsman, the *ranchero.* James Russell Lowell, pronouncing that *ch* like a *k,* wrote in *The Biglow Papers:* "These fellows are very propilly called Rank Heroes, and the more they kill the ranker and more heroick they bekim."

When the American adventurers passed the *mesas,* the 'table' lands, and reached the Pacific, they found the region already named by the Catalan monks: *California,* meaning 'hot as a furnace'. Citizens of that state today may point, for its origin, rather to a sixteenth-century romance in which a land named California is pictured as a paradise on earth. Both sources seem at different times correct.

Gringo, a Mexican term for a man from north of the border, springs from the well-known verses of Robert Burns:

> *Green grow* the rashes, O,
> Green grow the rashes, O,
> The sweetest hours that e'er I spend
> Are spent among the lasses, O.

—which was the chorus of a song popular with the homesick Yankee soldier.

A number of words the colonists had brought from England took on new meanings. *Lumber,* which originally described the pawnshops of *Lombardy,* in England meant old furniture; in America it was applied to cut-up trees. These were hauled out of the woods on rough *dirt* roads; back home, dirt was not 'earth' but 'filth'—a sense retained figuratively in the recently current reference to "a dirty old man." Dirt roads developed potholes or rough ridges, 'washboards'; in some places logs were laid crosswise, forming *corduroy* roads; improvements were therefore sought; to smooth the tops, roads were *macadamized*. This word, from the name of the man that invented the process, combines Gaelic *Mac* with Hebrew *Adam,* Greek *-ize,* and Old English (Germanic, Indo-European) *-d,* encapsulating in a word why the United States came to be called the melting-pot of nations.

For as the years rolled on, the welcoming torch of the Statue of Liberty in New York's harbor lighted the way to millions of immigrants and refugees. In the 1840s the potato famine in Ireland brought many Irish, who influenced the speechways rather than the vocabulary, but whose predilections are indicated by *shillelagh, whiskey,* and *mavourneen.* Later in the same decade, political turmoil drove many Germans to America, and their hearty appetites were accompanied with many terms from their kitchens: *pumpernickel, lager, dunking, pretzel, stein. Hamburger,* the first syllable misunderstood, was springboard to *beefburger* and *cheeseburger.* The *frankfurter,* also from the name of a German city, from its shape was nicknamed a *Dachshund sausage.* One baseball day at the New York Polo Grounds, the cartoonist TAD (T.A. Dargan), who couldn't spell, hit upon the term *hot dog.* So popular did this become that in 1913 the Coney Island Chamber of Commerce forbade the boardwalk concessionaires to advertise frankfurters as Hot Dogs.

After the Civil War, the increasing immigrants—Scandinavians, Slavs, Italians, Jews—gave lessening contribution to the language, which had learned to nourish itself from its own soil. Italian, like German, supplied some new items of consumption: *spaghetti* and other *pastas, pizza, espresso.* Spanish is becoming influential again, as U.S. citizens from Puerto Rico crowd into the States, giving us new words, as *bodega, machismo.* Yiddish, especially in New York, where in 1929 there were ten Yiddish theatres, has supplied various terms and turns of phrases: *I should worry; kibitzer, meshuga, kosher,* most of which have remained slang. Yiddish is still a source of ephemeral vogue-words, such as recently traced the growth of little Sammy. His parents wanted to name him Vincent, but Grandma exclaimed "Vincent Schmincent!" So they named the child Sadie. But Sammy came, and grew old enough to take music lessons. "Violin Schmiolin! What's wrong with TV?" A little later, Samuel had problems; his proudly up-to-date parents mentioned the Oedipus Complex, whereupon Grandma protested: "Oedipus Schmedipus, so long as he loves his mother!" As one of the earliest English poets comforted himself (in *Deor's Lament*): "This will pass also."

The use of colorful expressions will not pass. Individual words and phrases may go, but Americans continuously replace them with fresh locutions, keeping the language live and lively. To *cop out; splashdown, think tank, pantyhose, jetliner, waterbed*. Moonlight has long been in popular consideration, both in the mood of romantic lovers, leading to the *honeymoon,* and in the reputed influence of the full moon on dogs and humans (*lunatic,* from Latin *luna,* 'moon'); *moonlighter,* a recent coinage, in turn gave birth to the verb *to moonlight,* to work at a job in addition to a regular one. The list is long and, even as I write, changing.

Those desirous of copulation without population speak of "the pill," as though there were no others—as we all speak of *the* truth and *a* lie, as though on every occasion lies may be many and truth but one. Indeed, noting this, Mark Twain said, manifestly minimizing the number, "There are 869 different ways of lying, but only one of them is squarely forbidden: Thou shalt not bear false witness against thy neighbor." This leaves us widely free, and that freedom everyone not only employs but enjoys.

Some of the almost forgotten phrases of the last century are amusing and vivid enough to be, if not used, at least remembered. "I'll be there with bells on!" bespeaks an enthusiastic acceptance, from the days when one arrived with bells jingling on the harness of the horses that pulled the little buggy with the fringe on top. *Callithumpian* parties, which went on all night, are echoed in the fortissimo rock festivals of our day. Akin to the callithumpians were the *cowbellians,* who liked to "kick up a jollification"; the word is synonymous, and rhymes, with *hellions. To deacon* has gone, but no expression has replaced it, for the practice of putting the best berries at the top of the basket. In Billingsgate, such a practice is called *to dub. To acknowledge the corn* was a picturesque term for admitting guilt of a minor offense, to avoid punishment for a major crime. It arose when a man, accused of stealing four horses and the corn to feed them, declared: "I acknowledge the corn." The best we have for the continuing practice is *to cop a plea.* We continue, however, to find new vivid turns of the language; more will be mentioned in the discussion of slang.

A further frequent change in the United States came in the family name, the surname. Names from Old England—to look back for a moment—were seldom altered, although occasionally fancified, as with the *y* in *Byrd* and *Smythe*. British surnames, which became hereditary in the fourteenth-century, like those of other countries of Western Europe came mainly from five sources:

1. Family, of sire, ancestor, or tribe (clan, sept): *Johnson* (*Jones,* the most common name in Wales), *Tomkins, Fitzhugh, MacDonald, O'Keefe.*

2. Occupation: *Smith* (the most common name in England), *Baker, Chandler, Clark, Cooper, Fletcher* ('arrow-maker'), *Murphy* (the most common name in Ireland, the name of three septs, meaning 'sea-warrior'). Shakespeare had contemporaries named *Shakelance* and *Shakeshaft.*

3. Place of residence: *Atwell, Bradford, Shipley* ('sheep lea'), *Churchill.*

4. Personal peculiarities, perhaps at first nicknames: *Armstrong, Short, Longfellow, Whitehead, Kennedy* ('ugly head'), *Gray, Truman.* In the current London phonebook, the name *Mudd* occurs twenty-six times, *Muddiman* three, *Muddyman* one, and *Muddle* eleven.

5. Natural objects: *Berry, Buck, Fox, Oaks, Stone, Shaw, Burns.*

Of course, many changes in the nomenclature develop as families go on. The name *Bury,* twenty-five times in the London phonebook: does it mean what it says, from an earlier gravedigger or burial ground; or is it a turn from *Burg* or *Berry?*

The early Jews and Greeks were marked by a single name, which often to us seems chosen in anticipation of the person's career. *Adam* is the Hebrew word for man; actually, the one formed from *adama,* 'earth'. Similarly Latin *homo,* 'man', and *humanus* are related to *humus,* 'earth'. "Dust thou art." *Elizabeth,* the wife of Moses' brother Aaron in the Bible (Hebrew *Elishebha*), means 'My God is an oath'; the second element is related to *sheva,* 'seven'; literally, bound himself by the sacred number seven. The power of names and numbers was great in the early mind. God changed *Abram,* 'exalted father', to *Abraham,* 'father of a multitude': both Jews and Moslems claim him as ancestor. *Alexander* (the Great) was what his name means: 'leader of men'. The Greek hero Oedipus was named from his natal misfortune. It was prophesied that the newborn would kill his father and marry his mother; in the (vain) hope of preventing this, he was exposed—hung on a tree by his feet—and left to die. Rescued, he grew in the physical state caught in his name—used by Shelley in his translation of Sophocles' play: *Swellfoot* the Tyrant.

Oedipus means 'swollen feet'. Another nickname that has survived is that of the Greek whom his parents called Aristocles; from his broad shoulders, he is known to the modern world as the philosopher Plato. (The root recurs in *platypus,* named from its broad feet.)

The Romans seem to have been the first western nation to use three appellations. (The Chinese also use three: first, the family name, which is passed along; second, the generation name, shared by brothers, sisters, and first cousins; last, the personal name of the individual.) Among the Romans, the forename (*praenomen*) was the individual appellation; the (*nomen*) was that of the tribe, or gens; the third (*cognomen*) was that of the particular family within the gens. A family distinguished in the line of both parents might use two *cognomina.* And occasionally, in honor of an individual's distinguished achievement, he might be accorded an added name (*agnomen*). Thus the great leader Quintus Fabius Maximus Verucosus was given the last name *Cunctator* ('the delayer') for his constant harassing thrusts at Hannibal during the second Punic War (218–202 B.C.), while always avoiding a pitched battle. His policy gave rise to use of his name for the nineteenth-century English Fabian Society, led by the Webbs (Sidney and Beatrice) and George Bernard Shaw, advocating a gradualist socialism.

The favorite love poet of the Middle Ages, the Roman Ovid—banished by Augustus Caesar in 1 A.D.—was actually Publius Ovidius Naso, as W. S. Gilbert reminds us in *Iolanthe* when the Fairy Queen, stricken with love for the Parliament sentry, sings:

> Oh, amorous dove!
> Type of Ovidius Naso!
> This heart of mine is soft as thine,
> Although I dare not say so.

Shakespeare had earlier played on the nasal significance of the name, Holofernes speaking in *Love's Labor's Lost:* "Ovidius Naso was the man. And why, indeed, Naso, but for smelling out the odiferous flowers of fancy, the jerks of invention?" The most influential Roman writer through the first 1500 Christian years, author of the epic poem the *Aeneid,* was Virgil, who died in 19 B.C. Lines in his poem were supposed to have foretold the coming of Christ; St. Paul is said to have wept at his tomb. And for centuries, persons hesitant about the future sought the *sortes Virgilianae:* they opened the book at random, and were guided by what they read. The Roman Emperor Hadrian and the English King Charles I are among those that thus consulted the poet, whose full name was Publius Vergilius Maro.

Most of the name changes in America were made because of the difficulty, on American lips, in sounding the names of immigrants from Eastern Europe. These names, although their endings might mean 'from' or 'son of,' were frequently long, and unfamiliar to Americans. Often they were changed by ignorant or well-meaning immigration officials, registering the newcomers at Ellis Island, New York's reception center and long the main gateway to the States. Some newcomers, as the Kabachinsky family, went to court to legitimate the new name.

This family, in Boston, wanted to change its name to Cabot; the Cabots' attorney attended, to request a refusal. The judge ruled that no name, however distinguished, was the hallowed, exclusive property of a single line; that Kabachinsky was a difficult name, and not of an American tone; and he welcomed the new Cabots to citizenship in their new country. The next week, a columnist printed the familiar jingle pricking the pride of the "proper Bostonians":

> Here's to good old Boston,
> The home of the bean and the cod,
> Where the Lowells speak only to Cabots,
> And the Cabots speak only to God.

—save that in the column the last line was altered:

> And the Cabots speak Yiddish, by God!

Since then, there have been few objections to the simplifying of names.

A special problem developed in German-speaking countries when, in the early nineteenth-century, everyone was required to take a surname. In numerous villages, the clerk assigned an obscene or otherwise objectionable name, allowing himself to be persuaded, by an adequate gift, to substitute a more pleasant appellation. Two men, many years later grown friendly in New York, were Mr. Schmeiss and Mr. Schutz. One day the subject of names arose, and Mr. Schmeiss said: "You can't guess how much I paid to have that *m* put in." Mr. Schutz smiled back: "You can't guess how much I paid to have *m* taken out." (*Schmeiss* means fling; *Scheiss* is the vulgar word for excretion. *Schutz* means protection; *Schmutz* is filth.)

Some of these names were later Anglicized: *Geltwasser* became *Goldwater*, in apparent ignorance that this is a euphemism for urine. (In England, the man that cleaned out the privies was called the *goldfinder*.) Names in other languages have had similar vicissitudes; consider just the leading general in the 1821 Greek War of Independence: his name, *Theodore Kolokotronis*, means 'God's-gift Bullet-in-the-arse'.

The more fortunate received neutral names, like *Berliner*, *Eisenhauer* ('horse-shoer'); the wealthier acquired pleasant ones, *Rosenberg*, *Apfelbaum* ('appletree'), *Geltman*, *Adlerbloom*.

The study of names is *onomastics;* a bad name is a *caconymic.* Equally those that bear them have all joined in that most democratic of processes, the growth of the language.

[It might be of interest to consider a personal movement of word ways. For unsleeping hours, the night after I wrote of "Mark Twain modestly minimizing the number" of lies, I pondered the passage. That's when I added the words about our freedom. As all things not mentioned in the U.S. Constitution are left to the wisdom of the States, so all sins not mentioned in the Ten Commandments are left to the conscience of the mortal.

[Note that my first adverb was *modestly.* That didn't seem to fit. Then I tried *urbanely,* which added an *n* but lost the *m. Mournfully* had both letters, but not the meaning. Then *manifestly* thrust itself into my mind, and manifestly was the word. For clearly the number given is too small to encompass all man's methods of deceit. And the letters are in order: the *m* of *Mark* and the distant *n* of *Twain; m.n* of *manifestly; m.n.m* of *minimizing* (plus the faint twang of the participial ending: note that N-ding); then the reversal *n.m* of *number,* to close off the chain. And the repeated *m–m–m* may suggest the hemming of a man's hesitant moment before plumping to speak his lie, while the *n–n* is the sound of a doting yet disapproving mother.

[Excessive, perhaps, yet I trust not obsessive. Oscar Wilde once reported that he had spent a morning pondering a line he had written. Finally, he took out a comma. In the afternoon, he put it back.

[Years upon years ago, I held a poem of mine for nine months, seeking an adjective for the last, short line. Finally, I hit upon *bonny*—"My bonny mare"—the word *heath* in the line before justifying the suggestion of Scotland. Henry Seidel Canby, then editor of the *Saturday Review,* told me he liked the poem, but had to reject it because of one word—of course, my *bonny*. Every time he saw that word, he said, there flashed into his mind a song of the Scot comedian Harry Lauder. It began: "I love a lassie, a bonny, bonny lassie." The second stanza turns the line to "I love a lassie, a bony, bony lassie"; and in the final turn it becomes "I love molasses, New Orleans molasses." So I sent the poem to *Verse,* edited in Boston by Harold Vinal, who had probably never heard Harry Lauder. He printed it. Words too are known by the company they keep.]

Of course, not every passage wins the detailed consideration thus given in sleepless hours. Much of a writer's phrasing grows intuitive. But words repay the attention they are accorded.

4.

WORD DEVELOPMENT

THE WORDS OF OUR LANGUAGE have been contributed, without fear or favor, by persons in the whole range of human activity. The Romance languages, and all the words they have given to English, came not from the classical writings of Cicero but from the Vulgar Latin of the Roman soldier. And through the centuries eupatrid and helot, patrician and plebeian, priest and robber-baron, scholar and gentleman and ignoramus, butcher, baker, and candlestick maker, hobo and hooligan, have added their rude or polished terms to the speech of us all. In all language growth, *Vox populi, vox Dei*—"the voice of the people is the voice of God."

There are many ways in which words have come into being, have been granted a more or less permanent place in the language. Let us look at the major methods.

1. *Invention.* The simplest and most direct way of forming a new word is to make it up. In the slow growth of the language, however, this has been a rare activity, until the rapid advance of science and new products in the past century necessitated many new names. Among earlier inventions we may note *gas*, which in 1640 van Helmont declared he was forming by analogy with *chaos*. More recently have come *blurb* (Gelett Burgess, 1907), *kodak, pyrex, spoof, blimp, gimmick*. The Pfizer chemical firm, which develops some eighty products a year, has had a computer reel out thousands of letter combinations from which to choose. Most new terms, however, have been fashioned from the classical languages, as in the next group.

2. *Combination.* Some new words have been put together from already existing English words. Among these are *railroad, frog-man, paperback, teenager, handout, double-decker, long-playing* —the hyphen indicating that the coupling is not yet fully do-

53

miciled. Many others are combined from classical—Greek and Latin—roots, perhaps with a vowel (usually *o* for Greek and *i* for Latin) inserted to smooth the flow of the sounds. Thus *sine-cure, cornucopia, republic, carnivorous;* more recently *aureomy-cin, cellophane, homogenize, psychoanalysis, cosmonaut, ultra-sonic.* Some of the new words are hybrids, the two component parts from different languages: *automobile, tonsillectomy.* It was amusingly prophesied of one such word: "Television? No good will come of this device. The word is half Greek and half Latin." I myself fashioned a new word when the publisher asked me for a photograph, responding "I'm not especially *euphotic.*" The word popped out; on reflection, it seems more apt then the usual *photo-genic,* which has been twisted from its basic meaning, 'light-producing'.

Many good coinages came into English as progress made them necessary; a history of science might be written by tracing the words. Physics first: 1616 *magnetism,* 1619 *telescope,* 1622 *grav-ity,* 1646 *electricity.* Then living things: 1656 *microscope,* 1665 *cell,* 1696 *botany,* 1726 *zoology.* Then chemistry: 1789 *oxygen,* 1801 *atom.* Then 1832 *evolution.* Then health: 1847 *bacterium;* 1881 *pasteurize* . . . 1905 *hormone* (coined by Dr. Sterling from a Greek root meaning 'to set in motion'), 1905 *vitamin,* 1928 *peni-cillin.* Newton invented a mathematical language, the differential calculus, to construct his theory of gravitation; Einstein, the tensor calculus, for his general theory of relativity (1904). This capped the revelation of a strange world, beyond direct reach of our senses: we learned of the *X-ray* (1895), the *electron* (1895), *radioactivity* (1896), the *quantum* (1901), *relativity* (1904). New concepts may turn up at any moment, around any invisible corner —too minute or too distant for actual beholding. Thus Paul Jennings satirically pictures an Activated Sludge in which "two perfectly opposite forces are held in perfect equilibrium, like all those electrons, masons, neutrons, protons and morons in the atom."

Now we must deal in deadly earnest not only with human and terrestrial forces, but also with cosmic forces beyond earlier dreams. New words have come and more will, as we hesitatingly thread our way amid powers that, unless we handle them deli-cately and wisely, may end our days on earth.

There was, for a time, international rivalry in naming new-found elements; now there are international committees, in the effort to avoid confusion when creating new terms in science and technology, or for the mountains of the moon and other to-

be-mapped satellites and stars. The dangers of unorganized nomenclature are illustrated by the jingle H. B. and A. C. English
preface to their *Dictionary of Psychological and Psychoanalytical
Terms:*

> Ad-i-ad-o-cho′-kin-e-sis
> Is a term that will bolster my thesis
>   That 'tis idle to seek
>   Such precision in Greek
> When confusion it only increases.

The definitions of this octosyllabic word: a) incessant movement.
b) inability to make rapidly alternating movements.

3. *Borrowing.* There may be "loan words," taken directly into
English from another language, as *kindergarten, nucleus, collage,
apartheid, garage.* Some of these keep their original plural, as
memoranda, agenda; others may use either the original or the
English form. *Medium,* referring to communication devices, has
the plural *media* (sometimes misused as a singular); referring to
communication with the dead, *mediums.* There are also borrowings that are direct translations, as Bernard Shaw's *superman*
carries over Nietzsche's *Übermensch.* Others are *loudspeaker,
power politics, inferiority complex, wishful thinking.*

4. *General application of proper names,* of persons, places, or
commercial objects. *Volt, ampere, ohm, mho, diesel,* are all named
from men. So also *atlas, bloomers, saxophone. Volcano* is from the
Roman god of the forge, Vulcan. *Fahrenheit* is from the name of
the inventor of the mercury thermometer, who set zero at the
lowest temperature reached in his town, Dantzig, in 1709. *Boycott*
is one of a number of names used as a verb.

5. *Abbreviations and Acrostics.* Abbreviations were first employed in Sumerian, the earliest recorded language. The Romans
used initials; an acrostic is a word made up of the first letters of
other words. Roman dates begin A.U.C., 'from the founding of
the City', 753 B.C. Their standards bore the letters SPQR, 'the
Senate and the Roman People'. These were borne on top of the
fasces, a bound bundle of sticks with an axe-blade protruding, a
symbol of the union of the people in the Roman republic: united
we stand, divided we fall. Two thousand years later, the fasces
was adopted by Mussolini's *fascists,* twisting a good symbol to
an evil end.

A friendly letter in ancient Rome might end SVBEEV: *Si vales,
bene est; ego valeo:* "If you are well, that's good; I am well"—as

some today might sentimentalize an envelope SWAK, sealed with a kiss.

With the two world wars, initials proliferated; some of these are just spelled, as the U.N.; others are pronounced as words: UNESCO; the army and navy *Wacs* and *Waves; Socony. Zipper* is an echoic word, but the U.S. ZIP code is an acrostic of Zone Improvement Program. *Radar* and *scuba* are acrostics. The familiar *jeep* has on its dashboard GP; it is the army General Purpose vehicle. *Interpol* is the International Police, established in Paris in 1923. Our acrostical vocabulary draws upon several tongues: R.I.P. is Latin, R.S.V.P. is French, V.I.P. is English. Such terms have so multiplied that there are special dictionaries of abbreviations and acrostics. We shall meet the latter again in the discussion of words at play.

Some words have just been clipped: *phone, vamp, ad, fridge,* the *telly* or *T.V.;* college words such as *prof, lab, dorm, exam, gym.* Other shortenings may be compound: *fortran ('formula translation'), permafrost, laundromat.*

6. *Figures of Speech.* Some figurative words began as slang, then were accepted as standard speech. Thus *skyscraper,* partly superseded by the literal *highriser; bottleneck; eyewash; square, hip.*

A particular figure, often hidden in a word, is *metathesis,* the 'transfer (of a sound).' Old English *bridd* became our *bird.* Latin *scintilla* came directly into English, and also gave us *scintillate;* but by metathesis from the same Latin word came *tinsel* and *stencil.* Such changes, however, are more frequent today in accidental or (for humor) intentional Spooners: *Butterfly, flutter by.*

7. *Folk Etymology.* This is the transformation of a strange form into one that has a more familiar sound or meaning. Thus a *pentice,* originally a 'lean-to', became a *penthouse,* now a much more elaborate structure. The *crevisse* became the *crayfish.* In the Middle Ages, reading and writing were virtually a monopoly of the clerics; one could avert hanging by proving one's literacy, reading one's "neck verse," thus escaping from the king's to the ecclesiastical court. And when the general layman began tentatively to transfer words from his lips to paper, he was not always sure whether an *n* belonged to the *an,* or before the vowel in the following word. Thus folks began to write *an apron;* the less common *napery* and *napkin* retained the initial letter. There seems to have been a toss-o'-the-coin haphazard in these shiftings: the most common English venomous snake, *a nadder,* became *an adder,* while the little salamander, *an ewt,* became *a newt.* A

nonce-word was originally *an once-word; an umpire* was *a non-pair*, the odd man out, asked to referee between two others. For more than a hundred years (1400–1519) *an ox* might be written *a nox. An orange* is from Arabic *naranj;* it lost the *n* by the same process in the earlier French.

An odd interlingual instance of folk etymology lies behind the ubiquitous fruit we now call, after its Mexican name, the tomato. At first avoided as poisonous, it came to be sought as an aphrodisiac. For it was called, in English, the *love-apple;* in German, *Liebes-Apfel;* in French, *pomme d'amour*—from the Italian *pomi de Mori,* 'fruit of the Moors'! As literacy increases, although solecisms continue as more and more heedless or poorly educated talkers take the airways, such errors are less likely to slip into standard speech.

8. *Euphemism.* A word that seems indecent or disagreeable may be replaced by a more pleasing or innocuous one. Thus, as financial problems grew more increasingly widespread, the word *panic* (from the god Pan, god of nature, therefore universal) was abandoned in favor of *slump,* then *depression, recession, downturn.* Euphemism will have a later chapter to itself, with examination of the taboo four-letter words.

9. *Conversion.* Some words used as one part of speech were after a time also used as another. Nouns and verbs became interchangeable: "This is a must." Verbal forms such as *lay off, has been, sit in,* were hyphenated and used as nouns. Parts of the body—*elbow, hand, stomach, foot, toe*—were called into action as verbs. The word *down* has done yeoman service. It was, as I have noted, originally a noun, meaning highland: "I walked on the downs." Changing the meaning made it possible to say that life has its ups and downs (noun). In the football game, the team had its third down (noun). The stream cascaded down the slope (preposition). He waited on the down platform (adjective), to go downtown (combined noun, used as adverb). He took the elevator down (adverb). Down, Buster! (verb).

Shakespeare, in *Twelfth Night:* "Lady, you are the cruellest she alive!" makes the pronoun become the noun. In "He pooh-poohed the idea" an interjection has become a verb. Thus the resources of the language are multiplied.

10. *Backformation.* One part of speech is altered, usually shortened—an actual or seeming suffix dropped—to serve a different function. The noun *beggar* soon acquired the verb *beg.* Contrariwise, the noun *robber* followed the verb *rob;* but the verb *burgle* is a backformation from the noun *burglar.* The ad-

jective *greedy* came before the noun *greed*. This is still a live process: *sculpt* came in 1934; *televise*, 1950; *sightsee*, 1960; *bull-doze, escalate, baby-sit*. In the *Webster's New Collegiate Dictionary* of 1973, but not yet sanctified in the *Random House Unabridged* of 1968, from the armed forces and from "secret agent" fiction comes the verb *liaise*, backformed from *liaison*. (An even more recent word is the verb *backform*, coined in the previous sentence.)

Related to the backformations are the blend words, born when two common words coalesce: *bat* and *mash* produced *bash; clap* and *crash, clash; flame* and *glare* fused as *flare*. In the nineteenth century—Lewis Carroll's *chortle*, from *chuckle* and *snort*—these were called telescope or portmanteau words, both these articles being fashioned to press in, like the words. Others such are *snow-mobile, travelogue* (*travel monologue*), *pulsar* (*pulsating star*). The computer's *binary unit* is a *bit*. Not yet standard English are such telescopes as *disastrophe, insinuendo*. Some words, like *swellegant, sexploitation, sexcess*, flow directly from slang to cliché.

11. *Affixes*. One of the most frequent ways in which words are formed is by the addition of a prefix or a suffix, which may alter the application of the basic word in various fashions. Such new terms have come into the language at every stage of its growth, but many of the affixes are still live, ready for fresh use as the need arises. Among recent words with live prefixes are *decontaminate; prefabricated*, also *pre-Nixon; bemedalled, disinflationary, selfservice, selfstarter*. *Mini-* and *maxi-* have had their brief day, with the flurry of skirts above or below the knee. *Super-* has been overused in *superstar, superduper;* a *souped-up* auto is one with a *supercharger*. You may even have seen a shop that calls itself a *minisupermarket*, or a *superette;* the latter contains no root, being formed by joining two affixes.

A few prefixes require caution. *Anti-* obviously is used to mean 'against', and is widely available. But occasionally the *i* slips in where one should expect an *e, ante-* meaning 'before'. This occurs in *anticipate;* and *antipasto* is something eaten before the main course. *Para-* has threefold possibilities. From the Greek, it means 'beside', or 'outside of', in *paradox, parallel, parapsychology, paralanguage*. But it comes from Latin *parare*, meaning 'prepare for', in *parapet, parasol, parachute*. And from this last word a new series has sprung: *paratrooper;* the *paradoctor*, who drops down on emergency calls in remote places; and even the *parabomb*, thus dropped upon its victims. A *paramedic* may drop; more fre-

quently today, the word is used for one (*para-*, 'beside') trained
to assist a doctor.

The prefix *di-* has undergone some divagations. It means 'two',
as in (the horns of a) *dilemma; dichloride.* Even in the Latin, it
expanded in two other forms. *Dia-* means 'two apart, in succession'—hence, 'passing through'; as in *diagonal, dialogue, diarrhea.*
Dis- means 'two apart, in twain'—hence 'opposed'; as in *disagree,
disease* ('not at ease'). All three forms are live; the first two are
used mainly to form new scientific terms, but *dis-* is generally
available. It has been added to many words to mean their opposite; as *dishonor, disorder, displease.* The *Dictionary of Americanisms* lists a dozen words coined for an occasion, then lapsing
into disuse; such as *disretired, disquixotted, dissatisfactionist.*
Thus today we might note that many who voted for Nixon were
soon *disNixonized.* Some *dis-* compounds are still used although
the basic word has gone: *dispute, distort;* we can say *rupture,* but
not *rupt; disrupt* remains. In a few cases where the basic root is
no longer used, the prefix *dis-* is balanced by the prefix *com-*
(*con-*); thus *dissent–consent, discord–concord, dispute–compute.*
Also (as *in-* in *inflammable*) *dis-* is occasionally used as an inten-
sifier: hence the synonyms *dissoluble* and *soluble; disbar* and *bar;
disannul* and *annul.* With which we discontinue.

Suffixes, too, are live sources of words: *-ize,* as in final*ize; -wise,*
as in *economicswise* (*horresco referens!* 'I shudder at the mention!'), *percentagewise,* and more. An English airplane advertisement announces: "Malta is jetwise 4 hours from London."

The ending *-y* was used by Byron when he listed seven stages
to ebriety:

First silent, then talky, then argumentative, then disputatious, then
unintelligible, then altogethery, then inarticulate, then drunk.

This *-y* suffix, with its plural *-ies,* has given us *undies, talkies,
goalie, hanky;* also, the adjectives *squiffy, choosy, cagey, bossy,
balmy, batty. Summitry* and *gadgetry* try for admission to the dictionaries. Thus also *gamesmanship* (after *sportsmanship*), *brink-
manship, one-upmanship.*

Other affixes still alive are more special, as in *standoffish,
sixish; -ese,* as in *journalese; -esque.* There are many *manias* and
phobias listed in special glossaries, such as *triskaidekaphobia,* the
fear felt by builders who in high buildings omit the "thirteenth"
floor. The *New Gould Dictionary* lists 275 phobias. More mod-

estly, but trenchantly, H. B. and A. C. English, mentioned above, say in the Preface to their book:

> The editor fails to find a single case among over 180 listed terms where the compound with *phobia* is clearer, more convenient, more euphonious, or less ambiguous, than if the morbid fear had been characterized in English.

In a lively article in the *New England Journal of Medicine* (November 11, 1976) the head of the Section of Gastroenterology at Yale University School of Medicine, Dr. Howard M. Spiro, finds it hard to stomach the Greek coinages of doctors probably unfamiliar with the language:

> A heart surgeon is no good at fixing broken legs unless he moonlights as an orthopedist, and the physician should not expect to write clear English without practice; one of his most pretentious and easily corrected faults is his pride in making up new words without guidance, in the belief that he has a right to do so! That physicians expect good writing from their colleagues at all is testimony to the old ways that held a physician first a man or woman educated in a classical mode and only then trained in medicine. The end of that tradition is well known; in the current scramble for medical-school admission, faculties will not quickly change what premedical students will learn. Yet it is curious that the modern physician writer still prospects for new words in Greek or Latin as vigorously as Schliemann at Troy, even if he almost never comes up with coin as rich as that German's. The investigator who trains for months to do his experiments sallies forth when they are done, as ill trained as the Visigoths but as aggressive, to bring home new words for his new notions.

Specialists are seldom deterred by such considerations. A new term might bring an increase in salary or prestige. A mountain on Mars, or a disease, might even be named for its describer.

Affixes may be piled upon one another in a single word, as in one of the longest words in the language: *quasiantidisestablishmentarianistically*. They may, however, be usefully employed to distinguish shades of meaning, as *politic, political; elemental, elementary; emergence, emergency; commune, community; continuance, continuation, continuity*.

In the growth of the language, certain oddities of affix have developed. The noun *use* has spawned the opposed *useful* and *useless*. Several words have used one of the two opposed suffixes, but not the other. Only *-ful* for *fright, awe, bounty*. Only *-less* for *root, tail, voice, love, time, age, peer.* And still other words exist only in an affixed form, the basic word having lapsed from the language: *dismayed, insidious, disheveled, uncouth. Couth,* and *gruntled,* have made a tentative, humorous return. *Kempt* has fared even better: O.E.D. 1933 labels it archaic; its 1976 *Supplement* asks us to remove the label. One may be *disturbed,* or *perturbed,* or even *turbulent;* but no one today protests that he is *turbed.*

Affixes continue to play a major part in the development of new words.

12. *Meaning shifts.* As our words are continuously used, they may change their meaning in various ways.

There might be, through gradually shifting use, a complete change in meaning. *Silly* used to mean 'blessed' (as German *selig* still does). *Merely,* which today is a slighting term—'only and nothing more'—once meant 'wonderful'; then 'without admixture', 'purely'; in *Hamlet* it means 'completely', 'entirely'. *Beads* originally meant 'prayers'; nuns used to count their prayers by the tiny balls on their rosary. *To tell* was *to count; tellers* still count votes, or banknotes. *Sad* originally meant 'solid', as with the *sadiron,* opposed to a hollow iron into which one may pour hot water. The 1623 Shakespeare Folio, dedicated to William and Philip Herbert, states that they had *prosecuted* ('followed') the author and his works "with much favor."

Another sort of change, we might call semantic spread; it occurs when a common word acquires further uses. *To get,* for example, first meant 'to go and fetch': "Please get me the paper." But now you can get hurt. He's got to go. Let's get going. I got to know him better. Get up. You can't get away with it. The definition of *cell* depends upon the field of concern: politics, electricity, biology, or prison. The various meanings of *make* require thirteen pages in the O.E.D.

The change may consist in the breadth of reference. There may be a narrowing, a specialization, of the term. *Hound* once meant any dog (as *Hund* in German). *Deer* (as still *Tier* in German) meant any animal; in *King Lear* we hear of "mice, rats, and such small deer." *Meat* at first meant any food, as when men spoke of meat and drink; one man's meat is another man's poison. Again Shakespeare (*Romeo and Juliet*): "Thy head is as full of quarrels as an egg is full of meat." Or the reverse process may take place, a widening of the use, a generalization. We now can speak of a *carbarn; barn* at first meant a barley place. *Dog* was once limited to a strong hunter. *Junk,* to a sailor, once meant just old rope. Or there may be an emotional tinge added to a word—usually for the worse. A *hussy* was once just any housewife. *Collaborator, lust, appeasement,* have all taken on unfavorable implications. Finally, a word may slide to one side of a polarity. *Temper,* which once meant 'disposition,' becomes more precise in such phrases as "He has quite a temper." Every body has a *temperature,* but a mother becomes alarmed when told that her baby has one. The opposite slide occurs with *humor,* which now usually implies good humor, as a sense of humor indicates readiness to make or take a joke. *Humor* originally meant 'moisture', as in *humidity;* it was applied to "the four humours" of the body, as influencing a person's temperament: *phlegm,* predominance of which made one *phlegmatic; blood, sanguine; bile, bilious* or *choleric;* and *black bile* (Greek *melanos,* 'black'; *chole,* 'bile'), which made one *melancholy* or (from the Latin) *atrabilious.*

Changes of meaning often present a shift from something material, tangible, to something more general or abstract. *Climax* comes from the Greek word 'ladder'; *comet,* from 'long-haired'. *Scandal,* from 'snare'. A *trivial* matter is from the usual small talk where three roads (*tri-via*) meet. *To prevaricate* first meant 'to walk crookedly' (Latin *varus,* 'knock-kneed'). There may also be a shift from the physical to the feeling: *fear* at first meant 'trembling'; *anger* meant 'compression'. Or there may be a mingling of senses, as when one speaks not of sugar but of a *sweet voice* (taste to hearing); *warm colors,* a *sharp sound,* a *clear call.* In many uses, there seems a shift from basic spatial relations, as when one speaks of a *long* time, the *near* future, a *higher* temperature, *lower* expectations, the *height* (*peak, summit*) of one's career.

The way in which words of physical action are turned to mental activity is shown in the background of the words *amputation* and *reputation.* Latin *pavire,* 'to strike, stamp' (related to the Old High German word for 'castrate') gives us English *pave, pavement.* Related to it is Latin *putare,* 'to cut, trim, prune', whence English *pit* (a 'cut' hole), *putamen, amputate.* But even in Roman times *putare* was extended to mean 'clear up', 'adjust', 'regard', 'reckon', 'estimate', 'consider', and from this sense came more English words: *compute, deputy, dispute, putative, reputation,* etc. In the same way Latin *caedere, caesus; cidere,* 'to cut, lop', came to English *cement* (made with stone chippings), *scissors, caesura, circumcise, caesarian, Caesar* (cut from his mother's womb) hence *Kaiser, Czar,* and *sherry* (from Caesar's City, later Xeres, Jeres)—but also Latin *decidere,* 'to cut off', came to mean 'to put an end to', 'determine', whence English *decide, indecision, concise, precise,* and more.

There may, at times, be a misuse of words that tends to become fixed in the language, and may be regretted as marking a loss in discrimination. While some may still distinguish between *disinterested* and *uninterested, enormousness* and *enormity, adapt* and *adopt,* perhaps fewer persons know the difference between *comic* and *comical, economic* and *economical, politic* and *political.* The fictional detective Nero Wolfe once asked a prospective client: "Do you use infer and imply interchangeably?" (Her quiet "No" led him to take her case.) But *Webster's Third* identifies *to convince* and *to persuade,* although the first concerns ideas; the second, actions. Careless use has so often broken down valid distinctions that grammar has been cynically defined as the record of our grandparents' mistakes. As Pierre Claude La Chaussée phrased it back in 1747, *Quand tout le monde a tort, tout le monde a droit,* "When everybody's wrong, everybody's right." Word use shows democracy in action.

13. *Morphological shift.* Perhaps also under the head of ancestral slipshod utterance come changes in grammatical form, especially inflections. "It's me" is now almost universal. The objective *whom,* though still frequent in writing, is falling away from speech; we more commonly hear: "Who do you want to talk to?" For years the columnist F.P.A. (Franklin P. Adams) made valiant but vain struggle against this, quoting case after case under the heading: "Whom are you?" said Cyril. Two days after the 1976 presidential elections, there were spread across the front page of the *New York Post,* in large bold capitals, the words:

WHAT HE'LL DO
WHO HE'LL NAME

—remove the apostrophe to see where concern for the language has gone.

In writing, the opposite error may be more frequent. The late John Creasey, whose mysteries still sell at the rate of four million copies a year—The Bible, Shakespeare, Chairman Mao, John Creasey—has been printed in twenty-five languages; I hope the other twenty-four correct his *whom:* (in *Danger for the Baron*) "He was a tall, lean man whom even the cynics agreed was handsome." (in *A Period of Evil*) "a man whom I believe could be a murderer."

Such an error is called a *genteelism:* aware of the less frequent form, one shows one's "superior breeding" by the use of it—even where it doesn't belong. A man can be measured by his word ways.

Nor is the poor practice new, nor confined to one side of the Atlantic. Pope was moved to complain, 250 years ago:

> Some free from rhyme or reason, rule or check,
> Break Priscian's head, and Pegasus's neck.

(Priscian—"as every schoolboy knows," in Macaulay's overoptimistic phrase—wrote, about 500 A.D., the books of Latin grammar that were standard for a thousand years.) And George Steiner, in his 1975 Presidential Address to the English Association, re-emphasized the close relation between language and life, stating that Carlyle's fears for "the condition of England" must hang upon "the condition of English.... The vulgate is being swamped by the vulgar." Protests on both sides of the ocean seem like King Knut bidding the tide not to rise. One can but watch and hope that, as in the ocean, the tide of verbal disregard will show signs of an ebb. There is no present punishment for verbicide.

The comparative and superlative endings, *-er* and *-est,* are also dropping out of use. Milton used *elegantest, famousest, sheepishest*. On the other hand, prepositions turned adverbs are increasingly used as part of a verb. *To fall for* has a different meaning from *to fall;* but *to start up* an engine adds an unnecessary *up,* as *to meet up with* seems to mean no more than *to meet.* "Give me a ring" lengthens the expression, but means no more than "Ring me"—unless you're a young lady who wants her engagement made known.

Another error that has changed the form of words was the assumption that a final *s* represented a plural. The best known instance of this singular misunderstanding may be traced in the nursery rhyme "Pease porridge hot, pease porridge cold..." as *pease,* heard as a plural, took on the singular form *pea.* Other words created by mistaking a final *s* sound as plural are cherry, gentry, marquee, shay, sherry, shimmy.

There is some current confusion with *all,* withal. There should be a clear distinction between *all ready* and *already.* Of another pair, the O.E.D. Supplement (1972) primly states: "There is a common tendency to write *altogether* where *all together* is logically preferable." Fowler, back in 1926, declared that *alright* is "seldom allowed by the compositor to appear in print, but is often seen in ms." *Alright,* although still shunned by many, is granted "reputable" perch in the 1966 *Webster's Third*. Note that the preferred *all right* actually has two meanings. It may mean: "All things under consideration are satisfactory." Or it may mean: "It (the one thing under consideration) is completely satisfactory." This distinction parallels that between *all together* and *altogether;* and it may well be that, especially in the sense of "wholly correct," *alright* will come to prevail. Thus the language changes, almost beneath our eyes.

14. *Sound Change.* Another source of word development, deep-rooted in speech habits, is change of sound, especially as a word moves from one language to another. The variation of *s* and *sh* is the earliest such change on record, as the Bible tells us of the testing: 42,000 Ephraimites were slain beside the Jordan River, revealed because they could not pronounce the *sh* in *shibboleth*. The Arabic greeting, 'Peace,' *Salaam*, in Hebrew is *Shalom*. Similarly, German *schon* is English *soon*.

The sounds of *b* and *v*, also of *c* and *ch*, shift on the Romance tongues; the two together are heard in Spanish *caballo*, French *cheval*, 'horse'. The sounds of *t* and *th* were early confused: *author, catholic*, and other such words—*nothing*, even in Shakespeare's day—were sounded as we still say *Thomas*, as the Germans and the French still pronounce their *Theater* and *théâtre*.

The most widespread of such interactions is the shifting of *l* and *r*. There is no sound *r* in Chinese. If your waiter in a Chinese restaurant has not had long practice in English, he may still utter your order for "flied lice." Conversely, there is no *l* sound in Japanese. A composite fabulous monster, frequent on pottery, is Japanese *kirin*, Chinese *kylin*. Having flown over the waters of the Chinese Sea, I heard my Japanese host wish me a "Happy Horriday." My visit to Tokyo coincided with the meeting of the World Olympic committee. I was chatting with a new member of the Committee when a courteous Japanese came over to invite him to a little gathering "to cerebrate your erection." He glanced at me, then with a sober face accepted. When the gratified Japanese walked away, the committeeman remarked: "I suppose that's what an old codger often does."

Westward, the same transfer takes place. By a roundabout journey, Greek *serikon*, Latin *sericum*, traveling to China as the western word for an eastern product, came finally into English as *silk*. The famous Haroun al-Rashid of *Arabian Nights* was also ar-Rashid. The Persian *dulipan*, through Arabic and via Turkey, gives us two English words: *tulip*, and *turban*. Dutch *Amsterdam*, repeated in New York, was named from a dam on the Amstel

River. Our *glamour* (first used by Scott) and *grammar* come from the same Latin word. Latin *titulus, title* in Old French and Modern English, in Modern French is *titre*. A nickname of *Mary* is *Molly;* of *Sarah, Sally;* of *Dorothy, Dolly,* from which comes the little girls' companion, the *doll*. Shakespeare's Harry le Roi was Prince Hal.

That luscious fruit the *mulberry,* around the "bush" of which country children used to dance, from the ninth century through the fourteenth was a *moreberry;* and still the tree is of the genus *Morus*.

The American Indians, at least as interpreted by the whites, had the same *l-r* confusion, compounded with *n*. For the early explorers of Central America and the islands brought back from the Arawak tongue three soundings of the same word: *carib-, calib-, canib-,* giving us the *Caribbean,* the *cannibal,* and Shakespeare's savage in *The Tempest, Caliban*.

There is an army officer, in Spanish *coronel;* in French pronounced as it is spelled, *colonel;* spelled the French way in English, but sounded like the inside of a nut. When Chief Justice Marshall was asked by a young woman for an example of a paradox, he turned a trope into a toper, giving her a jingle:

> In the Blue Grass region
> A paradox was born:
> The corn was full of kernels
> And the colonels full of corn.

The same shift is seen in Greek a*ster* and Latin *stel*la, which have both come into English: in the star-flower the *aster;* in *asterisk* and *disaster,* in *astronomy,* in *stellar* and in *constellation*—for which an earlier English word was *asterism*. Malaysian: *Agar-agar, agal-agal* (seaweed); Turkish: *angola, angora* (cat). *Begora* and *By golly* are equal ways of avoiding *By God*. The transference is truly worldwide. Ripple *l* and *r* along your tongue, and you may feel the reason.

15. *Change of locale*. Finally, there are many local words or forms in various English-speaking regions. Scotland and Ireland have many words of their own; Australia has new words for its unique conditions. And there grew, in England and America, different words for the same thing, as the two lands went their separate ways. Rapid communication, and the increasing use of radio and television, are lessening these variations, and American English, frequently more crisp, colorful, or short and simple, seems

dominant. Differences, none the less, persist across the ocean; here are just a few of such terms:

England	United States	England	United States
lift	elevator	tin	can
leader	editorial	ironmonger's	hardware store
interval	intermission	face cloth	washrag
boot (of auto)	trunk	luggage van	baggage car
bonnet (" ")	hood	underground	subway

In Agatha Christie's *Murder on the Orient Express*, the detective Hercule Poirot knows that a woman has been in the United States because she says: "I can call long distance and talk to my attorney" instead of: "I can make a trunk call and speak to my solicitor." Even in the alphabet there is a divergence: the last letter, pronounced zee in the United States, in England is zed.

Despite these many avenues of accession, some words are still missing in the language. Prominent among the absentees is a pronoun that will include both man and woman. Despite the indignation of some active feminists, until such a word becomes current, grammatically as well as dramatically the male embraces the female. We have a *memory*, but not the equally important *forgettery*. We have the verb *to stink*, but none meaning *to smell fragrant*. And we have a number of words that must do double duty. Thus *right* pairs with *left* and with *wrong; old*, with *young* and with *new; thin*, with *fat* and with *thick; go*, with *stop* and with *come; soft*, with *loud* and with *hard;* and there is an odd chain linking *foul* and *fair, fair* and *dark, dark* and *light, light* and *heavy*.

Philologists are naturally interested in tracing words back to their earliest forms, their true (Greek *etymon*, 'true') source, in the study of etymology. In many cases, this hunt can be little more than an "educated guess." Cowper speaks of

> philologists who trace
> A panting syllable through time and space,
> Start it at home, and hunt it in the dark
> To Gaul, to Greece, and into Noah's ark.

Voltaire observed that, in the quest, vowels do not count at all, and consonants very little. And indeed the variations are great. Thus Latin *punctum*, which gives us *punctual* and *punctuation*, through the French comes to us in *point* and *disappoint*. In these, you note that the consonants remain the same. In words that we can trace back as far as the assumed Indo-European, however, there is a consonant shifting that differentiates the Mediterranean family from the northern branch, the regularity of which was established in 1863 by Jakob Grimm, more widely known as the collector of fairy tales. Simplified to cover English words, Grimm's law may be set down:

> Gutturals: g, k, kh, (h), g
>   *genus, kin; choler, gall; host, guest*
> Dentals: d, t, th (Latin f), d
>   *dual, two; trivial, three; fume, dust*
> Labials: (v), b, p, ph, (f), b
>   *pedal, foot; fertile, bear; fragile, break.*

In each instance, the word given first came to English by the classical route; the second, reaching us by the Teutonic highway, is one letter beyond in the series. Note that *c* is always hard (like *k*) in Greek, Latin, and German, as also in English and the Romance tongues save before *e* and *i*, or when especially marked as in French *français*. Before *e* and *i*, it may variously soften into *s*, *ch*, *sh*, or *zh*.

Before we move on, it may be of interest to look in greater detail at the stories of just a few words.

Palace. This abode of kings took its name from the location of the home of the First Roman Emperor, Augustus Caesar, on the Mons Palatinus, the central one of the seven hills of Rome. And the mount was so called because it was enclosed by a fence of stakes, Latin *palus*, from which we have also derived *palisade*, *paling*, and *impale*. To be *beyond the pale* is worse than having been born on the wrong side of the tracks: if there's no train (of prejudice) in the way, you may cross the tracks; but when Remus jumped the pale, his brother Romulus slew him, and gave his own name to Rome.

Intoxicate. Greek *toxin* was a bow; *toxicon* was applied to the poison on the arrow, whence English *toxic* and *antitoxin*. But just as we may ask a man what he wishes to drink by saying "Name your poison," so *intoxicate* came to describe the poisonlike but more temporary effect of too much liquor. *Ebriate* and *inebriate* are degrees of drunkenness, from Latin *ex-bria*, 'out of the cup'. *Sobriety*, of course, is the opposite; being *so* (*se*), 'apart from', *bria*. Latin *potare*, 'to drink', gives us *potion*, and also, from the medieval practice of supplying lethal beverages, *poison*. Name your poison.

Scholar. Athletics were part of the regular training of a Greek citizen. *Athleo* meant 'to contend for a prize', perhaps from an Indo-European root meaning 'to tire oneself'; the athletes trained naked, hence *gymnast* and *gymnasium*, from Greek *gymnos*, 'naked'. But the natural occupation of a citizen's leisure hours (Greek *schola*, 'leisure') was quiet talk and speculation; hence the *scholar* and his *school*. A *symposium* was originally a congenial gathering (Greek *sym*, 'together' + *posis*, 'drinking'), as pictured by Trimalchio in Petronius' *Satyricon* (first century A.D.); then it came to mean a gathering for talk. Plato held his symposia beside the athletic field, in a grove called the Academy. It was named from the story of young Helen (later taken by Paris to Troy); she had been spirited away by Theseus; her brothers Castor and Pollux went in search of her; a farmer, Academus, put them on the right track; his grove was therefore protected, and Athens grew around it. Lowell speaks of "that best academe, a mother's knee."

Achieve. This form comes from the French. (Latin *caput*, 'head'; *ad caput venire*, French *venir à chef*, 'to come to a head', 'to finish'.) Hence, 'to die'; Shakespeare (*Henry V*): "Bid them atchieve me, and then sell my bones." But one may also end successfully; thus again Shakespeare (*Twelfth Night*): "Some are born great, some achieve greatness." Middle English had the word *bonchief* ('good fortune'); we retain the *mischief*. A *handkerchief* (French *couvre-chef*) was at first a cloth held in the hand to cover the head. From the Latin *caput* comes *captain;* via the French, *chieftain*. We have a *capital letter, capital punishment* (Off with his head!), a *capital city*, and the *capitalist*. Also, that early form of exchange, *cattle*, as well as *chattel*. A *cape* is a 'headland', or a cloak with a head-covering, a hood. *Cap-a-pie*, 'head to foot' in fine fettle, became by folk etymology *apple-pie* order. Another type of cap was (Italian) *capella;* as worn by St. Martin, it became a holy relic, and was guarded by the *chaplain* in the *chapel*. There was no organ there, hence singing *a capella*, 'from the chapel', is without accompaniment. This headpiece was also worn by the knights of the Garter, attendants on the Queen; hence, a *chaperon*. There is much more on this head, but to come to an end, a fugitive grasped by the cloak might slip out of it and (*ex-cappa*) *escape!*

Cardinal. In Latin, this originally meant 'hinge'. It was then applied to the officers of the Catholic church upon whom hinged the choice of the Pope. The sacred college of seventy cardinals was assembled; the door was locked, not to be opened until smoke announced that they had made their choice; then the great doors swung upon their hinges, and one among them was proclaimed as the new representative of the Lord. The cardinals wore a cap and gown of a special shade of red; from the gown the color was named, and from the color the bird. There are also the *cardinal points* of the compass, NEWS; and the *cardinal numbers,* on which our calculations hinge.

Blimp. This was a word coined to describe the first nonrigid dirigible airship. H. L. Mencken stated that a group at the English airport were waiting for it to fly in, wondering what to call it. It was time for blunch (which this side of the Atlantic we call brunch); one Mr. Short, according to Mencken, said "Let's call it a blimp!" Mr. Mencken has shortchanged us. The airship was designed by the Goodyear Company; the first model, the A limp (nonrigid), was unsuccessful; the second, the B limp, survived as the blimp.

Jordan. This was a long-necked bottle, in which was carried water from the holy River Jordan. Jordan water is still available in Near East shops in New York City. In the middle ages, the jordan was used by alchemists in their experiments, and by doctors to hold a specimen of urine. Thus it came to be used for a urinal. Again Shakespeare (*Henry VI*): "They allow us never a jordan, and then we leak in the chimney." These expressions have become obsolete; all that's left in the language is the *jordan almond*—and that is a corruption of a *jardin* (garden) almond, a cultivated variety.

Taxi. This is an abbreviation of *taximetercabriolet*. Latin *capri-*, 'goat', named the island of Capri, for its wild goats, and Cape Capricorn ('goat's horn') from its shape. A *cabriolet*, a little cabriole, was a two-wheeled carriage that on the old dirt roads bounced like a leaping goat. From it was shortened our word *cab*. *Tax* is from Latin *taxare*, 'to censure', 'to charge': they taxed him with the offense, then taxed him for it. (Hence also English *task*.) *Meter* still means *measure*. Thus a little carriage that bounds like a goat, equipped with an instrument to measure and charge for its use, is named by the four-letter word *taxi*.

Eunuch. A eunuch, named from a Greek word for 'bed-guardian', was probably first created by Queen Semiramis of Assyria, about 2000 B.C. In the ancient Near East, the Grand Eunuch was often the power behind the throne. In Assyria, where the years were given the names of leaders, the new king was the first Eponym: his name was given to the year of his accession. For the second year of the reign, the Eponym was the Commander-in-Chief, the Tartan of the armies; for the third year, the Chief Eunuch. In Italy, a *spado* is a eunuch who has had just his testicles removed; a *castrato*, all the external sex organs. Young boys in the papal choirs were made eunuchs to keep their voices from changing. A group of such singers was forced to give up its attempt to capture the English audience. In 1761 Charles Churchill wrote:

> Never shall a truly British age
> Bear a vile race of eunuchs on the stage.

The practice, however, continues. In La Scala Opera House Museum in Milan, there is a note written in 1863 by Rossini, which I translate from the French:

> Little Solemn Mass for four parts, accompaniment of piano and harmonium, composed for my rustication at Passy. Twelve singers of three sexes, men, women, and castrati, will suffice, using eight for the chorus, four for the solos: total, twelve cherubim. The good Lord pardon me for the following association: twelve was also the number of apostles in the famous chewing-game painted *al fresco* by Leonardo, and called "The Last Supper." Who would have believed it! There were among Your disciples some who sounded false notes! Lord, be assured; I affirm that there'll be no Judas at my repast, and that my twelve will sing correctly and *con amore* Thy praises and this little composition, which is, alas, the last mortal sin of my old age.

In Denmark, between 1929 and 1959, some nine hundred men, mainly criminals, were made eunuchs, three hundred at their own request. In the last twenty years, almost four hundred rapists and child molesters in Los Angeles accepted the operation, in lieu of a long jail sentence. In 1975, however, the doctors there, when the American Civil Liberties Union opposed the practice, refused to eunuchize the prisoners, for fear of malpractice suits.

Prevent. This word comes directly from Latin *pre,* 'before', and *venire, vent,* 'to come'. The Latin verb has given us many words, including *convent, convenience, invention, circumvent.* But the meaning of *prevent* has changed since the pious English used to pray: "Prevent us, O Lord, in all our doings!"—"Come before us, and prepare our way." For in the more grasping days of commercial competition, one that came before was likely to secure the best prospects for himself and prevent—in the current sense— latecomers from enjoying the profits.

Salary. This word, itself a byblow, has had many relatives. It is from Latin *sal,* meaning 'salt'. In early Roman times, ice being available only to the very rich, salt was needed for preserving meat, and was given to soldiers as part of their pay: Latin *sala-rium,* English *salary.* We still may speak of someone as being worth his salt. Figuratively used of wit, *Attic salt,* refined but stinging, was contrasted with *Italic vinegar,* more insolent and biting. In the sixteenth and seventeenth centuries, *salty* was used to mean 'peppy'; *salt,* to mean 'sexual desire', whence also *sally,* and *salacious* (Latin *salire,* 'to leap', 'to be lustful'). But a lusty man was usually in good health (Latin *salus, salvus*), whence *Salute!* ('Good health to you!'), also *salutation, salubrious, salve,* and *salvation.* Various foods were prepared with salt: Latin *salsa,* 'sauce'; *salsicia,* 'sausage'; *salata,* 'salad', greens with salt. A wood was a salubrious place. Late Latin *salvaticus* gives us *savage,* a 'man of the woods'. This was earlier *silvaticus,* 'wooded', whence *sylvan.* And this is related to Greek *xyle,* 'wood', whence some English technical terms and the musical instrument the *xylophone,* now often made of metal.

Generate. From one of the most prolific of Indo-European roots, *gn, kn,* comes a great flowering of words. (Note that *g* is sounded hard—as in *good*—in Greek, Latin, and German; but before *e* and *i* like *j* in Italian and English, like *zh* in French.) Greek *gigesthai,* Latin *gignere, genitus,* 'to beget', begot *genus,* 'the family', and the head of the genus, the *general.* Hence also *genital,* and (procreation and the usual family relations being pleasant) *genial, generous; eugenics.* The *genius* was the spirit allotted at birth to preside over one's destiny. *Gentle* originally meant 'well born', hence *genteel.* One not well born was *ignoble,* the *i* being short for Latin *in,* 'not', as also in *ignorant* and *ignore.* From the same root sprang *agnostic* (this time Greek *a-,* 'not') and *cognizant, gnostic, recognition;* and, through the French, *reconnaissance* and *Renaissance. Gnaw, know*—"Chew upon this"—and *rumination* ('chewing the cud', 'pondering') show the progression from taking in to digestion, at first literal, then in the figurative sense of absorbing in the mind. The *Book of Common Prayer* (1549) says: "Read, mark, learn, and inwardly digest." Note the early, Biblical, sense of *know,* 'to have intercourse', hence to beget. Note also Latin *genu,* 'knee', French *genou,* English *genuflection.* For the father accepted his son as legitimate by placing it on his knee; hence, *genuine.*

The story is far from complete. *Kin* refers to birth together. The head of the kin is the *king* (Old English *cyning*); hence also

Slavonic *knez,* Russian *knyaz,* 'prince'. In German one's children are *kinder,* as in our *Kindergarten.* In Shakespeare's day, as in the German still, this *i* was short. In *The Merchant of Venice* copulation is "the deed of kind"; thus also "She comes of a gentle kind"; and Hamlet's first words, punning: "A little less than kin, and more than kind." And thus also *kindle,* one meaning of which was 'to give birth': "the coney"—once again Shakespeare, in *As You Like It*—"dwells where she is kindled." 'To rouse', 'to be animated', 'to glow'; hence, 'to kindle a fire': to *ignite.*

All this is still an incomplete tracing of the *gn, kn* root. Klein's *Comprehensive Etymological Dictionary* lists eighty-three more words in the family; among them are *benign, malign* ('ill born', 'born bad'); *natal, naive; pregnant* (literally, 'before giving birth'). The unrelated *impregnable* took in the irrelevant *g* from the neighboring potency of *impregnate.*

A word from this root, in an early English protest couplet, used by Wat Tyler in the 1381 Peasants' Revolt, goes to the root of the perennial problem of social inequality:

> When Adam delved, and Eve span,
> Who was then the gentleman?

Words will reward the questing. Edward Coke (1562–1634), the first Lord Justice of England, who established the Common Law, went even further, declaring: "Syllables govern the world."

5.

MEANING

LINGUISTICS, THE STUDY OF LANGUAGE, has become increasingly popular with the movement of this century. The field is so large that it has been broken into many little sections, each scholar attempting to be monarch of all he surveys, and in the process coming to be less aware, and often less tolerant, of the work in the neighboring regions.

Descriptive linguistics, sometimes called synchronic, attempts to give a general picture of a language as it is today. Historical linguistics, sometimes called diachronic, tries to show how it became what it now is. As George Watson, co-editor of the *Dictionary of American English*, said:

> A word bears within it some recollection of its origins, much as men and women do. It exists diachronically, so to speak, and not just from moment to moment, and it is understood as a friend is understood, partly in the light of its origins.

This remembrance of things past within a word is the basis of the linguist's objection to simplified spelling, which would wipe away traces of a word's history. The main argument for reformed spelling is caught in Bernard Shaw's remark that *ghoti* should be pronounced *fish*: *gh* as in rough, *o* as in women, *ti* as in notion.

Comparative linguistics has many subsections; it may survey two languages, or a whole family group, or language in general—either the present situation, or in historical study. Geographical linguistics concerns itself with the interaction of neighboring tongues, with dialectology, with the influence of trade, travel, and migration on the speechways.

Biolinguistics and its offshoot psycholinguistics deal with such matters as the language of children, problems of neurology, and

74

speech pathology. Although computational linguistics, the interaction of electronics and speech, has begun to draw some attention, the most active branch of the study in recent years has been sociolinguistics. This may seek to discern speech differences attributable to sex; or to wealth, comparing the educated and the rich with the "underprivileged" or socially "disadvantaged." In 1954 Professor Alan Ross, in England, sought to distinguish U (Upper Class) from non-U speakers by their choice of words; his monograph was popularized by Nancy Mitford. An American application makes a similar distinction between M (Middle Class) and U, listing such words as:

U	M
wash	launder
cheap	inexpensive
dinner-jacket	tuxedo
sweat	perspiration
rich	wealthy

and other expressions suggesting that the U speakers are more direct, less squeamish or pretentious.

In America especially, there has been considerable sociolinguistic discussion of Black English. Unlike Leroi Jones (Imamu Amiri Baraka, *imamu* being Swahili for 'spiritual leader', 'guru'), who turns to Swahili, David Dalby, a philologist in England who advocates the teaching of Black English in American schools, proclaims Mandingo as a noteworthy source of our words: "Over 80 Americanisms appear to have an African or probable African origin." He lists *jazz, jitterbug, boogie-woogie, jive; uh-huh* and *uh-uh* (for 'yes' and 'no'); *cocktail, guy, bogus,* and *O.K.* Most of Dalby's ideas find little favor with other linguists; Eric Partridge, for example, suggests:

cocktail is from the cocky male of the domestic fowl.

guy is with little doubt from Guy Fawkes, the ill-famed conspirator, arrested November 4, 1605, whose grotesque effigy was burned every year on the anniversary of the Catholic Gunpowder Plot to blow up the English Parliament.

bogus, short for dialect tantarabogus, a goblin; from bogey, the children's bogeyman, with a suggestion of hocus-pocus.

O.K. is possibly from Choctaw *okeh,* 'it is so'; but more probably popularized by the O.K. Club, for Old Kinderhook, used in the Democratic election campaign (1836) of Martin Van Buren, born in Kinderhook, N.Y.

In these days of increased self-consciousness of, and concern for, ethnic and other groups, with charges of discrimination and reverse discrimination, one of the most sensitive regions in socio-linguistics is the rundown urban area inhabited by a minority group. Outsiders may refer to this district as a *slum*, for that would put the blame for its condition on those that live inside. Insiders—and those on their side—may call it a *ghetto*, for that puts the blame on the indifferent or malevolent majority outside. Sociologists endeavoring to avoid these emotionally charged words grope about with such terms as *disadvantaged, underprivileged, substandard, less endowed*. The desire to be objective may lead to a bland "circumlocution syndrome" without vigor or substance, on the verge of gobbledegoop. Journalists and broadcast commentators, meanwhile, have so favored the term *ghetto*, with its implication of barriers—an emphasis of our time: Iron Curtain, Bamboo Curtain, Berlin Wall—as to put the word *slum* almost out of current use.

After one minority group, recently, chose to be identified not by Spanish *Negro* (Latin *niger, nigra*) but by English *Black* (with the same meaning), Ossie Davis and other interested persons retroactively counted the synonyms of black and white in *Roget's Thesaurus:* finding many of the former derogatory and the latter complimentary, they assumed or intimated a racial bias. This interpretation disregards the fact that it is natural—in nature—for white, the presence of all colors, to be associated with bright, sunshiny, pleasant objects and thoughts; while black, the absence of color, manifest in pitch, smoke, and the ominous dark of night, is linked with fiends and fears—long before any connection with, and wholly without thought of, human pigmentation. In every field, one should regard as well as respect the word. Kali, the name of the Hindu goddess of destruction, is the Sanskrit word for 'black'.

Incidentally, Egypt was called Blackland by the Greeks, *Chemia*, from Egyptian *Khem*, 'black', probably from the fertile soil of the Nile after the receding annual flood; hence also medieval *alchemy* and modern *chemistry*. As a deity, Khem was an important ithyphallic figure, "the bull of his mother," both son and husband. This is a symbolic outgrowth of the animistic nature myth, in which the New Year kills his father the Old Year, and marries his eternal mother Nature. It is probably quite fortuitous, sheer happenstance, that the most frequent coarse appellation used by the Blacks today repeats this incestuous relationship.

Subjects for Ph.D. dissertations are increasingly hard to find,

and the number of aspirants is constantly increasing, so that—
while there are no longer arguments as to how many angels can
dance on the head of a pin—we are given such conclusions of
lengthy survey and research as that in Detroit men are more likely
than women to say "I don't want none." There may be more value
in such findings, reported in the London *Times* of May 23, 1976,
as that viewers of crime plays on television become more aggressive when the program is interrupted for "commercials" than
when it is run without a break.

It is also declared that the speechways of women doctors, their
words and especially their paralanguage, give them a more pleasant "bedside manner" than men. Women's activities in many fields
are being surveyed. Why the terms and symbols of mathematics
should seem especially difficult for women has been the subject of
considerable research. Statistics seem to make the fact clear: in
Santa Barbara, in 1972, for example, at the University of California, seventy women and sixty-three men majored in mathematics; forty-eight men completed the course, but only twenty
women. This becomes important when we note that mathematics
is a "critical filter," sieving out women from careers in such fields
as physics, chemistry, engineering, architecture, and even medicine. Recent studies point to the conclusion that the observed
sexual differences in this case are sociological and psychological,
rather than genetic. The women seem disturbed and put off less
by the problems of understanding the terms than by the male
attitude toward their study.

Sociolinguistics has also examined the overtones of expressions,
marking some as "snarl" words or "purr" words; and has investi-
gated the verbal techniques of advertising, "like a citizen should."

This does not exhaust the names indicating staked-out regions
for specialized research. Theoretical linguistics attempts to establish a general framework for language study. Microlinguistics is
another term used for study of one language as it is; macrolinguis-
tics, for the wide study of the entire field. There is also applied
linguistics, the study of language in its practical enterprises, which
may cover teaching, or the manipulation of opinion and incite-
ment to action.

Most technical, perhaps, is parametric linguistics, which by
diagrams and details tries to present all the "characteristic elements," the parameters, of the language field, so as to fill in what
its proponents see as gaps in the structure of standard English.

One result of this narrowing specialization is the introduction
of new terms, or the varied use of old terms, so that even the

linguists may fail to understand their fellows, and the interested layman must grope in vain. Thus Noam Chomsky complains that other scholars "are constantly spinning off fantasies about my ideas."

An *idiolect* is an individual's "tongueprint," as recognizable as his fingerprint: the sum total of his linguistic and paralanguage equipment. This may also be referred to as one's personal *lect;* indeed, the word *dialect* has spawned a numerous progeny. The highest level of good English has been called the *acrolect;* the lowest level of poor speech, the *basilect;* both are contrasted with the *matrilect,* the general native language. "Satellite" tongues such as pidgin and creole may be called *satillect* or *acolutholect;* and there are further fine distinctions which punctilious perfectionists may select. The term *philology* is still sometimes used, especially in Britain, for linguistics; but now it is generally limited to the study of written records, seeking their first form, examining their authenticity, determining their meaning. The general field of speech and writing remains the domain of linguistics.

And at the core of linguistics lies the study of grammar. As civilization depends upon language, so language depends upon grammar. Grammar may be defined as the system of principles—the more rigid would say, the set of rules—*phonological* ('of sound'), *morphological* ('of structure'), and *semantical* ('of sense'), according to which words must be patterned in order to be understood.

For almost two thousand years, the Western model for the study of grammar was the structure of the Latin language. Indeed, until the mid-nineteenth century the term *grammar school* referred to Latin; it was assumed that every Englishman would grow up into proper use of his own tongue. In the United States, with its polyglot immigration, this was of course less true; and until recent years English grammar was a basic study in the schools, with its parsing of verbs, its seeking the syntax of the several words, and its diagramming of the sentence as a whole. For a full understanding of the language, some such basic analysis is essential. The genial essayist and critic Brander Matthews, in the first two decades of this century, used to remark: "A gentleman need not know Latin, but he should at least have forgotten it." Similarly, it would do no harm for anyone that writes, even an occasional letter, to have a lingering memory of good grammar.

Take but one instance of the loss of discrimination that comes with grammatical lapses. Teachers up to fifty years ago laid emphasis upon the two kinds of relative clause. "My brother that's

a doctor will be here next week." This structure indicates that I
have more than one brother, and I'm making clear which one is
coming. The pronoun *that* introduces a restrictive clause. "My
brother, who's a doctor, will be here next week." I have but one
brother, about whom I give a little extra information. The pronoun *who* marks a descriptive clause: *who* for persons, *which* for
things. But heedless or ignorant writers, associating *who* with
persons, have used *who* so indiscriminately but so persistently as
to win its acceptance for both types of clause, thus blunting one
method of making a distinction. So ingrained has the *who* usage
become that John Kieran, of "Information Please" fame, forgot
the past, and in his *Books I Love* spoke of "Mark Twain's *ungram-
matical* title, *The Man That Corrupted Hadleyburg*." Thus do the
winds of fashion blow dust in our eyes. The accumulative nursery
rhyme "This is the house that Jack built" shows the now-neglected
pattern:

> This is the cock that crowed in the morn, That waked the priest
> ... That married the man ... That kissed the maiden ... That
> milked the cow ... That tossed the dog ... That worried the cat
> that killed the rat that ate the malt that lay in the house that
> Jack built.

Not *who*, and not *which*—but restrictive *that*.

The rule for shall and will, with its reversal for the second and
third person, and its about-face for the interrogative, is probably
completely unknown to those that have gone to elementary school
(no longer called grammar school) since the First World War.

Practical grammar has been more or less disregarded in recent
years, with attention turned in two directions. There are the many
theorists, for the past twenty years dominated by Noam Chomsky,
who concern themselves less with the problems of the language as
it is than with general principles or patterns that might fit all
English utterances, or even all utterances of all tongues. And
there are the many shruggers of shoulders that, carrying Dewey's
permissiveness into speechways, bid us, as Robert A. Hall deliberately misputs it in the title of his book, *Leave Your Language
Alone*. (The pretty real-estate saleswoman knew the correct verb:
when asked by an impudent house-hunter: "Are you to be let
with the apartment?" she looked calmly at the hopeful customer
and replied: "No, I am to be let alone.")

Structuralism is a term for the study of grammar as it is, but
Noam Chomsky gave high repute to "generative grammar," the

search for all the material necessary for understanding the infinite set of sentences the human mind can put forth in a language. Much of our everyday speech, these speakers assert, is unnecessarily ambiguous. William Empson, in *Seven Types of Ambiguity*, has much to say in favor of passages that may be interpreted in more than one way, especially in poetry and satire. In straightforward discourse, however, there may be hidden dangers. The statement *She was a comic strip artist* would change meaning with a hyphen before or after strip. Look at the seemingly simple statement: "I like to watch my wife cooking." Then observe the similar structure: "I like to watch the pig cooking." It is clear that in the first sentence the wife is doing the cooking; in the second, the pig is being cooked. Rephrase the statement in general terms: "I like to watch X cooking," and it becomes evident that the structure is ambiguous. In a similar way the statement "X almost killed Y" may mean that X almost . . . caused him to die (spun the car at the last minute and Y was unharmed), or that X caused Y . . . almost to die (hurt him so badly that he nearly died). Thus Chomsky was led to seek a "deep structure" by which the surface form might be completely clarified, made free from any possible ambiguity; and to develop a "transformational grammar" that breaks an idea into its basic components so that we can discover how this deep structure (more or less conscious in our mind) turns into what we actually say. Break up a person's thought and you might find, for instance: "A-pig / the-pig-present-to-be-greedy / present-want-for-someone-to-give-a-potato-to-the-pig / the-pig-present-be-greedy"; this will come forth as the utterance, "The greedy pig wants to be given a potato."

Chomsky has made numerous shifts in details of his thinking, over this score of years, but has won staunch disciples as well as dissidents and rejectors. The *London Times* of May 16, 1976, entitled an article "Decline and Fall of Chomsky?" and Richard Hudson, author of *Arguments for Non-Transformational Grammar* (1976), declares that Chomsky's grammar "is unnecessarily complicated, and it's wrong." In a 1976 review of Chomsky's *Reflections on Language*, Eric Partridge iconoclastically expresses what many grammarians have hesitated to say, that transformational grammar merely restates in obfuscatory fashion principles that are abiding in our word ways. Look at Johnson's lines:

Let observation with extensive view
Survey mankind from China to Peru.

Deep grammar would analyze this structure as: "someone-observes / with-someone-observes-extensively / observes-mankind-extensively." Then one might reflect that too many pedants dwell, as Southey once remarked, among "the nugacities of hyper-grammatical absurdity."

Thus the quest for an ideal, universal grammar, announced by Roger Bacon, in the thirteenth century—"Grammar is one and the same in every tongue"—and zealously pursued by eighteenth-century linguists, goes unsuccessfully on.

Like a game, language is limited by its rules. These may be quite flexible; they may even be beyond complete grasping; but they exist. M. C. Beardsley has stated that some imaginable expressions completely break our English rules, defy any attempt at rational explanation; he instances: "a man in the key of A flat"; "a participial biped"; "consanguinity drinks procrastination." Hector Monroe, in an ingenious poem (in *Analysis* XXX, 1973) made a valiant attempt to use these expressions in a meaningful way, but failed to give them validity. Nor is it likely that anyone can confer sense upon the statement "All men melt weedwise when pyrzqxgl is poured on electricity." (*Pyrzqxgl* is the magic-power word in *The Wizard of Oz*.) Despite exceptions that "prove" it, a rule is a rule is a rule.

At the opposite pole from these grammarians' concern is the dismissal of all attention to grammar. In his *Leave Your Language Alone*, Robert Hall states that whatever a person says is suited to the social group or level in or on which he exists. If a man changes his structure and his diction, he will, to his fellows, seem affected, pedantic, pretentious, snobbish, high-hatty or just plain snooty. A hod-carrier, or some such bloke, lifting a mug with his mates at the corner bar, will use a jargon quite other than the speech of his educated son pleading before the judge at a different bar, though that lawyer son may modify his speechways when addressing a mixed jury. In a later edition, renamed *Linguistics and Your Language*, Professor Hall goes even further:

> There is no such thing as good or bad (or correct and incorrect, grammatical and ungrammatical, right and wrong) in language. A dictionary or grammar is not as good an authority for your own speech as the way you yourself speak.

This seems indeed permissiveness run riot, liberty descending into license. Such advocates, however, rush on to question the ethics of seeking to impose word ways upon others, such as a prestige dialect in the schools; a majority tongue on minority groups, as Hindi in India or Tagalog in the Philippines; or a nonindigenous tongue, as English in Ghana. Their policy has won wide support in the United States; in New York through the introduction of Spanish as the language of instruction in numerous public schools; in the country as a whole through new election laws requiring instructions and ballots in the language of large local minorities. The effect of this obtrusion of other tongues upon English has yet to be studied.

An apogee of permissiveness, one might say submissiveness, appears in an official policy statement of The Council on College Composition and Communication, entitled "Students' Right to Their Own Language." Itself exemplifying poor English, this document pontificates:

> Simply because "Johnny can't read" doesn't mean "Johnny is immature" or "Johnny can't think." He may be bored.... If we can convince our students that spelling, punctuation, and usage are less important than content. we have removed a major obstacle in their developing the ability to write.

Vitriolic scorn is poured on this by J. Mitchell Morse, Professor of English at Temple University, in an Op-Ed article in the N.Y. Times of October 21, 1976, quoting almost unbelievable examples of the writing of college students majoring in English. One sample should suffice:

> The blind and the death suffer unjustly because of there handicaped which are considered as being dim witness and are felt to be in a class for the retarded even when there not.... [One may agree that] The destruction of the language is caused by people attempting to decieve the writing and using bad speech practices.

Countering both these trends in language study, as a result in part of the protest that too many college applicants express themselves as though they still belong in elementary school, and the outcry of the business world that their recruits cannot speak or write or spell correctly, there is a reasserting tendency to impart at least the rudiments of grammar to the growing generation. It is urged by many that the basic pattern of subject, verb (transitive or intransitive), object, indirect object, and various modifiers be impressed upon the minds of school children.

Grammar deals mainly with words as they are structured in

sentences; larger units of discourse are commonly questions of rhetoric. The four modes of discourse, usually blended in actual use, have been distinguished for centuries: narration, description, exposition, argumentation, though recently classification and evaluation have been suggested as more accurate and comprehensive terms for the last two.

In the Middle Ages, studies were grouped in the Trivium, which comprised grammar, logic, and rhetoric; and the Quadrivium, arithmetic, geometry, astronomy, and music. The second group deals with numbers, which are in general out of our present scope; the first, with words. More particularly, grammar deals with words in their mutual organization; logic and rhetoric, with the organization of words to express ideas. Without the right words, one cannot express—can hardly have—right ideas. More will be said of these later.

Idioms, expressions that have a clear meaning in one language but make no sense in another, give little trouble to native speakers, who grow up hearing them, though they may confuse a foreigner. Look just at a formal greeting, in three languages. A German may ask: "*Wie befinden Sie sich?*" How do I find myself? I seldom lose myself. A Frenchman may ask: "*Comment vous portez-vous?*" How do I carry myself? Erect, I hope. An American: "How do you do?" Ah, wonder the Frenchman and the German, How do I do what? Casual greetings—"How's tricks?" "*Ça va?*" ("That goes?")—may seem even stranger to learning ears. But no native is likely to need help with an idiom.

Words remain basic, and their problems are considered in semantics, the study of meanings. When one seeks the meaning of a word, if no knowledgeable person is handy to tell, the obvious recourse is to a dictionary. One should note, however, that there are three sorts of dictionary: the proscriptive, the prescriptive, and the descriptive.

The proscriptive dictionary comes in the form of a handbook of *Usage and Abusage,* as Eric Partridge calls his survey (1961), subtitled "a guide to good English." Also standard are H. W. Fowler's *Dictionary of Modern English Usage* (2d edition 1968), adapted for American speakers by Margaret Nicholson, and the earlier *American Comprehensive Guide to Good English* (1927) by George P. Krapp. More recently, Theodore M. Bernstein, who began "Winners and Sinners" as a house organ to keep the writers of *The New York Times* alert to the linguistic quality of their work, has more widely published his findings and reflections in *Watch Your Language* (1948), *More Language That Needs*

Watching, and *The Careful Writer* (1965). Such books attempt to tell what words or expressions should be avoided. Unlike other modern dictionaries, they are the product of one person, and therefore inevitably reflect his training, temperament, and unrecognized bias. He may, like the astute Partridge, be aware of tendencies:

> Like persons, words cannot always be taken for granted. It just cannot be assumed that they will forever trudge along in the prescribed rut and forever do the expected thing! Journalists, authors, and the public whim . . . have raised lowly words to high estate or invested humdrum terms with a picturesque and individual life or brought to the most depressing jargon a not unattractive general currency.

Partridge instances *complex* (as a noun), *fantastic, reaction, sublimation*. Most space in such volumes, however, is devoted to warning the reader against using certain expressions that, for various reasons, are considered undesirable or incorrect. Self-constituted authorities on such matters, as these compilers are, always differ; Jespersen objects to some of Fowler's dicta; Partridge generously quotes, in later editions, writers who point out flaws in his own proscriptions. Also, aside from any idiosyncrasies of the author, the book is betrayed by the sheer passing of time. Too soon any such work becomes obsolete. Either words it discusses have so nearly dropped from general use that their presentation is no longer of interest, or one side of the controversy has established itself as standard, beyond reach of dispute. Thus, while we may agree with Partridge that "To ignore the useful distinction between *shall* and *will, that* and *who* (or *which*) is to set up ambiguity, without any fully compensating gain," the fact remains that the general practice has taken the alternative out of our mouths.

The usual dictionary, like the great O.E.D. or the *American Heritage*, is prescriptive, in that it indicates the level at which a word is regularly used: standard, colloquial, slang, derogatory, vulgar, dialectical; poetic, archaic, obsolete.

The descriptive dictionary, purporting to present what the public in general says and means, may degenerate, like *Webster's Third*, into a permissive vocabulary, allowing equal validity to the expressions of semiliterate speech and of masterly writing. Words in themselves do not mean. People mean. And such a dictionary reports the use of the people. But of course there are many "publics," and a dictionary might be expected to distinguish among them. Rex Stout's *Gambit* (1962) opens with detective Nero Wolfe tearing up and burning the whole of *Webster's Dictionary, Third Edition, Unabridged,* having found it "subversive and intolerably offensive." And indeed, a host of those concerned with the beauty and the discriminatory values of the English language cried out in strong protest when the work was published. Arthur M. Schlesinger, Jr., looked over from his historian's perch to comment on

> the indulgent compilers of modern dictionaries who propound the suicidal thesis that all usages are equal and all correct.... The alchemy that changes words into their opposites has never had more adept practitioners than it has today.

Such a dictionary, and the pronouncements of Professor Hall and the College Council on Composition, give point to the warning of Jacques Barzun, in the Preface to Bernstein's *Watch Your Language:*

> Unless some effort is made to arrest the black rot that we try to disguise by calling it "the problem of communication," it will presently bring us to the last stage of mutual incomprehension. ... Today, it is the educated who lead the way in destruction, it is they who in the name of freedom deny any social obligation to use decently that valuable common property, the mother tongue.

Permissive though it may be, Webster's in 1961, along with the *Random House Dictionary* of 1966, is the last important wordbook to exclude the chief four-letter taboo word.

Brief mention should be made of the many specialized dictionaries. In addition to lists of dialectal words are the *Dictionary of American English* and the *Dictionary of Americanisms,* presenting words that have originated, or have been given a different application or meaning, in the United States. Persons interested in interlingual word associations will enjoy Carl D. Buck's illuminating *Dictionary of Selected Synonyms in the Principal Indo-European Languages.* While the O.E.D. and other dictionaries, even in the shorter "college" or "concise" form, give the background of the words, there are several dictionaries of word origins: the excellent *Comprehensive Etymological Dictionary* of Ernest Klein; also the Oxford, and Eric Partridge's *Origins.* My own *Dictionary of Word Origins* and of *Early English* present tiny essays around a word, with sometimes surprising linkages:

"furious, See fur"; "Venus, See win." A representative entry in the second work is:

> prithee. An early variant of *I pray thee*. Also prithy, prethy, preethee. Shakespeare in *The Tempest* (1610) has "pre-thee no more: thou dost talke nothing to me." Suckling in his play *Aglaura* (1637) has a lively lyric, one stanza of which asks a shrewd question:
>
> > Why so dull and mute, young sinner,
> > Prithee, why so mute?
> > Will, when speaking well can't win her,
> > Saying nothing do't?
> > Prithee, why so mute?

An entirely different type of dictionary was begun by Ambrose Bierce in newspapers in 1881, collected in *The Cynic's Word-book,* and enlarged as *The Devil's Dictionary* in 1911. This contains such definitions as:

> Wit: The salt with which the American humorist spoils his intellectual cooking by leaving it out.
> Opportunity: A favorable occasion for grasping a disappointment.
> Positive: Mistaken at the top of one's voice.

This type of interpretation was occasionally ventured by Samuel Johnson:

> Patriot: One whose ruling passion is the love of his country. It is sometimes used for a factious disturber of the government.
> Pension: An allowance made to anyone without an equivalent. In England it is generally understood to mean pay given to a state hireling for treason to his country.

Such caustic wordbooks are likely to appear in every generation, as topical terms are misapplied by one's contemporaries. A recent one is Leonard L. Levinson's *The Left-Handed Dictionary* (1963), which includes:

> Education: One of the few things a fellow is willing to pay for and not get.
> Diplomacy: The art of saying "nice doggie" until you can find a rock.
> Free press: One hundred men imposing their prejudices on one hundred million.

Jazz: An appeal to the emotions by an attack on the nerves.

Highbrow: The kind of person who looks at a sausage and thinks of Picasso.

Lowbrow: The kind of person who looks at a Picasso and thinks of baloney.

Synonyms, antonyms, and homonyms will be discussed in later chapters, but it may here be mentioned that several books give lists of them, especially Roget's Thesaurus, and three works of J. I. Rodale, *The Word Finder, The Synonym Finder, The Phrase Finder*. Akin to these is Harry Shaw's *Dictionary of Problem Words* (1975), distinguishing between such words as decisive–incisive; baleful–baneful. There are several dictionaries of slang. Our earliest rhyming dictionary, published in 1570, is that of Peter Levens, *Manipulus Vocabularum*, "for such as use to write in English metre." Still available are J. Walker's, which Byron used, and the 1936 well-arranged one, with single, double, and triple rhymes, by Clement Wood.

Theodore M. Bernstein realized a bright idea in his *Reverse Dictionary*, which you can consult for the thought in your mind, to find the word for it. The first two entries under M are:

machine for giving gloss to paper or fabric: calender.
"Madam I'm Adam" type of sentence: palindrome.

Finally, there are dozens of dictionaries of terms within one or another special field: of Christian (christen) names, of last names (surnames), of science, art, literature, philosophy, geography, biology; of motion picture terminology, of "show business jargon"; of clichés, of idioms; of "5,000 adult sex words and phrases"; and uncounted more. Nor do I count the many lists of proverbs and quotations, which are often called dictionaries. The field is open for foraging.

It should be noted that no dictionary is complete. The O.E.D. lists some 420,000 words. *Webster's Third* offers over 450,000. But there are well over a million organic and inorganic chemical compounds, each with its own distinctive name. There are several million insects that have been named, with no one knows how many more still crawling or flying around unlabeled. There are at least a million different animals, and half that many plants, already identified. Of wild orchids alone, there are over 30,000 species. Dictionaries for general use simply have no room for all these. Van Nostrand's 2008-page *Scientific Encyclopedia* is one of many books that partially fill the gap.

While "concise" or "college" dictionaries often "define" by giving synonyms, and unabridged dictionaries sometimes add descriptive elements, the precise definition usually consists of three parts: genus, or the general class; species, the particular smaller group within the class; and differentia, the ways in which the item being defined is distinct from others of the same species. Thus defined, a stool is an article of furniture, for one person to sit on, without back or arms. To add "with either three or four legs" is to include a non-defining attribute; as to add "flying" to the definition of bird. Actually, not every creature that flies is a bird: the bat is a mammal; nor does every bird fly: the ostrich, the penguin, the kiwi, do not.

Sometimes the thing defined itself changes. A canoe is no longer made of birch bark; and the boats in a "canoe race" may turn out to be kayaks. A house and a ship of today may differ greatly from what bore those names three centuries ago. In the United States, what we still call a drug store is now an emporium where you can purchase beauty aids, beach toys, cigarettes, ice cream, and a quick lunch. "The comics" now offer adventure, science fiction, supermen, and superduper women like Varoom-shka and Modesty Blaise.

Definitions must also be devised so as to include the two major applications of a word, its denotation and its connotation. The denotation is the exact, objective significance of the word: the *thirteenth* is the one after the *twelfth*. More precisely, denotation covers the sum total of things (referents) to which the word can be applied: *tree* comprehends every such item that does, did, or will exist. A word's connotation is the aura of significance that has gathered about the word, because of its history, its earlier applications, or its associations in the mind of the user or hearer. Thus, to speak of "the thirteenth at table" makes the number a portent of misfortune, because of the thirteen assembled at the Last Supper before the betrayal of Christ. The remark "It doesn't feel like Sunday today" would make little sense in Moslem lands, where the holy day is Friday; nor would the joyous exclamation "I felt like a millionaire" have much meaning in China or the Australian bush. The expression "behind the eight ball" is mean-ingless to many; and some that know its meaning don't know why it has that sense.

Shakespeare has said that a rose by any other name will smell as sweet, and children chant "Sticks and stones may break my bones, but words will never hurt me"; but life has shown that this is far from true. The country landlady had served some tasty dandelion salad for her summer boarders; when her farmer husband, looking in, said: "I hope you folks are enjoying your pissabed greens," there was a sudden loss of appetite. A sinister jingle runs:

> For innocents' affliction
> Guilty deeds I must prepare;
> I'm the lovely fiend of fiction,
> With the yellow, yellow hair.

The classic heroine's hair is golden. Yellow is the color of cowards, of quarantine, of the labels once worn by Jews and prostitutes— of disease and impending disaster. Gold is beautiful.

It is clear that a dictionary cannot take note of connotations unless they are quite general; but some linguists go so far as to say that any complete definition is impossible. How, for example— in any but technical terms unhelpful to the layman—define *green?* How would you describe the difference between the taste of a peach and that of a pear? Certain terms have an inevitable vagueness: *freedom of speech; pornography; the public right to know:* the courts themselves have given such terms changing and conflicting definitions.

Before the presidential election of 1976, the magazine *Commentary* asked sixty-four persons to define liberal and conservative. The nearest they came to concord was the agreement that the terms are more often used for emotional effect than for intellectual discrimination. "These labels are used today simply as weapons in political power struggles." "They still serve, like neckties, as symbols of pretense or identification among the fashion-conscious majority of us." "The commonly fraudulent and intellectually useless terms liberal and conservative":—that is Alfred Kazin. "The words I have emphasized (conservative, liberalism, radical, reactionaries), and their cognate expressions, are today more often used as epithets of abuse or edification than of description":—this is Sidney Hook. Not one of the remarks makes a contribution to taxonomy, the study of scientific classification.

Where does outer space begin? Where the sky? The poet asseverates:

> Over our forehead spreads the sky,
> No higher than the soul is high.

But definitions fail.

Some scholars—especially with reference to poetry, as Dante's —find four levels of meaning: 1. Literal: the immediate fact or event. 2. Allegorical: symbolic meanings appropriate to this world. 3. Anagogical: symbolic meanings appropriate to the spiritual level. 4. Tropological: symbolic meanings personal, moral, yet universal. Thus, of *tree:* 1. This or that particular maple, spruce, or other individual tree under immediate consideration. 2. The tree as providing shelter (shade, or wood for housing) and warmth. 3. "The woods were God's first temples." 4. The sense of continuous growth in the world; the bridge of time; the ultimate rightness of nature. Thus each thing reaches out to all.

Sometimes it may seem that suggestion is more provocative of useful thought than definition. "Space is understood by what it separates; mind is understood by what it joins." Thinkers like A. H. Korzybski and S. I. Hayakawa, who have extended what they call "general semantics" from word meanings to life applications, insist that an *etc.* is to be understood at the end of every sentence, as the old alphabets for beginners ended with ampersand, &.

Persons planning to develop an argument or an extensive idea may begin by saying: "Let us define our terms." It often happens, however, that a definition is most convincingly presented as the culmination of a lengthy disquisition. The meaning emerges at the end. It is easier, for example, to write an essay on beauty than to capture its essence in a phrase.

When we move beyond a word to a sentence or paragraph, the question of its meaning takes on further complications. There is first, of course, its significance in the sense we have been considering, and its truth or nontruth. Then we must note the reference. The expressions "the author of *Macbeth*" and "the author of *Hamlet*" differ in reference but not in sense. There is also the force of the sentence to be recognized: is it an assertion, a question, a command, a prayer, an expression of wonder or dismay? Finally, one must judge its tone, expressed in voice as well as choice of word; it may be matter-of-fact, praising, scornful, querulous, pondering.

Beyond and because of such considerations, there is always the possibility of misunderstanding. A person may say one thing, and mean another; or a listener may hear one thing, and understand another. In either case, the duplicity may be unintentional, or deliberate.

In their book *The Meaning of Meaning,* Charles K. Ogden and I. A. Richards point out that the word itself has several senses.

1. Life has lost its meaning for me. (sense of purpose)
2. Nuclear war means the end of civilization. (will result in)
3. You mean a lot to me. (are worth)
4. He may not accomplish much, but he means well. (has good intentions)
5. Falling mercury in a thermometer means cooler weather. (is a sign of)
6. Democracy means government of the people, for the people, by the people. (is a symbol of the concept)

Meaning, J. P. McKinney suggests neatly, is *mean*-ing: taking the mean point of a whole range of individual experiences, thus giving a term common usefulness and validity. The O.E.D. devotes twenty-two pages to the noun *meaning* and the verb *mean.*

Don't ask for the meaning, said Wittgenstein, ask for the use. For all expressions call for interpretation on the part of the listener. Some speakers, on the other hand, make their interpretations first. A frequent and perhaps unwitting error of philosophers is the promotion of a limited concept to dominate a whole domain. Thus Aristotle chose moderation—his Greek term *meden agan* is on the temple at Delphi; Latin *ne quid nimis,* 'nothing too much': the golden mean—as the hinge upon which all virtues swing, instead of just one among the virtues. The materialist tells us that matter is not just one aspect of the universe, but its essential character. He will not be rebuffed by the neat attempt at disposal of his claim—What is mind? No matter. What is matter? Never mind—anymore than the philosophical idealist, his opposite number, was discomfited by Dr. Johnson's kicking a rock.

Still another danger involved in the quest for meaning is what has been called hypostatization or reification, the assumption that because there is a word for something (a noun) there must be a real something, an entity, that the word signifies. The mere existence of the word *vampire* adds to the number of awed believers, as do the expressions *flying saucers* and *Loch Ness monster.* From 1669 to 1822 scientists hunted for phlogiston, the substance within flammable materials that burned. Joseph Priestly, who in 1774 isolated oxygen, called it *dephlogisticated air.* As late as 1850 Baron von Reichenbach convinced many scientists that there was a basic force, which he called *od,* underlying many natural activities, such as magnetism (*magnetod*), crystallization (*crystallod*), light, the power emanating from the sun, and chemical reactions. He saw this odic force as "that which was wanting, to reply to most of the questions respecting life." The idea won wide acceptance; Elizabeth Barrett Browning refers to it in her poem *Aurora Leigh,* and even in 1895 a believer could speak of "the odic force whose existence science cannot deny, and speculation would not." Today the term *od,* if not forgotten, seems merely odd.

Even longer has been the search for the medium through which light waves travel. At least since 1676, when Olaf Roemer measured the speed of light, scientists have postulated a gas along which light waves can ripple. Ocean waves travel through water (which itself remains in place); sound waves travel through air; light waves travel through ether—except that no one has ever been able to detect any ethereal presence. Einstein's theory wiped it out of consideration; yet some still cling to the notion that some entity (rather than empty space) must serve to carry the many stellar radiations, one small range of which comes to us as light.

Around 1340, William Occam, "doctor invincibilis," issued a warning, known since as Occam's razor, that "entities should not be unnecessarily multiplied." This has too often been dulled in practice.

One type of word, the ghost word, is properly nonexistent. A ghost word is a misprint or other error, temporarily sanctified by inclusion in a dictionary. The First Supplement to the O.E.D. discusses 83 of these, and lists 270 more which are discussed in the body of the dictionary. Among such spurious words are alienatory, aristarchy, cherisance, conyne, corf, crevet, frenchmore, loudful, phantomnation, jimwhiskee. Allen Walker Read, in a December 1976 talk on ghost words at the Modern Language Association Meeting, suggests as "the most outstanding ghost word"*dord,* a recurrent misprint from the 1934 *Merriam Webster Dictionary* listing *D or d* as an abbreviation of density. My own favorite is *slughorn,* an early spelling of *slogan,* from Gaelic *sluagh,* 'army' and *ghairm,* 'cry'. Chatterton in 1770 rediscovered the spelling and misunderstood the second syllable; Browning in 1855 followed him, in "Childe Roland to the Dark Tower Came": "Dauntless the slug-horn to my lips I set, And blew." Most ghost words make fewer echoes in literary halls. Yet no doubt more spurious terms will insinuate themselves into print, if not into respectability. *Helpmeet* has remained in the language, from a misreading of the Bible, Genesis 2:18: "an help meet for him," *meet* meaning 'suitable'; in turn, it bred the form *helpmate.*

Professor Read included in his talk several other sorts of words, not born of error. The *nonce word* (for *then anes,* Old English for 'the once') is a deliberate coinage, a *hapax legomenon,* that found no further users. There are hundreds of these, fashioned in every period: 1447 *prend,* to 'take', from French *prendre* (the Latin comes to us in *apprehend* and *apprentice*); 1623 *rixation,* 'scolding'; 1709 *quackster,* midway between the 1579 *quacksalver* and the still current *quack;* 1864 *beehivy;* 1867 *Beelzebubian,* 'devilish', from the God of Flies; 1885 *rhythmize.* Akin to the nonce word is what Read calls the "individualism," also a coinage, but usually humorous and obviously for the one occasion; thus Diana Trilling described herself as "a less educated eclectic" than her late husband Lionel: "I don't have as many things to *eclect* from."

A nonce word occasionally catches the fancy, as *defenestration,* 'throwing someone out of the window'; *defeneration,* 'ruining someone through usury', fell flat. *Dentiloquent,* 'talking through one's teeth', and *doctiloquent,* 'talking learnedly', had their brief pedantic day; they are recorded in Thomas Blount's dictionary of difficult words, *Glossographia,* 1656. The jocular *capiloquent,* 'talking through one's hat', has yet to find perch in the wordbooks.

Often a highly respectable word, even a hallowed symbol (My Country) or the sign of one (The Flag) is so reified as to evoke emotions a rabble-rouser seeks to convert into action toward less hallowed ends. A word with admired connotations is frequently drawn to commercial use. *Atomic* being endowed with a sense of power, American cities have blossomed with the Atomic Launderette, Atomic Express Service, and more businesses of no visible connection with atoms other than the desire to attract customers by the name. In London I have noticed a seemingly prosperous firm with the name Rock Auto Parts, and the slogan "Try Rock— and roll."

While deviations and difficulties may obscure the meaning of a word in English, they are complicated when one approaches the problems of translation. It is easy to find ludicrous examples of error in translation, as when an earnest but unpoetic man learning French translated Hugo's sentimental *La rose, émue, répondait* ('the rose, moved, answered') into the possible but absurd "The pink emu laid another egg." Even computers cannot handle the problems. "Out of sight, out of mind," machine-rendered into Russian, returned to English by machine as "Invisible maniac." Columns have been filled with blunders made in the instantaneous translations of the experienced experts at the U.N.

Words that look alike in related languages may have deceptively different meanings. An international crisis was averted by a prompt explanation and apology when in a government document *La France demande* was translated *France demands* instead of *France requests,* which is the meaning. *Je me demande,* as the French say—I ask myself—what officious official perpetrated that mistake? The primary meaning of French *conscience* is English *consciousness.*

With all the time and talent one may wish, it must be recognized that full translation of a work of art is impossible. No version can carry into another tongue all the subtleties of sound, sense, and suggestion, the accordance of rhythm, the harmony of tone, the balance of structure, achieved in the original masterpiece.

Translation is impossible—yet essential. For most persons lack the capability, given the time and the desire, to master every language in which great works have been composed. Adequate translations of legal, commercial, and scientific documents can be made; in art, the best one can hope for is a comparable work in the second language. In fact, an inferior writer may seem better in translation, as his roughnesses are smoothed, his weaknesses strengthened, by an expert adaptation. This may help account for the exalted reputation of Byron on the Continent.

Contrariwise, some translators feel that they have made their author native, given him a new citizenship, as it were. The French claimed Poe as their poet. The Germans adopted as well as adapted Shakespeare: *Der Kaufmann von Venedig, vergrössert und verbessert,* 'The Merchant of Venice, enlarged and improved'.

The majesty, the intensity, of the Bible, of Dante, somehow survive translation. A great book attracts good translators; and if their own personality intervenes and colors their interpretation, the same is true of every reader of any work. The Italian saying *Tradattore, traditore,* 'Translator, traitor', is the anguished outcry of a victim. The essential worth of a book comes through.

A wholly different attitude is manifested in the words of the American publisher and philosopher Dagobert D. Runes:

> With the number of platitudes and irrelevancies spouted by mouth and pen in any one language, the acquisition of additional tongues should be roundly discouraged.

In other words, pick worthwhile books to translate.

I repeat: Words do not mean; people mean. But to most people, words are not treasures, they are merely tools. And the tools are employed not by careful workmen, but as free instruments handled carelessly and dropped aside as soon as used. Yet "to misuse the word is to show contempt for man," warned Dag Hammarskjöld, late Secretary General of the United Nations:

> Respect for the word—to employ it with scrupulous care and an incorruptible heartfelt love of truth—is essential if there is to be any growth in a society or in the human race.

People must not merely mean; they must mean well, and then find ways to make actual what they mean. Basic to man's goals is the proper use of words.

6.

SYNONYMS, ANTONYMS, AND MORE

TO WHATEVER DEGREE CARELESS USE may identify them, no two words function exactly alike. Synonyms allow us to indicate fine shades of difference; we may choose them as they fit our discourse in sound (tonal pattern, rhythm), in significance, in implication. It makes little difference, for example, whether we call someone *brave* or *courageous*—save in the harmony the term achieves with the rest of our remarks, *brave*, the Saxon term, being the more likely in casual conversation.

Synonyms differ in various respects. There may be shades of meaning, as with *forbid, prohibit, proscribe, prevent*. Such distinctions, in common parlance, tend to be lost. Thus *prohibit*, which once meant to keep someone from doing something, is now defined—Dumping Prohibited—as 'to forbid by authority', which is tantamount to an emphatic No!

The adjectives *alternate* and *alternative* are frequently confused; *periodic* and *periodical*, less often. But I wonder how many know that *pendant* is preferred for the noun; *pendent*, for the adjective. The word *fewer* has already been given a back seat; *fewer* is the *Random House Dictionary* definition 7 of *less*. Fewer, of course, should be used for things that can be separately numbered or counted; *less*, for things in the mass or lump, things in bulk or in degree. Although *demeanor* has kept its general sense, *demean* is so often used for a 'belittling' that *bemean* is almost forgotten. The verb *avert* is followed by *from*; for the adjective *averse*, O.E.D. gives a long list of noted writers using *from*, another long list using *to*. *Different to* is considered colloquial, but again O.E.D. gives two lists: you can follow Addison, Defoe, *et al*, and say *different from;* or Coleridge, Thackeray, and more, with *different than.*

When wordsman Noah Webster's wife came upon him as he was kissing the housemaid, the story goes, she exclaimed: "Why Noah, I am surprised!" Thereupon he drew himself righteously up, and informed her: "No, Madam: *you* are astonished; *I* am surprised." We may still speak of taking someone by surprise; but in general usage the difference is dictionaried as "astonish, to surprise greatly." The correct word, being used rarely, adds a touch of awe.

As our attention turns to outer space, we must learn to distinguish between a "cluster of galaxies" and a "galactic cluster." Our Milky Way is one of a local group, a cluster of thirteen galaxies: three spiral galaxies, including the Andromeda nebula and our own Milky Way, with our sun far out on one arm; six elliptical galaxies; and four irregular galaxies, including the Large and the Small Magellanic Cloud, our nearest galactic neighbors. (There is, indeed, question as to whether we do not belong in the cluster of several hundred galaxies in the constellation Virgo, which is only 8 million light years away.) A galactic cluster, on the other hand, is a closely knit group of stars, moving together in the swarm of stars within one galaxy. A galactic cluster—such as the cluster of some thirty stars in the constellation Taurus, in our Milky Way—is temporary, as the stars tend to speed apart; they are not likely to remain as a group for more than 10 billion years. If a cluster of galaxies ultimately separates, no sign of this has yet been susceptible to our measurements.

We should hear more, in the next few years, of a new use of the word *waterhole,* far from the hoped-for drink on a dry prairie. NASA (the National Aeronautic and Space Administration) is actively probing the waterhole, in its scientific Search for Extraterrestrial Intelligences (SETI). This waterhole is the spread between the frequency of an atom of hydrogen (H) and of a molecule of hydroxyl (HO). These combine to form water (H_2O). But H has a frequency of 1420 megahertz (a megahertz is a vibration of a million cycles per second), and HO a frequency of 1662 megahertz; the vibrations between constitute the waterhole. And it is in this range that our space scientists think messages from intelligent beings (if any) on planets of stars other than our sun are most likely to be transmitted. We are told that truth lies at the bottom of a well; perhaps there are new truths awaiting us in the heavenly waterhole. Meanwhile, here is an example of how an almost outused word can take on fresh significance.

At the opposite ends of the scale from galactic distances is another new world with which we should grow familiar. Computer and other calculations now work with items so small they used to be called *infinitesimal*, 'immeasurable'. For these, we have newly borrowed the Greek word *nanos*, meaning dwarf. A *nanosecond* is a thousand millionth of a second, 10^{-9} seconds, which means a dot followed by nine zeros before the digit 1. You can get some sense of the minuteness of this by considering that a nanosecond is to a second as a second is to 30 years. Yet measurements in that range—*nanogram, nanohenry, nanoliter, nanovolt*—have been utilized since 1940, are already in the dictionaries, and to the physicists of the coming century will be routine. The telephone company, which functions in mere microseconds (millionths of a second, 10^{-6}) nevertheless points out that there are more microseconds (60 million) in a minute than there are minutes (52.6 million) in the twentieth century.

Another way in which synonyms may differ is in affective qualities, in the associations commonly attached to the words. An *informant* is commonly looked upon with more respect than an *informer; to associate* implies more respectable companions than *to consort.* Have you an *assignment,* or an *assignation? Exceptional* and *abnormal* are synonyms, but parents would hope to apply the first word to their child. *Manly* is a favorable word; *manlike* is neutral; *mannish* bears the taint of disapproval.

Words within a single range may be used by writers to make their meaning more precise. Thus the curate says to the schoolmaster, in *Love's Labor's Lost:* "Your reasons at dinner have been sharp and sententious, pleasant without scurrility, witty without affectation, learned without opinion, and strange without heresy." Bernard Shaw—who is said to have claimed that he stood on Shakespeare's shoulders (as might a pygmy on a giant), and thus could see farther—was not to be outdone. (But, as Freud contemptuously silenced a preening defector: "A louse on the head of a philosopher sees nothing.") Don Juan, in *Man and Superman,* characterizes the friends of the Devil:

They are not beautiful: they are only decorated. They are not clean: they are only shaved and starched. They are not dignified: they are only fashionably dressed. They are not educated: they are only college passmen....

He goes on through seventeen more such oppositions—"they are not prosperous: they are only rich"—then crowds to a conclusion:

not intelligent, only opinionated; not progressive, only factious; not imaginative, only superstitious; not just, only vindictive; not generous, only propitiatory; not disciplined, only cowed; and not truthful at all—liars every one of them, to the very backbone of their souls.

In the Bible we find the use of synonyms as an emphatic element, as well as to achieve balance of rhythm; indeed, this forms a pattern in all early Semitic poetry:

> Hear, oh ye kings;
> Give ear, oh ye princes.

This grew into a device used by Marlowe in his plays. Faustus hails Mephistophilis as

> Archregent and commander of all spirits . . .
> Chief lord and regent of perpetual night.

The pattern finds rich expression in Shakespeare, with many synonymic lines:

> Within the book and volume of my brain. . . .
> The slings and arrows of outrageous fortune. . . .
> The whips and scorns of time. . . .
> Th' inaudible and noiseless foot of time. . . .

Sometimes these seem to have no more than emphatic and rhythmic intentions; but often a subtle extension of the thought may be discerned: the progression in whips and scorns from physical to mental; in the last above, from not hearing to the reason for not hearing. In general, however, a writer does not pile on, but selects among, available synonyms.

Still another way in which synonyms may differ is in degree. In fact, some sets of words may be arranged in a polarity, marked off more roughly than the degrees of latitude, but reaching at the ends two words of opposite meaning, antonyms. Most of us fit somewhere on a sliding scale between *good* and *bad*. *Hot* and *cold* have words below zero and above 100° Centigrade: *seething, scorching, scalding, white hot, red hot, boiling; warm, tepid, lukewarm; cool, brisk, chilly; raw, frosty, frigid, freezing, icy, glacial,* and the like. As the quotations from Shakespeare and Shaw indicate, distinctions can be made both by affirming an approximate likeness and by denying an opposite quality. In Roget's *Thesaurus,* the chief listing of such word choice, synonyms and antonyms are proffered side by side—though without any indication of distinctions. Distinctions are drawn in J. B. Opdycke's *Mark My Words* (1949).

Some words, in the vicissitudes of our language growth, have come to mean their own opposites. Such an autantonym is the word *fast:* a fast horse runs rapidly, a fast color will not run at all. Today the word *let* commonly means 'allow'; its use in the sense of 'hinder' is obsolete save in a *let ball*—often mistakenly called a *net ball*—in tennis, and in the legal phrase *without let or hindrance*. Seeded raisins have the seeds taken out; seeded rye bread has the seeds put in. Wind up a watch, it goes; wind up a business, it stops. If you think better of a person, you admire him more; if you think better of a project, you cast it aside.

Akin to the autantonym is a word that may indicate either cause or effect: *fearful* (as also *fearsome*) means either 'frightening' or 'frightened'. *Curious* may refer to something odd, or to the person that wonders about it. There is not quite an antonym, but a decided difference in the meaning of the word *think*, in the remark: The more I think of you, the less I think of you. The figure here, of an apparent but not actual contradiction, is an oxymoron (from Greek meaning 'foolish with a point').

A number of words, especially adverbs, while they do not range through a polarity, are used to indicate degrees of approbation or disapproval. Thus *ineffably, eminently, incomparably, irresistibly*, are used of pleasant things. *Deeply, incredibly, surprisingly, extremely*, are neutral; an act may be astonishingly successful, or astonishingly impolite. But *abysmally, grossly, inordinately, atrociously*, are used of disagreeable things.

Some such pattern may have led Bertrand Russell to his "conjugation of adjectives": I am firm. You are obstinate. He is a pig-headed fool. Such gradations caught attention; more were invited in several competitions. I am a social drinker. You sometimes overindulge. He is a lush. I am a creative writer. You have a journalistic flair. He is a thriving hack. I am curious. You are inquisitive. He is a snooper. Such removals of unpleasant qualities to the second and third person might produce more sobering reflection, if we reconsider them as indicating: What I think of myself; what those that like me think of me; what those that dislike me think of me.

Words may be classified in other ways. There are many reversibles, words that, spelled backward, make another word. *Deliver. Diaper. Gnat; star; desserts; rail; golf*. The title of the second Samuel Butler's novel *Erewhon* is to be taken as *nowhere* backwards.

Sometimes a man, playing a *part,* unwittingly sets his own *trap:* those that turn about *live* fall into *evil.* This marks the fate of Sir Walter Ralegh and of Christopher Marlowe, frequenters of the Elizabethan heretical School of Night, which reversed the idea of *God.* Marlowe was murdered; Ralegh was put to death. Their creed has been set in a palindrome: "Dog as a devil deified lived as a god."

A palindrome is a special type of reversible; it reads the same right to left as left to right. Some word palindromes are *redder, civic, tenet, rotator, repaper, kayak, Malayalam.* The palindrome has been expanded into a sentence; many such reversible sentences have been curiously and laboriously devised. The first words ever spoken were (of course!) in English: "Madam, I'm Adam." To which the new woman coyly responded: "Eve." A later young lady, when her suitor became too ardent, gently rebuffed him: "Ned, I am a maiden." Holding his ardor in check, he asked for her hand; she, still palindromically, amended: "Now, Ned, I am a maiden won." Perhaps there is an admonition to officeworkers in the palindrome: "Sex at noon taxes." There are many such sentences; wordmasters try to concoct the cleverest or the longest.

Palindromes are by no means new; they are sometimes called sotadics, after Sotades, a Greek poet of the third century B.C., who wrote (mainly scurrilous) palindromic verse. A neat Latin palindrome is the lawyer's boastful promise: *Si nummi immunis,* "Pay me your fee and you go scot free."

An even more complicated, and more significant, Latin design is the palindromic square

```
S   A   T   O   R
A   R   E   P   O
T   E   N   E   T
O   P   E   R   A
R   O   T   A   S
```

which is a palindrome read top to bottom, bottom to top, left to right, right to left. This may be translated: "Arepo the sower holds the wheels to the work." It means, however, much more. Found scratched on a Roman wall in Cirencester, England, and among the ruins of Pompeii, it is also engraved on amulets and charms, which in early Christian times were laid upon the belly of a

pregnant woman to ensure safe delivery. In the days of persecu-
tion of Christians, such a charm might have been a secret means
of identification. For centered in the palindromic square, the
word *tenet* ('he holds'; now used in English of a *held* belief)
forms a cross. All the letters in the square, moreover, form a
larger cross, making the words

```
                    P
                    A
                    T
                    E
                    R
    P A T E R       N     O S T E R
                    O
                    S
                    T
                    E
                    R
```

which are the first two words of the Lord's Prayer—save that
four letters are left out. These are A,O,A,O. Place these at the four
ends of the Cross; they are the first and the last letter of the
Greek alphabet, alpha and omega. You will find them in the Bible
(Revelations 21:6): "I am the alpha and the omega, the beginning
and the end." And all the letters of the square—this time with
no omissions—can be rearranged to form the Latin *Oro Te, Pater;
oro Te, Pater; sanas:* "I pray to Thee, Father, Thou healest." A
solid set of Christian symbols crossed in a square! Thus, like
other games, as we shall see, what has ended as wordplay began
long ago with more serious intentions.

There being reversible words, it follows that there are irreversible words. Most words in the language, of course, when spelled
backwards do not form other words. But there are compounds
that are irreversible in another sense; separate and reverse the
two components, and they have a different meaning. One may
look a document *over*, and somehow *overlook* a vital clause.
One need not *understand* the mechanics of a shower to *stand
under* it. Many of the *over-* and *under-* compounds, and a number
of the *in-* and *out-* words—*income, output, inborn, outrun*—thus
present different senses with the different grouping.
words that appear always in the established order. They might
Even more frequent are the irreversible binomials, paired
make equal sense if turned about, but would sound strange if not
ludicrous. There are so many of these that they have been classified in six groupings.

1. With rhyme. *By hook or by crook. Town and gown.*

2. With alliteration. This is a large group; the identity of opening sounds is both pleasant and an aid to memory, a mnemonic. *Bag and baggage. Bed and board. Spick and span. To have and to hold.*

3. Synonyms. *At one's beck and call. Law and order. Assault and battery. Null and void.* These may also be alliterative: *hale and hearty. Safe and sound. Pots and pans.* (One does not say *Pans and pots.*) *Rack and ruin.*

4. Antonyms. *To be or not to be. Win or lose. Sink or swim.* (It would seem a more appropriate sequence to say *Swim or sink,* as in the more erudite *Survive or perish;* yet that is not the order.) *Now or never. Profit and loss.*

5. Complementary. *Knife and fork. Soup to nuts.* (At the ancient Roman table, it was *Eggs to apples;* among gamblers, it used to be *Soda to hock,* these words meaning the top and the bottom card in the dealing-box.) *On hands and knees. Meat and potatoes.* There is an old English saying: "Take care of the pence, and the pounds will take care of themselves," which Lewis Carroll converted to "Take care of the sense, and the sounds will take care of themselves."

6. General expressions. *Male and female. Husband and wife.* But *Ladies and gentlemen.* And "I've lived here, *man and boy,* for sixty-five years." Thus also *cat and mouse, hammer and tongs.*

In these couplings, the shorter word usually comes first: *rough and tumble; slow and steady;* the *strait and narrow* path. There are a few exceptions: *hither and yon;* and (because of the nursery rhyme) *tattered and torn.*

The Germans have made a trinomial linkage describing woman's domain: *Kinder, Kirche, Küche,* which may keep the alliteration in English as *kids, kirk, and kitchen,* or *children, church, and chores.*

There are also verbal expressions that differ on reversal, as when you are *booking a place* on a plane or *placing a book* on a shelf; *thumbing a lift* or *lifting a thumb* (thumbs up at a Roman arena, to spare a life).

Another kind of word has been variously labeled: swallowword, kangaroo word, or marsupial. This consists of a word within which a synonym lies cuddled, the letters not necessarily adjacent but in proper order. Thus *calumnies* contains *lies; respite, rest; evacuate, vacate.* There is a surprisingly large number of such words. *Container* holds both the British *tin* and the American *can. Masculine; rapscallion; catacomb; deliberate.*

Three other sorts of words have been distinguished, on purely literal grounds. A charitable word is one that can give up any letter, and still form a valid word. *Seat* thus becomes in turn *eat, sat, set, sea.* So also *spay; boat.* A hospitable word is one that, contrariwise, can accept a letter in any place: *rap: trap, reap, rasp, rapt. Pat: spat, peat, part, path.* Thus *hat; far.* An amenable word is one that can exchange any letter for another: *load: road, lead, lord, loan.* Thus *bond; lane.*

To these may be added the turnabout or unending word, one that can transfer its first letter to the last. The *heart* clings to its native *earth. Each* tooth, alas, can severally *ache. Speculation* may lead to *peculations. Echoic; emanate.* Sometimes the process can be continued: *stable, tables, ablest; emit, mite, item; tea, eat, ate, tea . . .*

The wide and varied field of anagrams will be lightly looked upon in the chapter on wordplay. Here we may note the familiar type, in which the letters of one term may be rearranged to form another. Twenty trees lie hidden, in this manner, in the following passage:

> In a cabin a mile north along the River Wye, lives old Lem with his pet lamb. Old rags take the place of window panes and door panel. Possessed of ample means, he has not cared to wear other covering than a ragged dolman, nor to drink from aught but a cheap blue mug. At dusk he goes to reap the harvest of his melon patch. He will take a lamp in one hand to allure insects, and a lump of rock in the other with which to slay a possible weasel.

> The twenty trees, in order, are lime, thorn, yew, elm, balm, aspen, plane, maple, ash, cedar, almond, peach, gum, pear, lemon, teak, palm, laurel, plum, cork.

A single word can be made from *roast mules.* Quite another word is an anagram of its singular, *roast mule.* These may be found at the end of Chapter 13. Meanwhile we may note that some believers in the magic potency of words have hailed *anagrams* as *ars magna,* the 'great art'.

The longest one-word anagrams seem to be *conservationalist–conversationalist* and *interlaminations–internationalism.*

A subdivision of this type of anagram is the aptagram, wherein the two terms formed by the same letters are in some way related. Thus *neat leg* is *elegant; no more stars*—also, *moon-starers*—turns into *astronomers. Into my arm: matrimony. Sly ware: lawyers. I cry that I sin: Christianity.*

In various ways, this pattern has entered into politics, literature, court proceedings, even religion. Followers of Disraeli anagrammatized his name as *I lead, Sir;* whereupon his opponents countered by lampooning his fastidious ways: *Idle airs.* Elleanor (so she wrote!) Davies set herself up as a prophetess when the Stuarts reigned, claiming to be foreordained by the anagram of her name: *Reveals, O Daniel!* She was disposed of by the Court of High Commission, which turned Dame Eleanor Davies into *Never soe mad a ladie!* Scripture has been better served by the aptagram. When Pilate, looking at Jesus, asked "What is truth?" he did not wait for an answer. He already had the answer. At the Roman court, proceedings were in Latin. Pilate asked: *Quid est veritas?* And the anagram of these words is *Est vir qui adest,* "It is the man who stands before you."

For some centuries, *i* and *j* were treated as one letter; so were *u* and *v.* Thus John Bunyan could write, in 1682:

> Witness my name, if anagrammed to thee,
> The letters make "Nu hony in a B."

Not many years later, more permanently, François Marie Arouet (*le jeune,* 'Junior'), added the initial *l* and *j* (*i*) to his family name, and has thenceforth been known to the world as Voltaire. François Rabelais anagrammatized his name, signing both *Pantagruel* and *Gargantua* as by Alcofribas Nasier. The strict Calvin disapprovingly turned Rabelais' last name, in its Latin form Rabelaesius, into *Rabie laesus,* 'afflicted with madness'. Misogynists have turned the first woman's name, Eva, into *Vae,* Latin for 'woe', which, they say, she brought onto the earth. The tables are neatly turned on this by hailing her who brought redemption into the world, *Ave* Maria. The first to link Eva and Ave in print was the Jesuit Father Robert Southwell, who was hanged in England in 1595. George Herbert in 1633 built his anagram of *Mary,* mother of Jesus, into a couplet:

> How well her name an *Army* doth present,
> In whom the "Lord of Hosts" did pitch his tent.

In the same century two Latin works in prose, and one in meter, had each over three thousand anagrams about the Holy Family. Swift, in an unusual romantic moment, noted that some lovers form anagrams out of their name combined with that of their beloved. The practice of making anagrams, observed Henry Wheatley in his book on the subject (1862), was by no means uncommon among the Greeks. Louis XIII of France, although ruled by Cardinal Richelieu, on his own appointed one Thomas Billon as Royal Anagrammatist. As late as 1965, David Stevenson, in *The Meditations of William Shakespeare*, supplies hundreds of anagrams to lines from the sonnets and plays, suggesting that the Bard of Avon bared his true nature in such patterns.

Scientific terminology has occasionally enlisted the anagram. The *mho* is the electrical reciprocal of the *ohm*, both names from the German physicist George Simon Ohm (1787–1854). The monkshood plant, the aconite, yields *aconitic* acid; on decomposition it forms another, anagrammatically named *itaconic* acid. Two varieties of calcium silicate are *okenite* and *nekoite*. The range of the device is wide.

Some that make much ado about words have presented claimants for the proud position of the longest word in the English language. Borrowing from a rule in Latin grammar, William Shenstone in 1741 coined a word, saying: "I loved him for nothing so much as his floccinaucinihilipilification of money." The poet Southey and the novelist Scott took this word, with its *i* nine times, into their vocabulary; but its 29 letters are exceeded by the 34 of a word meaning the practice of using long words: *hippopotomonstrousesquipedalianism*. Science, which reaches out to swallow all reality, can gobble these down like minnows. Medicine speaks (not often!) of *diaminodihydrocyarsenobenzenedihydrochloride;* this word of 44 letters is better known as *salvarsan*, familiarly called 606 (605 compounds tried before had failed). Biochemistry can leave such terms wallowing in the wake. *Tryptophen synthetase A protein,* spelled in full, would run to 1,913 letters. Fortunately, the scientist can resort to symbols.

Literature, while not stretching our jaws this far, has tried some lengthy words. James Joyce, who turned Homer's *Odyssey* into a framework for his tale of a Dublin day, took the title of a bawdy ballad for his *Finnegans Wake*, and in it perpetrated ten "thunderwords," each built up with 100 letters. While these are not likely to become familiar words in the language, they are proffered to the readers of what presents itself as an English book. The seventh thunderword, we are told, compresses within it, symbolizes, celebrates, or bewails four falls: the tumble of the Irish hod-carrier Tim Finnegan from his ladder—in the ballad, it is Tim's wife with her lover (at Tim's wake) that falls from the couch of their coupling; they jostle the "corpse" and wake the supposedly dead Tim from his coma—the spill of Humpty Dumpty from the wall, the banishing of man from his primeval garden, and the lapse of Lucifer from bliss. How much of this can you surmise from Joyce's word? Here it is: bothallchoractorachumminatoundgansumuminarumdrumstrumtruminalumptadumpwaultopoofoolooderanaunsturnup.

The Japanese, aware of life's vicissitudes, if not of Finnegan's, may wish a man good fortune by saying: "May you have twelve falls, and thirteen risings."

What is by all odds the longest word in Indo-European literature is that used by the Greek Aristophanes to describe the main course at the banquet which closes his comedy *Women in Parliament*. This word, which takes almost as long to pronounce as to eat the dish, runs through 182 letters. In case you wish to try this treat, I set down its ingredients, as translated in Oakes and O'Neill's *Complete Greek Drama:*

> limpets, slices of salt fish, thornbacks, whistle-fishes, cornelberries, a remoulade of leftover brains seasoned with silphium and cheese, thrushes basted with honey, blackbirds, ringdoves, squabs, chickens, fried mullets, wagtails, rock pigeons, and wings ground up in wine that has been boiled down.

A more complacent contender for the longest English word is *smiles:* between its first and last letter, there is a mile.

Sometimes, amid the vagaries of English, the shorter may be the longer: We speak of a person as having a heavy head of hair; use the word in the plural, *hairs,* and it seems that you can count them. Or the nearest may outdo the farthest: Along London's Savile Row, in the imperial days, a proud shopowner put up a sign: "Best Tailor in the Empire." His neighbor, in sharp reaction, set out a placard: "Best Tailor in England." A third, not to be surpassed, displayed a more modest card: "Best Tailor on This Street." The longest way round is not always the sweetest way home.

Length does not invariably involve difficulty; and sometimes short words are hard to understand. Simplicity and shallowness, complexity and profundity, are ideas that should be dissociated. One of the classic riddling questions, "How old is Anne?", sets its problem in words that, save for a number, a common name, and a simple plural, are all familiar monosyllables: "Mary is twice as old as Anne was when Mary was half as old as Anne will be when she (Anne) is three times as old as Mary was when Mary was three times as old as Anne. The sum of their ages is thirty-two. How old is Anne?" Simple though the words may be, the problem is a bit bewildering. You may skip the mathematics if you wish, and jump to the answer.

> (My classmate the mathematical wizard, inventor, and prize-winner, Edward T. Frankel, has worked out the neatest solution:
> Let X equal Anne's age when Mary was 3 times as old as Anne. Thus Mary was 3X. Note that the difference between their ages will always be $3X-X=2X$.
> When Anne is 3 times as old as Mary was then, Anne will be 9X.
> One-half that is $4\frac{1}{2}X$, and when Mary was $4\frac{1}{2}X$, Anne was that minus 2, or $2\frac{1}{2}X$.
> Mary is now twice that, or 5X; so Anne must now be 3X. The sum of their ages is 8X, which is 32. Thus $X=4$.)

Mary is now twenty, and Anne is twelve.

Which words seem difficult depends, of course, upon the level of one's literacy. Writers have often sought to amuse their readers by having their characters make mistakes. Shakespeare's Mrs. Quickly says *canaries* for *quandaries,* and *honeyseed* for *homicide.* His clown Costard looks at the coins he has been given, and reflects: "Remuneration. Oh, that's the Latin word for three farthings." The same ploy occurs more recently, as when Groucho Marx promises his brother a nice commission, and Chico asks: "How about a little money?" Such a blunder is committed by a man that, as the curate in *Love's Labor's Lost* declares, "hath never fed of the dainties that are bred in a book; he hath not eat paper, as it were; he hath not drunk ink; his intellect is not replenished." How plenished one's intellect turns out to be, is after all a comparative matter. Of most literary critics the London *Times* once observed: "What is arcane to them is lucid to Dr. Leavis." And what is recondite to Dr. Leavis may be the daily portion of the compiling clerk of an active lexicographer. Some such thought may have suggested to Heathcote William Garrod his revision of Wordsworth's sonnet:

> Milton, thou shouldst be living at this hour,
> England hath need of thee . . .

which he changed to:

> Thou shouldst be living at this hour,
> Milton, and enjoying power.
> England hath need of thee, and not
> Of Leavis and of Eliot.

Most words of our six hundred thousand, of course, are not in the active vocabulary of even the usually educated reader. Perhaps you know *syzygy*, or *ipses*, or the difference between *neonate* and *neoned*, or: apsides, or iracundious (which let's hope we're not) or agelast (which I know I'm not), or wordfacturologist (which you may think that at this moment I am, but all these are dictionary vouched-for terms). Look for zumbooruk, or zygmosimeter, or xanthocyanopia (in which I have a son expert), or dolman, or dolmen (which is not its plural), or dokimastic (which addicts should consult), or puteal, or puy, or yttiferous. Try wyliecoat (where Burns expected lice to abound). Orignal (from the Basque) is not a misprint. No businessman should snuff at nundination (not related to inundation). If you're thirsty, askos for some wine. If you read astrological charts, you probably know your own dodecatemory (which rhymes with memory). Megacity in several ways does not chime with veracity; nor is a nuditarian allied with a nudifidian. The two-syllable manes may once have been a maness—or even a menace; but a nunatak is not likely to attack a nun.

And if you think these are difficult words, the next time you are in England listen to the program "Call My Bluff." It has been weekly on BBC television for over seven years, although the U.S. networks deem it too esoteric for American viewers. Two teams, of three persons each, alternate in offering a word, with three seemingly equally preposterous putative definitions, for the opposing team to tell which is correct. One recent program presented the words *carrapato, switter, cartoush, mambu, skillion, gowly, cumulet,* and *kreeker.* Other words the teams have had to do their best with are *zinke, thoky, reaks, crith, calamistrum, massymore, pedrail, tardle, yohay, hersillon, lockchester. Griffinage* and *griffonage* appeared on the same program. *Griffonage* is of special concern to this volume; it shows that obfuscation is no new device; it is an early English word for *gobbledegoop.* And for over a century after Steele invented *grimgribber,* in 1722, it also was used to mean gibberish, gobbledygook, gobbledegoop. Under whatever name, it's trashy.

I stop, lest I be accused of epeolatry. All these words lie snug in the O.E.D. Once they were part of the living English. But as Friedrich Schlegel pointed out, only through former words are better words possible. Many of today's familiar words, replaced by timely successors, will in their turn be far-fetched or forgotten.

7.
SPEAKING AND WRITING

OF THE WORLD'S ALMOST SIX THOUSAND LANGUAGES, before modern scholars tried to record them, scarcely 5 percent had developed a written form. Even today, there are many tongues that have never been set on paper. When the U.S. Voting Rights amendment was passed in 1975, stating that election instructions and ballots should be printed in the languages of concentrated minority groups, the Secretary of the Oklahoma Election Board was baffled: of the more than forty Indian languages in that state, only one has been reduced to writing. This is Cherokee, set down by the partly white Indian, Sequoia, after whom the longest-living American tree has been named.

Of course, for thousands of years spoken languages sufficed for all human needs. Even today, save perhaps for the dryasdust scholar amid his antique tomes, speech plays a far greater part in every life than the written or printed word. And during those millennia, as men spoke with constant fluency, certain patterns of sound developed.

Early English tended to throw the accent on the first syllable of a word. Latin usually stressed the next to the last syllable, the penult; Greek, the antepenult. In French words there is a fairly even stress, so that to English ears there is more emphasis than they're accustomed to on the last syllable. In 1204 England lost Normandy, its hold on the continent; in 1244 King Louis IX of France ordered those that held property in both countries to choose one allegiance; the many French speakers that chose England brought thousands of French words to the island, and English ears grew attuned to every variety of accent. This further increased the tongue's adaptability to new words from any source.

In Greek, and in English words from the Greek, one can often speak of "the triumph of the antepenult": the syllable before the next to the last receives the accent. Thus *hippopot'amus, meta-mor'phosis, kleptoma'niac, aphrodis'iac, euthana'sia*. Occasionally this is also true of a word from the Latin: *opportu'nity, notori'ety*. But in current English the more established stress comes upon the next to the last syllable, the penult. When Aristophanes' comedy *Lysis'trata* was revived upon the New York stage, its mispronunciation was so general that the company itself shifted the heroine's name to *Lysistra'ta*.

It seems difficult, for many, to sound the stress as far back as the fourth syllable from the end. You are likely to hear—rather, not to hear—a lost syllable, so that *lab'oratory* becomes *labratory*, or the British *labor'atory*. *In'tricacy*, not being a word on the common tongue, is seldom stressed on the *trick;* but *despicable* and *applicable* are frequently stressed on the *-ic*. Even an *ex'-quisite* lady may be pronounced as though she were a blurred apology— Exquis'ite, please!—and I have heard an expensively dressed woman near me in the theatre twice refer to a person as *hospitable*, each time expelling the accent on the *spit!* An indication of public pressure on word use was given in England a few years ago, in a periodic guide to pronunciation issued for broadcasters by the BBC: "formidable, accent on the first syllable, except for H.M.S. Formid'able." Popular error persisted until the *mid*-way was deemed correct.

As a word takes different forms, some fairly regular shifts may be noticed. Thus there is an onward progression in *de'mon, demon'ic, demoni'acal; fam'ily, famil'iar, familiar'ity; pho'to-graph, photog'raphy, photograph'ic*. Or the vowel may shorten as the word lengthens: *equal, equable; grave, gravity; omen, ominous; crime, criminal*. Sometimes both changes may occur in one sequence: *compare', compar'ison, com'parable*.

As most persons tend to adopt the easiest way, some more complicated sounds fall into disuse. Although *few* retains the *y* sound, it is harder to form in the word *new*, and has been largely lost; almost invariably one speaks now not of Nyoo but of Noo York. A pirate might consider a *beauty* to be proper *booty*. Gerald Ford, in his 1976 campaign debates, joined the great majority in several times pronouncing *opportunity* with a toot-toot-*toon*, instead of a merrier *t(y)une*. He defended the *Con-stitooshn*.

Shifting accent, on words rather than syllables, may be a deliberate device, for emphasis or altered shades of meaning. This is often used by public speakers—though seldom to the extent of W. S. Gilbert's use in his light opera *Patience*, emphasizing a different word in each of the four times a verse ends with the line "He was a little boy."

There are some words that will cause no confusion if heard, but when read require the words around them, the context, to make clear both sound and meaning. In some such cases, one pronunciation is that of a native word; the other, that of a foreign word used in English. Thus *said*, in two syllables, is the title of an Arab chief; *sake*, in two syllables, names a Japanese drink. *Pace, cave, vale, vice*, are all Latin words used in English, with the final *e* sounded.

There are also English words of one spelling, but different sounds and meanings. Some of these, homonyms, will be discussed in the next chapter. But figures that a college mathematics student is asked to *multiply* may be *multiply* complex—the second use, as an adjective, is pronounced *multiplee*. Also, if a man holds a hand out of the window of a moving car on a cold day, a *number* of his fingers may be *number* (pronounced *nummer*) than those of his other hand. A *co-ward* is saved by the hyphen from being a *poltroon*. [*Poltroon*, for 'coward', by the way, has a curious history. The French classical scholar Salmasius (Claude de Saumaise) in the early seventeenth century said the word was a corruption of Latin *pollice truncus*, 'cut-short thumb', from the self-maiming of the Roman proletarian to avoid military service. From this came the use of *poltroon* in falconry, to mean a bird of prey with the talons of its hind toes clipped. Modern etymology has dismissed the Romans, but is divided as to the word's source. O.E.D. traces it to Italian *poltro*, 'sluggard', 'lazy good-for-nothing', from an assumed *poltro*, 'couch' or 'resting place'. Klein's *Comprehensive Etymological Dictionary*, which is generally sound, traces it to Italian *poltrone*, 'colt' (Latin *pullus*) from the known timidity of the young horse.] Similarly, if a man strained his back reaching for something, he might find, if he *reached* again, that he *re-ached*. Though the two words grew from one root, a *stingy* fellow sounds unlike a *stingy* nettle. An inquisitive cleric might be cautioned: O priest, thou priest into secular matters not thy concern!

Wholly within the range of spoken English are the varieties of vocal, even vociferous, competition, in the use of abuse. The roarers of London have already been discussed; but the practice of cursing is of course most widespread. It is found in ancient Greece, as in the lines attacking the Athenian leader in Aristophanes' comedy *The Frogs*:

> On the lips of that foreigner base
> Of Athens the bane and disgrace,
> There comes shrieking, his kinsman by race,
> The impudent swallow of Thrace.

Curses—"May your field and your wife be barren!"—have been found on lead tablets buried in fourth-century B.C. Greek farms. In the Roman Empire, personal invectives in the crude Fescennine verse grew so extensive and intensive that their circulation was forbidden by law. Among pre-Islamic Arabs, the poet led his tribesmen into battle, to hurl his imprecations, like so many spears, at the foe.

Actual combats of curses, logomachy, are found in many lands. Even earlier than the roarers were the *flytings* (Old English *flyte*, 'to wrangle', 'to jeer') of the Scots, scurrilous fifteenth- and sixteenth-century verses pouring invectives upon an equally scornful opponent. The verses of King James V of Scotland (aged twenty-four in 1526) are lost, but the "Answer to the King's Flyting," by his former tutor, then his Lion King of Arms, Sir David Lindsay (aged forty-six) has been preserved; one of its ten stanzas is quoted in the discussion of obscenity, Chapter 9. Here is a stanza out of thirty-two pages of abuse, by Captain Alexander Montgomery, poet laureate to the same king, who was defeated by the (lost) flyting of Sir Patrick Hume of Polwart:

> Purse-peeler, hen-stealer, cat-killer, no I quell thee;
> Rubiator, fornicator by nature, foul befal thee.
> Tyke-sticker, poisoned Vicar, Pot-licker, I mon pay thee.
> Jock blunt, dead Runt, I shall punt while I slay thee.

Traces of the flyting continue in English literature. Nashe, in Elizabethan days, raised railing to a fine art, and he threatened to damn any "excrementitious dishlicker of learning" who presumed to dispraise his work: "I have terms . . . laid in steepe in Aquafortis and Gunpowder, that shall rattle through the skyes, and make an Earthquake in a Peasant's eares."

When Cromwell was rising to power, an anonymous prayer of eighteen stanzas included:

> From those that would divide the General and the City,
> From Harry Martin's whore, who is neither sound nor pretty,
> From a faction that has neither brain nor pity,
> From the mercy of a fanatic Committee,
> > Libera nos, Domine.

As might be expected, Dean Swift has several poems in this vein; here is a sample from "The Yahoo's Overthrow" (1734, issued anonymously, so that he praises himself in the first line), directed against an attorney named Kite:

> The Dean and his merits we every one know,
> But this skip of a lawyer, where the de'l did he grow?
> How greater's his merit at four Courts or House
> Than the barking of Towser, or leap of a louse?
> Knock him down, down, down, knock him down.
>
> If you say this is hard, on a man that is reckoned
> That serjeant at law whom we call Kite the Second
> You mistake, for a slave who will coax his superiors
> May be proud to be licking a great man's posteriors.
> Knock him down, &c.

[Swift was so widely and vehemently castigating in his epigrams that his enemies sought revenge. Not matching him in vituperative or invective power, they made him the butt of public laughter—in the presence of the Queen. Let me recount the anecdote by means of a modern instance.

[The late American critic George Jean Nathan wielded a caustic pen. He once wrote that what the illustrious gentlemen of the Pulitzer Prize Advisory Board (usually made up of three of his colleagues) knew about the theatre "might comfortably be put in a quinine capsule, with plenty of room left to spare for a copy of the Lord's Prayer, a tinted photograph of Major Bowes, and one of Anna Held's pink garters." One of George's genial ways of putting a playwright in his petty plagiaristic place was to unearth some obscure earlier drama and declare that this of course was where the new work had borrowed its plot. Turning this practice upon Nathan himself, we may observe that "of course" he borrowed the above idea and image from what had happened to Swift. For Queen Anne was a devotee of private theatricals and other entertainment; and one night, before a large aristocratic assembly, in the royal presence, a conjurer who had been hired plucked from the tall hat of Dean Swift two gold watches, a bawdy ballad, "When Susan Went Over the Stile," and the Duchess of Marlborough's garters. It was an embarrassed head that swiftly reclaimed that hat!]

In the early nineteenth century, the poet Blake wrote to one Flaxman:

I mock thee not, though I by thee be mockèd;
Thou call'st me madman, but I call thee blockhead.

This is rather mild; and after Victorian reticence, the tone was lighter, nearer what has come to be called black humor. Thus Hilaire Belloc:

Lord Finchley tried to mend the electric light
Himself. It struck him dead. And serve him right!
It is the business of the wealthy man
To give employment to the artisan.

And Edmund Clerihew Bentley:

What I like about Clive
Is that he is no longer alive.
There is a great deal to be said
For being dead.

From these, for fresh full-bodied flyting, one must turn to the Irish. In 1907, when Synge's *The Playboy of the Western World* opened in Dublin to a week of rioting in the theatre, over—said Arthur Griffith, future President of the Irish Free State—"a vile and inhuman story told in the foulest language we have ever listened to on a public platform," an abusive sister of one of the playwright's mockers was treated to this prayer:

Lord, confound this surly sister,
Blight her brow with blotch and blister,
Cramp her larynx, lung, and liver,
In her guts a galling give her.
Let her live to earn her dinners
In Mountjoy with seedy sinners:
Lord, this judgment quickly bring,
And I'm your servant, J. M. Synge.

Far from dying in our more chastened if not civilized days, invective has recently swung into a fresh spurt. In 1974 a paperback *Book of Irish Curses* was issued in Cork, to aid the aspiring generation; and the next year, there was founded Maledicta, an International Research Center for the Study of Verbal Aggression, with president Reinhold Aman, in Waukesha, Wisconsin. The London radio, in the fall of 1976, announced an Open University course in Invective. The comic strip *B.C.* currently features a "Curse Exchange." Words, fashioned for use, lend themselves generously to abuse.

The Bible and other ancient books record the practice of hurling abuse at one's enemies. In Africa, among the Galla, Tuareg, and other peoples, there developed the game of howling reciprocal abuse, its purpose being a challenge, to provoke the victim from verbal to more physical encounter; who first lost his temper and resorted to fisticuffs—lost. This exchange, brought to America by the slaves, is called *the dozens*—not from any twelve, but from *bulldoze,* originally *bull dose,* meaning a thorough dose of a bullwhip to a recalcitrant slave. Possibly the slaves indulging in the dozens fantasied that they were thus belaboring the slave driver. A humorous side-product of the dozens was the "insult dialogue" of the minstrel show.

The Romans noted the same progression, *a verbis ad verbera,* "from words to blows." Most of the railing, fortunately, was what they termed *bruta fulmina,* 'bootless thunder'.

A nonvehement, harmless activity of pure sound in the language is the creation of double-tones, words mouthed as echoes, lingering pleasantly on the tongue. These are so numerous that they may be grouped in four main varieties:

1. The word is exactly repeated, as in *pooh pooh, ha ha.*
2. The initial consonant is changed: *razzle-dazzle, namby-pamby.*
3. The vowel is changed: *flipflop* (extended in *flippety-flop*), *chitchat.*
4. Both consonant and vowel are changed: *pish tush, skilligal-lee.*

Such words can make a long higgledy-piggledy list. When you give someone tit for tat, then you may cry Even Steven.

In examining the nature of sounds, each vowel is considered as an individual unit, long or short. Some, however, are combined in diphthongs: *ah ee* becomes long *i; au* is the conjoined *ah oo.* Consonants have usually been classified according to the organ most significant in forming the sound, as guttural, labial, dental; or according to the nature of the sound, as plosive, stopped, voiced, etc.

Such considerations did not come into the mind, however, until long after words were set down, on stone, on bark, on papyrus, finally on paper; carved, scratched, painted, written with stylus or split-quill feather; then pencil, crayon, and pen, slit point or ball point or nylon fiber.

The Sumerians, whose first dynasty, near the Euphrates, ended in 3575 B.C., are the earliest people whose writings have come down to us. These are wedge-shaped, *cuneiform*, scratched into stone, incised at first from top to bottom. In the course of two millennia they came to be carved from left to right, as the inscriptions were adopted in turn by the Semitic Eblans and Akkadians, by the Assyrians, the Babylonians, and the Indo-European Hittites.

These writings used symbols for groups of letters, sound groups such as *pr*, *gd* rather than single tones; but they set down consonants only. Even today in Hebrew and Arabic, and mostly in Indic and Ethiopic writing, vowels are indicated by accents and other diacritical marks. The names used to label these symbols had other meanings in the language, as the Hebrew alphabet begins with *aleph*, 'ox'; *bet*, 'house'. The Greeks took over some of these labels, but to the Greeks they had no significance other than to denote the sign. And the Greeks used some of the signs for vowels, and invented other vowel symbols, thus achieving the first full letter alphabet.

It should be noted that, though sticks and stones are contrasted with words in the childhood jingle, they both were used in primitive recording. Counting sticks, with grooves, developed into the familiar abacus, which is still in use in the Orient, and which an expert can use almost as rapidly as a bookkeeper his adding machine. The early farmer counted his sheep by dropping a pebble into a sack as each went forth to pasture in the morning, and tossing it out as each came back to the evening fold. Latin *calculus*, 'pebble', gives us our *calculation*. The Incas developed quipu writing, records kept by knots in strings of various lengths and colors. Signs for words and phrases, used early in Phoenician, Hebrew, and Aramaic, returned in English in the forms of stenography.

Toward the end of the fourth millennium B.C. the Egyptians also developed a sort of carved-picture writing, although recent scholars tell us the pictures were chosen not to represent specific objects, but rather the sounds made in naming those objects. Thus the writing was actually phonetic, not merely pictorial. (Eskimo and American Indian written forms were mainly intended as pictures of objects.) Their symbols were known to the Egyptians—only the priests wrote—as "the god's words"; we call them *hieroglyphics* (Greek, 'sacred writings'). We have found 960 different hieroglyphic forms; the animals and other objects usually face the right, and are read from the side they face.

About 3100 B.C. the Egyptians developed the hieratic script, for faster writing, with reed pen on papyrus. This form was more cursive, using only the essential outlines of the older characters; it was written and read at first downward, then from right to left. About 650 B.C. an even more freely flowing form, the demotic script, came into use, for business transactions and some literary writing. As it was employed by traders as well as priests, it is often slovenly and hard to decipher. The interpretation of these writings was a mystery to the European world until Napoleon's soldiers, alerted by the Emperor to seek antiques, came upon a stone in the Rosetta delta of the Nile, with the same material in hieroglyphics, demotic characters, and Greek. You may now see the Rosetta Stone in the British Museum.

The Chinese, perhaps influenced by South Semitic symbols, also developed a picture writing, which soon, however, became stylized beyond pictorial significance.

Jonathan Swift, in *Gulliver's Travels*, covers the possible ranges of script upon paper, in his statement that the Lilliputians

> write neither from the left to the right, like the Europeans; nor from the right to the left, like the Arabians; nor from up to down, like the Chinese; nor from down to up, like the Cascagians; but aslant from one corner of the paper to the other, like the ladies in England.

(The Cascagians, it should be mentioned for puzzled geographers, abide some 370° north by south of the Lilliputians.)

We read from left to right, our eyes following the text as to the manner born, but more than half the world reads otherwise. Indeed Swift, who might have included the Hebrews as writing from right to left—so that their books begin at what to us is the back—omitted one possible style: in early Hittite and Greek carvings the lines run alternately right to left and left to right, as an ox moves in ploughing. The path of the ox gives such writing its name. In Greek, ox is *bous;* the Latin form has given us the word *bovine:* writing that alternates direction is called *boustrophedon*.

There have been some 250 alphabets in various times and places; about 50 are currently used. Sabaean, in Yemen in the sixth century B.C. had twenty-nine letters; Arabic (Kufi, the alphabet of the Koran), twenty–eight; Hebrew, twenty–two; Greek, twenty–four. The Roman (Latin) alphabet, upon which ours is based, had twenty–three letters; *i* and *j*, as well as *u*, *v*, and *w*, although distinguished in the late Middle Ages, did not until the eighteenth century become fully established as separate letters, giving us our twenty–

six. The British Museum Reading Room catalogue, indeed, did not separate *i* and *j* until the 1920s.

Futhorc (so named from its first six letters) is the twenty–four–letter Runic alphabet, used by the Scandinavians and the Anglo-Saxons from the third to the thirteenth century. It is based upon the Latin, but adds *edh,* ð; *thorn,* þ; and *wen,* w. Note that the thorn looks like a closed *y.* When you see a store called *Ye Olde Goodie Shoppe* or the like, the first word has the Runic thorn and is pronounced not *ye* but *the.* Ogham, the twenty–letter alphabet of the Old Irish inscriptions of the fifth to the tenth century, is carved along the edges of tombstones, and uses lines across the edges for consonants, notches for the vowels.

Naturally, the scholars that burrowed into the ancient tombs to decipher the inscriptions have given their activities technical names. *Epigraphy* is the study of inscriptions; *paleography,* more specifically the study of ancient written documents. *Semasiology* (literally, 'meaningful wording') is applied to pre-alphabetic indication of ideas, or *ideography. Logography,* writing whereof each sign is a complete word, is most closely approached in Chinese, but never fully developed as a writing system, for phonetization invariably slipped in, the sign being given not a meaning but a sound value. We see a form of this in the English rebus (Latin *rebus,* 'by things'), in which sounds are represented by objects; thus an eye and a carpenter's saw would mean *I saw* (e.g., the train coming); a bonbon and a date (the fruit, or e.g., 1893) would mean *candidate.* Through a thousand years, early signs came to stand for sounds, and alphabets were born.

Like man's acquisition of fire and man's extraction of iron, man's invention of the alphabet has been hailed as a prodigious conquest—and looked upon as fraught with constant danger. From the beginning of writing, indeed, its value has been questioned. Aristotle, pointing out that speech is the representation of the experiences of the mind, writing is the representation of speech, gave early recognition to the secondary role of the written word. Plato was more trenchant in his criticism. He put objections into the mouth of the Egyptian King Thamus, reporting that when the god Thot expressed pride at having invented writing, the King declared that it was a quite questionable gain:

You, who are the father of letters, have been led by your affection to ascribe to them a power the opposite of that which they really possess. . . . You offer your pupils the appearance of wisdom,

not true wisdom, for they will read many things without instruction and will therefore seem to know many things, when they
are for the most part ignorant and hard to get along with, since
they are not wise, but have only the semblance of wisdom.

Indeed, with the increasing demand for universal literacy, the
protests also increase. A. K. Coomaraswamy in *The Bugbear of
Literacy* speaks with approval of the *analfabeti* of Italy who cannot read yet know cantos of Dante's *Divine Comedy* by heart;
one of Plato's objections to writing is that it discourages the use
of memory; just as today the increasing use of the pleasure car
discourages the use of the legs. And Walter Shewring, in the article on Literacy in my own *Dictionary of World Literary Terms*
writes roundly and soundly:

> There is no doubt of the quantitative increase of literacy of a
> kind, and amid the general satisfaction that something is being
> multiplied it escapes inquiry whether the something is profit or
> deficit. . . . For some it helps commercial advancement; for most it
> facilitates exploitation by political propaganda and business ad-
> vertisement. Society at large is not intellectually enriched mean-
> while. Learning and wisdom have often been divided; perhaps
> the clearest result of modern literacy has been to maintain and
> enlarge the gulf.

That the recent demand for opening a college education to all
comers has resulted in a lowering of the standards is the common
protesting cry. And the opening of the airwaves to sound and
sight have led some "social scientists" to announce the decline of
the written word. Marshall McLuhan is perhaps most prominent
among these prophets of a benign illiteracy, with wisdom radiat-
ing into every home via radio loudspeaker and television screen,
guaranteed by the check–check–check of the computer. (The
novelist Norman Mailer made vehement protest: "When no more
good novels are written and the hum of the TV set is the only
resonance in our ear . . . civilization will enter hell.")

"One picture is worth a thousand words." Sight is a daylight
boon. For hundreds of centuries, man has learned to depend upon
his vision. *Voir, c'est croire,* say the French; seeing is believing. We
recognize what is coming toward us; if it is dangerous, we may
prepare and hope to counter it. Thus kings ordained the "mile
walk" before their palace: visitors had to dismount, to be observed, over open ground to take that last slow mile on foot. Thus
Macbeth had the dangerous Banquo slain. Sight is assurance.

But vision dies with darkness. Sound comes on. The tread of footsteps approaching in the night: friend or foe? The howling of beasts in the encroaching forest; the whipping of branches in the wind, the furtive sound of unseen scurrying: the unknown terrors of the dark, hints of hostility, ominous indications, give rise to fantasies of demons and defending gods. The voice of the unseen Lord admonished and instructed the prophets. The unseen counsel of godly spirits led Joan of Arc to the fire, and to sainthood. The unseen voice along the airways roused panic in the States with word of invasion from Mars.

Sound thus plays directly upon the passions. For centuries, man has learned to respond rapidly to heralding sounds. A clap of hands behind a man's back when he is unaware, and he will startle; in front, when he can see, he will smile. Ingrained in our nerves is the reaction. Sound wakens reflexes that bypass the restraints of reason. The loud-voiced speech of a dictator wins the responsive Hitler *Heil*. The loudspeaker magnifies the call of a Billy Graham, the summons of a Reverend Moon, to twang the heartstrings of receptive millions. Sound is commanding.

All sound plays upon the feelings. The whispered words of the lover, the shouted cry, the thunder that rolls after lightning or cannon fire; each in its way lights a spark in a man, or starts a conflagration. Words are not needed; a lilting melody or a battle call, music from Beethoven to the Beatles, all have an immediate effect, driving directly at the nocturnal readiness, the essential dependence upon sound. Sound is commanding.

Sound, however, is limited. It is instant, but it dies in the utterance; thus it is narrowed by time. And for the millennia before modern inventions brought it to wider ranges, it was limited—as still in private circumstances—by space, by the span of our hearing.

The written word is slower, and more subtle. I first saw the explication of Einstein's theory of relativity in the form of nine mimeographed pages—of which I managed to understand, if I remember accurately, the first eight lines. Yet out of these pages loomed the devastation of Hiroshima, and shone the promise of atomic energy. The written word persists. It radiates slowly, but its power grows. Where the spoken word, having done its temporary damage (or served its good purpose) is forgotten, the quiet page recalls the emotion as experience, and points the way to a better world. That is why the first impulse of a despot is to burn the books. They outlast his mortal days.

In the night terrors, sound takes temporary charge, but with the dawn of a new day, sight takes over. Sight, and its soon companion, insight, will survive. That is why, in the new edition of my *World Literary Terms,* I was impelled to append a note to Shewring's words about the value of literacy:

> On the other hand, since wisdom must be based upon some measure of understanding of the world, the complexities of which the scientific disciplines have made clear, without widespread literacy there can be little hope for a wider spread of wisdom. . . . It is no easy task for humanity to lift itself by its own bootstraps. Mortal men are in a greater hurry than mother nature, and often rail at the present stage of a continuing process. The wiser are more patient. Although the achievements of the enforcedly literate remain dim, literacy remains the surest broad way to ultimate light.

Let us attempt, not an anthropomorphic, nor yet a global, but a cosmological view. Astronomer George Gamow has measured the time: "It took less than an hour to make the atoms, a few hundred million years to make the stars and planets, but five billion years to make man." How infantile the dreamers (who enslave millions in their quest) that hope to find utopia just around the corner, or even peace in our time! Our sun will sustain us for another five billion years, if we in our passion-sprung striving do not first destroy ourselves. Wisdom has time to expand, to enable our days. The One that made time made plenty of it.

Be our present wisdom as it may, it has in English an alphabet of only twenty-six letters, from which to fashion all the words that we employ. This may seem a small quantity, but mathematics smiles: using each letter only once, the number of combinations possible is 1,096 followed by 24 zeros (1.096×10^{27}). The actual possible number is incalculably larger, since many words use a letter more than once; as we have noted, in floccinaucinihilipilification the letter *i* occurs nine times. Of all these combinations, those that can be sounded as possible words are likely to suffice for any man's vocabulary—or all mankind's.

Letters, indeed, have been used for other purposes than to form words. In many tongues, they also represent numbers. Roman numerals, which are letters, are still used in English, on large clocks and on the cornerstone of many buildings. They are also employed in games and in acrostics; the number letters beginning the words "My day closed is in immortality," for instance, form a chronogram, MDCIII, the year of the death of the first Queen Elizabeth, 1603. Assigning values to letters, to consider their influence on human life, as in numerology, yields 666 as the number of the Antichrist; believers have therefore sought to find it in the name of their enemy, Mahomet, Luther, Napoleon, Hitler. Isidore of Seville, about 600 A.D., said: "Take from all things their number, and all shall perish."

It may be noted that virtually every letter in our alphabet

Letter Word		Silent in
a, aye	A	deaf, dread
be, bee, Bea	B	dumb, plumber, debt
see, sea	C	victuals, lascivious, duck
dee, River Dee	D	addle, Wednesday, grudge
(base in logarithms)	E	neurosis, cue, height
(note in music)	F	different, ineffable
gee (a horse)	G	gnat, phlegm, although
aitch-bone	H	phthisis, Thomas, honest
I, eye, ay	I	weight, either
jay, Jay	J	hajj, hajji
(early) quay, Sir Kay, cay	K	back, know, knife
ell	L	llama, salmon, alms, could
em	M	mnemonics, ammunition
en	N	gunning, hymn, condemn
O, owe, oh	O	souvenir, wound, should
pea, pee	P	pneumatic, raspberry
cue, queue	Q	lacquer, racquet
are	R	whirr, myrrh, irretrievable
(road turned in a great) ess	S	viscount, demesne, kiss
tea, tee	T	whistle, often
you, ewe	U	guilt, somersault, glamour
vee (neck)	V	flivver
"I double you"	W	who, wrong, sword, window
Marks the spot; in algebra	X	Sioux, billet-doux
why; Wye River	Y	crayon, key, sayyid
zee-bar	Z	jazz, fuzz

sounds like an English word. Also, as the table on page 123 shows, every letter, in some words, appears but is not sounded.

Six of the letters also have their plurals in words: seize, ease, pease, tease, use, wise.

There are also many combinations that we may call letter-words, as NME sounds enemy. Thus also XTC, XPDNC, NV, EZ, XL, DK, and more, to give all of which might be XS.

The alphabet, naturally, is run through in rhymes for children. The Opies' *Oxford Dictionary of Nursery Rhymes* gives five different alphabetical jingles, with variations, dating from the seventeenth century, with parallels in other languages; as well as counting-out songs and riddle rhymes going back over nineteen hundred years. Alphabet verses have been used in many school primers, and are still reprinted; the twenty-six illustrated letters beginning

> A was an apple pie,
> B bit it, C cut it

and ending

> X, Y, Z, and Ampersand
> All wished for a piece in hand.

cover a full page in the *New York Times* Children's Books issue of November 14, 1976.

The early writers probably had few problems. If a symbol they needed did not exist, they had but to invent it. Once an alphabet was established, however, difficulties cropped up for unaccustomed users. The chief of these persists, in the complications of spelling. Unfortunately, the gradual growth of the language produced so many irregularities that no rules for spelling can be set down without at once the need for announcing exceptions. Thus to state that words ending in *y* form the plural by changing *y* to *ies*, makes it necessary to add that if a vowel precedes the *y*, we merely add an *s*, as in *monkeys*. Then someone may note that we may use both *moneys* and *monies*.

Plurals are arrived at in various ways. The usual added *s* has three distinct sounds: *s* as in *cats; z* as in *dogs; iz* as in *Charles's* and *horses.* Seven words are mutated—the vowel changed—to form the plural: *man, woman, tooth, foot, goose, mouse, louse.* Some words use the same form for singular and plural: *deer, sheep, moose, grouse.* Collective nouns, such as *fleet* and *assembly* (which also have plural forms) may be followed by a singular or a plural verb form, according as one thinks of the unit or the separate parts: "The assembly were divided on the question." *Fish* is the plural form unless we are thinking of different varieties of *fishes.* Note also *children, oxen; brothers* or *brethren.*

The plurals of foreign words brought into the language are still more troublesome. Many forget that *media, memoranda, bacteria,* are the plurals of Latin words, the singulars ending -*um. Phenomenon* and other such words from the Greek also form the plural with -*a: phenomena. Genus,* however, from the Latin, expands to the plural *genera.* Latin *genius,* for an exceptionally brilliant human, has the plural *geniuses;* for an attendant spirit, *genii.* This is akin to the Arabic *jinn,* which is a plural, with a singular, masculine *jinnee* (often, in English, *genie*), feminine *jinneeyeh.* Even college graduates have complications with their appellations: a male graduate is an *alumnus;* a female, an *alumna;* groups of them are male *alumni;* female, *alumnae.* What to do when they are co-ed is their problem.

Medium, in the sense of the roughly halfway mark, or of a go-between from this world to the next, is more Anglicized than it is in the communication field, and forms its plural by adding the English *s.* So too, in ordinary parlance, with *hippopotamuses,* as spectators watch their placid ugliness at the zoo; in zoological consideration, they are *hippopotami.* With such words—*indexes, indices; amoebas, amoebae;* even *plateaus, plateaux*—the plural form is chosen to fit the casual or technical level of discourse.

Spelling was emphasized, in the earlier days of our country, with spelling bees, contests in which class was lined up against class, county against county, in the attempt to "spell down" the opponent. Each misspeller had to sit down until only one was left standing, the champion of the hive—often, it must be stated, the queen bee, for girls seemed more efficient with the words than boys. Tricks have been devised to trap a proficient speller. Ask her to spell *joke . . . folk . . .* the white of an egg. The white of an egg is not the *yolk,* but the *glair.* A male is more likely to slip on that one.

The problems of spelling are rendered no easier by the fact that some sounds have many spellings, or that one spelling may represent many sounds. Thus the sound of short *e* appears in *let, heifer, leopard, leather, says, said, many.* Not only vowels may be represented by many combinations of letters; the consonant *t* is sounded in *cut, kissed, butt, butte, right, site, debt, ctenoid, ptar-*

migan, Thomas, phthisic. The consonant sound *sh* has even more spellings: *anxious, shun, issue, mansion, fuchsia, position, coercion, sugar, complexion, schist, nauseous, ocean, conscience, expatiate, eschscholtzia, pshaw.* On the other hand, the spelling *ough* may represent several sounds: *though* (long), *thorough* (short), *hough* (*ock*), *cough* (*off*), *ought* (*aw*), *bough* (*au*), *rough* (*uf*), *hiccough* (*up*); *slough* is pronounced *slau* if it means miry ground, as in Bunyan's Slough of Despond; *slew,* if it means a backwater or pond; *sluff,* when a snake sheds its skin.

It is thus no wonder, despite the frowns of word lovers, that spelling reform is a frequent quest of persons concerned with education of the masses. In 1977 The Simplified Spelling Society in England inaugurated a test of six different alphabets for children learning to read and write. The proponents of such "orthographic reform" believe that their chosen system more closely approximates the phonetic realities and (an essential qualification) can be shifted in due time and without mental confusion, so that the learner can come back with more quickly gained capacity to read books printed in the standard forms. Among the six systems are New Spelling; the already touted ITA (Initial Teaching Alphabet); Torskript; and The Spel, which is supported by sums from the will of Bernard Shaw. Hitherto, the heavy load of inertia, from the sheer weight of all the books that exist in our usual spelling, has prevented any substitute system from long thriving.

It took a long time for writers to agree on how to spell their words. In Shakespeare's days there was wide variation; in the 1609 first printing of his *Sonnets, mistress* is spelled in five ways, and there are thirteen known spellings of his name. While most differences have been ironed out, and to some extent the "proper" form has been fixed by the dictionaries, even in these, alternative spellings are sometimes found. Thus *esthetics* is countered by a return to the more classical form *aesthetics;* contrariwise (once *contrarywise*) a compendium of general information is now called an *encyclopedia,* except in the title of the *Encyclopaedia Britannica.* Certain differences appear as one crosses the Atlantic: British *theatre* is American *theater* (sometimes quaintly pronounced with a long *a*); most of the *-our* words—*harbour, honour, succour*—drop the *u* as they come over the ocean. An exception is *glamour,* probably because of its association with *amour.* But for most English words, there is now one "correct" spelling.

In the days when hunting and fishing took a larger portion of a gentleman's time and concern—there is still hunting to hounds;

and in some parts of the world in addition to the British isles fishing rights along streams are carefully guarded—there grew up
separate specific terms for a number of creatures of a kind. These
nouns of assemblage include forty-two for birds: a siege of herons,
a walk of snipe, a covey of partridges; forty of animals: a bury of
conies, a business of ferrets, a knot of toads; and fourteen of
fishes: a pod of whiting, a bale of turtles. Farmers still speak of a
herd of cattle, a flock of sheep. Wordsmen, like Eric Partridge,
enjoy extending such terms to assemblages of humans. Among
these terms are old ones like a boast of soldiers, a gaggle of gos-
sips, a dignity of canons, a galaxy of milkmaids. More recent attempts at apt clusters are a flutter of spinsters, a prowl of proctors,
a column of journalists, a procrastination of plumbers, a quantum
of scientists, a frown of critics, a noise of musicians, an obsoles-
cence of lexicographers. To which the reader might add, a plethora of scribblers.

A need that arose with writing, beyond spelling, was for
punctuation. In speech, pauses, tone changes, gestures, all the
devices of paralanguage—the wave of a dismissing hand, the indignation of a pointing finger, the doubt of a lifted brow—help
create mood and meaning. The written character needs other resources. At first no solution to this difficulty was found: early
inscriptions show carved letter after carved letter, with no space
even at the end of a word—although as early as the fourth century B.C. a stroke might indicate the conclusion of a section.
Spaces between words were not regularly made until the eleventh
century A.D. But gradually, beginning about the ninth century,
punctuation points were introduced, to mark pauses of various
lengths. Their first full use in English was in Wycliffe's translation
of the Bible, in 1382. In fact, the terms we now use for punctuation marks—comma, colon, period—originally named elements of
sentence structure: a phrase or short clause was a comma; a long
clause was a colon; a period was the stretch of two or more colons.
Thomas Nashe, attacking a letter of the scholar Gabriel Harvey,
wrote:

> I talk of a great matter when I tell thee of a period; for I know
> two several periods in this last epistle, at least fortie lines long
> apiece.

We may still say that an orator talks in rounded periods.

Perplexity about significance, nevertheless, did not die with
the use of punctuation. American economic history records the

twelve-million-dollar comma, a mark misplaced in a tariff law
that cost the government that sum in uncollectable duty before
the error was corrected.

Even in the early days of their use, punctuation marks were
turned by playwrights to humorous ends. About 1553 Nicholas
Udall, headmaster at Westminster School, wrote *Ralph Roister
Doister*—the earliest English comedy—probably for his pupils to
play. In short rhymed doggerel, it shows Ralph courting the
widow Dame Custance. A scribe—you can still see his like, sitting
with writing tablets in long rows outside the post office of cities
in the Near East—prepares a letter for Ralph to send Custance,
addressing her as "mine own dear coney, birde, swete-heart, and
pigsny." The clown Merigreeke reads her the epistle:

> Sweete mistresse, whereas I love you—nothing at all;
> Regarding your substance and richesse chief of all,
> For your personage, beautie, demeanour and wit
> I commend me unto you never a whitte.
> Sorry to hear report of your good welfare. . . .

After listening to thirty-six lines of such insults, Custance turns
upon Ralph in righteous wrath. Ralph rushes in a rage to the
scrivener, who takes up the letter with wide-eyed innocence, and
reads:

> Sweete mistress, whereas I love you—nothing at all
> Regarding your substance and richesse; chief of all
> For your personage, beautie, demeanour and wit—
> I commend me unto you. Never a whitte
> Sorry to hear report of your good welfare. . . .

and Ralph is more bewildered than before. Shakespeare similarly
seeks humor in misplaced punctuation, as in Quince's prologue to
the Pyramus and Thisby burlesque in *A Midsummer Night's
Dream*.

Other puzzling punctuation problems have been devised. The
sentence "Charles the First walked and talked half an hour after
his head was cut off" needs but the judicious insertion of a semicolon and a comma to make sense. There is a well-known twelve-
line poem, published in *The Westminster Drollery* of 1671, of
which I give the beginning and the end:

> I saw a peacock with a fiery tail
> I saw a blazing comet drop down hail
> I saw a cloud . . .

  ...big as the moon and higher
I saw the sun even in the midst of night
I saw the man that saw this wondrous sight.

Of this strange boast the poet Walter de la Mare remarked: "So
may the omission of a few commas effect a wonder in the imagination." I should be more inclined to set a semicolon after the first
noun, in every line except the last. But I shall be careful not to
lose the comma in the remark: "Women are pretty, generally
speaking."

By proper punctuation, it is possible to make sense of a sentence
with the word *had* eleven times in a row; speaking of a corrected
English exercise, we may say: John, where Thomas had had "had
had," had had "had"; "had had" had had the teacher's approval.

In serious writing, punctuation may serve either of two purposes. It may be used for structural reasons, to keep clear the
meaning of a passage. Or it may be used for rhetorical reasons, to
bring out the writer's special emphasis or otherwise to help color
the meaning with his feelings, and to establish his desired rhythm.
Certain simple rules may serve as structural guides: commas when
there is a series, or a short descriptive clause; semicolon for longer
stretches or sharper breaks; the colon to indicate a list, or the
beginning of a quotation.

In the last half century, speech has in one respect grown more
limited, as more and more families are content to gather of an
evening in front of a little box that does the talking for them.
Wistfully, the English thinker about words Julian Franklyn has
remarked: "In an age clean of the cinema and free of the incubus
of wireless, the art of conversation was not dead." In other respects, however, words continue to proliferate, and present their
many problems.

Ever since the Tower of Babel brought "confusion of tongues"
upon the world, with the problems of language interpretation
complicated by unfamiliar forms and spellings beyond the grasp
of the widest polyglot, there has been a need for international
communication. Less important when outsiders were ipso facto
enemies, this grew in the days of commercial interchange to a
desire for a universal language. Descartes in 1620 proposed that
one be sought; Thomas Urquhart some thirty years later, in the
curiously named *Logopandecteision,* set forth the requirements
for a language so scientifically constructed that the sounds and

syllables of its words would at once inform a stranger of the words' meanings and use. He sought a "proportion between the sign and the thing signified"; but neither he nor any other striver has managed to set down this ideal ubiquitous language. Other attempts in the eighteenth century were more specific. Some ventured into pasigraphy, the use of symbols other than letters, or sought to express ideas rather than words, so that (like the figures 1, 2, 3) they would be comprehensible throughout the world; this was first tried in 1796. Letters, indeed, have limited value, as they vary with different styles of writing, such as Chinese, Arabic, Hebrew, Russian, German, Turkish—though the last two named have in recent printing adopted the Roman script, which is essentially ours.

Beginning in the nineteenth century, several so-called world languages have been worked out, for commercial purposes: Ido, Novial, Interlingual, Volapük, Esperanto. Most of them are limited by vocabulary based on Indo-European roots. Interglossa, developed by Launcelot Hogben in 1943, tried to combine the simple Chinese syntax with Greek and Latin roots. Ido, launched in 1907, is an attempt to simplify Esperanto. The linguist Otto Jespersen in 1921 wrote *Historio di mia lingua* in Ido; this and *Artificial Languages after the World War* have been translated from Ido into English. Esperanto, concocted in 1887 by L. L. Zamenhof, although it has become the most widespread, with a journal, even aspiring to literary works, and with an annual international convention, uses mainly Latin and English forms; to wide ranges of the world, it is just another foreign tongue.

Recognizing the far-flung influence of our language, in 1934 Charles K. Ogden and I. A. Richards put forward their *System of Basic English*. They presented a basic list of 850 English words, as competent for all important transactions: 600 things (nouns), 150 qualities (adjectives), and 100 operators (verbs and structural words, prepositions and conjunctions). They noted that Basic is an acrostic: British American Scientific International Commercial. Despite considerable ballyhoo, however, and the approbation of both Winston Churchill and Franklin D. Roosevelt, Basic English has made no great stir in the international business world.

For most people, whatever their own tongue, have recognized the importance of the English language, and in schools throughout the world, where it is not the native language it is the second one learned. Meanwhile, at the United Nations, five languages are recognized with simultaneous translations: English, French, Russian, Chinese and—more recently—Arabic. You switch your earphones to the tongue you want, and listen, not to the actual speaker with his personal eccentricities and desired emphases, but to the even voice of the translator. Later, you may read the remarks, set down in the language you desire, and try to understand.

The substance of what you read may seem an oft-told tale. "There is nothing new under the sun" is an age-old observation. "Everything's been said," said a cynic. André Gide found the riposte: "But nobody listens." Hence the world repeats itself, time and again. Samuel Johnson remarked that, as an evil period enacts many laws, so an ignorant period publishes many books. He mentioned the proliferation of how-to volumes, and of popularizations; but the latter are always required, for no man can be a specialist in every field yet every man should desire a conspectus of current knowledge. Too often a prominent figure speaks like an oracle— and wins acceptance as such—in fields beyond his ken. (By chance, his dictum may hold a grain of truth, as when assembly-line automobile manufacturer Henry Ford uttered his pronouncement: "History is bunk.") It should be observed, despite the maxims, that in science there is frequently something new to be said, and in literature sometimes a new way of saying. Spoken or written, English words await the occasion. And new occasions will continue to breed new words.

8.
HOMONYMS, ON TO SLANG

THE LIMITED NUMBER OF VOWEL sounds that humans can utter makes repetition inevitable. The O.E.D. has eighty-seven columns of words beginning with *can-*. Many words, as a consequence, seem in some respects the same. Such words, from Greek forms meaning "same name," are called homonyms. As there are three major aspects of a word—sound, spelling, and significance—so there are three sorts of homonym.

Two words (or more) may have the same sound, but different spellings and meanings. Thus a farmer may *sow* while his helpmeet may *sew*. *Red* letters may be easily *read*. *To, too, two*, are three words with a single sound, as are *rain, rein, reign*. Such words may more specifically be called homophones.

Two words may be spelled the same, with different sounds and meanings. A man may *bow* to a woman wearing a pretty *bow*. The farmer may *sow*, then feed his *sow*. Naturally, this distinction depends upon the spoken word. If you merely see the word *tearing*, you need the context to tell whether one is ripping something, or growing moist at the eyes. Because they are written alike, such words may more specifically be called homographs.

Two words may have the same spelling and sound, but different meanings. The general term, homonym, covers this type. Such words, however, are of two sorts. They may actually be one word, which has developed several meanings. *Spirit* may mean a mental disposition, or a disembodied essence, or a volatile liquid, an alcohol. The various senses of *make* fill thirty-five columns in the O.E.D. Such words may, on the other hand, be quite different in origin, accidentally come together in the centuries of speech. The flying mammal, the *bat*, is of different origin from the baseball *bat;* so is *mine*, 'belonging to me', from the salt *mine;* and there are three entirely separate words that spell and sound *fine.* Some of these words, as pointed out in the discussion of antonyms, as our language developed have come to mean their own opposite: the butcher may *cleave* ('cut clean through') a bone; the minister may enjoin a bride and groom to *cleave* ('cling close') to one another through rain as through shine.

Chinese, in the main monosyllabic, has attempted to avoid such confusions by varying the pitch, or tone, to give a sound a different significance. Mandarin employs four tones: high, low, rising, falling; but some dialects use more; the most widespread, Cantonese, has nine tones. English may use tone to indicate questioning, irony, or other subtlety; but changes in use are sometimes indicated by accent.

There is an increasing group of words, including *conduct, progress, rebel, transfer, convict, record,* that when used as a noun are accented on the first syllable; as a verb, on the second. This shift is spreading. Two generations ago, the dictionaries allowed only one stress—on the second syllable—whether you said "Please address this to me" or "Please tell me your address." Now the noun is *ad'dress.* At present the shift is in process; listen to any sports reporter on the air speaking of *defense* and *defeat.* The change is more or less complete in *refund, relay, relapse.*

What in some cases may produce ambiguity, however, may also be turned to valid use. Oriental poetry frequently employs a "pivot word," which has one meaning when taken with the words that precede it, but another with the words to come. In English, homonyms may be employed occasionally in poetry, but they find fullest use in wordplay. What we call wordplay, however, is not always intended as humor.

The most common play with homonyms is the pun, which depends upon a shift of meaning with one sound. And the Catholic Church is founded on a pun. In the Bible, Matthew (16:18) quotes Jesus saying to Simon Bar-Jona: "You are Peter, and on this rock I will build my church." In Greek and Latin (as in French with *pierre*) the name *Peter* and the word *rock* are the same: Peter was "petrified" into St. Peter's at the Vatican.

Puns are of ancient lineage, and lilt from many tongues. A legended pun is credited with the triumphs of Alexander the Great, who sighed that he had no more worlds to conquer. Early in his career, he almost failed. He sat so long before the city of Tyre, in vain siege, that he was about to call off his army and return home frustrated. That night he dreamed that he had caught a satyr—in Greek, *satyros*. And his dream-interpreters (oneiromancers) exclaimed: "*Sa Tyros!*" "Tyre is his!" In the morning he attacked, took the city, and marched on to subdue the known world.

The Latin pun *Amantes amentes*, "Lovers are lunatics," anticipated Shakespeare's linking.

Shakespeare often used puns in serious situations. When the light-hearted Mercutio, in *Romeo and Juliet*, is dying, he says: "Look for me tomorrow, and you shall find me a *grave* man." When Antonio, in *The Merchant of Venice*, is ready to yield his pound of flesh to Shylock, for his friend's sake, and says: "I'll pay it instantly with all my heart," out of the figurative expression the literal meaning leaps.

In *Love's Labor's Lost*, after punning on *sore* and *sorel*—the L multiplying the sore by (Roman numeral) fifty—Holofernes modestly explains:

> This is a gift that I have, simple, simple, a foolish extravagant spirit, full of forms, figures, shapes, objects, ideas, apprehensions, motions, revolutions. These are begot in the ventrical of memory, nourished in the womb of pia mater, and delivered upon the mellowing of occasion.

The *pia mater* seems fit *venter* for the pregnancy of a pun—as Holofernes' self-picture fits his author.

(In *Sly Fox*, a 1976 adaptation of Ben Jonson's *Volpone*, Foxwell J. Sly's love of God is fifty-fold increased when, with the L, GOD is revealed as GOLD.)

It should be noted that Shakespeare's puns and other word play are seldom ornaments or divagations; they add to the intensity of the feelings, or—as on the tongue of Lear's Fool, and of Olivia's—they bring out the underlying theme of the play. Note may be made of Shakespeare's use (as later, Lewis Carroll's) of a sort of pinched pun, the portmanteau: two meanings and two words packed into a single term. Laertes, bent on vengeance for Ophelia's death, rushes into the palace with the "ocean's impittious haste": *impetuous* and *pitiless*. Cleopatra calls upon the asp to untie "this knot intrinsicate of life": *instrinsic* and *intricate*. (One recalls a French production with a mechanical asp that, before the fangs dug, raised its head and hissed. And the critic Sarcey wrote: "I agree with the asp.") When Shakespeare speaks of Ariachne, humorless scholars cry that he has nodded. On the contrary, he has caught into one name the two great thread-bearers of antiquity, Arachne and Ariadne. The arguments of those that presume to correct Shakespeare are often threadbare.

Helge Kökeritz, in his study of *Shakespeare's Pronunciation*, takes 89 pages to list the playwright's homonymic puns. M. M. Mahood, in *Shakespeare's Wordplay*, counts 114 puns in the short and savage *Macbeth*.

Shakespeare had a royal exemplar for his puns. Queen Elizabeth once rebuked her chief Secretary of State: "Ye be burly, my Lord of Burleigh, but ye shall make less stir in our realm than my Lord of Leicester."—If you think of a pun on a man's name, refrain; he's heard it a dozen times before.

A pun may turn upon the meaning of a word, or upon the sound. It may swing between two ideas, or be purely—some would say merely—verbal: *Vox et praeterea nihil*. The first type survives translation. Thus Cicero remarked in Latin that the man who ploughed his family graveyard was cultivating his fathers' memory; the pun remains fruitful in English. Thus too with the Frenchman who boasted that he could pun instanter on any subject; someone called out "The King" and at once he replied "The King is not a subject." Sarah Bernhardt's neat response to a reporter, on the other hand, involves a purely verbal pun, and must be explained in English. When the young actress burst like a nova in the theatrical heaven, French society wondered whether "the divine Sarah" was married to the man she was living with. No one, of course, would put the question bluntly; one clever reporter asked her where she had been married. Well aware of his intent, the actress responded: "Naturellement, à l'autel." This means, "Naturally, at the altar"; but the same pronunciation means, "at the hotel." A bitter pun of Danton silenced a fellow prisoner of the Terror. Awaiting the guillotine, the man tried to dam up his fear by stammering poetry. Finally Danton cried: "*Plus de vers! Dans huit jours tu en feras assez.*" "No more verses! In a week, you'll make enough of them"—but *vers* also means 'worms'.

In the duplicity of a pun, the mind recognizes the two possible senses; startles; for a moment see-saws; wins the pleasure of finding that either will fit, then the increased pleasure of seeing that both will fit.

This verbal double-dealing may be found in many tongues and places. Erasmus, when he entitled *In Praise of Folly*, was punning on the name of his host, Sir Thomas More: the Latin title of the book is *Moriae Encomium*. More's own *Utopia* is also a punning title: it fuses the Greek prefixes *eu-* and *ou-*, thus signifying "the beautiful place that is no place." We are told that the irrepressible

Rabelais, when sick, asked to be wrapped in his domino (hooded cape), because *Beati qui in Domino moriuntur,* 'Blessed are they that die in the Lord'. The poet Thomas Hood, in a similar situation, protested that the undertaker was too eager to earn a livelihood (urn a lively Hood).

The early eighteenth century, in Augustan decorum, turned from the pun. There is hardly a pun or a quibble in the playwright Congreve's wit. The Spectator opposed the use of the pun in society; Addison listed twelve varieties of false wit. (He noted, however, that wit may arise from resemblance or from opposition. If from resemblance, it should add surprise: "My mistress' bosom is as white as snow—and as cold.")

Naturally, such animadversions were ignored by the language lovers. Jonathan Swift and Thomas Sheridan (grandfather of the playwright) had punning bouts together. Swift wrote *A Modest Defense of Punning* in 1716; three years later appeared Sheridan's *Ars Punica.* In this book, Sheridan invented ancient aficionados: thus Pythagoras had his disciples plant beans everywhere, because in Greek beans are *punnoi.* The book lists thirty-four rules for the art of punning. Rule 32, "Never speak well of another punster," has become the general practice. An exception is the praise essayist Richard Steele accorded composer Daniel Purcell, dubbing him Pun-Master General.

A little later, when Boswell suggested that Samuel Johnson disliked puns because he couldn't make them, the pundit at once retorted: "If I were punished for every pun I shed, there would not be left a puny shed for my punnish head." Johnson was usually pungent.

Sir Charles Napier is said to have sent back a one-word punning dispatch from India, when in 1843 he captured Sind: his message was the first word of the penitent in the Confessional, *Peccavi* (Latin, 'I have sinned').

Purely verbal puns, as I have said, defy translation. Here is a particularly neat one in French:

> On s'enlace.
> Puis, un jour,
> On s'en lasse.
> C'est l'amour.

(Literally: They embrace. Then, one day, they weary of it. That's love.) Similarly untranslatable is the English tale of the wealthy lady who told her suitor he must stop smoking. It ends:

"To have your Anna, give up your Havana."
But he, when thus she put him to the scratch,
Lit his cigar, and threw away the match.

Occasionally, however, another tongue lends fortuitous assistance. Take the English query and response: "Is life worth living?" "It depends on the liver." Turn this into French; "*La vie vaut-elle la peine?*" "*Question de foie.*" And while *foie* means liver, its homonym *foi* means faith.

No matter how flat your words may be, a woman would like to have them flatter. Which reminds me that even here sex rears its restless head. Oliver Wendell Holmes, on his "Visit to the Asylum for Aged and Decayed Punsters," finds only male inmates. For, he avers, "there is no such thing as a female punster. I have once or twice heard a woman make a single, detached pun, as I have known a hen to crow." At this, we may listen for a loud cackle.

Some solemn soul has always been ready to point a finger of scorn at the pun. In 1676 Sir Roger L'Estrange mocked the "quibble, pun, punnet, pundigrion, of which fifteen will not make up a single jest." In 1727 Alexander Pope, in *The Art of Sinking in Poetry*, mocked it: "A word, like the tongue of a jackdaw, speaks twice as much by being split." Several critics have lamented that "even Shakespeare's magic is not proof against the artillery of puns." And in truth they crop up in strange places in his plays; Hamlet's first two speeches turn upon puns. The wordplay of Polonius is rhetorical affectation; the puns and mixed metaphors of Hamlet are emotional condensations; his puns are Attic salt rubbed on a wound.

Among the staid Victorians, aspersions were again cast upon the pun. Scott, Thackeray, and Dickens took other roads to popularity. Edward Lear wrote his limericks; Lewis Carroll, his Alice tales, for children. But again the frowns were ignored by less earnest writers. Thomas Hood was extravagant in his humor, enough to write that

Cleopatra died, historians relate,
Through having found a misplaced asp-irate.

Whatever the punishment, puns march hardily along. There is, indeed, some sort of continuity in the humor. Of the recent remark that "the druggist is a piller of society," the punster was probably unaware of the background of his jest. Back in Elizabethan days, a piller was a robber (hence our word pillage).

Bishop Latimer preached against "extortioners, caterpillers, usurers"; the bishop was burned at the stake at Oxford, in 1555—for heresy, not for his railings. Then Walter Scott in 1828 spoke of "caterpillers, not pillars of society." In devious ways, language turns on, and turns us on.

It is still the fashion to belittle the pun. Often it is received with a groan, though punsters claim this but shows that the groaner wishes he'd thought of it first. The pun has been called the lowest form of wit, to which the retort is that then it is wit's foundation. Despite its many detractors—"He that would make a pun would pick a pocket"—serious writers have recognized its value in seasoning discourse. Addison in 1711 went so far as to say that "the seeds of punning are in the minds of all men." The German physicist and satirist G. C. Lichtenberg, in 1799, observed: "When the common people like puns, and make them, the nation is on a high level of culture." A little later, Charles Lamb wrote to Coleridge: "A pun is a noble thing *per se*. It fills the mind." And in another letter he stated: "I never knew an enemy to puns who was not an ill-natured man." The pun is, indeed, like a two-edged sword, and often enables one to puncture an opponent's argument with a "punch line."

While it may help to put something across, the pun seldom serves to put someone down. There is a vogue, still current, of the type of humor that takes delight in belittling. The closer a remark verges upon insult, the funnier it may seem to those that are not the victim, who therefore can bask in the sunshine of their superiority. Thus "the man who came to dinner," in the Kaufman-Hart play of 1939—based upon the nature of the journalist and caustic wit Alexander Woollcott—hails his conscientious and pleasant nurse: "Good morning, Miss Bedpan." From the site and nature of the "Three Hours for Lunch Club," to which Woollcott belonged, this sort of humor may be called the Algonquin quip. A pretty actress comes in, and is greeted: "Good evening, Miss-cast." Like the pun, this sarcastic humor is usually spontaneous, but it is invariably cruel. The pun is in general less taunting; it is content to be neat. The Algonquin quip, Alfred Adler would claim, rises from a sense of inferiority, which seeks to denigrate others to exalt itself—although indeed the notion that humor springs from derision was enunciated by Plato. Quite another sort of humor, rising from what Hobbes called "a sudden glory" and Hegel "a hale condition of the soul," is the good humor of a healthy mind; this sparks the innocuous but amusing homonymic play we call the pun. And the pun is unquestionably the most persistent, prevalent, and serviceable variety of wordplay in general speech.

Utilizing the pun, though only for a puzzle, is the conundrum. A conundrum is a riddle solved with a pun. Being merely playful, its double meanings are of a lower level, directed mainly at children. What's the difference between things bought and a load of coal? Most things bought go to the buyer, a load of coal goes to the cellar. The grandfather of conundrums had two answers. When is a door not a door? When it's a jar (ajar). But if you guessed that, the correct answer, instead, was: When it's a Negress (an egress). This shift of the *n*, as we have seen, is a factor in language growth—both ways. When words only spoken for uncounted years were at last put upon paper, who knew whether the *n* came first or last? For a time, some words fluctuated; we find a message that called for *a nanser;* the Fool in *King Lear* says Nuncle, for Mine uncle. An aitch-bone (originally natesbone, of the buttocks) has persisted. When a man has to "eat humble pie," he is mortified; but verbally the phrase is a folk transformation of *an umble pie,* which itself was originally *a numble pie,* numbles being the innards of a deer. And this itself, by a further transfer, comes from the Latin *lumbulus,* diminutive of *lumbus,* 'loin'. Quite a vernacular journey!

Since egress (by the way) sounds like a feminine form, perhaps of egret, Barnum, who said that the public likes to be fooled, took advantage of it when spectators overcrowded his circus sideshows: he put up a sign "This way to the egress," and curious customers found themselves in the street.

Homonyms may be used without punning, as when the priest tried to teach the wheelwright to write the right rite. Probably the neatest homonymic sentence is the Latin *Malo malo malo malo,* translated "I'd rather be in an apple tree than an evil man in adversity." When I was in Iran, I visited the Kurds, who ferment the milk of mares, and I admired the way they weigh their whey.

An outgrowth of the punning homonym, moving by leaps and starts, by absurdity and impertinence, is the homonymble, or nymble. The classic instance of this is the case of the bookkeeper who wore out the seat of his trousers, notwithstanding. This type of word play may start with the request to use a word in a sentence. *Translator:* The medium said she would go into a trance later. *Satisfaction:* The leader of the dissidents entered the room sat his faction on the left. Or the nymble may start with a question. How can a man escape from a solid, sealed room, containing only himself and a table, far from home? He rubs his hands till they are sore. Then he saws the table in half. Two halves make a whole. He crawls through the hole, shouts until he is hoarse, and gallops away.

Usually the maker of nymbles soars along as fancy flies, until he finds a good question to put first. Why is a ruled sheet of paper like a lazy dog? A sheet of ruled paper is an ink-lined plane. An inclined plain is a slope up. A slow pup is a lazy dog.

But let us not forget the man who referred to his wife Susan as Peggy. Peggy, short for Pegasus, an immortal horse. And an immortal horse is an everlasting nag.

An elderly man did not rise when an old friend, a stately if not stout woman, entered the room. She chided him: "I see you're not so gallant as when you were a boy." He retorted: "And you are not so buoyant as when you were a gal."

Practical use has been made of the nymble. Shirley MacLaine records that for her first film, directed by Alfred Hitchcock, she was quite nervous; he sought to soothe her: "Genuine chopper, old girl!" She naturally looked bewildered; he said "Try some synonyms." When she reached *real* for *genuine*, and *ax* for *chopper*, Hitchcock smiled: "That's it. Real ax. Relax, old girl." She smiled, and found that she did.

The nymble embodies the same principle as the remark Shakespeare gives Cassius, of Julius Caesar:

> Now it is Rome indeed, and room enough,
> Since there is in it but one only man.

A frequent type of verbal blunder occurs when a person, talking beyond the scope of his learning, stretches out for a word but reaches only what sounds like the one that he intends. This error has been played upon by Shakespeare and by many since. For a time such a ludicrous misuse of one word for another was called a *slipslop*, from Mrs. Slipslop in Fielding's *Joseph Andrews* (1742), his intended burlesque of Richardson's *Pamela* Andrews. Fielding's frail matron made such neat blunders as "When he's had one drink, he gets all erotic"—meaning erratic. She was followed by the equally aberrant Mrs. Winifred Jenkins, in Tobias Smollett's *Humphrey Clinker* (1771); but the term we now use comes from the malpractice of Mrs. Malaprop (French *mal à propos*, 'ill-fitting') in Richard Sheridan's comedy *The Rivals* (1775), who described someone as "headstrong as an allegory on the banks of the Nile," and prided herself on her "nice derangement of epitaphs" (arrangement of epithets).

Mrs. Malaprop and her numerous kinsfolk may slip and muddy their words in two quagmires. They may fall upon a word that sounds like the one they are seeking: "Illiterate him from your memory." Or they may tumble onto a word in the polarity of significance: "We will not anticipate the past; our retrospection will be all to the future."

Much the same as malaprops are boners and bulls. Boners, in England called howlers, are usually attributed to schoolboys, but may often be the invention of their teachers. "In Scott's *Ivanhoe*, Brian de Bois Guilbert asked Rebecca to be his mistress, and she reclined to do so." The Irish Bull has been traced to Obadiah Bull, a nineteenth-century solicitor in London; but Milton used the term bull in this sense two centuries before, and it is of Sir Boyle Roche, a Dublin politician of the 1770s, that it was first said: Every time he opens his mouth he puts his foot in it. "Half the lies our opponents tell about us are not true." There is sound counsel in the saying: An author should always make his own index, let who will write the book. It is at once description and illustration to state that the Irish bull is pregnant.

Other terms, frequently overlapping, have been used for these varieties of word play. Fluff, either noun or verb, is applied to making a mess of a message; frequently, to muddled memory: He fluffed his lines. If an error can be interpreted as revealing something, especially something embarrassing, it may be referred to as a Freudian slip. A recent telescoped coinage, for a verbal malfeasance with a mixed metaphor, is *malaphor*, apparently rife in governmental bureaucrap. Among many malaphors recorded in Washington are: "He threw a cold shoulder on that idea." "I'm not going to bail out his chestnuts." "The problem started small, but it is baseballing." "We're breaking previrgin territory." This is indeed a bull!

Sometimes an individual seems to be a wellspring of the humor of a generation. Thus countless ribald jokes he never fathered were foisted upon Chauncey Depew. After him the ladies had their turn, in Dorothy Parker, who once, they say, told a horticulturists' convention: "You can lead a whore t' culture but you cannot make her think." Similarly, motion picture magnate Samuel Goldwyn—abetted by his publicity department—actually gave his name as a label to a variety of boner uttered by a bonehead. Among Goldwynisms are: "Anyone who goes to a psychoanalyst ought to have his head examined." Told that a story was rather caustic, he exclaimed: "I don't care what it costs; if it's good, we'll make it." As may be said of many a bad book, "I read part of it all the way through." One may agree with his dismissal of a piece of dialogue: "Let's have some new clichés!"

A book of boners has been published entitled *Pullet Surprises,* because "In 1924 Eugene O'Neill won the Pullet Surprise." The Pulitzer Prize is still a source of controversy; dissatisfaction with it led in 1935 to the founding of the New York Drama Critics' Circle and its annual award to the "best" new play produced in New York City. Speaking of plays, one naturally thinks of Shakespeare: a comic remarked that he once knew a speech from *Julia Sees Her.*

Since the renewed emphasis on speech, in simultaneous translation at the U.N., and over the airways, unintentional boners have abounded; these oral ones are frequently referred to as bloopers. U.N. translator Alexander Schwartz, who can work in fifteen languages, has through the years made a collection of such inadvertent blunders. One of them seems too close to truth to be funny: "The Secretariat's sphere ..." by a sadly misplaced juncture, was translated into four languages as "The Secretariat's fear of competence."

As might have been expected, among the aired pronouncements of the 1976 Olympics were many precipitate howlers. Among them: "And this lad, with all the world in front of him, finished fifth." "Now we can see Goralov coming around the corner, just out of sight." "Since then, she has filled gymnasia all around the world with aspirates." (So precise with the foreign form of the plural, and then the misplaced breathing!) "In a little while, we hope to have the pole vault over the satellite."

Another sort of verbal misplay, the Spoonerism or Spooner, draws its name from the Rev. W. A. Spooner (1844–1930), Warden of New College, Oxford. This consists in a transposition of sounds at the beginnings of words. "I have a half-warmed fish in my mind" (half-formed wish). The Dean is supposed to have told an errant student: "You have hissed my mystery classes; you have tasted the whole worm. You will leave Oxford tomorrow by the town drain." (missed my history classes ... wasted the whole term ... by the down train.) And he nudged a nervous bridegroom: "It is kisstomary to cuss the bride." Earlier, a Spooner had been called a Marrowsky, from a supposedly thus-afflicted Polish count. Here again we have a process, mentioned before, of language growth, metathesis. Thus *fringe* is from an earlier *fim-bria;* conversely, *dirt* was earlier *drit* (German *Dreck*).

A more flowery if not hifalutin pattern of verbal play is the Wellerism, named after Samuel Weller in Dickens' *The Pickwick Papers,* on whose lips Dickens makes the form frequent. This is a tangential flight of fancy, soaring off on an absurdly relevant image. Urging a slow-speaking man to give him the news, Weller cried: "Out with it, as the father said to the child when it swallowed a farthing." A mini-echo of Milton is in the cry, on the way to a party, "Away with melancholy, as the little boy said when his schoolmissus died." The pattern, known before Dickens, has been fashioned since. "I've been struck by the beauty of the place, as the fresh young man said when the pretty girl slapped him." "I'm thirsty myself, as the lady remarked when the baby fell into the fishpond." One could continue lengthily in this vein, but might pause with the thought that a character in Helen MacInness's mystery *Friends and Lovers* had *very close veins.* As Goldwyn is said to have said, Include me out.

These triflings with the language may seem trivial, but they are fun. And beyond this pleasure in the juggling of words, they have a further value. For they serve to waken, or to keep alive, a concern for the meaning of the words we use. To understand and enjoy the wordplay, one must be alert to the distinctions involved, to the differences or alterations on which the humor depends. Thus one learns, and by the best method of learning, through an enjoyment in which the educative element is undiscerned.

The words we have been discussing are all part of the vernacular, the speech native to a person or place. *Vernacular* comes from the Latin *verna,* which means a slave born in the house of his master. The heedless and illiterate wordways of the slave made it natural for *vernacular* to come to mean plain, ordinary, everyday speech, and then substandard speech, as opposed to literary or learned language. Thus the word is gathered, in *Webster's New Collegiate Dictionary,* into a list of synonyms that includes dialect, argot, cant, colloquialism, jargon, slang.

It is good to know that English is, beyond most tongues, rich in synonyms. This affords us the opportunity for fine distinctions, for selecting among various similar terms the one that most precisely captures our immediate intention. It is less pleasing to recognize that the majority of persons are heedless or ignorant of, and indifferent to, such minutiae, are unable or unconcerned to discriminate among synonyms. They therefore use one for another haphazardly; they blunt the edges of words, they confuse and confound ideas.

Such carelessness has made the terms *Webster's* lists overlap. Most distinctive is *dialect*, which refers to the speech ways of a particular region within a language group. *Argot* consists of the special terms and idioms of a subgroup—criminals, English cockneys, railroad workers, homosexuals—developed often as a sort of secret code, to identify and set apart the members of that group. Thus we are told that the Negro has developed his own argot "partly to put the white man off, partly to put him down." Word-use-man Fowler, however, declares that *argot* is a French word, without justification in English.

So far, so good. Come now to cant. *Cant* has a distinct significance, as language insincerely expressing pious or ethical sentiments. But Webster's definition 2a is "the argot of the underworld."

Jargon likewise has its special sense, as confused, almost unintelligible language. But it is also defined as the "characteristic idiom of a special activity or group"—which identifies it with both cant and argot. Varieties of jargon in its proper sense, such as officialese, commercialese, expertease, bureaucrap, or gobbledegoop, may be postponed until our remarks on obfuscation.

Colloquial language is that of informal conversation, a mixture of standard English and slang, with frequent abbreviations and slurred syllables. The word comes from a Latin compound meaning 'talking together', and such speech rarely appears in writing, except in fiction as dialogue, and in the lines of newspaper columnists and purveyors of ephemeral gossip.

Most important of these terms is *slang*, for slang pervades the speech and writing of every level of society. But the first definition in Webster is "language peculiar to a particular group, as (a) argot (b) jargon." Only thereafter is it called "an informal nonstandard vocabulary composed typically of coinages, arbitrarily changed words, and extravagant, forced, or facetious figures of speech." The *Random House Dictionary* reverses the order, ending with the identification (confusion!) of slang with argot and jargon. It begins: "very informal usage in vocabulary and idiom that is characteristically more metaphorical, playful, elliptical, vivid, and ephemeral than ordinary language, as *Hit the road*."

Slang terms leap into the language from various sources, often on the spur of the moment's thrust of an individual fancy. They may be melodious manufactured words, sometimes indicating their origin, as *slantindicular* from *perpendicular,* or *splendiferous* as a lilting leap from *splendid.* Or they may be just gleeful expansions of sunny sound, as *rambunctious* or *absquatulate.* Occasionally there may be an echoic term, the sound suggestive of the idea. Perhaps *tin Lizzie* sought to mimic the squeaking of the old-time Ford car. *Whiz-bang* speaks for itself; the *wiz-kid* (whiz kid) is more probably a cutting of *wizard,* speeded, no doubt, by the Wiz, the Wiz, the wonderful Wizard of Oz.

Curtailing, or shortening, gives us such slang as the epidemic *flu,* made more familiar by the jocose remark that somebody opened the window and influenza. Similarly, *looney* (for *lunatic*) had a flurry of literate popularity when J. Thomas Looney published his book proclaiming that the author of Shakespeare's plays was really not Bacon but Edward de Vere, Seventeenth Earl of Oxford—and the orthodox Stratfordians cried: "Who's looney now?"

The converse of curtailing, expanding, has also given us some slang expressions, as when "Hot dog!", as an exclamation of joyous approval, grows to "hot diggety dog!", or a positive attitude is made more forceful by the insertion in *absodamlutely* or the blend of *posolutely.*

Another source of slang is exaggeration extended to a figure of speech, hyperbole. This may be no more than an excessive adverb, such as *awfully* or "I was terribly excited!" or other over-emphatic exclamation. "I almost died!" This familiar piece of hyperbolic emphasis was travestied in a bit of doggerel by Oliver Wendell Holmes, in the story of a man who, listening to a joke of the poet's, did die laughing. Holmes mournfully assures his readers:

> Since then I've never tried to be
> As funny as I can.

The exaggerated slang may, however, be a genuine creation, such as "out of this world" or "on cloud nine."

Then there are the perhaps deliberate mispronunciations, sung at times in popular songs: *loverly, bimeby.* Or the older *nincompoop,* transmogrified from Latin *non compos mentis,* 'of unsound mind'. Another early corruption is *hocus pocus,* perhaps a prestidigitator's change from *hoc est corpus,* the beginning of the Latin religious phrase "This is the body . . ." as the priest symbolically changes bread and water into the body and blood of the Lord. Then the magician changes a white handkerchief into a green and red scarf. *Hocus pocus* itself has spawned the slang *hokum,* and *hokey,* as well as the now standard word *hoax.*

Many slang terms are borrowings from other languages. *Pronto!* is from Spanish; *boloney,* from Italian. Yiddish seems indeed a fertile source, especially of American slang, with *mazuma* (money), *schlemiel* (blockhead, *Dummkopf,* this from the German), *goniff* (thief), *chutzpa* (nerve!). The *Random House Dictionary of the English Language* somehow includes *hock a tchainik,* defined as to gossip incessantly, to make a fuss about trivial things, and gives the example: "My little Elsie, all she does is sit on the phone and hock a tchainik all day," with a note that the Yiddish means, literally, 'to chop at a teapot'. Indeed, *Random House* gives, in close succession, seven separate entries of Yiddish words: *schlemiel, schlepp, schlimazel, schlock, schmaltz, schmaltzy, schmalzy.* Not to mention *schmo, schmoose, schmooze* (separate entries, all), *schmuck, schnook, schnorrer, schnozzle*—but despite Cyrano's nose, no proudly outthrust Jimmy Durante *schnozzola.* Still, this is somewhat of a proboscideous, though Random, English listing.

Finally, a slang expression may be a transfer of a general term into a particular field. Instead of bidding someone Hurry! we may cry Step on the gas! A *bluffer* may become a *four-flusher.* For a well-informed, deft how-to person, we may go back to the days of the four-masted sailing craft, and say "He knows the ropes." "I won't stick my neck out," a man may exclaim, as though not to invite the executioner, or the garrote. An unwelcome intruder may try to *butt in,* like a goat, or to *horn in,* as though with a stag's horns—or a shoe-horn. "Keep your eyes open" may strain to "Keep your eyes peeled," as though the lids were a fruit skin. Those that subsequently repeat such phrases may not be aware of their literal origin.

These are the major sources of slang terms. Sometimes, however, there is a blank wall behind a word, and on it, like graffiti, etymologists write stories of its origin. There are two dozen explanations of the origin of *O.K.* (*okeh, okay*), ranging from an initial misspelling of "all correct" to the initials of Old Kinderhook. It has been traced to other tongues, from American Indian Choctaw to black African Mandingo. And it has, from its still unknown beginnings, become the most frequently used English term around the world, and has developed its own offshoots, such as *okeydokey.* The usual slang for a *knock-out* in boxing, *kayo,* is sometimes used as reverse slang for okay.

Another such term of disputed origin is *bunkum,* which has been shortened to *bunk,* which in turn has been built into the

verb *debunk,* a frequent journalistic process. The favored origin
of *bunkum* traces it to a congressman from North Carolina, who
used to make long speeches in the House not to persuade his
fellow-members, he told them, but to impress his constituents
back home in Buncombe county. An informed New Englander
may tell another tale. In our eastern northwoods, near the Cana-
dian border, lived many French-speaking Americans. They en-
dured hard physical labor, six long days a week, felling trees, or
clearing stumps and rocks from fields for farm or pasture. And
on the day of rest, if the housewife suggested that something
might need repair, the man might shrug his shoulders and wearily
declare: "It's good enough as it is"—"*C'est bon comme ça!*" And
the wife would mutter, in resignation or subdued scorn: *Bon
comme ça!: Bunkum!*

Slang that can be traced to a definite source seems seldom to
well from a natural spring of sparkling folk-terms; rather it is the
conscious creation of a wordsman. Sports writers and gossip columnists are in the van of such innovators, peppering their articles
with new-coined turns and fancies. The widely syndicated Walter
Winchell was noted for his inventions, such as *Renovated,* of persons parked in Reno, Nevada, for a quick and easy divorce. He
was, however, anticipated by the English in this sort of transformation. Thus a nugatory, worthless ne'er-do-well might be
labeled Newgatory, bringing to the English mind the notorious
Newgate Prison and the noted Newgate Calendar of crime. The
thrillers of the mid-nineteenth century are known as the Newgate
novels; Thackeray (envious?) put Dickens' works in that category.
Many such terms seem to die with their makers—*Renovated,* and
the pregnant *infanticipation,* seem to bear the sign "Copyright
by W.W."—but the process goes on, and on.

Slang has been described as ephemeral, and indeed much of it
is. Few persons today would speed (or impel) the parting guest
with the once ubiquitous "Twenty-three, skidoo!" *Tommyrot!*
even *Nuts!* (and the euphemistic *Nerts!*) have fallen from fashion. Slang dictionaries grow quickly out of date, with a long trail
of outmoded or obsolete expressions. Shakespeare used *costard*
(a large apple) to mean 'head', *claybrained* and *knotty-pated* to
mean 'slow of wit'. Ben Jonson used *bid-stand* for a *highwayman;*
smelt for a *simpleton.*

A comparative few of our slang expressions have managed to
maintain a longer hold on the public fancy. Some, indeed, survive
the centuries, always remaining slang. When Julius Caesar crossed
the Rubicon to become ruler of Rome, his words *Alea iacta est*

"the die is cast," may have referred to actual knuckle bones, the earliest form of dice. When Chaucer, in the fourteenth century, wrote of tossing the bones, the expression was probably figurative, and definitely slang. It remains both of these in the twentieth-century "Roll dem bones!"

Jonson's *coffin* for 'pie crust' still finds use among chefs. Shakespeare's *sand-blind*—although the sand is a corruption of *sam-*, *semi-*, meaning 'half'—has grown more ominous in *gravel-blind* and *stone-blind;* the last of these persists. Calling Cleopatra Antony's "dish," Shakespeare found a term still applied to a lovely lass. (*Stevenson's Book of Shakespeare Quotations* quaintly lists Enobarbus' remark, of Antony: "He will to his Egyptian dish again" under the heading of cookery. This, despite the warning, in Caroline Spurgeon's *Shakespeare's Iterative Imagery*, not to list "the blanket of the dark" under household effects.) A "whither-go-ye" for a nagging wife, from her persistent question to a wandering husband, has died, but the equally eighteenth-century *riveted* for 'married' would be understood today, and its figure is carried on in the terms *spliced, hitched,* and the like. The parson still *ties the knot.*

Just a few years ago, persons noting a lapse of logic or memory might tap their head and say "Nobody home!" They had in all likelihood never read the eighteenth-century epigram of Alexander Pope, aptly entitled "An Empty House," which tells:

> You beat your pate, and fancy wit will come:
> Knock as you please, there's nobody at home.

This persistence may be observed in another fashion, when a slang word makes the grade, and passes into the standard English vocabulary. For its slang replacement, a new word, attempting to find fresh vividness when the old term has become standard but trite, will rise again right out of the same region. Ancient physiology, for example, assigned the emotions to various parts of the body. Love, of course, wells from the heart, hence one's *sweetheart,* and the heart-shaped boxes of sweets for St. Valentine's Day. Courage dwells a little lower, in the viscera. One definition of *visceral* is 'dealing with crude or elemental emotions'. The Bible in several references presses this home: "His bowels were loosed with fear." In this light, consider the word *pluck,* meaning 'courageous readiness to fight or continue against odds'. A century ago, you would not have found this meaning in any dictionary. Then, *pluck* meant the part of a fowl the butcher would put his hand in and pluck forth, the liver and lights; namely, the viscera. About 1870 sports writers, reporting boxing matches, began to use the term *pluck* figuratively, the seat of courage standing for the feeling. The word caught the public fancy, and gradually grew to be the standard term. And nowadays, when someone wants to put fresh vigor into his admiration of a plucky fighter, he goes right back into the viscera, and exclaims "That guy's got guts!" More grandiloquently, he might speak of *intestinal fortitude*.

[Pluck, incidentally, has unexpected relations. It comes from the Latin *piluccare*, to pull out the hair, from Latin *pilus*, 'hair'. From the same word come *plush* and *pile* (of carpet), the verb *to peel*, the medical *pill*, and the wartime *pillage*. From the sixteenth into the nineteenth century, a scornful term for a bald man was *pilgarlic*. Words may take odd pathways.]

Of some terms that have become standard English, the slang was present in the Latin originals. There are many such slang Latin words promoted to standard English. *To insult*, for example, literally in the Latin means 'to jump upon'. *Perplexed* is, in Latin slang, 'balled up', literally 'braided together', 'tangled'. *Precocious* is 'half-baked'; *delirious*, 'off one's trolley', literally, 'out of the furrow', in ploughing. An *interloper* is a 'jump-betweener'; a fool is a bellows, a windbag. Oddly, *gams* has remained slang for *legs;* it comes via French from Latin *gamba*, 'hoof', but Late Latin slang for a leg. Cowboys today may speak of cattle on the hoof, meaning on their legs, alive. Leaping on legs, rolling on wheels, soaring in rockets, slang keeps pace with the times on many tongues.

The importation of slang also occurred in French: the standard French word for so universal and important a thing as one's head, *tête*, comes from the Latin *testa*, which means 'pot'.

A special type of slang, originating among the cockney English in the early nineteenth century, spreading to Australia and in lesser degree to America, is rhyming slang. A simple sample of rhyming slang is "Let's get down to brass tacks," meaning, the facts. This has survived in the States, helped by the actual presence of two brass tacks, pricked a yard apart into the edge of the counter, for measuring cloth, in the now vanishing country store. Usually there are two terms, the second making the rhyme. But in the argotic desire to be different, apart, incomprehensible to outsiders, the cockney went a step further: he dropped the rhyming word. Thus, when a likely lass walks by, the coster's "Have a butcher's at her" is understood by his pals: butcher's hook, have a look. "Lost me titfer!" complained a tyke on the morning after (*tit for* tat: hat). "Don't be stupid! Use yer loaf," he said to his bumptious son (loaf of bread: head). In the nineteenth century, the Khyber Pass was in the military news, and swiftly became rhyming slang: when a cockney cried "Up your Khyber!" he had to be ready for a blow.

A few of these rhyme-lost terms have taken hold in the United States. *Sugar and honey,* and *bread and honey,* are appropriate rhyming slang for *money,* that sweetener of many situations. And *sugar,* and *bread,* without the rhyme, are both used to mean the desired dollars. More distinctive, perhaps, is the expression for that rude noise, the raucous blare of disapproval, known in local circles as the Bronx cheer, more widely sounding in "They gave him the razz." You may recall the whole word for this: *razz* is a shortening of *raspberry.* The full rhyming slang is *raspberry tart.* The scornful sound imitates an audible expulsion of anal wind. (Hamlet intends this, when he says "Buzz Buzz" to Polonius.)

An interesting bit of rhyming slang is *Dickey dirt;* this was first used of a worn-out shirt; but now *dickey* is the standard English word for a detachable stiff shirt front, as worn by waiters and once by men unprepared for an "evening dress" occasion. *Do and dare* is cockney rhyming slang for frivolous feminine underwear; "She's wearing her do and dare" has obvious implications.

Many such terms were drawn from the theatre, which spreads through London's cockneytown. Thus Terry (from the actress Ellen Terry) is rhyming slang for Jerry, short for Jeroboam, slang for chamber-pot.

Some Jewish terms have come into cockney slang, at either end of the rhyme. Thus *flour mixer* is rhyming slang for *shicksa,* Yiddish for a non-Jewish girl. On the other hand, *mozzle and brocha,* Yiddish words, are rhyming slang for *on the knocker,* said of a *forty-four* ('door-to-door') salesman. These two Yiddish words not only rhyme but are appropriate, as they incidentally name the last two of the six "goods" a house-to-house salesman should have: good looks, good manners, good voice, good temper, good luck (*mazel, mozzle*), good health (*brocha*).

A less frequent but occasionally used variety of slang is back-slang, the sound of a word reversed. Thus, if someone has angered a person by a stupid action, he may be told: "Your name is mud" (dumb). Among thieves, a *birk* is a *crib;* that is, a place to be burgled. Back-slang, however, usually calls for greater ingenuity than slangsters have or desire to expend.

Virtually all slang is figurative. Adam Smith, in a discussion of rhetoric as far back as 1762, observed that "there is nowhere more

use of figures than in the lowest and most vulgar conversation."
Since the rude and semiliterate garnish their talk with slang, one
may wonder why it also plays a large part in more polite conversation. Eric Partridge, in his study of *Slang Today and Yesterday,*
gives fifteen reasons for its popularity. Five of these seem major.

Slang may spring from sheer exuberance, gay high spirits that
impel one to break into extravagant figures. It may, as already
noted, stem from a desire for private speech, to mark one's distinction from the common herd. Especially among sports writers,
columnists, and other commentators on passing events, it marks
the search for variety, for a different way of putting a recurrent
word or notion. Think of the attempts to vary such baseball terms
as *ball* and *bat* and *base.* Once a slang term has found flavor and
favor, it is slipped as it were casually into many a person's talk to
show that he is "with it," that he is *au courant,* in the know, hip.
And very often, among sophisticates as well as sophomores, slang
—especially a taboo word—is used to make manifest one's "advanced" attitude, to defy the laws of decorum, to rebel against the
parent or "pig" or the social order.

Slang being thus pervasive and persistent, one is led to inquire
whether it is healthful, like good exercise, or harmful, like the
common cold. The Fowler brothers, H. W. and F. G., in their
magistral study of *The King's English* make no bones about their
condemnation:

> As style is the great antiseptic, so slang is the great corrupting
> matter; it is perishable, and infects what is around it—the catch-
> words that delight one generation stink in the nostrils of the next.

Grudgingly they concede that a few slang expressions ultimately
establish themselves; "but during probation they are accounted
unfit for literary use." This is akin to the injunction not to go into
the water until you know how to swim. Words can grow into
literary use only by being so used. The counsel of Pope seems
relevant:

> Be not the first by whom the new are tried,
> Nor yet the last to lay the old aside.

The general excoriation of slang, without particulars, is empty.
The chief cogent objection, beyond the mere observation that a
gentleman should use restraint, not slang, is that it becomes the
lazy man's speech. He takes up the vogue word, which rapidly
becomes the common phrase, the commonplace, loosely used

cliché. Mouthed as a catch-all, it lacks precision, it blurs distinction, it pauperizes the vocabulary. It marks the misty if not musty mind.

Against this objection, iconoclast Chesterton bluntly set the remark: "All slang is metaphor, and all metaphor is poetry." Logically, of course, this has as much validity as the observation that all donkeys are mammals, and all mammals are men. Despite inaccurate analogues, however, there is little question that slang, if fresh and vivid, may be effective and arresting—and therefore justified. When the freshness fades, it is likely to be discarded, like an old bouquet. Yet its figures are often colorful and strikingly apt. *Pie in the sky* lights an alluring illusion. *Put on the bracelets* seems a gentler way to fasten the handcuffs in an arrest.

Slang is part of the American word way of life. As our humorist Finley Peter Dunne has his Mr. Dooley remark: "When we Americans get through with the English language, it will look as if it had been run over by a musical comedy." And musical comedies are America's liveliest and perhaps loveliest gift to the gaiety of nations. But of course there are bad ones, quickly defunct ones—as with slang.

Whatever one may think of the use of slang, like the drinking of liquor it will not submit to prohibition. It is rooted in man's continuous search for vivid and vigorous expression; if it strikes home, it will endure for its triumphant day. And the usually anonymous creators of slang will succeed one another along the corridors of time, keeping the pedants in their petty place and the language alive.

9.
EUPHEMISM

EUPHEMISM, THE USE OF A pleasant substitute for a term with unpleasant or objectionable associations, appears in almost all our talk. It grows from the assumption that "the voice with the smile wins." If you are called to comment on a woman whose countenance is forbidding, do not say to her, "Your face would stop a clock." Make that face smile by saying, "Whenever I look at you, time stands still." There are, however, three major hunting grounds of the taboo: the creator of life, the beginning of life, and the end of life; that is, God, sex, and death.

There was a time, now for many gone by, when the name of the Lord was strong enough to be taken in vain, and even the great Adversary, the Archfiend, was not referred to with impunity. "Speak of the devil" now marks a casual coincidence, but once showed fear of a dreaded appearance. Pope tells of a minister "Who never mentioned hell to ears polite." W. S. Gilbert pokes fun at the Captain of The Pinafore, who protested:

> Though "Bother it!" I may
> Occasionally say,
> I never use a big, big D—.

For centuries, it was deemed blasphemy to violate the religious taboo on the name of the Lord. The four-letter word that has been under taboo for the longest time in history—it is even called *the* four-letter word, Greek *Tetragrammaton*—is the Hebrew word for God, YHVH, still never spoken nor written by a pious Jew. The Greeks called the Furies, to whom even the gods deferred, the *Eumenides,* the 'good-natured ones'.

In the Christian world, the practice of swearing led men to curious transformations of the holy name. *Odds bodkins,* 'God's

153

little body'. *Zounds*, 'God's wounds'. *Gorblimey*, 'may God blind
me'. *Lumme*, '(Lord) love me'. *Bloody*, long a fearful taboo word in
English, combines the spilling of gore with the suggestion of *By
Our Lady*. W. S. Gilbert quickly changed a title from *Bloodygore*
to *Ruddigore*. Mrs. Pat Campbell, fresh from country companies,
became a London star when the reigning stage beauties refused
the role in Shaw's *Pygmalion*, because Eliza had to say "Bloody"
—now frequently heard in the musical adaptation *My Fair Lady*,
with the word accepted as matter-of-fact.

There have been changing attitudes toward swearing. Elizabethan gentlemen, encouraged no doubt by the Queen's frank if
not foul tongue, swore roundly. Hotspur, in Shakespeare's *Henry
IV*, reproaches his wife:

> Swear me, Kate, like a lady, as thou art,
> A good mouth-filling oath, and leave "in sooth"
> And such protests of pepper-gingerbread
> To velvet-guards and Sunday citizens.

Elizabeth's courtiers must have laughed at that!

After Elizabeth, James I, always at odds with the fund-grant-
ing Parliament, initiated the practice of selling peerages, but also
sought to bolster the royal exchequer by setting a fine of twelve
pence for every curse uttered at court. John Marston has a character in *Antonio's Revenge* exclaim: "Sneaks, an I were worth but
£300 a year more, I could swear richly!" In the next century, in
Sheridan's *The Rivals*, Bob Acres suggests the "oath referential,"
fitting the expression to its object. Thus with Ensign Beverley he
swears "Odds triggers and flints!" So today, one might, with a
lawyer: "By habeas corpus and torts!" Such an oath averts the
wrath of the deity, while it adverts the curse to the person.
Sheridan's contemporary, Sterne, in *Tristram Shandy* (1761),
indicates the gamut of his day: "From the great and tremendous
oath of William the Conqueror, *By the splendor of God*, down
to the lowest oath of a scavenger, *Damn your eyes*." How far we
have lapsed from any serious swearing is shown in the off-hand
dismissal of a pious wish, by B. and C. Evans, in their *Dictionary
of Contemporary Usage* (1957): "The use of the phrase *D.V.*,
the initials of *Deo Volente*, or the English form *God Willing*,
as an interjection after an expressed intention, is a verbal counter-
part of knocking on wood and has about the same value." The
coining of colorful oaths has gone temporarily out of fashion.

Euphemisms for the burier have already been listed. For the
dead, the *deceased*, the *dear departed;* more colloquially for

died, *gone west. Cemetery* itself is a euphemism; the Greek word
means 'dormitory'. In such expressions, precision gives way to
what the time deems good taste.

Sex has been by far the richest range of taboo, of the supposedly obscene. Strangely, this has altered from the days of the
ancient Greeks. For *obscene* meant 'off the scene', not presented
on the stage; and what was kept off the ancient stage was violence, always reported by messenger—while in the comedies and
satyr plays the men would strut about with a big artificial phallus
outthrust before them. Addison in 1711 (*Spectator,* 44) observed
that "murders and executions are always transacted behind the
scenes in the French theatre." Thus there is etymological support
for those that in our days protest that true obscenity lies not in
sexual performances but in the indecencies of racists and the
atrocities of licensed killers. "Make love, not war."

Be that as it may, down the years the strongest taboos have
been in the field of sex. A pious priest, now a saint, long ago observed that we are born between urine and feces, and excrement
became involved with execration. Thus obscenity and scatology
have come hand in forbidden hand along the ages. Swinburne
noted a third hand in the holy prohibitive alliance: "Thou hast
conquered, O pale Galilean; the world has grown grey with thy
breath." Religion, making woman a secret and a sin, intensified
the other taboos. Mockers in every generation have tended to
associate the religious with sex. Boccaccio is but the best known
of a host of medieval and renaissance writers to picture the priest
as pornophiliac. His "Putting the Devil in Hell" shows a hermit
using the mask of piety to seduce an innocent maid. Indeed, the
pictured practice of the priest has come into the language. The
only ones that do not call a priest Father, we are told, are his own
children. They call him Uncle. And often, just as royal bastards
were made nobles, so priestly by-blows were lifted to high posi-
tions in the Church. Giving exalted posts or sinecures to relatives
is called *nepotism;* and *nepotem* is the Latin word for 'nephew'.

In 1750, Bishop Warburton made the often quoted statement:
"My doxy is orthodoxy; your doxy is heterodoxy." The learned
Bishop was no doubt aware of the Elizabethan description:

Doxies, i.e., she-beggars, trulls, wenches, whores, being neither
maids, wives, nor widows, will for good victuals, or a very small
piece of money, prostitute their bodies, protesting that they never
did so before, and that sheer necessity drove them to it—though
they are common hackneys.

They are described as bargaining, often with lewd propositions and provocations,

> till at last few words are best, the bargain's made, and the pox is cheaply purchased at the price of a guinea.

Nowadays, better protected by prophylactics and "the pill," doxies may be referred to as secretaries.

Swift turned a pious wish into a venereal curse: *Pax vobiscum,* "Peace be with you," became in his advice: "Tell your enemies, *Pox vobiscum!*"

The linkage of sex and sewage has also been made in our day. The critic Robert E. Fitch, D.D., speaks of the *mystique de la merde,* the preoccupation of writers with "mud, blood, money, sex, and merde." This has taken sustenance from Freud's dictum that "embryologically the anus corresponds to the primitive mouth," and his linking of feces, *merde,* with the penis, with gold and money. Shakespeare, in *King Lear,* set these in the devil's realm:

> But to the girdle do the gods inherit,
> Beneath is all the fiend's.

And the English critic Alan Pryce-Jones sees much of what is called art today reduced to

> the status of a bowel movement. The artist senses a vague itch or urge, he squats, he evacuates, he flushes, he starts over again. During my own lifetime I seem to have heard very little, in the palace of art, except the roar of the flush, carrying away the latest detritus.

Before making a cursory survey of changing attitudes toward the sexual taboos, let us look at some of the words that mark the field. What to us is the blunt word *whore* was actually a euphemism; it comes from the Latin *cara,* 'darling'. *Pornography* first meant writing about whores (Greek *porne,* 'whore'), with probable reference to the description of proffered charms and promised activities posted before the harlot's house. Its current wider sense has still not been made precise by the courts, nor has *obscene* been made satisfactorily specific. The "appeal to prurient interests" implies that the judge or other censor can look into a person's mind and determine the nature of his feelings. A little thought should lead to the conclusion that such terms are subjective, varying according to the nature (and to some extent the age) of the person involved. Back in 1596 Sir John Harrington—of whom more in a moment—observed:

> It is not the baseness, or homeliness, either of words or matters, that makes them foule and obscenous, but the base mindes, filthy conceits, and lewde intentes of those that handle them.

A euphemism for *pornography* is *erotica;* the difference between the two terms is of style rather than substance. For example, as reported in a *London Standard* 1976 interview, the actress Sarah Miles declared: "I'm fascinated by erotica—as I am appalled by pornography. Eroticism is rejoicing in love; pornography is debasing love"—which seems to say that if you like it, it's loverly. The woman was speaking about a scene in which she masturbates in front of a mirror. You choose the appropriate word. As Uncle Remus counseled: "Ef you bleedzd ter eat dirt, eat clean dirt."

The word harlot was originally (thirteenth century) used of a boy, a knave, a vagabond, a greedy-guts; in the sixteenth century, of a male fornicator. By the fifteenth century, it was also applied to a female juggler and dancer; then, especially in Biblical references, to a strumpet—though Wycliffe preferred to call such women *hooris*—and the application to men dropped away.

The word *fornication* developed from the structure of ancient Rome. *Fornax* is Latin for 'furnace'; *fornix,* for 'vault' or 'arch'. Under the vaulted arches of the Roman viaducts were constructed the great furnaces for baking the bread that was freely distributed to the poor, on the principle that "bread and circuses" would keep them from violent protest and rebellion. These vaults were therefore pleasantly warm, and became the trysting grounds of lovers and the haunt of whores. The early meaning of *fornicator* was 'whoremaster', whom we more curtly call *pimp.* The word *pimp* seems to be a nasalized form of *peep,* meaning a bird call—a neat figurative term, although we no longer speak of a bird "in a gilded cage." There is no connection between *fornication* and *formication* (the tickly feeling of ants crawling on the skin) save that the god Zeus, the lusty protean lover, changed himself into a swarm of ants to seduce the nymph Clytoris.

Among early English words for copulation were *swive, occupy, ride,* and *sard.* The O.E.D. gives, as sense 8 of "*occupy:* to deal with, or have to do with, sexually; to cohabit." It appends a special note:

The disuse of this term in the 17th and most of the 18th century is notable. Against 194 quots. for the 16th century we have for the 17th only 8 (outside of the Bible of 1611, where it occurs 10 times), and for the 18th only 10, all in its last 33 years. . . . This avoidance appears to have been due to its vulgar employment in sense 8. Cf. Shakespeare, 2 *Henry IV*, 2,14,161: "A Captain! God's light, these villains will make the word as odious as the word occupy, which was an excellent good word before it was ill-used."

A letter of 1544 expresses horror at thought of a man who "from the fylthy occupying of a harlot cometh straight to the altar." Ben Jonson in 1637 protested that "many, out of their own obscene apprehensions, refuse proper and fit words. as occupy." Grose in his *Vocabula Amatoria* quotes a ballad of the time:

> All you that in your beds do lie
> Turn to your wives, and occupy;
> And when that you have done your best,
> Turn arse to arse, and take your rest.

Sir John Harrington explained the word's source in an ironic epigram "To Lesbia, a great lady":

> Lesbia doth laugh to hear sellers and buyers
> Cald by this name; Substantiall Occupyers:
> Lesbia, the word was good while good folks used it,
> You mard it that with Chaucer's jest abused it:
> But good or bad, how ere the word be made,
> Lesbia is loth, perhaps, to leave the trade.

Similarly Leonard Bloomfield in *Language* (1933) comments:

In older French and English there was a word, French *connil, connin,* English coney, cunny, meaning rabbit [whence New York's Coney Island]; in both languages the word died out because it resembled a word that was under a tabu of indecency. . . . It is a remarkable fact that the taboo word itself has a much tougher life than the harmless homonym.

On the contrary, it is not remarkable but natural: Gresham's law in economics, that the baser coinage drives out the simon pure, applies also in linguistics. When the homosexuals commandeered the word *gay*, its earlier meaning at once dropped out of use; a man can no longer state that he went to a party, and everyone was gay—unless the special, new meaning is intended. *Gay*, in

the sense of 'light and lively', is obsolescent; if the homosexual
use continues, the other meaning will become obsolete. *Fairy* had
a similar strain before *gay*. R. Reisner, in his *Graffiti* (1974)
adverts to a more technical but less lasting term: "The inverts
(a word preferred by homosexuals to perverts) attempt to win
converts."

The most striking example of such obliteration is in the history
of the word *fuck*. Since the word came into the general dictionaries (*Penguin* in 1965; *American Heritage* in 1969; the
O.E.D. *Supplement* in 1972), efforts have been made to trace its
etymology. They all come up against a blank wall: there is no
such word in the several centuries of Middle English. The English then did not fuck; they swived. An early English version
of the Old Testament called the Book of Genesis the Book of
Swiving. Into the apparent vacuum, of course, folk etymology
has leered. There have been three fanciful suggestions—reported seriously in nonlinguistic publications—that the word
grew as an acronym; the most widespread such notion claims that
the letters are the law clerk's abbreviation for a man convicted of
sodomy or rape: *for unnatural carnal knowledge*. There are, of
course, no such court records to adduce.

There was, however, a very common word, *firk*, used from the
eleventh into the seventeenth century, which (like *get* and *make*)
developed a number of meanings, among them, as noun, 'a sharp,
sudden blow'; as verb, 'to strike', 'to stroke', 'to move rapidly up
and down'. Also, note the quotations in O.E.D.: 'firkerie, an odd
prank, or jerk, in whoorisme. . . . These five years she has firked
a pretty living. . . . Your soberest jades are firkers in corners." In
Thomas Dekker's play *The Shoemaker's Holiday* (1600) the
master cobbler introduces his worker: "Here's Firk, my fine firking journeyman." Eric Partridge euphemistically explains firking
as "given to caressing women." In those days, *f.i.r* and *f.u.r* came
to be pronounced alike. Also, in many words, the *r* has been lost:
the fish *barse* is now *bass*, as indeed *arse* is most often *ass*. Shakespeare puns on *ford* and *food*, on *arms* and *alms*. Try repeating
fur coat rapidly; the *r* is driven into silence by the commanding *k*.
And *firk, furk, fuck*, grew in its present sense, and the old meanings were wiped out 350 years ago by what has remained the
most powerful sexual vulgarism in English speech.

—Save that, in some quarters, it is losing that power, having
become in various forms a mere emphatic expletive, an "empty
modifier." Allen Walker Read, who back in the December 1954
American Speech was the first to give scholarly attention to this

"obscenity symbol," has recently surveyed its use since, noting how widespread and often meaningless it has become. Dorothy Parker is supposed to have told an inopportune telephoner: "I'm too fucking busy, and vice versa!" Kenneth Tynan, a theatre critic until he concocted *Oh! Calcutta!*, was the first to blurt the word to astounded BBC listeners. At a New York theatre one evening, the actors stepped from the stage to draw the audience into the spirit of the play; one of them unwittingly sat on the arm of a critic's aisle seat. The critic whispered to him; the actor rose, exclaimed: "Do you know what he said?" and called "He told me to fuck off!" to the titillated audience.

While the word *fornication* has a Roman history, the practice that named the *testicles* goes back to early Hebrew days. The word is a diminutive of Latin *testis*, 'witness', whence also English *test, testament, testimony*, and more. The original meaning of *testicle* is explained in some dictionaries as "witness or evidence of virility," but the fact is just the reverse: the virility is offered as evidence, as guarantee, of one's sincerity. For in the Bible, when a man took a solemn oath, he laid his hand, as the euphemistic phrase runs, "under the thigh"; actually, on his ballocks, meaning: "If I prove false, may I become impotent (You may cut off my balls)." The noted eleventh-century Jewish commentator Rashi sought an explanation:

> When one swears, one takes a sacred object in his hand.... The circumcision was the first precept of God to Abraham, and had also come to him through great pain; hence it was particularly precious to him, and so he ordered his servant to put his hand upon it when taking the oath.

Rashi came near the explanation, but balled it up. It is by euphemistic extension of this practice that Christians swear on the Bible.

John S. Farmer, in *Slang and its Analogues* (1890; ultimately, by Farmer and E. E. Henley, expanded into seven volumes) was the first to deal frankly and courageously with usually taboo terms. He gives some six hundred substitute terms for fornication, and about the same number for the penis; the listing of alternative terms for the vagina takes seventeen packed columns with over one hundred terms per column. Among the illustrations Farmer supplies is Fletcher, *The Spanish Curate* (1622): "They write *sunt* with a C, which is abominable"; he also lists the dash that ends Sterne's *Sentimental Journey* (1768), of the intrusion of a maidservant into the narrow space beside his bed, "so that,

when I stretched out my hand, I caught hold of the fille-de-
chambre's ——."

For the female pubic hair, Farmer lists Falstaff's call to Mrs.
Ford, when he is disguised as a stag in *The Merry Wives of
Windsor:* "My doe with the black scut." Falstaff's words just
before that mark Shakespeare's most vivid reference to ejacula-
tion: "Send me a cool rut-time, Jove, or who can blame me to piss
my tallow?" Farmer also lists a ballad of 1720:

> I heard the merry wagg protest
> The muff between her haunches
> Resembled most a magpie's nest
> Between two lofty branches.

Purely scatological terms, without sex, came more readily into
general use, although they too are covered with euphemisms.
An illustration of how long such a word may linger on the lips
before it finds print is provided by the leader of the "rude me-
chanicals" in *A Midsummer Night's Dream* (1594). Bottom, the
weaver, is fitly named, for one of the meanings of *bottom* is the
bit of wood or whatnot on which a ball of thread was wound.
But when, in the play, Bottom is transformed into an ass, it seems
safe to say that the name is still appropriate. Yet the earliest
quotation in the O.E.D. for *bottom* in the sense of the human
posteriors is dated 1794, exactly two hundred years later!

An odd euphemism is *night soil*. Night soil does not mean
earth ploughed or seeded in the dark; it means human excrement
(usually collected in the morning) used as fertilizer. It seems a
macabre pun: *soil* meaning 'fertile earth' and also 'soilure': the
end product used to help the beginning. Equally odd is the fact
that, if at a butcher's you ask for lamb *fries,* what you get is
testicles.

There are many euphemisms for the excrementorium. *Toilet*
(French *toile,* 'cloth') was originally a lady's dressing room.
Privy means just a private place. In Kronborg Castle, at Elsinore,
once Hamlet's home, I was shown the King's "secret": a small
room jutting out over the castle moat, with a round hole in the
floor; the moat, originally flowing with the water of a diverted
stream, would carry excretions away. In Shakespeare's time, the
privy was called a *jakes* (Jacques), as recently it has been called
the *John.* Queen Elizabeth's godson, Sir John Harrington, was
banished from court for his *The Metamorphosis of Ajax* (*a
jakes*), reporting his invention of the flush toilet. He begins by

telling of a maidservant who, when Jacques Wingfield identified himself at the door, informed her mistress that Mr. Privy Wingfield sought the pleasure of her company. When Touchstone, in *As You Like It,* greets the melancholy Jacques, "Good even, Mr. What y' call it," the audience did not misunderstand.

Yesterday, when someone said "I have to see a man about a dog," he was playing a variation on Autolycus' words in *The Winter's Tale:* "I shall but look upon the hedge, and follow thee"—though perhaps the actor sounded the *look* like *leak. Stevenson's Book of Shakespeare Quotations* labels this "a famous euphemism."

Some words come into this field by curious divagations. Marie Angelique de Scorraille de Roussilles, Duchesse de Fontanges, mistress of the French Sun King, Louis XIV, was horseback riding in his company one day, when a gust of wind ruffled her hair. Nonchalantly she took off a garter to bind the disheveled locks. Soon all the court ladies were wearing their hair *à la Fontanges.* The word, as a singular, came into England, but the style changed, into a headdress framework adorned with lace and flowers; Addison speaks of a fontange an ell (45 inches) high. But since the device of the Duchesse was convenient, it was also called a *commode (Random House* definition 4), and a commode (*Random House* definition 1) is also a *flush toilet—* which was also called a *convenience.*

Today there is no lack of euphemistic terms. *Lavatory* is a Latinized word for 'wash room'. This may be shortened to *lav;* as also *lat,* for *latrine;* also, especially in England, the *loo,* possibly in punning reference to the place where Napoleon was put down, *Water*loo. At the roadside filling station you may find the *W.C.,* or a *Comfort Station;* at a hotel or theatre, it's more likely to be the *Powder Room, Cloak Room,* or *Rest Room,* with perhaps inner doors discreetly marked *Ladies* or *Gentlemen.* In the London Parliament, for the House of Lords it is cutely labeled *Peers.*

Also today, you may smell on French streets a urinal, which the natives commonly call a *pissoir,* although the more respectable may refer to it as a *vespasian.* The Roman Emperor Vespasian sold the accumulated liquid of the public urinals to the launderers, who used it for whitening garments. When Vespasian's son Titus objected, the Emperor had some of the gold brought to him, to show him that "money doesn't smell." (The ammonia used for bleaching takes its name from a similar source: it was first extracted from the urine-steeped sand at the hitching ground of the many camels, while their riders worshipped, near Thebes, at the Egyptian temple of the great god Ammon.) The outdoor urinal, and the imperial name for it, crossed the Channel. Christopher Morley, on a tour of the old pubs that survived the Blitz, saw "the loveliest of all London's vespasians, opposite the door of The Anchor"—across the Thames from St. Paul's.

The French seem to have been heartier than the English in their use of taboo terms, although Urquhart sometimes added expressions when he translated Rabelais, as in his list of four-hundred-odd terms for the cod, the scrotum. (Instead of a zipper, men's garments in Elizabeth's days had a droppable codpiece.) Boston is known as "the home of the bean and the cod"; Mark Twain, in a letter to a society there, deliberately turned from the fish and wrote bawdily of "the mammoth cod," as the male appendage.

Early English used *tickle* as meaning 'to touch in the sense of generating'; the French have a similar linkage of *chatouiller*, 'tickle', and *chat*, 'pussy', 'vagina'. *Vagina* itself, though technical in English, was slang in Latin; its literal meaning was 'sheath', which of course is the intended receptacle for the sword, and Latin *gladius*, 'sword', was slang for 'penis'. *Penis* itself originally meant 'tail'; with a diminutive ending it also comes to us in *pencil* and *penicillin*.

A Frenchman, now and for many years past, in a moment of disappointment or anger, might use the word *merde* without any hesitation, quite without consideration of its literal sense. To be different, Alfred Jarry, in his play *Ubu Roi*, the first flatulency of the theatre of the absurd, opens with Ubu crying *Merdre*, which may be Englished as Shittle. Cocteau, in his best play, *Orphée* (1926), hides the basic word in an acrostic. The favorite horse of Orpheus comforts its master, with sudden miraculous speech: "*Madame Eurydice reviendra des enfers*," "Your wife Eurydice will return from the underworld"; but it expresses its own jealous feelings through the first letters of the French words.

The English, though not so free and easy with such words, have still made use of them. The Cavalier poet Sir John Suckling, whose knightly lyrics—"Stone walls do not a prison make" —are in every anthology, has also written:

> Love is the fart of every heart:
> It pains a man when 'tis kept close,
> And others doth offend when 'tis let loose.

Jonathan Swift pictures Strephon, slipped into his Celia's dressing room, noticing "a noisome cabinet":

> So things which must not be exprest,
> When plumped into the reeking chest
> Send up an excremental smell
> To taunt the parts from which they fell,
> The petticoat and gown perfume,
> And waft a stink round every room.
> Thus finishing his grand survey
> Disgusted Strephon stole away,
> Repeating in his amorous fits
> Oh! Celia, Celia, Celia shits!

The poem, chiding the lover, ends with a more pleasant thought:

> When Celia all her glory shows,
> If Strephon would but stop his nose
> He soon will learn to think like me,
> And bless his ravished eyes to see
> Such order from confusion sprung,
> Such gaudy tulips raised from dung.

"Two lips," of course, are made for kissing. Sir Thomas Browne, author of the richly anecdotal *Vulgar Errors* (1646), spoke admiringly of "women largely composed behind," and in our tense and troubled times it is a pleasure to see a woman composed.

The practice of out-of-doors excretion, predecessor to the outhouse, was still usual in the eighteenth century; Swift objected to Celia's indoor "reeking chest." He wrote, in 1745:

> I am very much offended with those ladies, who are so proud and lazy, that they will not be at the pains of stepping into the garden to pluck a rose, but keep an odious implement, sometimes in the bedchamber itself, or at least in a dark closet adjoining, which they make use of to ease their worst necessities.

John Gay, in his *Trivia* (1716), had turned his attention to the other sex, with a different euphemism:

> The thoughtless wits shall frequent forfeits pay,
> Who 'gainst the sentry's box discharge their tea;
> Do thou some court or secret corner seek,
> Nor flush with shame the passing virgin's cheek.

Two common terms in the sexual field are drawn from names. *Sadism*—pleasure, even sexual climax, in inflicting pain—is from Comte Donatien Alphonse François de Sade (1740–1814), who called himself Marquis. His novel *Justine* pictures an innocent woman subjected to every defilement, whereas her sister, shown in *Juliette,* finds sexual ecstasy in every crime. Sade himself spent some time in an insane asylum at Charenton; his activity there was made into a play by Peter Weiss, a hit in the 1960s, with the first naked man (rear view) on the English and American stage. *Masochism*—pleasure in suffering, in being subjugated, humiliated, maltreated—takes its name from Leopold von Sacher-Masoch (1836–1895), whose best known work is *Venus in Furs,* although the fullest picture of a masochist appears in *The Story of O* (1954). The English have written many stories that emphasize pleasure in inflicting, or receiving, flagellation—long a common practice in the public school and the Navy. When Winston Churchill was First Lord of the Admiralty (1911–1915), he grimly remarked that the traditions of the Navy were "rum, sodomy, and the lash." Psychologists have asserted that sado-masochistic impulses are in all of us, the morbid state is a matter only of degree. This is tantamount to saying that the germs of all evil—and the seeds of all good—are in everyone; our heredity and environment (in measures still disputed) dispose us severally to contagion or spiritual health.

Let us glance at the sexual verbal taboos along the years. The early English freely used either scatological or sexual terms. Sometimes, indeed, in patterns still employed, they played upon anticipation. The *Exeter Book,* collected by an Anglo-Saxon monk about 975, is an anthology of pious and devotional pieces. It also contains a number of riddles, and some of these as they move along stir sexual thoughts, but at the end present an everyday commonplace solution. Here is one such, translated from the Old English:

> An odd thing hangs by a man's thigh
> under its master's cloak. It is pierced at the tip,
> is stiff and hard, and has a good fixed place.
> When the man lifts his garment
> up over the knee, he desires to visit
> with the head of this hanging instrument
> the familiar hole which it,
> of equal measure, has often been filled before.

Answer: a key.

Some sexual terms were bluntly presented to the citizen on his daily walk around town. A twelfth-century list of London streets includes Gropecunte Lane. Today, in different sections of London, the activity is disguised in eight Love Lanes, one Love Walk, one Lovers Walk. There is also a Little Love Lane; I have traversed it, and can state that the Little refers to the length of the road, not the strength of the feeling. But in all of these, the activity of those that lingered in the once-leafy lanes has been sentimentalized, euphemized, in the name. Historian John Stow, in 1598, remarked that the Westminster Love Lane was "so-called of wantons." The 1970 *Dictionary of City of London Street Names* says of the Love Lane running to Aldermanbury, inside the old London Wall: "In the Middle Ages the wanton women of the City gathered in this lane, seeking customers, and the street thereby acquired its name." Farmer's dictionary lists *love lane* as early slang for the vagina.

James I of Scotland, like Haroun al Raschid of Baghdad before him, and Charles II of England after, frequently walked incognito among his subjects. On one such occasion, dressed as a bagpiper, he was carried across a ford by a *gaberlunzie* ('beggar girl'). He must have given her a double reward, for when they parted she gave him her benison: "May your purse ne'er be toom and your horn aye in bloom!"—which Grose in his 1785 slang dictionary translated: "May your purse and your prick never fail you."

Our earliest English lyric, the delightful song

> Summer is y-cumen in,
> Lude sing cucu!

does not blanch at direct expression; it contains the lines

> Bulloc starteth, bucke farteth,
> Merrie sing cucu!

Our first great English poet, Chaucer, declared he must speak bluntly of things as they are, so as not to "false" his material. He does this especially in *The Canterbury Tales:* the Miller's tale, and the Wife of Bath's complacent self-description in her Prologue.

The Miller's tale is of fair Alisoun and her lover Nicholas,

> And privily he caught her by the queynte
> And sayde, "Y-wis, but if I have my wille,
> For derne love of thee, leman, I spille,"
> And held her harde by the haunche-bone. . . .

By a trick they have gotten her husband out of the way, and Nicholas is spending the night with Alisoun. But the clerk Absalon, also in love with her, comes to the window and begs for a kiss; obligingly she goes over—and squats:

> And with his mouth he kissed her naked ers
> Full savourly, ere he was ware of this—
> Aback he started, and thought it was amiss,
> For well he knew a woman hath no beard. . . .

In a vengeful fury, the clerk goes to a blacksmith, gets a hot poker, and returns to beg another kiss:

> Then Nicholas had risen for to piss
> And out his ers he putteth privily:
> "Speak, sweetest bird, I wot not where thou art":
> This Nicholas anon let fleen a fart—

and at the same moment, the red-hot poker strikes the down-spread Nicholas, whose consequent howling breaks up the party. Note that the Miller is telling this tale to a group on a holy pilgrimage, including a nun, an abbess, and a pious monk.

The lusty Wife of Bath, who has worn out five husbands, makes no bones about her predilections. Here are a few of her frank remarks to the company:

> In wifehood I will use my instrument
> As freely as my Maker hath it sent;
> My husband shall it have both eve and morrowe. . . .
> And truly, as my housbands told to me,
> I have the beste quoniam mighte be. . . .
> What aileth you to grucche thus and groan?
> Is it for you would have my kent alone?
> Have thou y-nogh, what thar thee recche or care
> How merrily that othere folkes fare?
> For certeyne, olde dotard, by your leve,
> Ye shal have queynte right y-nough at eve. . . .

(Spelling was not fixed in Chaucer's day: *kent, queynte, quaint*— and the Latinized *quoniam*—all meant the same. Florio, in 1600, defined "*Quaint,* a woman's privities." James Clavell, in his 1966 best-seller *Tai-Pan,* put the word *quent* into the mouths of his rough mid-Victorian seamen. Writing in Victoria's prime, Sir Richard Burton, in his unexpurgated but privately printed translation of *The Arabian Nights,* pictures each of the three tipsy ladies of Baghdad asking the Porter what he calls "this article, pointing to her slit, her solution of continuity." Among the names he gives are *cleft, womb, vulva,* and *coynte; machine,* and *genitory.* They tell the Porter more poetic names: "the basil of the bridges . . . husked sesame seed . . . Khan of Abu Mansur"— *khan* being a caravanserai, which gives shelter but not bed or board. The Porter then refers to his "prickle, pintle, pizzle" as "mule Burst-all, which browseth on the basil of the bridges, muncheth the husked sesame, and nighteth in the Khan of Abu Mansur.")

The Wife of Bath talks on:

> A likerous mouth must have a likerous tail;
> That madeth me I coulde not withdraw
> My chamber of Venus from a good fellawe. . . .

Her fifth husband was a young and lusty lad:

> In our bed he was so fresh and gay
> And therewithal so wel could he me glose
> That when he wolde han my *belle chose*
> That though he had me beat in every bone
> He coulde win my love again anon.

In the century after Chaucer, eminence—and vehemence— in verse shifted to the Scots. Of the Lion King at Arms Sir David Lindsay's "Answer" to the lost flyting of his roisterous bachelor monarch, here is one stanza (*shell* is one of the thousand-odd terms for the female intercrural foramen):

> I give your Council to the feynd of hell,
> That would not with a princess you provide,
> So that you run shutand from shell to shell,
> Waistand your corps, lettand time overslyde:
> For like a boisterous bull ye run, and ryde,
> Royatouslie, like a rude rubeator,
> Aye fukkand lyke a furious fornicator.

Sir David was indeed a "Lion" King at Arms, to speak thus to his royal master—and paymaster!

Also in this period came a number of popular ballads, hawked and sung in the streets, with frank relations:

> Because she loved riding
> At the stews was her abiding.

The ballad "Heigh for Bread and Cream" sings:

> She poppit into bed, and I poppt in beside her;
> She lifted up her leg, and I began to ride her.

The playwright John Fletcher wrote:

> The Phrygian boys in secret spent their seed
> As oft as Hector's wife rid on his steed.

There is a bit of sarcastic advice, still occasionally offered, dismissing someone who has made a simple and obvious suggestion: "Go teach your grandmother to suck eggs." In the days before Shakespeare it was worded more bluntly: "Go teach your grandam to sard."

Helge Kökeritz has said: "The Elizabethans were wont to call a spade a spade, and they evinced no squeamishness in matters of sex or bodily hygiene. On the contrary, they relished a risqué innuendo or a salacious jest—and so did Shakespeare."

A book has been written by Eric Partridge, on Shakespeare's bawdry (this word has become archaic, the adjective *bawdy* having taken on also the functions of the noun). But no capture of Shakespeare's ribald references is complete. Note just a few of the common words that, to the Elizabethan, might mean the vagina: *breach, commodity, aperture, circle, O, notch, slit, nick, case, cut.* The last of these (with an *n* tucked in) is spelled out in the letter that lies awaiting Malvolio, Olivia's overweening and overambitious steward in *Twelfth Night.* As he enters upon the scene, he is dreaming aloud of his happy future: "Having come from a day bed, where I have left Olivia sleeping"—when he sees the forged missive the watching pranksters have set for him. "By my life, this is my lady's hand! These be her very C's, her U's 'n' her T's; and thus makes she her great P's." This last statement needs no interpreting; but to make sure the audience grasps the rest, Shakespeare has the dense Sir Andrew ask his cronies: "Her C's, her U's, 'n' her T's—why that?"

Love's Labor's Lost, an early work of Shakespeare's, is virtually built upon wordplay. Two nobles watch unseen as the Spaniard affectedly compliments the Princess:

ARMADO: I do adore thy sweet Grace's slipper.
BOYET (ASIDE TO DUMAIN): Loves her by the foot.
DUMAIN (ASIDE TO BOYET): He may not by the yard.

For some two hundred years, *yard* was the favorite euphemism
for the penis—a sheer case, of course, of masculine arrogance.
Rosaline, in the play, written at about the same time as the
sonnets, is described as

> A whitely wanton with a velvet brow,
> With two pitch balls stuck in her face for eyes,
> Ay, and by heaven, one that will do the deed
> Through Argus were her eunuch and her guard.

In *The Merry Wives*, the Welsh parson Evans is questioning his
pupil:

E.   What is the focative case, William?
W.   O—vocativo, O....
E.   What is your genitive case, plural?
W.   Genitive case?
E.   Ay.
W.   Genitive: horum, harum, horum.
MRS. QUICKLY *breaks in:* Vengeance of Jennie's case; fie on
  her! Never name her, child, if she be a whore.

Only the foothills can be glanced at here, of Shakespeare's
mountain range of sexual allusions. Comedies, tragedies, history
plays, all are tinged with lubricious implications. In *Henry V*,
when the French princess Katherine is trying to learn English—
her marriage to Henry being a term of the treaty of peace—the
words her maid helps her to (mis)pronounce are bawdy in one
language or the other: *foot* sounds like French *foutre; gown* is
sounded like French *con; neck* is here pronounced *nick*. Katherine cries out that English is a dirty language (much as an English girl might exclaim on hearing a swimming-pool called
French *piscine*).

Long overlooked by producers and ignored by scholars is the
comic climax of the Pyramus and Thisby burlesque in *A Midsummer Night's Dream*, presented as part of the wedding celebra-
tion of Theseus, Duke of Athens, and Hippolyta, Queen of the
Amazons. Thisby wins a preliminary chuckle by telling the man
who stands before her, representing the Wall: "My cherry lips
have often kissed thy stones." Pyramus has come, and bids the
Wall "Show me thy chink, to blink through with mine eyne."

What probably happened was that Wall spread his legs, Pyramus kneeling in front, and Thisby behind. For now all talk of *cranny* and *chink* is abandoned; Pyramus cries "O kiss me through the hole of this vile Wall"—and Thisby laments: "I kiss the Wall's hole, not your lips at all."—As if to compensate for the coarse play, Shakespeare introduces at once one of his rare bits of aesthetic criticism:

HIPPOLYTA: This is the silliest stuff that ever I heard.
THESEUS: The best in this kind are but shadows, and the worst
  are no worse, if imagination amend them.
H. It must be your imagination then, and not theirs.

As our imagination has probed other shadows than the Elizabethans', we have lost we know not how many of their references and allusions to sex. It seems almost safe, when the sense of a passage escapes us, to paraphrase Tacitus' adage: *Omne ignotum pro obscoeno*, "everything not understood, assume to be obscene." Thus in *Love's Labor's Lost, nutmegs* reminded an Elizabethan of testicles; *lemon,* of *leman,* a loose woman; "cloves —no, cloven" of a woman pretending to be a virgin.

Viola says to the Clown in *Twelfth Night:* "They that dally nicely with words will quickly make them wanton"; and most of Shakespeare's word play exemplifies her remark. When it is not wanton, it is usually aggressive, as when Pistol threatens his French prisoner, Monsieur Fer: "I'll fer him, and firk him, and ferret him," with obscene undertones. Remember that *e* was pronounced as *a: Fer, far; clerk, clark.* And note that, as today with the words *thistle* and *whistle,* the Elizabethans pronounced *Pistol* with the *t* silent. Likewise *epistle.*

In several of the comedies, of a couple engaged in love's sweet combat—Berowne and Rosaline, Beatrice and Benedick, Petruchio and the shrewish Kate—the wordplay is at once hostile and seductive. Shakespeare himself declares (*2 Henry IV*):

'Tis needful that the most immodest word
Be looked upon and learned.

Two biographical sexual concerns turn us to the Sonnets. Those that are told Shakespeare was a homosexual should reread Sonnet 20, which clearly rebuts this charge. It ends:

And for a woman wert thou first created,
Till Nature, as she wrought thee, fell a-doting,

> And by addition me of thee defeated
> By adding one thing to my purpose nothing.
> But since she pricked thee out for women's pleasure,
> Mine be thy love, and thy love's use their treasure.

The 1952 *Complete Works,* edited by G. B. Harrison, naively glosses "pricked thee out" as "selected you."

The second biographical flaw is the matter of Shakespeare's "dark lady." There's none so blind as he that will not see. So eager have scholars been in their quest for, and proclaiming of, a real-life woman to be this nonexistent flame of the bard, that they have neglected to ponder the references to this supposed mistress. In the first place, the woman in the Sonnets is not dark, but 'black": the word black is applied to her ten times, the word dark but once, and then obviously to avoid repetition:

> For I have sworn thee fair, and thought thee bright,
> Who art as black as hell, as dark as night.

Note also that the words here refer not to physical but to spiritual characteristics. Indeed:

> In nothing art thou black save in thy deeds.

To an Elizabethan, this emphasis on black had a significance we should recapture, to understand. Sir John Harrington, in one of his epigrams, makes it quite clear:

> These thirty things that Helen's fame did raise
> A dame should have that seeks for beauty's praise:
> Three bright, three black, three red, three short, three tall,
> Three thick, three thin, three close, three wide, three small. ...
> Her brows, eyes, privy parts, as black as jet. ...

Shakespeare, in this tenfold triple concordance of beauty, ascribes to both Rosaline in *Love's Labor's Lost* and his equally supposed mistress in the Sonnets, brows and eyes of black; the third region he reserves for his privy thoughts. But nowise is she dark. Nor, save as his genius animates her, is she out of the long tradition of the imaginary deceiver whom many poets of Renaissance Italy, France, and England hopelessly "loved." Words may fashion a "reality" more abiding than the facts. The mistress was wanton, but scholars want her actual in vain. Weigh the words, and the word ways will not mislead you.

Shakespeare's poem *Venus and Adonis* is likewise sexually clear: The Queen of Love urges the unwilling mortal:

> I'll be a park, and thou shalt be my deer.
> Feed where thou wilt, on mountain or in dale.
> Graze on my lips, and if those hills be dry,
> Stray lower, where the pleasant fountains lie.
> Within this limit is relief enough,
> Sweet bottom-grass, and high delightful plain,
> Round rising hillocks, brakes obscure and rough,
> To shelter thee from tempest and from rain.
> Then be my deer, since I am such a park....

The Passionate Pilgrim speaks more cynically:

> The wiles and guiles that women work,
> Dissembled with an outward show,
> The tricks and toys that in them lurk
> The cock that treads them shall not know.

Shakespeare, of course, could be as direct as he desired. It may therefore be suggested that his bawdy remarks are couched in roundabout terms not because of any social taboo—censorship in his day was partly religious but mainly political—but, quite the reverse, because to the men and women of the court suggestion was more amusing than explicit statement. The meaning is hardly hidden, but the mental jump is left to the audience, which is thus doubly tickled—by the humor itself, and by its own perspicacity in seeing through the phraseology of the speaker. Each looks at his neighbor, and shares the knowing smile.

The noble contemporaries of Shakespeare were equally free in their expression. That colorful courtier Sir Walter Ralegh (he never spelled his name with an *i*) had an unpredictably obstreperous son. One day, as John Aubrey relates the incident in his *Brief Lives*, they were invited together to a state dinner, and Sir Walter admonished his son to behave. He did—until a silence midway of the meal, which he broke: "I was with a whore this afternoon. She let me tug and kiss her, but when I wanted to ride her she drew away, and exclaimed: 'Fie! I fucked your father not half an half ago!'" In the moment, Sir Walter boxed his son's ears. It was of course unthinkable for a son to strike his father. So he slapped the man next to him, crying: "Box about, and it will come round to him." Aubrey was a frank forerunner of today's gossip columnists.

George Pettie in 1581 warned: "I am of this minde, that the making of rime should not make a Poet use naughtie wordes." His warning was ignored by Massinger and Dekker, who in their play *The Virgin Martyr* made punny rhyme: "A pox on your Christian cockatrices! They cry, like poulterers' wives, No money, no coney."

In 1593 Philip Stubbes complained that books "full of all filthiness, scurrility, bawdry, dissoluteness, cosonage, cony-catching and the like ... are either quickly licensed or at least easily tollerate, without any denyall or contradiction whatsoever." And in 1609 Henry Chettle protested that ballad-mongers on the London streets hawked lascivious ballads, spoiling the market for honest men's wares. The preservation of order was then more important than the regulation of morals; in all those days, there is record of only one ballad forbidden "until the indecentness be reformed." Ben Jonson wrote of a critic:

> I have not salt: no bawdrie he doth mean,
> For wittie, in his language, is obscene.

In his 1618 play, *Amends For Ladies*, Nathaniel Field has a widow exclaim: "O man, what art thou when thy cock is up!"

Freedom of reference was not confined to the playwrights and the playboy cavaliers. John Donne, the Dean of St. Paul's, as noted for his polished sermons as for his metaphysical verse, was direct in his desires though decorous in his diction, as when he wrote "To His Mistress Going to Bed":

> License my roving hands, and let them go
> Before, behind, between, above, below....
> To teach thee, I am naked first; when then
> What needst thou have more covering than a man.

Another cleric that wrote about sex, definitely but with verbal decorum, was Robert Herrick, Vicar of Dean Prior, Devonshire, in his *Hesperides, Works both Humane and Divine* (1648). In those days before toilet tissue or Sears Roebuck catalogues, he begins by addressing his book:

> Who with thy leaves shall wipe (at need)
> The place where swelling Piles do breed:
> May every ill that bites or smarts
> Perplexe him in his hinder parts.

Most of the poems in the volume are short, and human all too human. One "To His Mistresses" (Note the plural) is a plea for renewed potency. One of his verses to Anthea ends diffidently:

> Anthea bade me tye her shooe;
> I did, and kist the Instep too:
> And would have kist unto her knee
> Had not her blush rebukèd me

—but he promises more: "The rest Ile speak, when we meet both in bed." To Julia he wrote fifty-three poems: to her leg (which also he longed to kiss), to her breasts, to the nipples on her breasts. He mocks betrayed and angry husbands in a quatrain:

> Scribble for whordome whips his wife, and cryes
> He'll slit her nose; But blubb'ring she replyes:
> Good Sir, make no more cuts i' th' outward skin,
> One slit's enough to let Adultry in.

His most detailed poem relates a penic dream, of still another damsel:

> I dreamed this mortal part of mine
> Was Metamorphoz'd to a vine;
> Which crawling one and every way
> Enthrall'd my dainty Lucia.
> Methought, her long small legs and thighs
> I with my tendrils did surprize,
> Her Belly, Buttocks, and her Waste
> By my soft Nerv'lets were embraced . . .
> But when I crept with leaves to hide
> Those parts which maids keep unespy'd,
> Such fleeting pleasures there I took
> That with the fancies I awook;
> And found (Ah me!) this flesh of mine
> More like a *Stock* than like a *Vine*.

During the years when the Roundheads were casting their gloom upon the land, and the theatres, as "antichambers to the brothel," were shut down, Andrew Marvell was Milton's assistant as Latin Secretary to Cromwell. After the Restoration, he was an active member of Parliament; but under both regimes his poetry was quiet and reflective, full of praise of gardens and country life. Yet, considering the context, and how odd the choice of the term, it is difficult to believe that, in his lines *To His Coy Mistress,* he did not have in mind Chaucer's use of the word *quaint:*

> But at my back I always hear
> Time's wingéd chariot hurrying near:
> And yonder all before us lie
> Deserts of vast eternity.
> Thy beauty shall no more be found,
> Nor, in thy marble vault, shall sound
> My echoing song: then worms shall try
> That long preserved virginity
> And your quaint honor turn to dust;
> And into ashes all my lust.
> The grave's a fine and private place,
> But none, I think, do there embrace. . . .

With the Restoration, the shrewd but lusty King Charles II, called the merry monarch, brought reveling courtiers home from France. The epitome of Restoration license was John Wilmot, Earl of Rochester, whom the *New Century Handbook of English Literature* describes as "a favorite of Charles II and of various court ladies and their waiting women." No man in high position has been freer in his speech; alternately he was banished from court for his insolence and welcomed back for his wit. His play *Sodom* (1689) is supposed to be a satire of homosexuality at the courts of James I of England and of "Monsieur," the brother of the King of France. (Even so staid a volume as Geddes Mac-Gregor's 1968 *Literary History of the Bible* refers to James I as "Queen James." In Kenneth Tynan's 1976 *Carte Blanche,* a brief travesty of *Sodom* shows three court courtesans excited over two men with exaggeratedly extended phalluses. Rochester named two of the courtesans Fuckadilla and Cunticula.)

More representative of the play's theme is the following passage:

> I would desire you to make a pass
> Once more at Pocherello's Royal arse;
> Besides, Sir Pin has such a gentle skin
> 'Twould tempt a saint to thrust his pintle in.
> Come my soft flesh of Sodom's dear delight,
> To honoured lust thou art betrayed tonight,
> Lust with thy beauty cannot brook delay;
> Between thy pretty haunches I will play.

For each of Charles's mistresses, Rochester found admiring words, as "Her hand, her foot, her very look's a cunt." Of Nell Gwyn's hold on the royal heart he wrote a poem, "The Angler," with the lines:

> However weak and slender be the string,
> Bait it with Cunt, and it will hold a king.

This time, he was banished from court for a whole month; on his return, he found himself pilloried in anonymous verses, written by or for the King, which pictured him

> Through all the Town, the common Fucking Post,
> On whom each Whore relieves her tingling Cunt.

Rochester was verbally more restrained, but politically no less daring, in his comments on King Charles himself, as in his mock epitaph:

> Here lies our sovereign lord the King,
> Whose promise none relies on;
> He never said a foolish thing,
> Nor ever did a wise 'un.

To this Charles responded, not with banishment, but with agreement: "This is very true, for my words are my own, and my actions are my ministers'."

While all the court buzzed with such activities and taunts and teasings, the common citizens were sufficiently aware of the licentiousness, and the consequent debilitating of the treasury, to carry through, when the astute Charles was succeeded by his more austere but more pig-headed brother, the bloodless revolution.

It must not be supposed, however, that bawdy recreation was the exclusive prerogative of the courtly circles. In the seventeenth and eighteenth centuries, licentious chapbooks were sold on the London streets by "flying stationers" and "running booksellers," and were purveyed through the countryside by wandering chapmen and hawkers.

With Augustan sobriety more Latin terms came into use, and blunt Saxon words were more frequently limited to books proffered by peddlers crying their wares, or in shops "under the counter." But while the words might be more decorous, the ideas,

especially in the theatre, were sexually explicit. A song in John
Dryden's *Marriage à la Mode* (1671) runs:

When Alexis lay prest
In her Arms he loved best,
With his hands round her Neck
And his head on her Breast,
He found the fierce pleasure too hasty to stay,
And his soul in the tempest just dying away.

When Celia saw this,
With a sigh, and a kiss,
She cryd, oh my dear, I am rob'd of my bliss;
'Tis unkind to your love, and unfaithfully done,
To leave me behind you, and dye all alone.

The youth, though in hast,
And breathing his last,
In pitty dyed slowly, while she dyed more fast;
Till at length she cryd, Now, my dear, now let us go,
Now dye my Alexis, and I will dye too.

Thus entranced they did lye,
Till Alexis did try
To recover new breath, that again he might dye,
Then often they dyed, but the more they did so,
The Nymph dyed more quick, and the Shepherd more slow.

This song was so popular that within the year it was reprinted in
Covent Garden Drollery, then in *New Court Songs* and *Westminster Drollery* (both 1672) and in two more collections. Another song in *Covent Garden* proclaims the pleasures of promis-
cuity:

Away with this legal fruition,
The pennance of flegmatick love,
Devised by some old Politician
Whose sinewes no longer could move;
Since wenching is modish, and beauty is common,
Why should we wed the defects of a woman?

The Husband has all the vexation,
The quarrels and care of the sheets,
Fair Perriwigs and Fops, in the fashion,
For nothing, enjoy all the sweets.
Since wenching is modish, etc.

If the Wife has witt, beauty, or portion,
Fine Cloathes and Gallants must be had,
She followes the Court for Promotion:
And heigh for the new Masquerade.
Since wenching is modish, etc.

When the Chaos was made a Creation
And all things in order did move,
The wisest in every nation
Went in unto all they did love.
Since wenching is modish, etc.

Each bout is a feast of new pleasure
To those that may any where feed;
The bees have all nature's sweet treasure,
But drones are confined to a weed.
Since wenching is modish, and beauty is common,
Why should we wed the defects of a woman?

(By a probably unconscious censorial slip, the first printing of
the *Covent Garden Drollery* worded the refrain: " Since wenching is modest . . ."!) The *Drollery* also contains a song by Aphra
Behn, that ends:

My greedy eyes no ayde required
To tell their amorous Tale:
On her that was already fired
'Twas easie to prevail.
I did but kiss and claspe her round
Whilst they my thoughts exprest,
And laid her gently on the ground:
Ah! Who can guess the rest.

The next year, in her comedy *The Dutch Lover,* Mrs. Behn has
Francisca sing this (with the necessary sex changes) to divert
her mistress. The song was reprinted in six anthologies; the last
of them suggested that it is autobiographical, "made upon her
Self and her very good friend Mr. Boyle," and it adds:

As amorous as these Verses may be thought, they have been reduced to bring them within the Rules of Decency, which all
writers ought to observe, or instead of a Diversion they will become a Nuisance.

An amusing turn of the sexes developed from the fact that
with the Restoration, actresses appeared for the first time on the

English public stage. All Shakespeare's feminine characters were in his day portrayed by young men; Shakespeare smiles at this practice when Rosalind, delivering the Epilogue to *As You Like It,* ends:

> If I were a woman, I would kiss as many of you as had beards that pleased me, complexions that liked me, and breaths that I defied not. And I am sure as many as have good beards or good faces or sweet breaths will, for my kind offer, when I make curtsy bid me farewell.

The new actresses were equally amusing, but less modest. Usually a woman, dressed as a man, addressed the audience. The Prologue to Dryden's *Marriage à la Mode* ends with an invitation to the three types of spectator:

> We'll follow the new Mode, which they begin,
> And treat them with a Room and Couch Within:
> For that's one way (how e'er the Play falls short)
> T' oblige the Town, the City, and the Court.

The Epilogue to *The Parson's Wedding,* by Thomas Killigrew, is even more outspoken:

> When boys played women's parts, you'd think the Stage
> Was innocent in that untempting Age.
> No; for your amorous Fathers then, like you,
> Amongst those Boys had Playhouse Misses too:
> They set those bearded Beauties on their laps,
> Men gave them Kisses, and the Ladies Claps.
> But they, poor hearts, could not supply our room:
> They went but Females to the Tyring-room;
> While we, in kindness to ourselves and you,
> Can hold out Women to our Lodgings too.

Dryden's cousin, Jonathan Swift, was less concerned with verbal propriety; he wrote many poems that are quite blunt in their wording. He wrote pseudonymously a comparison of a woman and a cloud, then composed an answer, the Cloud speaking:

> Even Jove, and Mercury his pimp
> No higher climb than Mount Olymp,
> (Who makes you think the Clouds he pierces?
> He pierce the Clouds! He kiss their arses!) ...

And when Apollo struts on Pindus
We see him from our kitchen windows:
Or, to Parnassus looking down,
We piss upon his Lawrel Crown. . . .

The poem ends, condescending to the other author (Swift himself) with what is now a cliché:

We own, your Verses are melodious,
But such Comparisons are odious.

Among the several verse riddles Swift wrote is one on the posteriors, and one of ninety-five lines on a privy, beginning

Come hither and behold the fruits
Vain man, of all thy vain pursuits—

itemizing the noisome odors and noxious works that find resolution in the mephitic atmosphere.

While most English writers "conformed," frank expression was to some extent maintained in Scotland, rising from doggerel and ballad into the realm of poetry in the work of Robert Burns. Note, in the third of these stanzas from Burns's "Holy Willie," behind the spurious piety the unrepentent arrogance:

O Lord—yestreen—Thou kens—wi Meg—
Thy pardon I sincerely beg.
O may't ne'er be a living plague
To my dishonor,
And I'll ne'er lift a lawless leg
Again upon her.

Besides, I farther maun avow
Wi' Leagie's lass, three times, I trow.
But Lord, that Friday I was fou
When I came near her,
Or else, Thou ken, Thy servant true
Wad never steer her.

Maybe Thou lets this fleshy thorn
Buffet Thy servant e'en and morn
Lest he o'er proud and high should turn
That he's sae gifted:
If sae, Thy hand must e'en be borne
Until Thou lift it.

Pornography need not be verbally obscene. The three international classics in the field—though coarser versions have proliferated—were in their original form free from any words that
could not be spoken, in other context, in a Victorian drawing-
room. Yet Cleland's English *Fanny Hill*, we are told, helped
warm the tents of both blue and gray in the American Civil War.
The French *Gamiani* is supposed to have been written by Alfred
de Musset in revenge, after George Sand contemptuously replaced him as her lover; others state that he wrote it to sub-
stantiate a boast that he could detail the wildest of sexual activities in the most genteel of words. (When Musset fell sick in
Venice in 1824, George Sand left him for the doctor she had
called to treat him; in his publicly printed *Confessions of a Child
of the Century*, 1836, he acquits her of all blame.) The German
Letters of a Soprano similarly contains no word that a modest
Victorian maiden would have blushed to hear.

The authors of these works were of course aware of their
verbal discretion. When Cleland, his printer, and his publisher
were arrested, Cleland generously tried to exonerate his associ-
ates; he wrote to Lovel Stanhope of the Secretary of State's
office (November 13, 1749) that "they were deceived by my
avoiding those rank words in the work, which are all that they
judge obscenity by."

It is interesting to note that, in 1706–1709, when lewd parodies
of the devotional book *The Fifteen Joys of Our Lady* were published—*The Fifteen Comforts of Matrimony, The Fifteen Comforts of a Wanton Wife, The Fifteen Plagues of a Maidenhead*—
the only one prosecuted was the last: virginity must not be trifled
with. But their writers laundered the language of the bawdy
books.

The language of speech and song was still free. Tom D'Urfey,
in his 1720 *Pills to Purge Melancholy*, says in song: "All my
delight Is a cunny in the night." The *School of Venus* (1744)
testifies to the freedom of speech: "(You) can now without
blushing call prick, stones, ballocks, cunt, tarse, and the like
names." Apart from ballads and other bawdy broadsheets, however, the printed word was more restrained.

What went underground in print found vent in the private
clubs of the Georgian rakes. The oldest of these, The Medmenham Monks, commonly known as the Hell-Fire Club, became a
public scandal when the papers of John Wilkes were examined
on his arrest for antigovernment activities in 1763. The motto of
Medmenham Abbey on the Thames was borrowed from Rabelais'

Thélème: *Fay ce que voudras,* "Do what you will." The other two clubs, starting in Scotland but soon meeting also in London, lasted beyond Victoria's reign, we are told, to the brink of the First World War. They fuse legends of three peoples. Founded in Anstruther, Fife, in 1732 was The Ancient and Most Puisant Order of the Beggar's Benison and Merryland, the name of which recalls the adventure of King James and the gaberlunzie. The Sovereign of the Order, at its ceremonies, wore a wig of fabulous repute, traced to Cleopatra. When Mark Antony was growing bald, Cleopatra and her maids laughingly presented him with a wig—made of their pubic hairs. This was borne back to Rome as a trophy by Augustus Caesar, and worn on revel evenings by a succession of emperors until in 328 Constantine, moving his capital to Byzantium (Constantinople), presented it to the Bishop of Rome, the Pope. In the Vatican, it was augmented by the thick sporran of pubic hair that the Queen of Sheba had forfeited to Solomon, which also was among the papal treasures. The wig was sent by Pope Clement X as a gift to Charles II, in the Church's endeavor to win England back to Catholicism. Charles refreshed it with hairs of his mistresses, then presented it to his close friend, loyal through all his misfortunes, the Earl of Moray, who was an officer of the Order of the Beggar's Benison. At each new member's initiation, in addition to public auto-eroticism, he had to proffer hair of his wife or mistress, to keep the wig in state.

The wig's importance in the rites is shown by the fact that, when in 1775 some of the members of the Order broke away, they carried it with them and named their group The Wig Club, which became even more successful in England. Among its known members were George IV, four dukes, seventy-three peers of the realm, thirty baronets, and at least two bishops. Women, while not members, were needed and welcome at the meetings —masked until they saw all the attending men, so that if any had a husband or a brother present she might, if she wished, be excused for the rest of that evening. Complete verbal freedom, as well as physical, was enjoined on all present, so that words seldom printed were kept alive by the ribald rakes and their doxies.

The word *rake,* incidentally, is an abbreviation of *rake-hell,* the word implying that soon the person will be busy raking the hot coals to keep hell's fires burning.

Thus we approach the Victorian regime, with a queen whose most noted aesthetic expression was "We are not amused." On the threshold of the nineteenth century, Tom Morton wrote the play *Speed the Plough;* a query in it, "What will Mrs. Grundy say?" became the watchword Thomas Bowdler and his rigid sister came chillingly to apply. Leigh Hunt went so far as to change Chaucer's direct "Thy breath full sour stinketh" to "Thy breath resembleth not sweet marjoram"! Thackeray, as editor, rejected a poem of Elizabeth Barrett Browning because it contained the word *harlot.*

Thackeray, despite his accordance, characterized his time as "if not the most moral, certainly the most squeamish." Recent books such as *The Other Victorians,* and the Victorian, but recently released, sex-obsessed *My Secret Life* expose the volcanic fires of lust beneath the quiet decorum of the surface; but the language was subjected to a temporary scouring. Tables and pianos no longer had *legs,* only *limbs.* Gentlemen did not wear such innominable articles as *breeches* or *trousers;* over a dozen terms such as *unmentionables* were employed; Dickens used this, also *unwhisperables* and *etherials.* Other items were similarly genteelized. Ladies at table might ask for the *bosom* of the fowl. The harmless animal the *ass* became a *donkey;* the *cock* of the walk came up as a *rooster;* the farm *haycock* turned into a *haystack.* "Sam Slick" jokingly turned a *coxswain* into a *rooster-swain,* but that plump fruit the *apricock* is now and forever an *apricot*—the *Random House Dictionary,* rather naively for 1966, says "by mishearing." It was no doubt for fear of miss-hearing that Bronson Alcox changed his name to Alcott, a blessing for his daughter Louisa May, who wrote the girls' best-sellers *Little Women, Jo's Boys,* and more.

The laundering of literature began before the Bowdlers. James Plumtre in 1805 published a Shakespeare song-book, in which "Under the greenwood tree, who loves to *lie* with me" became *work;* "With everything that pretty is *My Lady sweet arise*" was turned into *For shame thou sluggard rise!*

There was an unofficial censorship exercised by the major Victorian booksellers. "Moral" Mudie, who began in the 1840s, by 1861 had 800,000 books in stock at his New Oxford Street store. H. W. Smith (the "ruler of the Queen's Navee" who never went to sea, pilloried in *H.M.S. Pinafore*) in 1851 acquired monopoly of the train-station bookstalls, and the firm has stores all over England; he was nicknamed Old Morality. The pressure of such monopolists on the Victorian writers can hardly be overemphasized. Although Humphrey House in his study of *The Dickens World* called the nineteenth-century underworld "drenched in sex," you see little indication of this in Dickens's writings. On the contrary, in his introduction to the 1841 edition of *Oliver Twist*, Dickens declared that he had "banished from the lips of the lowest character I introduced any expression that could by possibility offend." In that same decade, pornographic books and snuffboxes with obscene pictures were sold not only at Oxford and Cambridge but at boarding schools for young ladies. What is comparatively open today was carried on covertly in Victoria's time. As Scribe in nineteenth-century France expressed it in one of his vaudeville songs:

> *Cela ne se dit pas,*
> *Mais cela peut se faire.*

> Such things aren't spoken of,
> But they may be done.

Among works still buried in Victorian cupboards, according to *Obscenity and the Law* (1956) by Norman St. John-Stevas, is an obscene opera by Gilbert and Sullivan. This work, *The Sod's Opera*, we are told, includes the characters "Count Tostoff, the Brothers Bollox, a pair of hangers-on, and Scrotum, a wrinkled old retainer. For many years a copy of the opera was kept in the guard room at St. James's Palace." St. John-Stevas gives no authority for this, and I find it hard to believe that Gilbert, who as director allowed his chorus girls no costumes more revealing than those in a Victorian drawing-room, and Sullivan, who composed sacred songs and was favored by Queen Victoria, wrote such a work. Indeed, the tightrope of their relationship demanded such delicate balance that neither would have wanted the other to have such knowledge of him. If *The Sod's Opera*— *sod* being short for *sodomite*—existed, the unknown author (in fashion familiar down the ages) probably sought the prestige of attribution to such noted names. I record the report, and my dubitancy.

This brings to mind, however, the changed attitude, and the freer use of words, in the field of male and female homosexuality. While *The Ballad of Reading Gaol* resulted from Oscar Wilde's incarceration for homosexual activities in 1895, on release he lived outcast from society. A satirical obituary had wide underground circulation:

> When Oscar Wilde, as all men must,
> Went off to meet his God,

He found, to his extreme distress,
The nether pit was bottomless.
For him that was not odd,
For each man's punishment is just,
And he returned, not dust to dust,
But barren sod to sod.

In less "advanced" countries, the stigma still holds; in Yemen, for example, a man convicted of homosexual activity was executed in 1966. But before then, in France, noted authors discussed their own (as one used to say) urning predilection without loss of fame or favor; in England, persons of that ilk appear on the list of the Queen's honors, and are to be addressed as Sir; and in the United States, there is a national gay association, to which persons prominent in public life announce their affiliation, and colleges have set aside lounges for the tribe and the tribade. *The New York Times* (January 9, 1977) gave a full-page spread to the headline protest "Candidate for the Priesthood Says Jesuit Superiors Bar His Ordination Because He Is a Homosexual," and a picketing parade for him was shown on television news the next weekend; and *The Times* on January 11 announced that an avowed lesbian, officer in a homosexual organization, had been ordained as an Episcopal priest—adding that in various parts of the country there are more than thirty congregations composed of homosexuals.

The changed moral attitudes reach into other areas as well. Not only do increasing numbers of young couples live together "without benefit of clergy," as the phrase used to go, but prominent women—a stage star, a member of Parliament—openly become unmarried mothers; and virginity has lost its hallowed hold. Contrast Goldsmith's verses in *The Vicar of Wakefield* (1762):

When lovely woman stoops to folly
And finds too late that men betray,
What charm can soothe her melancholy,
What art can wash her guilt away?

The only art her guilt to cover,
To hide her shame from every eye,
To give repentance to her lover
And wring his bosom—is to die.

—with the nonchalance pictured by T. S. Eliot, two hundred years later. Eliot repeats Goldsmith's first line, trivializing it by sticking *and* on the end—and has the woman turn on some music, perhaps in pleasant reminiscence or anticipation of further follies, perhaps a bit bored by it all. What once was ruin has become routine.

The cockney, of course, was never bound by middle-class prudery. Although the cockney's contributions to the language did not become significant until the nineteenth century, he was marked out some three centuries earlier, as "one ignorant of country matters." The word cockney is from early English *cocken,* the plural of *cock,* and *ey,* 'egg'. A malformed egg was called a cock's egg; then the term was applied to a silly child, and finally to one that in the United States would be called a greenhorn. *The Beggar of Bednell Green,* a play of 1600, speaks of a London cockney asking whether a haycock is better roasted or boiled. A cockney, is, in English parlance, one born within earshot of Bow Bells, of St. Mary-le-Bow on Cheapside—which, around 1400, called Dick Whittington back to be Lord Mayor of London. The term, like Quaker, first given in scorn, has become the normal appellation.

The talk of the cockney, including his rhyming slang, has the color of the London streets, rough, and muddy—and sexy. I draw as illustrations three words granted entry into the 1972 *Supplement* of the O.E.D. *Berk,* defined as a fool, is given as rhyming slang from *Berkshire Hunt:* the rhyme word is *cunt,* which is also slang for a fool (male or female). *Bristol* is given as slang for 'breast' (rhyming slang, *Bristol City: titty*); *cobblers,* slang for 'nonsense' (*cobbler's awls: balls*). He's fond of a plate (of ham) rhymes with gam, short for *gamahuche,* a French term for fellatio.

> The monkey he got drunk,
> He sat on the elephant's trunk;
> The elephant sneezed and fell on his knees
> And what became of the monk, the monk,
> And what became of the monk?

Elephants is good rhyming slang for *drunk.* But if a cockney says "He's a nelephant!" that is a different story. It's good argot, too; an outsider would never guess. For the rhyme is the well-known London pub The Elephant and Castle, and the base word is the cockney pronunciation of *arsehole* (*arsle*). Vulgar is not a word in the cockney vocabulary.

The cockney may also use letter-words: "Ef you see Kate, I'm leaving." "See you any Tyoosday, comin' down the street." Comparable are the current Brooklyn snub words: "I have a new car license, 4 Q."

Jerk, now also slang for a fool, was originally a masturbator. Henry Miller's 1976 book *J'suis pas plus con qu'un autre* is translated, "euphemistically," says the *International Herald Tribune, I Aint More of a Jerk than the Next Man.* Release from the Victorian restraint came slowly. Frank Harris, who had made quite a name as essayist, raconteur, and editor—he hired Bernard Shaw as a critic for *The Saturday Review*—found himself dropped into mere notoriety on the publication of *My Life and Loves* (1923). Of his "life," he wrote that it developed in three stages: How I got on; How I got honour; How I got honest. His "loves," though decidedly plural, were more limited: How I got on her. But Harris complained that, after the book was published, the sale of all his works fell off. And indeed, when I met him shortly after, for his year in New York as editor and lecturer, he was quite short of funds.

Frank told of a lecture he had just given. At the end, a woman asked him to define a word he had used: *virgin.* He responded: "*Vir* is Latin for 'man'; *gin* is an old English word for a 'trap': a virgin is obviously a mantrap." Another woman protested: "A trap begins open, and ends closed; the reverse is true of the virgin." And so on. When Frank was through—there were three of us in his little office on lower Fifth Avenue—the other man snorted, and said: "You've concocted the whole story." I demurred: "You've corroborated it. *Concoct:* the first syllable is the French word for the trap, and the second syllable tells how it is sprung."

The freshest call for a more affirmative approach to the pleasures of sex has been voiced by D. H. Lawrence, who proclaimed: "Sex is a very powerful, beneficial and necessary stimulus in human life, and we are all grateful when we feel its warm, natural flow through us, like a form of sunshine."

But the fight for full freedom of speech and print was slow—and is not over. In America, the Supreme Court has acted on the question in varying ways. It upheld the conviction of Samuel Roth for selling pornography, and of Ralph Ginzburg apparently for his "lascivious" promotion of his magazine *Eros,* which he wanted to mail from Intercourse, Pennsylvania. But in the cases of *Ulysses* and *Lady Chatterley's Lover,* it ruled that no single word sufficed to make a book obscene; it must be judged by its general tenor and tone. This opened the floodgates to the four-letter taboo words, which are now almost ubiquitous in fiction and drama—save perhaps in the Gothic romance—and seem to be growing acceptable over the air, a little more rapidly in England, perhaps, than in America.

The American Supreme Court in 1960 set a threefold test of obscenity (recently allowing for the difference in local standards, which at once raised problems for publishers and film producers whose works are sold throughout the land): 1. the dominant theme taken as a whole appeals to prurient interest in sex; 2. the material is patently offensive because it affronts contemporary community standards; 3. the material is utterly without redeeming social values. A work must fit all three counts, to be barred.

There was a consequent gathering, at court cases, of critics who, earnestly believing in the freedom of the press, put forward for almost any book attacked the claim that it had artistic merit, hence social value. To such asseverations is largely due the reputation of Henry Miller, whose hyperbolic sexploits are proudly paraded in several supposedly autobiographical volumes. To him might be addressed the words written by Owen Seaman in Victorian times:

> The erotic affairs that you fiddle aloud
> Are as common as coin of the mint,
> And you merely distinguish yourself from the crowd
> By the fact that you put them in print.
>
> You're a prentice, my boy, in the primitive stage,
> And you itch, like a boy, to confess;
> When you know a bit more of the arts of the age
> You will probably talk a bit less.
>
> For your dull little vices we don't care a fig;
> It is *this* that we deeply deplore:
> You were cast for a common or usual pig,
> But you play the invincible bore.

In 1930, when John Ford's play *'Tis Pity She's a Whore* (1633) was revived in New York, the *Times* refused to print the title; it was advertised as *'Tis Pity*. For the 1960s revival, the name was used in full. Also in 1930, on the opening night of the revival of Dekker's *The Shoemaker's Holiday*, the audience heard the line: "She has a secret fault: she farts in bed"; it froze, and the line was at once cut from the production.

One may feel relieved that squeamishness has gone out of

fashion. In a delayed but, when it did come, a swift reaction, "we have long passed the Victorian era," Somerset Maugham summed it up, "when asterisks were followed after a certain interval by a baby." One need not, on the other hand, approve of the extent of the counterswing of the pendulum. I shall mention but four of the new plays of our day, to indicate the current freedom, or, if you prefer, license. *The Beard*, presented first in Los Angeles; then in New York and London in 1970, is a one-act play, its two characters Billy the Kid and June Harlow; it ends with the woman sitting with her legs spread, while the man nuzzles between. (When the same posture occurs in the film *Deep Throat*, the naked woman says: "Do you mind if I smoke while you eat?") The first full nudist show to become a hit on both sides of the Atlantic was Kenneth Tynan's *Oh! Calcutta!* The title is a play on the French *Oh, quel cul t'as!;* and in the show's advertisements, a flower adorns the indicated portion of the female anatomy. (One is reminded of Paul Valéry's remark, of the French literary radicals: "When one no longer knows what to do to astonish and survive, one offers one's pudenda to the public gaze.") More expansively sexual is the play that for its title with irreverent effrontery reverses the heartfelt plea of the ancient Jewish leader, "Let my people go!" to form the lewd solicitation *Let My People Come*. While this show flaunts the four-letter taboo words, listing them loudly in a song that protests There Are No Dirty Words, it by no means neglects the Latinized terms that even the circumspect *Times* admits to its pages. It presents a skit of a college (or perhaps just a prep-school) course in fellatio; one of the students is a male. Each tyro is practicing with a banana; the high point is attained when an overzealous student bites off the tip. Another skit displays the cunnilingus champion of a summer camp. The purpose of such "plays" seems to be (if I may employ a euphemism) to keratinize the spectators.

A play entitled simply *X*, presented at the London Royal Court Theatre in 1974, proposes that such activities be taught in the kindergarten, so that children may grow up to become properly fulfilled adults, instead of inhibited, frustrated, neurotic misfits. Are not more than half the hospital beds in England and the United States occupied by mental patients? And is not sexual maladjustment the major cause of mental strain? Let my people come early and often.

If the word *fellatio* had come into the language through normal channels—instead of being scooped up as a quick euphem-

ism to make the unprintable pass—it would have been *fellation*.
Incidentally, our writers are not so precise as the Romans, who
named two modes of buccal copulation: in *irrumationem*, the
mouth is a passive receptacle; in *fellationem*, the mouth employs
inciting force.

The extent to which frankness even about one's own sexual
life has reached is indicated by remarks of the First Lady in
1976 about her sleeping habits and her expectations of her
daughter; and by the (successful) presidential candidate about
his lustful thoughts. [It is an interesting psychological point
(determined by sex or party affiliation?) that the Republican
woman's euphemisms—*sleep with; having an affair*—are standard
English, while the Democrat man's—*shack up with; screw*—
are slang.] A scant generation ago, the public expression of such
thoughts, and the words of their expression, at the highest level
of our political life, would have been unthinkable.

While such thoughts are now publicly uttered, and motion
pictures and books have literally no holds barred, verses on the
subject, especially limericks, have had currency for many years,
passed along by mouth-to-mouth transfusion. The spooner,
though taking its name from a nineteenth-century victim of
metathesis, was much earlier a literary device—in French amusingly called the *contrepet:* French *pet*, 'fart'—and utilized as far
back as Rabelais, who turned *à Beaumont le Vicomte* into *à bon
con le vit monte.* One such spooner in English is in the form of
a conundrum: What is the difference in a boarding-house maid,
in the day and in the night? In the daytime, she's fair and
buxom; at night, she's . . . This sort of oral enjoyment of sex is
at least as frequent as the act itself.

One may, of course, be aware of the taboo words, even
cognizant of their origin and literary use, without making them
part of one's usual verbal equipment. Toward the extreme
polarities of illiteracy and supersophistication, their expression
may be frequent. They may occur in conversation among persons
of the same sex, more commonly, perhaps, among males. They
may be on the lips of fledgling rebels trying their wings. They
may find utterance in the intimacy of amorous engagement. By
most persons, they will be known, digested, and eschewed.

Contrasted with direct speech, which calls a spade a spade, and
with euphemism, which calls a spade a digging instrument,
plumps dysphemism, which calls a spade a dirty shovel. Dysphemism is intended as a stimulant; it seeks to increase the
relevant emotion. This emotion may, as in racial slurs, be anger,

or contempt. The English slurs against the Dutch have been mentioned. Syphilis, which the English used to call the French disease, was in France called the Italian sickness. *To take French leave* is, in French, *filer à l'anglais*. Neighbors are often the ones caught in derisive or derogatory phrases: "Taffy was a Welshman, Taffy was a thief." It's not good to *welsh* on a deal. In America there was for a time a host of terms contemptuous of the newly come Irish. *Irish confetti* meant 'bricks'. An *Irish buggy* was a wheelbarrow—"an invention which taught the Irish to stand on two feet." Nor are these slurs wholly gone from our coining: a July 1975 issue of the comic strip *Wizard of Id* spoke of the "famous seven-course Irish dinner: a boiled potato and a 6-pack." Such "fun" is always condescending. The technical term, *ethnophaulism* (Greek *phaulos*, 'ugly, mean'), seems to have been first used in 1944, in the subtitle to A. A. Rodack's *Dictionary of International Slurs*.

While dysphemism in the realm of sex may bring arousal, euphemism, intended to avoid offence, may prove a sedative. Chesterton protested that it lightens the evil, equating, for instance, one who sells her body with a girl walking along the street. Chief among those that have sought to color all our lives with the hues of hidden lechery are the pansexualists who have followed the questionable trail of Freud, who at every stage of life's journey tugs man into the mire.

If a man takes the advice of the ancient Greek which Alexander Pope framed as "Know then thyself . . . The proper study of mankind is man," what is he—ask Freud!—but a more or less aware narcissist? If he recognizes that the race and the individual, from their infancy, have survived by virtue of the exercise of curiosity, and if he somehow manages to keep that quality unextinguished through his days, he is manifestly a ("psychologically castrated") voyeur. If he plays, or enjoys watching, games, he is indulging in a symbolic reenactment of sadomasochistic desires. When a mother says of a happy babe: "Oh! I could just eat it up!" this is obviously a vestigium of cannibalism. And as the child grows, the mutual family affection, if not an Oedipus complex (the very name ill-chosen!) is nonetheless clearly a repressed incestuous desire. Thus the Freudian smudge bemeans every act and attitude, carrying beyond life to the mourners, who visit the cemetery on anniversaries in necrophiliac longing.

Psychologists used to explain our laughing at the man that slips on a banana peel as a sudden release of energy: we grow tense in empathy with the falling man; then, as we are still steady on our feet, our gathered emergency escapes as laughter. But now we are told that what we feel is *Schadenfreude,* a malicious joy in the discomfiture of others. Verbal wit is, in this view, a comparatively safe "sublimation," a harmless outlet for our suppressed and conventionally forbidden impulses. A neat travesty of this claim is the one-act play *Suppressed Desires* (1914) by Susan Glaspell, which reveals Stephen Brewster's suppressed desire caught in his name: Step hen, be rooster. This does not mean that all men are chicken-hearted.

The pertinent fact about the Freudians, who tar everyone with the same brush, is that a word spread thus universally loses its particular force. When we say that all men are mortal, we mention an objective and obvious, an indisputable and neutral, fact; but what value is there in calling John Doe a voyeur, if you and I and everyone else are all of us voyeurs? Though one may control or conceal the impulse better than another, if the lust is in all our hearts, who shall cast the first stone? Thus individual sins are glossed over by a general guilt. If everybody's wrong, everybody's right. A good Christian sentiment, if everyone were as Jesus. But in human terms, along with condemnation, discrimination has been washed away. In a comedy of 1923, by Frederick Lonsdale, the next to the last line is "I'm a goddam fool!" The last line, which gave the play its name, is *Aren't We All?* But then, down came the curtain. Thus, too general application of a term ends its valid use as a characterizing word. It is not merely the language that loses, but the mind.

The Nice Nellies of Victoria's days were in all likelihood well-meaning; but their innocence or ignorance prissyfied the language. Nor have scholars been untinged by this prudery. Thus in the O.E.D. there are definitions one today wonders how any informed lexicographer could have proffered. In Urquhart's translation of Rabelais, for instance, we are told that the infant Gargantua "would rock and loll in his cradle and nod his head, monocordising with his fingers and barytonising with his tail." The O.E.D., quoting only this passage, and changing the spelling, defines the two main words: "*Monochordize:* to perform on the monochord." Look, and you find: "*Monochord:* a musical instrument with a single string." For *barytonize:* "[?from preceding]." Preceding is "*Barytone:* the male voice of compass intermediate between tenor and bass. . . . But cf. French *baritonner,* to wag, or dangle, up and down." Gargantua wagging his tail, forsooth! The precocious infant was masturbating, and venting audible expulsions of anal wind.—Nor has this misdirection been corrected in the 1972 Supplement.

Unfortunately, such innocence is not limited to mid-Victorians; it persists in our own day. To the antipapist Tudors, *nunnery* was a slang term for a *brothel;* it is when Hamlet turns in disillusion upon Ophelia, set by her father and the King as a trap, that he bids her "Get thee to a nunnery!" But *The Reader's Encyclopedia of Shakespeare,* in the enlightened year of 1966, speaking of the dark lady of the Sonnets, lists "a certain Lady Negro, Abbess of Clerkenwell," with no hint that Clerkenwell was not a convent, not a genuine nunnery, but the red-light district of London, nor any indication that Abbess was Elizabethan slang for *whoremistress.* Slang may be informal, but innocence in a reference work is in no sense informing.

The O.E.D. *Supplement* editors seem trying to atone for previous omission by a generous sprinkling of the formerly taboo terms, not only in separate entries, but in illustrative quotations. One wishes they were as expert as they are expansive. They give separate listings to such variant spellings as *muthafucka, muthafukka;* but they supply an incorrect definition of *mutual masturbation;* they should have consulted the O.E.D. for the meaning of *mutual.* It is good, however, to see the "harmless drudge" grown bolder than Bowdler.

One normally uses euphemisms not for oneself, but for the listeners. For the very choice of a comely term, the selection of a seemly alternative expression, indicates that the basic word, with all its frank and natural implications, is in the speaker's mind. Probably no one is misled, but the good taste of the time may be preserved. Only, as the Roman said, and you of course have noticed, *Tempora mutantur, et nos mutamur in illis,* "Times change, and we change with them." The next line, in the Latin, says that men invariably change for the worse.

10.

POETRY AND PROSE

WORDS OF POETRY may be reached through thoughts of communication. There is no question that the basic function of language is to serve as a means of communication. What it communicates is more open to dispute.

Most linguists concur as to the three basic needs for which men use their language. There is, immediately, the need of finding out. We must recognize what to do, and how to do it, in order to keep alive and thriving. As immediate is the need of pointing out, of calling attention to a source of food, or of information, or of danger. Close upon these comes the need of crying out, of commanding, beseeching, uttering a prayer. In more sophisticated terms, these functions may be described as the seeking, and then the representation, of facts, of regularities and idiosyncrasies in nature and society, and then the triggering, guidance, or modification of actions regarding them. These basic needs have created three moods in the structure of the language: interrogative, indicative, imperative.

These needs, which are apparent by day, become more urgent in the dark of night. Primitive man was perhaps never free from the recurrent fear that the onset of the dreaded darkness might not be followed by the happy glow of dawn. That is why, as the heortologist reminds us, the important holy days, of the gods of light and life, as, even, the birth of Jesus, are celebrated when the year's darkening is checked and turns, and the days begin to grow longer.

The French thinker Alain saw enwombed in man's need of sleep the source of most of his progress. In the first place, man in the hours of slumber needs protection from savage beasts, from hostile neighbors; hence his clustering together; the organization of guards; the erection of walls: the beginnings of the city and of civilization. And while man sleeps, he dreams; and in those dreams the terrors multiply: monsters and demons, and friendly heroes and gods, do battle for man's body and awakening soul, and he has found religion. In the less fearful dreams imaginings persist, what today might be called "wish fulfillment" fancies; ideals and visions of glory are superimposed upon man's workaday labors, and he has created art. Thus, much of what we have established, what we cherish and prize, has risen from what Charles Lamb has called "night fears." Man's most earnest prayers are for tranquillity at night and of thankfulness in the morning.

While these basic needs, and their appropriate responses, were essential to man's survival in an indifferent world—populated, he long believed, by supernatural forces that had to be placated, won over, or warded off—there are other functions that words must perform, of almost equal importance. They must serve to express our emotions, sometimes on the spontaneous urge of our feelings, sometimes to convey and impart these to others. This, too, reaches out to the wide range of literature, of oratory, poetry, and drama. Fiction suggests a further use of words, in the development of fantasies, deliberate turnings from, or approximations of, the factual world, for relief and hopefulness and entertainment. And this in turn brings to mind the frequent if not pervasive use of words, in daily life, to hide our thoughts, disguise our feelings, conceal our past or intended actions: the vast range of deceptions and lies.

Some linguists make still another division of word use: naysaying, refusal, the negative. Others regard such an utterance as actually a positive statement, an "affirmation of the opposite." Indeed, every negative remark can be rephrased positively, with little change of meaning. There is no less force in the declaration "I will go" than in "I will not stay."

Unfortunately, these various uses of words are often confused. What is intended as a factual observation may be not only tinged with, but distorted by, feeling; and often a seeming truth, or a semitruth, will have the effect of an undetected lie. That is why in court one swears to a triple oath: to tell the truth, the whole truth, and nothing but the truth. Thus, as words build into ideas, it is important that they be clear, correct, complete.—But take note of the difference between a clear but potent liquid and a clear but empty glass.

Words in themselves have already been considered, in their threefold growth of sound, spelling, and significance.

The use of words in the expression of ideas calls for the application of logic. The earliest studies of logic enunciated three basic laws: *The law of contradictions:* Nothing can be both A and not-

A. *The law of the excluded middle:* Any thing is either A or not-A. *The law of identity:* A is A; any thing is itself. These may seem self-evident, but they are the basic conditions for all rational thinking. They are so basic that William James, in his *Pragmatism* (1906) felt it necessary to set down "the scholastic adage": Whenever you meet a contradiction, you must make a distinction. This permits the solution of many long-troubling problems, including, for a simple example, that raised in the query: When you walk around a tree on which a squirrel scrambles to be always facing you, do you walk around the squirrel? The distinction called for here involves the precise use of words demanded in logic.

Aristotle long ago arranged ideas in a hierarchical order, each stage preparatory to the next: 1. necessary and conceptual ideas, as in logic, mathematics, and analytical philosophy; 2. factual and empirical observations, as in science, history, and the law courts; 3. evaluative pronouncements, as in morals, government, and the criticism of art. Consideration will reveal that ideas of the first type provide the rules governing inquiry, the essential preliminary to the second type. And those of the second type yield corresponding technologies or applications, to serve in the realization of the desired ends developed in type three.

In this quest of the essence of reality, and our proper behavior in the search, the nineteenth-century French philosopher Comte sought also to arrange a hierarchy of the sciences, with arithmetic at the base. Following, in order of decreasing exactitude, he set geometry, mechanics, astronomy, physics, chemistry, biology (including physiology), and—least precise of the sciences—sociology. Psychology, as it grows scientific, will be absorbed in the final two; it remains outside the pale as long as it must depend upon introspection (of oneself, or reported) instead of objective observation, which may be repeated and checked by others. So deeply into all human activities has science penetrated, that it is hard to believe that the word *scientist* was not coined until 1840.

Underlying science spreads metaphysics (so called because it literally came *after* [Greek *meta*] physics in Aristotle's discussion), which seeks the principles, ideas of type 1, upon which science must rest. And beyond these, making no claim to cognition or representation of reality—save perhaps through a glass, darkly, as it holds "a mirror, as it were, up to nature"—is the vast range of art.

The fundamental value of art is the entertainment it provides. This is fundamental, not because it is the most valuable aspect of the work of art, but because without it no one would attend.

Although art of some kind, however rude or refined, comic strip or high tragedy, plays a part in every person's life, it is an optional enterprise. One may enjoy it at home, in a periodical or a book, or on a screen—I am considering only the verbal arts, though the point presses for them all, and for sports as well—or one may go to a motion picture or a play; or what you will. Thus, if you are not entertained, you may leave at intermission, or simply close the book, press the button, or turn the switch. To hold your attention, the work must entertain.

Beyond entertainment, out of the work of art wells also a greater awareness, an enlightenment. This is frequently blurred, as in blunt propaganda. Many books, plays, and motion pictures are drawn from current concerns, such as questioned conflicts or questionable conduct in high places. A friend of mine, a high official in Turkey, once told me of a disgraceful incident in the government; he paused a moment, then added: "I was so mortified I went home and wrote a poem!" Indignation may indeed be a valid impetus to art, at least as valid as personal ambition or as greed. Samuel Johnson said that only a fool would write for anything except money; Byron, on the other hand, often refused payment for his poems, writing for the pleasure and the glory. The objection to works that press an angry point is not that they are propaganda, but that too often they fail to be art. In fact, a work is not called propaganda unless the receptor senses that the author is biased, is pressing one side of the scales. Then the characters are likely to seem mechanical figures carrying the author's creed, mouthing his message; they are likely to be damned villains or shining heroes. But this is not the present consideration; the usually one-sided information that a thesis novel or a propaganda play proffers is not the enlightenment art in itself provides. There rises from a work of art not an indignant fervor, but an increased awareness of man's basic drives and fantasies and feelings. When Dido weeps at the departure of Aeneas, we do not feel sad because Dido is sad, or because author Virgil is sad. We are, rather, awakened to a fuller comprehension of the depths of human sadness; we become aware of potentialities in our own heart as in the hearts of others. In all likelihood, during the experience we are not conscious of any increased understanding. We go from the work of art stimulated, and enlightened unaware.

The final gift of all great art is exaltation. Before a tragedy, we quicken with a sense of man's resolution, holding his head high in the face of insuperable odds, taking death as a glad sacrifice in the defense of his ideals. Even a "villain" may elicit this response. We watch Macbeth, caught in a momentum he cannot control, deluded and led on by false assurances, in his final moments standing erect, defying fate and, if not so living, nobly dying. As psychiatrist Joos A. M. Meerloo has stated: "Man does not have to be victorious to be accepted by the gods."

High comedy erects a carefree front before the insignificance of man's endeavor; life is a game we play to our inevitable losing— but we will lose bravely, with a smile and a jest and a final lift of the head as our last chips are swept away. Doomed though we are to mortality, we hold a gladness and a pride at being human.

Entertainment, enlightenment, exaltation.

Among the verbal arts that grant these boons, the oldest is poetry. Some students of early man believe that the first speech was song. But poetry, like beauty, is easier to elucidate in an essay than to confine in a sentence. In fact, poetry is doubly difficult to define, because it has two distinct meanings, one for the general reader, even the college graduate not specializing in literature, and quite another for those of especially literary concern. To the general reader, poetry is mainly a question of How; to the specialist, mainly of What. One considers the form; the other, the substance.

Most persons regard poetry as involving a special form, which we call verse. The word *verse* comes from a Latin word that means 'turning' (as shown in the word *reverse*): While prose runs on and on, and across a page to the edge of the paper; verse moves along to a particular extent, then turns to begin again, as on a new line.

Most readers of verse will be aware of three varieties: verse, blank verse, and free verse. The first two of these arrange their words in *meter*. In them, the natural but unorganized rhythm of all speech is patterned into measured units. A cluster of normally two or three syllables, one of them accented, makes a *foot*. The most common foot is the *iambic*, which consists of an unaccented syllable followed by an accented one. The meter is determined by the number of feet in a line. For short lyrics, the most common meter is of three or four feet, but for longer poems, the five-foot or *pentameter* line is more frequent.

Gray's "Elegy in a Country Churchyard," long the most popular poem in English, is written in iambic pentameter. It begins:

> The curfew tolls the knell of parting day,
> The lowing herd winds slowly o'er the lea,

> The ploughman homeward plods his weary way,
> And leaves the world to darkness and to me.

The general reader will recognize in these lines, not only the iambic measure, but a pattern at the line-ends that is also a regular concomitant of verse, namely the chiming of accordant sounds that we call *rhyme*.

The word *rhyme* developed along a confusion of terms. It comes from Latin *rithmus*, from Greek *rhythmos*, meaning 'measured motion'—much as *rhythm* does in English today. In medieval Latin, *rithmus* was applied to the new accentual verse, as distinguished from the Greek and classical Latin poetry, the lines of which are measured by quantity, by the length of the syllables, the time taken to pronounce them—not, like the new poetry, by accent and counted feet. Then a double change occurred. Since the new accented poetry ended in chiming sounds, *rithmus* came to be applied to this terminal identity. And in the Germanic languages the word was cut to a monosyllable, in English merging with the old Saxon word *rime*, which meant a 'number', or 'counting'. Finally, in the Renaissance, when many words were altered to match the ancient Greek spelling, the English unwittingly approached the classical origin, and established the word as *r.h.y.m.e.* Rhyme in Greek and Latin poetry is rare, accidental; and indeed in Renaissance criticism, which looked upon the ancients as models, rhyme was frequently attacked as an unwanted jingling. It is both so pleasant, and so helpful in marking various changes, that it has persisted as a characteristic of verse.

Blank verse is simply verse without rhyme; but one pattern of this, the unrhymed iambic pentameter, is so frequent that often when the term *blank verse* is used, this particular pattern is understood. Most long poems in English, like Milton's *Paradise Lost*, are written in this blank verse, as is the greater part of every play of Shakespeare, as well as most other poetic dramas before this century. Within the basic pattern of iambic pentameter, however, blank verse avoids monotony by the frequent shifting of pause and stress, as in these words of Prospero toward the end of *The Tempest:*

> Our revels now are ended. These our actors,
> As I foretold you, were all spirits and
> Are melted into air, into thin air:
> And, like the baseless fabric of this vision,
> The cloud-capp'd towers, the gorgeous palaces,
> The solemn temples, the great globe itself,

Yea, all which it inherit, shall dissolve
And, like this insubstantial pageant faded,
Leave not a rack behind. We are such stuff
As dreams are made on, and our little life
Is rounded with a sleep.

There are added variety and beauty with the interplay, sometimes the counterplay, of the set meter and the rhythmic flow of
the words as they develop the sense. Two falls pictured in Milton's
Paradise Lost illustrate this variety. First is the (to Milton and
his contemporaries) actual fall of Lucifer:

Him the Almighty Power
Hurled headlong flaming from the ethereal sky
With hideous ruin and combustion down—.

Second is the merely fabled fall of Mulciber (Vulcan),

flung by angry Jove
Sheer o'er the crystal battlements; from dawn
To noon he fell, from noon to dewy eve,
A summer's day; and with the setting sun
Dropped from the zenith like a falling star
On Lemnos, the Aegean isle: thus they
Relate, erring. . . .

The two passages are in the same meter; yet in the second the
final words are hardly needed to show that it is sheer fancy.
"There is no escape from meter," said T. S. Eliot, "there is only
mastery."

The French, for their poetic dramas, have not used blank verse;
their lines, in rhyming pairs, are of six feet, *hexameters*. These are
regularly arranged so that a pair of single rhymes (*sphere, sou-
venir;* also called *masculine rhyme*) alternates with a pair of
double rhymes (*martial, impartial;* also called *feminine rhyme*).
Italian, with most of its words ending in a vowel, revels in feminine rhyme. There are also triple rhymes (*cynical, pinnacle*), but
these occur seldom in serious English poetry—Byron is a bright
exception:

But—Oh ye lords of ladies intellectual,
Inform us truly, have they not henpecked you all?—

though trisyllabic rhymes are playfully exuberant in musical comedy and in the lively lyrics of humorous versifiers. Byron has even

stretched a syllable farther, rhyming *Orientalism* with *sentimentalism.*

Note that in English the concordance of sound goes back only to the accented vowel; the preceding consonants are different; in French, if the meaning is different, the entire word may rhyme. Thus *meet, mete, meat*, being a perfect match in sound, are imperfect rhymes in English; their counterparts would make good rhyme in French.

Poets using regular verse forms in English may violate one or another of these principles. Such a violation is referred to as poetic license. This is not, however, like a driver's license, a certificate of permission; it is a case of liberty overstepping its bounds, into license. This may occasionally be allowed a good poet, for his greater accomplishments; it may even at times achieve a felicity beyond the reach of rule; yet the warning remains, that

> Although few tyros seem to know it,
> It's not one's license makes one poet.

Verse and blank verse were the two patterns of modern poetry until about the second quarter of the nineteenth century, when the French began to take a few liberties with their forms, calling the looser lines *vers libre*. Then Walt Whitman burst upon the American scene with what has since become the most frequent form, *free verse.*

The opposite of verse is *prose*. But between free verse and prose, except for the manner in which they are set upon the page, it is sometimes hard to tell the difference. For free verse abandons both meter and rhyme, and may consist of a single figure, as Carl Sandburg's "much admired poem, Fog":

> The fog comes
> on little cat feet.
> It sits looking
> over harbor and city
> on silent haunches
> and then moves on.

Set that in lines across the page, and who would discern that it is verse? The barriers break down completely in the work of some writers, who label their products "poetic prose," "polyphonic prose," "poems in prose." In fact, Whitman referred to his own *Leaves of Grass* as prose. Robert Frost once remarked that writing free verse is like playing tennis with the net down.

The *Leaves of Grass* began in 1855 as twelve poems, but through several years and editions grew to a thick volume; it is saturated, as Whitman wrote,

> with the vehemence of pride and audacity of freedom necessary to loosen the mind of still-to-be-formed America from the folds, the superstitions, and all the long, tenacious and stifling anti-democratic authorities of the Asiatic and European past.

[The formation of words being, as I have said, the basic democratic process, working unperturbed within whatever political regime may oppress the people, it seems inevitable, as we pass America's bicentennial year, that Whitman's hopes for democracy come here into brief consideration. Whitman was over-optimistic. As James Fenimore Cooper pointed out when our nation began, government by the people depends upon the quality of the average man, and the "average" is necessarily low. It goes but halfway. Thus actual democracy is less an attainment than an ideal, the nearness of our approach to which depends upon the quality of human nature. Democracy, like other abstract terms, exists in only two ways: as an idea in the mind; and in the actions of individuals who exemplify the idea. Perhaps one may hope that, as in the first thirty thousand years (say) of civilization's struggle, man has advanced tremendously in control of the natural forces without; so, in the next thirty thousand, he will attain similar control of the human forces within. Holding fast to the ideals, we may trust that there is truth in Winston Churchill's words from war-torn Europe in 1940 (quoting a poem by Arthur Hough Clough): "Westward look, the land is bright."

[A spiritual atlas will include Utopia. Rabelais in *Pantagruel* set ship for it around the Cape of Good Hope. Meanwhile, we express our hopes poetically, and labor prosaically to bring them into being.]

Prose normally differs from verse in that its rhythms are more haphazard, less regularly patterned. Rhythm exists not only in what we write; it is ubiquitous; it is the substance of all things. Psychologist Havelock Ellis, in *The Dance of Life* (1923), emphasized it as the base of all living creatures. Today we know that it establishes all relationships. Tiny particles deep in the atom give it its substance as they spin their several ways within their infinitesimal microcosmos; while in the majestic spread of the sky the stars and the galaxies move in their measured patterns of steady flow. However still a human may seem to be, the systole and diastole of the heart, the pulse beat and the flow of blood, the electric signals of his brain, are as continuous as his very being. While he is awake, he is stirred by constant motion; every emotion is a state of "being moved." Rhythm thus flows naturally through all man says or writes.

Choice of words is another aspect of all writing, verse or prose. In Chaucer, and in the ballads of the century after him, there is little discernible difference between the diction of poetry and that of prose. With the word-conscious Elizabethans, and increasingly from the Renaissance until the nineteenth century, there developed a number of terms used especially in verse, but less and less in more prosaic writing. In 1798 Wordsworth and Coleridge, publishing in one volume some of their separate poems, set themselves each a particular task. Wordsworth's aim was to write of simple, everydaily things in simple, everydaily language, lifting them onto the level of poetry; Coleridge was to bring the far-off realm of fantasy into the scope of the common man. The resul' was good poetry from both of them, at their best. But in Wordsworth the simple sometimes verged upon the simpleton; it would be hard to find another great poet that has written such a body of bad verse. Much of "Peter Bell" is unbelievably banal; in "Simon Lee the Old Huntsman" the bathos is almost self-parody. And in Coleridge there is a plethora of words since dropped from the vocabulary even of poetasters. The words *stoppeth, stoppest, may'st, grey-beard loon, eftsoons,* occur in the first three stanzas of his best-known poem, "The Ancient Mariner." A special poetic diction seemed to be developing.

There is a danger in the use of archaic words; they may seem strange, even ludicrous, to the general reader. Wordsworth himself was snared by them, as evidenced one evening at the Lambs'. Charles Lamb read the first line of a new Wordsworth poem, "The Force of Prayer":

What is good for a bootless bene?

—and his sister Mary at once cried out: "a shoeless pea!"

(By no means incidentally, the Ancient Mariner suffers because of his disregard of natural things, and he wins release when his *state of mind* changes: "and he blessed them unaware ... he blessed them unaware." This is precisely the condition, and the need, of oil-drunk man in the polluted world today. As it has been pithily put, our future is metanoia or paranoia. R. Buckminster Fuller calls it (his 1967 book's title) *Utopia or Oblivion.* H. G.

Wells earlier saw us in a race between education and catastrophe. It is a question not of knowledge but of attitude.)

A reaction against this double excess of word use was manifest in the abrupt and occasionally harsh diction of Browning, as also in the smoother, precise observation of Tennyson. Today, after the wide ranging, from slang and prizefighter's jargon to lyric rapture, in such a work as Masefield's *The Everlasting Mercy* (1911), the full resources of the English vocabulary have again been opened to the poet, who shrinks neither from vulgar profanity nor from scientific terminology, weaving a variety of expression unequaled in earlier days. It should be remembered, however, that the quality of a work of art has no relation to the quantity of different words employed in its production; as we have noted, Shakespeare's works, and the King James Bible, were achieved within a small span of words. As the Bible reminds us, indeed, "a fool is known by the multitude of words." If they are well chosen, so that they fit—fit the idea, the occasion, the mood, the speaker, and the audience—with sufficient variety to avoid the monotonous, few words will suffice for power and for beauty. Almost worn words are used, and the point illustrated, in Keats's opening line:

A thing of beauty is a joy forever.

One further frequent characteristic of modern verse was a required element of Old English (Anglo-Saxon) poetry. This poetry consisted of lines of four heavy beats, strongly accented syllables, about which unaccented syllables were grouped. There was usually a slightly longer pause after the second beat. As these poems were recited, chanted, by the bard at the banquet hall, celebrating a triumph or exalting a hero, it is easy to imagine the thumping of the tankards on the table—much as an audience today may clap hands keeping time to a favorite song of a favorite singer. To emphasize this beat, at least three of the four stresses in the Anglo-Saxon line are marked by the same initial sound. This practice lasted into the fourteenth century, as in the dream of *Piers Plowman*, who saw

> Of alle manner of men, the mene and the rich,
> Working and wandering as the world asketh.

This similarity of initial sounds continues, as alliteration, in most poetry since. Quite obvious in some poets, as in Swinburne, its more subtle use adds to the savor of a work. Observe, in the lines above from Gray's Elegy, the various alliterative tones. The *l* sound, present in every line, is emphasized by the following long *o* sounds in line 2 and by the rhyme word *lea*, as well as by the *pl* combination following. The later *leaves* recalls the tranquil *lea*. The *w* also, premonitory in line 2, is pressed home to the rhyme in the next line, with the echoing *world* in the last. And the lull of the *l* and the woo of the *w* accord with the quiet dusk of the evening.

Sometimes alliteration is fortuitous, appearing with words chosen for different reasons; at other times, it seems one of the reasons for the choice, as, deftly, in Shakespeare's line, "The fresh green lap of fair King Richard's land," with the overlapping *f* and *l*, and the undertones of *r*.

Alliteration may of course be used in prose as well, as Bernard Shaw confesses after a mess of it—in hell:

> DON JUAN: Are we agreed that Life is a force that has made innumerable experiments in organizing itself, that the mammoth and the man, the mouse and the megatherium, the flies and the fleas and the Fathers of the Church, are all more or less successful attempts to build up that raw force into higher and higher individuals, the ideal individual being omnipotent, omniscient, and infallible, and withal completely, unilludedly, self-conscious: in short, a god?
> THE DEVIL: I agree, for the sake of argument.
> THE STATUE: I agree, for the sake of avoiding argument.
> ANA: I most emphatically disagree as regards the Fathers of the Church; I must beg you not to drag them into the argument.
> DON JUAN: I did so purely for the sake of alliteration, Ana; and I shall make no further allusion to them.

Perhaps the most frequent prose use of alliteration is in slogans, for propaganda or advertisement: "Tippecanoe and Tyler too!" "Not a cough in a carload." Brief messages after battle may take that form: Julius Caesar's *Veni, vidi, vici;* Donald F. Mason's radio to the U.S. Navy base, on January 28, 1942: "Sighted sub; sank same." Epigrams and other brief statements may gain emphasis by alliteration; thus Anthony Hope said of W. S. Gilbert: "His foe was folly and his weapon wit."

In verse, alliteration has coursed through the alphabet, as in the well-known jingle beginning

An Austrian army, awfully arrayed,
Boldly by battle besieged Belgrade ...

But, judiciously applied, "apt alliteration's artful aid" is a major device for lightening and enlivening poetry, and subtly enhancing the mood.

Various other forms of rhyme or near-rhyme have been increasingly used in the freer verse forms. *Beginning rhyme,* also called *head* or *initial rhyme,* comes at the start of the lines, sometimes accompanied with *middle* or *internal rhyme,* as in Lanier's "The Symphony":

> We weave in the mills and heave in the kilns,
> We sieve mine-meshes . . .
> And thieve . . .
> To relieve. . . .

Carrying alliteration a letter farther, to include the vowel, has been called *reverse rhyme* (at the beginning instead of the end of a word): *many* a *menace; quick–quiver. Assonance* occurs when different consonants enclose the same vowel sound: *frame–late. Consonance,* also called *pararhyme,* occurs when a different vowel is enclosed within the same consonants: *draining–drowning; dim–damn–dumb. Mosaic rhyme* is the use of two or more words in one or both of the rhyming partners, as in Lowell's:

> Unqualified merits, I'll grant, if you choose, he has 'em,
> But he lacks the one merit of kindling enthusiasm.

There are further, but less frequent, variations of sound accordance that poets have found, and probably more await the ingenuity of future writers.

If the general reader were pressed, he would probably admit that not all verse is poetry. He would accept the dismissal of mnemonic devices:

> Thirty days has September,
> April, June, and November

—of humorous jingles and coarse doggerel. But he would cling to the notion that all poetry involves verse.

The student of literature makes quite a different distinction. He marks the two modes, not as poetry and prose, but as poetry and matter of fact. The earliest English *Apology for Poetrie,* by Sir Philip Sidney, who died in 1586, states unequivocally: "The distinguishing mark of poetry is not metre, but a certain feigning." He elaborates: "One may be a poet without versing, and a versifier without poetry." And, in fact, in Arabic even dictionaries have been compiled in verse.

Poetry, for such persons, includes only, but all, imaginative writing, whether in prose or in verse: drama and fiction as well as the products of those specialists known as poets. Matter of fact includes the wide range of everydaily writing, from business records to the news report, the gossip page to the editorial, the science notes to the advertising. (Some of these may of course be highly imaginative, but they are not intended to give that impression; they are or pretend to be fact.)

Another way in which this distinction is noted is by the division of all writing into the literature of knowledge and the literature of power. The former, we are told, may advance man somewhat upon the worldly plane of his human activity; the latter exalts him to a richer plane of spiritual arousal. Pursuing other word ways, we may speak of scientific as opposed to emotive language. Science seeks to present an objective, an uncolored, dispassionate view of the world around; opposed to this is the subjective, the personal, point of view, colored by the opinions and the feelings of the speaker. Some skeptics have declared that everything a person writes or speaks must be influenced by his individual genes and his particular environment, must therefore be subjective. This is, however, to deprive the word of significance. One can no more usefully picture a completely subjective world, than one can sanely declare that all things are short: *short* has no meaning without the contrasting possibility of the *long*. The truly subjective is inexpressible; as soon as something is expressed it is objectified; it is part of the outside world, open to exact examination. Nevertheless, much that is presented as objective observation is unfortunately tinged if not permeated with personal inclinations or bias.

The development of thermodynamics suggested another division of qualities: *additive,* and *nonadditive.* Two men can lift twice the load of one. Power is additive. Distance is additive. One impregnated woman can produce a child in nine months; nine women cannot do it in one month. Your normal temperature, and mine, cannot be combined to obtain 197°F. These are nonadditive. Reason and emotion present a more complicated case. While a team of scientists may accomplish more than one person, each does his thinking alone. Reason is essentially individual. Thought is each man's private universe. Emotions are more generally shared; feelings can be caught in common. In a crowd, feeling may grow to passion and turn the crowd into a mob, in which the

rouse is shared and multiplied, and often sweeps to violent un-
reasoned action.

"Scientific" language is further complicated by the fact that
the questions men may ask are of two main and distinct types.
There are questions of fact, as asked in laboratories and law
courts. And there are questions of policy, important in daily
affairs, in legislative bodies, and the councils of government. The
former deal with past or permanent events, the latter deal with
future conduct.

In the exact sciences, questions of fact may be answered by
experiment and demonstration, which may be repeated and thus
checked by various persons; by prophecy and its fulfillment. Scientific hypotheses are called seriously into question when predictions based upon them fail to eventuate. The intellectual world
was agog with expectation before the eclipse of 1919, because the
truth of Einstein's formula for the deviation of light would be
confuted, or confirmed, while the sun was obscured. Einstein was
right.

Proof is so important to some scientists that they declare that
questions which cannot be empirically answered are non-sense
questions, and should not be asked. Such questions include the
existence of God, of free will, of life after death. "Sir," exclaimed
Samuel Johnson, "we *know* our will is free, and *there's* an end
on't." But these matters are *unknowable;* they belong to the range
of faith, not of science. Scientific knowledge involves the possibility, if not of proof, at least of disproof; and the correctness of
prediction. As Comte observed: *Savoir pour prévoir pour pouvoir,*
"Knowledge permits prediction, produces power."

In court cases, truth is established by a different process. In
addition to physical evidence, there are the words of witnesses,
which the language sets in a series of increasingly definitive terms.
A *statement* is the presentation of something as a fact. An *assertion* is a statement backed by, but only by, the authority of the
speaker. Most of our remarks in the course of a day are assertions.
Testimony is an assertion offered as helping to establish the truth.
Evidence is testimony accepted as helping to establish the truth.
Finally, *proof* is evidence, the accumulation of evidence, accepted
as establishing the truth—beyond, as the phrase goes, reasonable
doubt.

Questions of fact, as I have said, may deal with what always
happens—as when hydrogen and oxygen are combined, H_2O, to
form water—or they may deal with what has happened. The law
courts and the history books are here akin. Questions of policy, on

the other hand, inquire about a course of action to be taken, about what should be done. Dealing with the future, such questions are not susceptible of conclusive answer; they must be decided in terms of likelihood, degree of probability. On them must be brought to bear the weight of authority, the nearness of analogy, the summoning of statistics. And each of these is a weak thread to tie an action.

An *authority* has been defined as a more or less well-known individual who shares your opinion. As many an important court case has made manifest, an equally impressive assumption of authorities can be gathered on either side of many questions. And while a layman may properly defer to an expert, he may reserve— as does a jury—the right to draw his own conclusions.

Analogy consists in the presentation of an established case, supposedly similar in essential respects to the matter under consideration, with the inference that what was true in the analogous instance will be true in the proposed one. Its weakness lies in our inability, in the complex of human activities, to be sure that the cases are significantly alike, that the aspects considered are both essential to and sufficient for the drawn conclusion. Can, for example, the lack of any rise in serious crime after the abolition of the death penalty in Australia be a valid argument for its abolition in the United States?

As to *statistics*, one may note the cynic's listing of the three degrees of the lie: lies, damn lies, and statistics. The collected instances of a case may be presented fairly; even then, there is a great gap between what they show and what should be done because of them. If statistics show, for example, a striking increase in crime, shall we make our jails bigger and our punishments more severe, or take more perceptive measures to reduce the basic causes of crime? And do these basic measures mean a change in our educational system, or do they extend to the complete reorganization of our competitive society? Statistics cannot point the way.

Even in themselves, statistics may be malleable to the compiler's purpose. There are, for example, four ways of estimating the value of a series or set of figures: by the average, mean, median, or mode. As we have learned to expect, the dictionary is of no help; it simply compounds the confusion. *Webster's New Collegiate Dictionary* defines *average* as "a single value (as a mean, mode, or median) that summarizes or represents the general significance of a set of unequal values." And it defines *arithmetic mean* as "a value that is computed by dividing the sum of a set of terms by the number of terms"—which is the usual acceptation of the word *average*.

Let us look at the deviations produced by figuring according to these four words, giving each its specific—distinct—significance. Suppose fifteen candidates have taken a test, achieving these percentages:

30; 45; 47; 62; 68; 70; 77; 80; 81; 85; 85; 87; 89; 92; 97.

The *average*—the sum of all the figures divided by the number of figures—is 73%.

The *mean*—the mean between the extremes: the lowest and the highest figures added, then divided by two—is 63.5%.

The *median*—the middle point, with the same number of figures below as above—is 80%.

The *mode*—the most frequent value, this time occurring twice—is 85%.

Take your choice. And note that, according to Webster, any one of these final figures may be called "the average"!

Consider another avenue of approach, along the line of probability. If one sees, say, four or five animals with a neck over a yard long, one may be entitled to assume the existence of a distinct species, and to call the creature by a special name, such as *giraffe*. The same principle underlies the endeavors of the various pollsters who have insinuated themselves into the public's imagination, who take samples of the people's thinking, and on the basis of the sampling assume the same grouping for the entire population. They then apply the sample percentages to the whole, to prophesy, for example, the decision to vote for a certain candidate. To some extent, it must be recognized, such prognostications tend to make themselves come true, because undecided voters may plump for the one heralded as successful. But *The Literary Digest*, a nationwide weekly since 1890, lost its readers and ceased publication because it had forecast a landslide for Landon in 1936 when instead Franklin D. Roosevelt won handily. This indicates one of the dangers of reasoning by induction.

Induction and deduction are commonly considered the two basic logical and complementary methods of seeking truth. *Induction* consists in the examination of what is deemed a sufficient number of similar specific cases, and from them reaching out to announce a general truth. The assumption is: If so many objects with these characteristics have this nature, then all objects with these characteristics will have this nature. Thus we arrive at a general conclusion, or "law"—for an obvious instance: all men are mortal.

Deduction, conversely, begins with a general law, arrived at by common sense, or by induction. Since, for centuries, any man with "common sense" was aware that the sun revolves around the earth —we still say that it rises and it sets—it seems well to limit ourselves to general laws arrived at by induction. Deduction then seeks to establish that a particular object or incident falls within the class covered by that general law, so that the law must apply to it. Thus, to continue with our obvious instance: Socrates is a man. Therefore, Socrates is mortal. With this conclusion, few will quarrel.

Note, however, the assumption that I mentioned concerning induction: "If so many objects . . . , then all. . . ." This itself is a general rule. And thus induction, which is supposed to permit us to arrive at a general rule, itself depends upon one. Such an argument is circular; its validity may be cogently challenged. And of course, if one can count the entire set of things being considered, as the persons in a room, the general law is unnecessary. For such reasons, logicians in the past century have tended to avoid the terms *induction* and *deduction,* although they are still commonly regarded as fundamental.

Induction fails if a single negative instance can be advanced, but all affirmative instances cannot add up to positive proof of a universal law. They may, however, as the American logician C. S. Peirce put it, "lead to a result indefinitely approximating the truth in the long run." This is perhaps as close as mere mortals may hope to attain.

The pattern above, establishing that Socrates is mortal, is called a *syllogism.* It consists of two premises—the general law, and the setting of the particular case under that law—followed by the incontrovertible conclusion. Yet it may be faulty; it is open, indeed, to three types of fallacy.

There may be a *material fallacy,* an error in substance, a misstatement of fact: the supposed law may not be valid, or the particular case may not belong under it. There may, secondly, be a *verbal fallacy,* in that the terms of the case are incorrectly applied. Thus a general principle, that all creatures with eyes can see, obviously overlooks the blind; or, more subtly, it fails to recognize that sight may have different meanings: some insects, though their eyes are sensitive to light, show no possibility of forming images; the many-faceted eye of the fly enables it to see much farther around than its major enemies—that's why it's so hard to swat!—and many men (not women) are colorblind. There may, finally, be a *formal fallacy,* disturbing the organization of the argument. For a sound syllogism, the subject of the first premise must be the predicate of the second. "All cheese is edible. Corned beef is edible"—we have run off the track! We must continue! "Limburger is a cheese. Therefore, limburger is edible."

This is rather obvious. What is less apparent is that discussion very frequently involves this pattern, though with one of the premises omitted. Such a shortcut is called an *enthymeme*. Thus, if we declare that John is untrustworthy, we may go on to tell what he has said or done. This assumes the general law, that a person exhibiting such qualities or performing such acts is untrustworthy; therefore, John.

The problems of *fallacy,* 'erroneous reasoning', are given considerable attention in studies of logic, and numerous types have been specified. Perhaps the most frequent fallacy is the one labeled *Post hoc ergo propter hoc,* 'after this therefore because of this'. If two events occur in close succession, there is a natural tendency to assume that the first is the cause of the second. This of course may well be true; but the warning is valid: look before you leap to a conclusion.

The earliest English challenge to these processes of reasoning came from Roger Bacon, who died in 1294, and who was several times in trouble with the Church for challenging the deductive method, the general rules (first premises) of which were often established by authority. Bacon listed authority as one of the chief causes of error, the others being custom, the opinion of the ignorant majority, and ignorance that cloaks itself in the assumption of knowledge. Instead of authority, Roger Bacon urged experience. It was almost four centuries later that Francis Bacon, in his *Novum Organum,* of 1620, added his emphases. He declared that the syllogism "is no match for the subtlety of nature." He too listed four main sources of error, of false mental images, which he called idols. Idols of the Tribe are those inherent in human nature, such as the tendency to select, among observed facts, those that favor one's own preconceptions. Idols of the Cave are errors springing from one's own make-up and training. Idols of the Marketplace are verbal fictions and confusions rising from men's dealings with one another. Idols of the Theatre are errors involved in philosophical systems, which, like dramas, develop unreal worlds of their own. To correct such errors, Francis Bacon laid emphasis on direct observation, experiment, and induction. These are even today considered bases of the scientific method.

By still another path, logic (which is the organization of words so as to attain valid ideas) has attempted to go beneath the surface of ideas to their basic patterns. Considering the nature of a *proposition*—a form of speech that affirms something—it marks, first, the obvious distinction between a true proposition (John H. Higginbotham is a man) and a false proposition (Platinum is a peanut). This is preliminary to the new term, the *propositional function*, of which the truth or falsity depends on the meaning of the terms (X is a Y; God is love). Then the notion advances to the statement that every proposition is a value of a propositional function, expressed or understood. This notion of Bertrand Russell may be seen as a challenge to science, to examine and define its basic terms.

While such rigor is less easy than it may seem, both this and the syllogism, usually in its implicit form, are more urgently of concern in what, by contrast with the natural or physical, are called the social sciences. The latter are much less rigorous; some scientists, indeed, assert that they are not sciences at all, since we cannot, as yet, submit them to proof. The social sciences are, therefore, increasingly seeking ways of more exact measurement and more fully controlled experiment, with the use of computers and other freshly fashioned devices. History has taken the name of its Muse to label a recent school *Cliometrics*. But in sociology, economics, and psychology, science must still be regarded as an aspiration rather than an achievement. As the bright Brazilian beauty remarks, in Josephine Tey's *Miss Pym Disposes*, explaining why she studies not psychology but anatomy: "An idea today may be nonsense tomorrow, but a clavicle is a clavicle for all time."

While the language of science ideally is objective, emotive language is by choice subjective, springing from the feelings of the user, or aimed by him to sway the feelings of the receptor. The contrast is neatly demonstrated by the different approach of psychology and of publicity, of advertising. Psychology studies, among other things, the lusts and greeds and unacknowledged fears that lurk within us; it seeks to bring them forth into the light of day, so that we may recognize, understand, and perhaps disarm them. Advertising also examines the ingrained appetites and apprehensions—but in order to play upon them, to use them in persuading the public to buy. "Promise, large promise," said Samuel Johnson back in the eighteenth century, "is the soul of an advertisement." Various automobiles are given names that suggest high social rank, or even wild-beast power. Pictures of pretty young women urge: "Fly me to Miami!"

Cosmetics marks a high point of this verbal insinuation. T. S.

Eliot, in lines omitted from *The Waste Land*, tells us that the artful French concocted alluring odors to mask the female "stench"; but perfumes were the queen's and the courtesan's delight long before the French were a nation.

Cleopatra on her burnished barge was probably sweet-smelling, and incense was wafted through the air around. During the largely unwashed Middle Ages, artificial scents were probably necessary, to keep unpleasant odors from even royal courts. Until the late nineteenth century, the occasional bath was in a carried tub, into which water was poured. The American bathtub, then the shower, changed all that—the artful French bidet offering an assist—and cleanliness and consequent freedom from persistent malodor are now not only possible but frequent. Nevertheless, we have been taught to beware of the "hearty female stench," and pressured to substitute for it the anal and genital secretions of the deer (musk), the skunk (civet), and the beaver (castor), and the diseased sperm whale (ambergris). All other males than human are attracted by the genital odors of their female kind. "Mad Avenue" (actually Madison Avenue, New York), the denizens of which design our so-called public relations, is aptly named.

The trade names given to items in the field of feminine allure are chosen to add to this attraction. *Cosmetics* itself is derived from *cosmos*, which means the ordered universe. Cosmetics are preparations to bring order to your personal world. Their opposite is *chaos, chaotic*. (In these days of the brushing off of law and order, one awaits the thrust of a rock group calling itself The Chaotics.)

An early deodorant had the blunt name *Odorono* (Odor? Oh, no!); but that was soon outmoded. The word *deodorant* itself has been largely replaced by the less repellent term *antiperspirant*—pronounced on television with a sweet accent on the "purr" followed by a short *i*, so that no one will dwell upon so disdained a social blemish as perspiring. Perfumes more temptingly tease, with such names as *White Shoulders* and *My Sin*. *Cupid's Quiver* is a name that euphemistically—mistily and crassly—indicates a woman's douche: she may have it in orange blossom, raspberry, jasmine, or champagne.

An even more striking example of insidious allure through words is found in the naming of habit-forming drugs. *Opium* comes directly from a Greek word meaning 'poppy juice'. But some time after De Quincey wrote his *Confessions of an English Opium-Eater* (1821), opium was subjected to official condemnation. Thereupon a derivative of it was proffered instead, made inviting—Try me, and have happy dreams!—under the name of *morphine*, after Morpheus, god of dreams. In its turn, morphine fell into disrepute and legal restriction. Another derivative was developed, technically known as *diamorphine;* but who wants to die o' morphine? So it came upon the market—Try it, little fellow; one dose and you're a big shot!—as *heroin.* A truly heroic effort to blank out resistance!

Fortunately for the human race, emotive language can be put to better use. Beyond the physical and the social sciences, far from the false lure of advertising, lies the great field loosely called the humanities, where humanity may happily abide. And at the core of this field, in the crown of art, shines beauty.

The attempt to explain what beauty is leads us into a largely barren range of philosophy. For no one has ever beheld beauty; we experience only beautiful things. Beauty is a quality within such objects; its nature can in some measure be deduced from them, but it cannot be deducted and observed as a separate entity. Does beauty, then, exist? Is there such a thing, such an entity, as beauty? Or are there only disparate objects, which because of some characteristics we call beautiful? Remember that for two hundred years scientists talked about phlogiston, the entity in things because of which they could burn.

Plato, and his followers today, claim that such essences—ideas —exist, have always existed, and will persist. Gravitation, for example, some scientists assert, was inherent in the "big bang"—if it was a big bang—that started our universe on its journey through space-time. And certainly Einstein did not create the relationship expressed in his formula $E = mc^2$ (Energy is equal to the mass times the square of the speed of light). The relationship existed. We may say that Einstein discovered it. We may with more assurance say that he set it forth, made it apparent to others, and thus paved the way for the explosion of the atomic bomb.

The Hindus share the Platonic belief in the reality of a "heavenly" paradigm of earthly items. As the most significant interpreter of the East to the West, Ananda K. Coomaraswamy, saw it: "Man has always co-related his own constructions with cosmic or supernatural prototypes. For example, the Indian seven-storey palace has always been thought of as analogous to the universe of seven worlds."

Others would state that the question of the eternal existence of such relationships is a non-sense question, in that it cannot be proved or disproved, and therefore wastes our time in the asking, diverts us from more profitable probings. "Which came first, the chicken or the egg?" is a searching, perhaps a tantalizing, but a bootless, query.

Beauty, however, more than color, like kindness or greed, seems less a relationship than a quality, an aspect or element of a larger whole. Relationships may often be set down in mathematical terms, but despite Edna St. Vincent Millay's declaration that "Euclid alone has looked on beauty bare," qualities are less amenable to such extraction or abstraction. We call them *abstract*.

When we look upon objects that we call beautiful, we may, of course, seek within them what they have in common, what in them justifies our feeling that they embody beauty. There have been listed some sixteen major definitions of beauty, which fall into three groups: beauty as essence, as relation, or as cause.

In the first group belongs Clive Bell's assertion that "significant form is the quality common to all works of visual art." Coomaraswamy ironically extends this remark: "We who can call an art 'significant', knowing not of what, are also proud to 'progress', we know not whither." But Roger Fry speaks like Bell: "I must be dogmatic and declare that the aesthetic emotion is an emotion about form." And T. S. Eliot is not only dogmatic but elitist when he puts us in our place: "Very few know when there is expression of significant emotion, emotion which has its life in the poem and not in the history of the poet."

While we may agree with Keats that

> A thing of beauty is a joy forever;
> Its loveliness increases, it will never
> Pass into nothingness—

we prefer to be in the position of the person who, saying "I know what I like," can continue "and I know why I like it."

The quest for specific characteristics that beautiful objects share, in a measure does take us back to the question of form, for form is measurable. In relationships, whether of lines and shapes or words and figures of speech, form takes value as proportion. And proportions are not hard to find, especially in the nonverbal arts. In music, for example, from the first to the last note of the octave, double the vibrations. In the analysis of ancient architecture and sculpture, and in much painting, we have been made familiar with proportions, perhaps not mathematically known to the artists themselves but unerringly interwoven in their art. Thus the golden mean—of a line ABC so divided that AB is to BC as BC is to AC, the shorter related to the longer as the longer to the whole—and the golden section (similar relations in a plane) establish a "divine proportion" approximated in the Fibonacci sequence, a series of numbers 1, 1, 2, 3, 5, 8, 13, 21, 34 ... ∞, each number of which is the sum of the two before it. The same ratio is found in the plane sequence known as the whirling squares; and it exists in nature, as in the whorls of sunflower seeds and the spiral growth of a conch-shell, as well as being a proportion basic in much art.

One must, however, be careful not to confuse an accompanying with a defining characteristic. All men are mammals, but not all mammals are men. The diagram of the whirling squares is a perfect example of what has been named dynamic symmetry, but though beautiful things may have dynamic symmetry, in the whirling squares there abides no beauty. All beautiful things may exhibit proportion, but not all things that exhibit proportion are beautiful. Edna Millay's pretty figure about the mathematician Euclid goes not far enough. What mathematics lays bare is the framework, as it were the skeleton of beauty, which the artists must body forth with flesh and blood and sinews. Nor has any scientist analyzed the godlike boon that makes a man Pygmalion, to bring the work to imaginative life in the receptor. Beauty may dwell in the eye of the beholder, but what the mind perceives is a blend of the creator's art and the receptor's sensitivity.

Also considering beauty as a relation, some critics down the ages have linked beauty and nature, mainly in the dictum that art imitates life, art consists in the imitation of nature. Aristotle, followed by many, suggests an idealizing imitation, a showing not of what is, but of what ought to be, of the best that may be. As to direct imitation, Nietzsche declared that "From an artistic point of view, nature is no model," and more recent iconoclasts have declared (as Rebecca West worded it): "One of the damned thing is ample." Baudelaire, Pater, and Wilde lead a group of aesthetes that reverse the tilt of the see-saw, claiming that life does, or should, imitate art.

Still others have put into more philosophical language what Keats phrased in poetry:

> Beauty is truth, truth beauty; that is all
> Ye know on earth, and all ye need to know.

—declaring that beauty reveals truth. Beauty, or art, in the realms of the imagination, may thus be a flame-tipped arrow shot into the future, while science more laboriously blazes a trail to the forward goal.

How prophetic an imaginative writer may be is shown in Jules Verne's description of a periscope, in *Twenty Thousand Leagues Under the Sea*, so accurate that later the actual inventor was refused a patent. The author of an early science-fiction account of an atomic bomb was visited by government agents, to determine the source of the leak. These, of course are fortuitous coincidings. But even if we concede that beauty is truth, we are far from a capture of the basic nature of beauty. First we must learn how to answer Pilate's question: "What is truth?"

Edgar Allan Poe, moreover, bluntly contradicts the idea of such an association:

The demands of Truth are severe. She has no sympathy with the myrtles. All *that* which is indispensable in Song, is precisely all *that* with which *she* has nothing whatever to do. In enforcing a truth, we need severity rather than efflorescence of language. We must be simple, precise, terse. We must be cool, calm, unimpassioned. In a word, we must be in that mood which, as nearly as possible, is the exact opposite of the poetical.

Thus a poet breaks a poetic figure from a scientific fact, a delight from a definition.

To many readers, and to some of the artists themselves, indeed, absorption in the creation or contemplation of beauty may involve not a capture of but an escape from reality. As it has been sharply put, "Art is the quickest way out of the Bronx." This equates art with what millions see within the frame of their television set.

Critic Leo Stein (Gertrude's brother) suggests a different relationship, pointing out that an engineer may speak of a beautiful piece of work; a surgeon, of a beautiful operation. "The surgeon does not mean that the sight is beautiful, but he does mean that the operation is a perfect expression of a felt interest, and therefore he has the right to call it beautiful."—But what a perfect expression of a felt interest many an urchin achieves by thumbing his nose!

Benedetto Croce carries the concept of art as expression to the extreme notion that all expression is art. Others would go almost as far, stating that all art is the expression of the artist's personality. Thereby one is reminded of the French teacher of painting who asked a student what she thought she had put on the canvas, and when she protested that it was an expression of her personality, coldly informed her: *"La personnalité de ma'amselle n'intéresse que maman."*

James Joyce, thinking of his *Ulysses,* put into a neat figure the idea that an artist must hold back nothing, must put his complete personality into his work. Joyce was walking in Dublin Park with Padraic Colum; Padraic passed the episode on to me. "When the Cyclops asked Odyszeus his name, the wily warrior replied: 'No man'—in Greek, *Odys*. And if a writer attempts to conceal any part of his self, it is inevitably the *Zeus,* the god in him, that is sloughed, and no man indeed that remains."

The ultimate human remains, among the excesses of our time, were displayed at a recent art exhibition in Paris, a literal *reductio ad arseturdom.* Whistler's *Mother* is a classic of the presentation of *Mère de l'artiste;* in Paris, under a small glass dome, lay what was correctly labeled *Merde de l'artiste.* All expression claims the glamour of art.

While Joyce made a figure of the need for full and free expression, Croce questioned what else art could provide: If art is anything more than expression, "no one has been able to indicate of what that something more consists." That "something more" has been stated, very simply: revelation. We are not merely caught into the author's or the character's emotion; we are made richly aware of its essence, its potentiality, and depth. Expression may rouse us; revelation exalts. Joyce himself has described this as an epiphany.

Today, many aesthetic thinkers are inclined to state that art is not an expression of, but a release from, personality. The concerned artist forgets himself in the tumult of the forces within him: of tradition, of background and breeding, of spontaneous surge of emotions, of contemporary opinions and movements, all struggling in a welter of fancied shapes and clashing symbols— until somehow they find fusion, and bring him release, in the finished work of art. Calm of mind, all passion spent.

We may, then, turn to the third type of definition, beauty defined by its effect. Before examining this range, however, we should note that some current critics of repute, headed by W. K. Wimsatt, Jr., and Monroe C. Beardsley, dismiss all such definitions as the "affective fallacy"—considering beauty not as a thing *per se,* but merely as a cause of some reaction. Critics at all times, nonetheless, have pondered the effects of art. Aristotle declared that drama results in a catharsis, purging the spectator of terror and pity. Longinus said that "transport" is the test and conse-

quence of great literature. More recently, both Ruskin and Santayana have sought its significance in pleasure: "Beauty is pleasure
regarded as a quality of a thing." Even the aesthete Baudelaire
thought this incomplete, endeavoring to transform his pleasure
(*volupté*) into understanding.

The doctrine of empathy may be drawn upon here, the notion
that beauty enables us to "put ourselves inside" the contemplated
object. We look at the statue of the discus thrower, and our
muscles flex. We read a book, or hear and see a play, and in its
spell we are the characters. The familiar phrase "There but for
the grace of God go I" withholds its grace; during the spell, verily
there go I. The fact that this temporary identification may come
with any best-seller or claptrap melodrama or ephemeral song—
"I met a million-dollar baby in a five-and-ten-cent store"—makes
it seem less than a binding definition of beauty.

Two more cogent claims have been made for beauty in terms
of its effect. One of these is termed *synaesthesis*, which means
the coming together of feelings. Feelings normally opposed or
incompatible are conjoined, aroused together, by beauty. We are
deeply stirred at a tragedy, yet we remain calmly in our seats, for
our diverse emotions rise together and maintain an equilibrium:
we may feel moved, but we neither cry out upon the villain nor
write a check for relief of the distressed heroine. And at the same
time our mental awareness, our keenness of judgment, which
usually are swirled away by powerful emotion, hold alert and
expectant: that we are moved by Ophelia's death or Hamlet's
dilemma and doom makes us no less conscious and appreciative
of Shakespeare's verbal felicity. When our emotions and our
thoughts are thus companionably aroused and enriched, we are
confronting beauty. For those content to define the quality of
beauty in a work in terms of what it does to those that contemplate it, this seems a sound definition.

There is one further. For the effect of beauty may be seen as
akin to love. The painter Picasso, indeed, dismisses the whole
problem: "What is beauty anyway? There's no such thing! I love
or I hate!" And unquestionably art may be roused by love, as
many a poet has proclaimed. Thus Dante:

> I am one who, when Love
> Inspires me, note, and in the way that he
> Dictates within, I give the outward form.

Sir Philip Sidney made the same idea more personal:

But if (both for your love and skill) your name
You seek to nurse at fullest breasts of fame,
Stella behold, and then begin t'endite . . .
'Fool!' said my Muse to me, 'look in thy heart and write.'

In this sense, through the poet, beauty makes universal what love keeps personal. In the presence of beauty, as Thomas Aquinas noted, desire is stilled. Beauty, then, is love content to contemplate, rather than eager to possess. As I have expressed the idea:

Beauty's the form love gives to things.

Like love, art combines the stirring of constantly fresh surprise and instantly familiar recognition. New beauty is at once a welcome stranger and a cherished friend.

Familiarity, we are told, breeds contempt; in a better-tempered spirit, it breeds contemplation. And as we ponder the difference between matter-of-fact prose and poetry, we come to recognize that prose, once it is understood and absorbed, may be rephrased or discarded; what matters is the idea to be conveyed. With poetry, on the other hand, the form is an integral part of the substance; it must be kept intact; the work can be experienced, be enjoyed, again and again. He is a poor reader that has not read his favorite books more than once, a poor playgoer that has seen but a single Hamlet—no lover of poetry that has not had lines by heart. Thus prose is the Sphinx, that dies with its enigma; poetry is the Phoenix, reborn of its consumption.

It remains a matter of faith, not open to proof, that beauty is a reality apart from particular things, existing in itself, abiding. It remains a matter of fact, not open to doubt, that our only glimpses of this ideal beauty come in its imperfect realization in material things—in this beautiful statue, this beautiful poem, this beautiful play. It is part of our glory that we can fashion such a multitude and such a variety of beautiful things, to enliven and enrich, and in a deep sense to justify, our otherwise spendthrift being.

11.

THE LITERARY FORMS

AS THE COMPLEX IMPULSIONS, of passive receptivity and active participation, involved in absorbing a work of art have been increasingly recognized, an almost forgotten word has been revived: *receptor*, to include listener, spectator, and reader, in all their acceptive and reactive attitudes. We are also more aware that Shakespeare and a current bedroom farce, Dostoevski and the latest best-seller, reach out to different levels in the receptor. Roughly, three levels may be marked off, according as the work appeals, *whatever the chronological age,* to the mental and emotional child, adolescent, or adult.

To the child, all persons are starkly seen as black or white. A work that thus pictures them meets the child's expectations and demands; he relishes the deep-dyed villain—who may have a high old time and keep everybody on tenterhooks, but gets his due come-uppance at the end. This is "poetic justice."

To the adolescent, all persons are black and white, but this troubles the adolescent. He wants to remodel the world. To the adolescent, as Aristotle remarked, all things are didactic. He is in the van of all revolutions. George Washington took command of the American Army in 1776, but in 1770 the students at Princeton (New Jersey College) pledged to buy no goods made in England. The youth of today are equally dissatisfied, but with less precise goal. They may, therefore, react with purely destructive violence; or attempt in various ways (drugs, or commune, or meditation) to withdraw from the contemporary world; or, more cynically, plunge for a share of life's baubles. Hence their reading may be of idealistic dream-stories, of science-fiction fantasies of other worlds; or of satire, propaganda, and the cruel or absurdist or sex-obsessed plays and pictures—all of them, ways out of direct and positive concern.

The weary adolescent—of whatever physical age—is taken a step farther by Vincent Canby, in his 1976 Thanksgiving survey of current films in the *N.Y. Times*. He pictures "the shrugged shoulder. The street corner sage who avoids thinking, avoids making judgment or any commitments by saying that everybody's crooked so what's the use?" Some emotional adolescents thus remain in the dumps through much of their life.

The adult knows that all persons come in shades of gray. He seeks to avoid moral judgments, to reject delusive slogans. Tragedy and high comedy are his mettle. He may, with Anatole France, look upon life with irony and pity; but in any case he will try to view events with some measure of detachment, recognizing (with Dickens) that great expectations must often find content in lesser ends. Few of us, of course, are fully adult, save at moments. As within the wasp's hive curl all its earlier layers, so within the mature man, ready to respond to the appropriate appeals, lie low the adolescent and the child. Some works rouse only the undeveloped aspects, the child in us. Most books and plays appeal to the adolescent mind and feelings. A great work reaches out to every level of the receptor's appreciative powers, satisfying the child's delight in triumph, the adolescent's desire for justice, and the adult design to see life steadily and see it whole.

[This grouping of ideas in a threefold pattern, we may note, has marked man's word ways through the centuries. Man has always been drawn to and baffled by numbers, which in several senses have seemed, and may still seem, magic; but no number has assumed greater significance than three. The triad, as already exemplified several times in this book, is a natural, and undoubtedly the most frequent, grouping. Things just seem to arrange themselves in threes. The ancient Greek poet appealed as often to the three Graces as to the (three times three) Muses. The Greeks tried to outwit the three Gorgons and placate the three Furies, but bowed to the three Fates. The Fates of the Northlands, the Norns, had names meaning "What was," "What is," and "What shall be," marking, of course, the irretrievable past, the elusive present, and the implacable future. The Greek poem the ode had three parts: strophe, antistrophe, and epode. Aristotle said that every work must have a beginning, a middle, and an end, which the rhetoricians discuss as introduction, body, and conclusion. Aristotle also gave impetus to the demand for the three dramatic unities, of time, place, and action.

[The Hellenic trinity of beauty and laughter and love may be measured against the Persian teaching of "three good things": to ride, to draw the bow, to tell the truth; and the ancient Chinese quest of gentleness, frugality, humility—capped by the triune Christian call for faith, hope, and charity, and the pious belief (enunciated in Hooker's *Ecclesiastical Polity*, 1594) that three is "the mystical number of God's unsearchable perfection within Himself." And in continued chorus are aligned the three hierarchies of the heavenly hosts, each with its own three orders: Seraphim, Cherubim, Thrones; Dominions, Virtues, Powers; Principalities, Archangels, Angels.

[Early writers sought the good, the true, and the beautiful, which they linked with the body, the mind, and the spirit. Psychoanalysts prate of the ego, the superego, and the id; earlier, they watch the three critical periods of growth to maturity: oral, anal, and genital. Freud, in "The Theme of the Three Caskets," examines the three daughters of King Lear and the three chests in *The Merchant of Venice*. He is following the pattern of the fairy tale; Cinderella also has two evil sisters; and it is the youngest (not the younger) son that wins the prize.

[The Muslim, before entering the mosque to pray, ceremonially cleanses his eyes, which may behold temptation; his feet, which may lead him toward it; and his hands, which may take it in. There come to mind the three monkeys, symbols of our guard against evil. The Wheel of Life—on which men may turn through many rebirths before they rise to become one with the World-Soul—has at its hub, conjoined, the hog, the serpent, and the dove, embodiments of ignorance, anger, and lust, at the poison-core of man's misfortunes. (Note that ignorance means what a man can know, but through sloth, or heedlessness, or willfulness, does not.)

[The Parsi, descendant of the Zoroastrian sun-worshipper, still prays every morning for good thoughts, good words, good deeds. This encapsulates an admirable lifetime. And, fundamentally, thought and knowledge, along with their vehicle, language, are conscious, common, and communicable.

[Dear to the Marxians is Hegel's description of the three dialectical steps: thesis, antithesis, and higher synthesis. A novel may range among the upper class (aristocrats), the middle class (plebeians), or the workers (proletarians). A vogue in the arts moves through three periods: innovation, imitation, irritation. A great work—I repeat—affords the receptor entertainment, enlightenment, exaltation. It has been said, indeed, that all good things come in threes. Having bowed toward the three R's, we may now turn to three literary forms, the drama, the novel, and the essay.]

A play is obviously something that is played, usually before an audience. *Drama* has been harder to define. The French Ferdinand Brunetière states that the essence of drama is *conflict*. The English William Archer calls it *crisis*. The American Clayton Hamilton plumps for *contrast*. This seems to me too placid, almost passive; I prefer *opposition*. In drama we watch two opposing forces, striving for a common goal; or one attempting to reach a goal, the other blocking the way. The presence of an audience introduces a third element: sympathy with (not for) one force. This sympathy the author sets.

The same organization is true of the novel; the difference being, of course, that in the drama we watch and hear the characters themselves working toward their desires, whereas in the novel this is just told to us, in ways we shall note later.

In most plays down the ages of dramatic writing, but especially in the nineteenth century, the opposing forces are centered in two persons, the hero and the villain, with the heroine either the goal, or the prize for him that attains it. In many plays, on the other hand, the forces opposing the hero may be social: the finger of fate points the path; or the background—heredity in Ibsen's *Ghosts;* convention or restrictive laws in thesis and propaganda plays—tugs the reins. In more subtle or more searching drama, the opposition is within one person, whom we then call not hero but protagonist. The contrary drives within him may be as conventional as the *pundonor*, 'point of honor', in classical Spanish drama, when the demands of honor (vengeance) run counter to the call of love. In Shakespeare, this opposition sets the doom of Romeo and Juliet. Classical tragedy sprang from a violation of natural or human laws; today disaster often springs from their very existence. The deepest tragedy perhaps lies in the deliberate choice a man makes—for tragedy implies free will—holding his head high on the road to death, for the sake of his ideals. Thus also Joan of Arc, in several plays, notably Shaw's. Thus too, with a problem pertinent today, Joyce's *Exiles.*

Such a character looms as basic in the play, and thereby brings us to a critical opposition. For Aristotle says that the action is fundamental in the drama; and certainly in melodrama, particularly in mystery thrillers, the plot is what matters, and in propaganda and discussion plays the characters may be little more than puppets mouthing the author's ideas. In most serious drama, how-

ever, attention turns rather to the persons involved, so that
Dryden could protest: "The story is the least part." Critics today
tend to think that this opposition is a false one: as the drama
moved from outer to inner conflict, action rousing passion, passion
spurring to action, it became clearer that character and action are
inseparable. We know a person by his deeds, because his deeds
are determined by his nature. Given Lady Macbeth's character,
once she has heard the witches' prophecy, *she* makes it come true.
As Hegel phrases the situation: "the character that is dramatic
plucks for himself the fruit of his own deeds." It is the wine we
press that we must drink.

Two types of tragedy have thus been distinguished, each described—again—by Shakespeare. In the tragedy of circumstance,

> As flies to wanton boys, are we to the gods,
> They kill us for their sport.

Contrariwise, in the tragedy of recoil,

> The gods are just, and of our pleasant vices
> Make instruments to plague us.

The second type involves the concept of the tragic flaw, the
weakness in an otherwise good man—his indecision or his ill-
decision—that leads to his downfall. For this we have borrowed
the Greek term *hamartia*, although to the Greeks themselves
hamartia meant a mistake in identity, followed by the fateful
recognition on the part of the character; the audience knew all
along. Also *hubris*, which we understand as inordinate pride—the
major tragic flaw—was to the Greeks an act: an abuse of power, a
criminal or morally heinous deed. For a third (and final) altered
application, *nemesis* to the Greeks was a righteous indignation, a
sense of injustice, which might lead to—but which we have identified with—the retribution. In many cases, however—as Medea's
slaying of her own children to punish her faithless husband—we
lose sight of the justified grievance in the horror of the revenge.
Yet the German playwright Hebbel had point in his remark that,
in a good play, every character is in the right.

Terror and *pity*: again there has been a critical quarrel over the
terms. Aristotle declared that the effect of tragedy is to rouse terror and pity in the receptor, thus producing a *catharsis*, purging
him of these emotions. The Christian world, on the contrary,
deems pity a proper feeling to harbor in the breast of a moral
man. And the radical playwrights of today speak alternately of

alienation and commitment: *alienation* of the audience from the emotions of the characters in the play, so as to grasp the meaning of its attack upon the mores: *commitment,* then, to the policy the playwright would have his hearers pursue. It has been said, of Ibsen, that his plays rouse only pathos, they but simmer with small souls; yet on their first presentation they were vilified, howled down, as obscene threats to the existing order. A mild turn of phrase upon the author was to label him Ibscene.

Such considerations hang upon the assumption that the theatre is a weapon in the class war; they consider not its aesthetic but its social arousal. This is the attitude of certain playwrights, not that of the usual critic, nor of the general public. Few are pleased with propaganda that were not persuaded before the play. It gives believers a prod to righteous indignation, a push toward action; others are more likely to feel embarrassed, condescendingly tolerant, or just unconcerned. Put such considerations aside, there remains a fundamental value: beyond the quickening of one's powers that is the gift of all art, tragedy gives man a pride and an assurance, a song to sing against despair. I have called this exaltation.

The three *unities*, of time, place, and action—story limited to one day, one location, and one main drive—were observed by the French until Hugo broke the bonds in 1830; in Elizabethan England, Jonson was observant, but Shakespeare ignored them, as have most playwrights in English since. The five-act division of a play, however, was the norm up to the last half of the nineteenth century. It has been shaped in Freytag's pyramid (Gustave Freytag, in 1863):

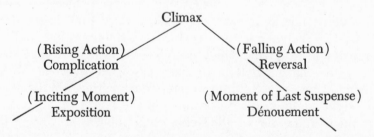

The climax is the decisive moment, in which one force triumphs; the opposition is dissolved. Recent plays have shortened the dénouement, the tying together of loose ends after the struggle is over; the curtain now usually falls close upon the climax, with the play written in three acts, or even but two.

Comedy, loosely defined as a play with a happy ending, has

been less controversial than tragedy. It is said that comedy ends in the church; tragedy, in the churchyard. The terms have also been applied outside the theatre. Homer's epic *Iliad* is tragic; its last line is: "So wrought they the burial of Hector tamer of horses." His *Odyssey* is comic; its last line (as recorded by Aristarchus in the second century B.C.; more has been added) is: "So came these two to the rite of the ancient marriage bed." Dante's great poem, ending in Paradise, is known as *The Divine Comedy*; Balzac's many novels have been linked as *La comédie humaine*.

Some critics state that comedy presupposes tragedy, and indeed in ancient Greece the serious trilogy was followed by the mocking satyr play. More picture the two as opposite sides of the one coin of human nature, rising out of the same quest, serving together to strengthen the spirit against deviation, desperation, and despair. The great works are thus neither conservative nor radical. They do not seek to affect temporary contemporary troubles, but may move toward a more humane outlook, a wiser approach to the perennial problems of living and living together. It is in this sense that Santayana declared: "Every artist is a moralist, though he need not preach."

The earth has been here a long time; the forces of gravity, stability, inertia, are strong; our development has been tentative and slow—too slow for any individual in any generation to discern the upward trend from still-bestial drives to more mutual concern. Therefore the impatient ones, who in these last years of the second Christian millennium desire utopia by sunset and the earthly paradise in the dawn, create in the verbal arts what they themselves call antidrama, antinovel, antiart. This rebellion takes two directions. They may seek to rub the raw flesh of feeling, to rouse the gut-passions; to strike out at current ills and by destruction end them. Or they may seek to probe beneath the surface of things, to reach the essence within the manifest form. This second direction leads to abstract art and dissected language, in the attempt to draw out leviathan's heart with a hook, to snare a quiddity with a symbol. A pyramid of tomato-soup cans piled on the floor or painted on a canvas shows that the industrialized world is tinny rather than tuned. A man onstage, grunting to an audience of empty chairs, demonstrates (as does the U.N.) the futility of man's attempt to achieve understanding and harmony along the usual avenues of communication. And while these impatient efforts have their blatant and more or less exciting day, art maintains its slow yet exalting movement through the centuries.

Another controversy that has divided opinions on the drama is whether a play is to be judged in the performance, or in the reading. Aristotle said: "Terror and pity may be induced by spectacular means; but it is much better to produce them by the writing." Insofar as stage effects are concerned, they can now be far surpassed in the motion pictures. Playwrights increasingly expect their plays to be read. Bernard Shaw wrote long prefaces developing the ideas in his dramas. James M. Barrie often printed confidential asides for his readers. Eugene O'Neill wrote stage directions beyond any production's capture. In the printed copy of his *Desire Under the Elms* we are told, of the two overhanging trees: "They are like exhausted women resting their sagging breasts and hands and hair on its roof, and when it rains their tears trickle down monotonously and rot on the shingles." It does not rain during the play.

It might be suggested that a good play should be both heard onstage and read in quiet. Yet the response of the players to an appreciative audience, and the reaction of each receptor to the general rouse, add something that solitary reading cannot bestow. Nor can stage directions in cold print convey the effect of the motions and even wordless sounds onstage, such as the quickening heartbeat that comes with the insistent primitive drumbeat as the Emperor Jones seeks refuge in the forest through the night.

When O'Neill's *The Iceman Cometh* was being readied for Broadway, the press agent sent a note to the critics, stating that they had often declared it was hard to judge an O'Neill play from one performance, and offering to send copies to those that wished to read it in advance. Two of the twenty-five requested a copy. (Eugene had sent me one six months before.) I asked one of my colleagues in the Drama Critics' Circle why he had not wished to read the play; he responded that he wanted to go to the theatre like the ordinary playgoer. This struck me as both impossible and undesirable: no ordinary playgoer sees every play for many years; and the editor hires the critic as presumably an expert, to view, judge, and report.

Knowledge of the plot need not destroy interest in a good book or play. Virtually all the ancient Greek dramas tell stories already familiar to their first audiences. Roman plays have a prologue summarizing the plot. The reading of a play should kindle anticipation of a vivid performance. And in the theatre, when we hear Lady Macbeth say:

A little water clears us of this deed

we are the more involved in her emotions if we know that soon she will cry:

> All the perfumes of Arabia will not sweeten this little hand.

Such awareness helps create the sought-for tension.

There are three degrees of tension in the theatre: surprise, suspense, dramatic irony. Sheer surprise is seldom used alone. Shakespeare employs it once in a critical moment, when Othello cries, of the turban'd Turk:

> I took by the throat the circumcisèd dog
> And smote him—thus!

as he stabs himself.

Imagine a situation. An elderly man, sitting in his study at night, hears a footfall in the next room. He, and the audience, are surprised. He reaches in his desk drawer for the revolver, and awaits the next step. He, and the audience, are in suspense. But if the audience knows—as he does not—that the approaching intruder, about to slip through the door and face the frightened old man with an aimed revolver, is that man's own son, who ten years ago had left to live in a commune and was forthwith disowned: that is dramatic irony. Like the gods on Olympus, the audience watches the unwitting man onstage as a crisis in his life draws near. The receptor is lifted to a plane of understanding beyond that of those whom he is watching.

Dramatic irony is found in the Bible. Job is unaware of God's challenge to Satan; Joseph's brothers in Egypt do not recognize him as the potentate before whom they bow. The same effect is frequent in lighter mood. However the persons in *The Comedy of Errors* mistake the twins, the audience knows them apart, the more to enjoy the onstage confusions.

This involvement of the spectator raises the question of the extent to which he should be caught in the play's emotions. In these days of widespread radio and television dramas, we are far from the naive reaction burlesqued in *Show Boat*, when two cowboys, watching the play, draw pistols and order the villain to desist. Yet some propaganda plays have ended with the audience captured or moved into singing the *Internationale*. Good plays establish what is called *psychic distance*, so that the receptor is at once carried along with the emotions of the characters and kept intellectually free and alert for subtler significances of which these characters may be unaware; both enjoying the play and appreciating the playwright's powers. Sometimes this distancing is effected by special devices: in Obey's *Lucrece* (1931) the ravishing of the matron is presented in dumb show, while a narrator comments. Usually, however, the playwright works more subtly, with dialogue and measured restraint.

In hybrid drama, the appeal to the receptor is more complicated. Of the many compounded forms suggested by Polonius— tragical-comical-historical-pastoral—one term we continue to use: *tragicomedy*. In this, "hornpipes and funerals" mingle; horror succeeds farce, or indeed is lumped into farcical cruelty, as when we turn from Marlowe and his fellows to contemporary drama, Anouihl, Beckett, Ionesco, still summoning us to laughter and tears. This "new craft of dark comedy," we are told, "eventually sours the laughter and redoubles the emotion; it is likely to be drama at its most cheerless and uncompromising." As it evolves today, it seems to move toward bad taste, rebellion, annihilation of significance. Its authors, indeed, find no significance in our living. And, J. L. Styan goes on, "Bad taste is the essence of every rebellion, and rebellion is the essence of artistic vitality." Eric Bentley sees it from another perspective: "Dark comedy will drag us passionate through the mud." Comedy and tragedy were on occasion fused; now they seem often confused.

Bentley states that dark comedy may seem to have a bitter ending, because it does not really end at all. It is at home in polemical drama, in drama of commitment, for it says, in effect, "What happens after this is up to you, the public." Such drama, as has been noted, is likely to appeal only to those already committed. Many may throng to bitter plays, plays of violence, attacks on the social system, identifying themselves with either side in what has been called a sadomasochistic enjoyment; but an Aristotelian catharsis is achieved: they work off their impulses at the play, then go home to a quiet bed.

Ancient, and Shakespearean, tragedy ends with an achieved resolution, a calm within the play after the storming passions. The hybrid form, dark comedy, exposes the social sore, and hopes the receptor will turn physician. The receptor is usually neither trained nor interested in that role. The contribution of art to our living is indirect; by challenging our sensitivity and enlarging our understanding, it makes us more attuned to justice; action may be its ultimate result, but is not its immediate goal.

Much of what has been said of the drama applies also to that more private form of fiction, the novel. Both of them, at their best, spread around the specific plot an aura of universality. What happens to a king affects the entire kingdom. With less prominent figures, the author must win the receptor to recognize his neighbors, indeed himself, in the characters. Verily, there go I. Many persons have stated that they see Hamlet in themselves. *Mutatis mutandis*—in our lesser scope—we may see, around if not within, an incipient Shylock, a miniature Macbeth. But also, an ocean-spanning Lindbergh; the first man to land on Mars. Florence Nightingale; Eleanor Roosevelt; the new Marilyn Monroe. Who has not read, and dreamed a dream, may close the book.

The novel, with its greater length and therefore more leisurely development, can more readily than the drama convey this sense of universality. The first chapter of Dickens' *A Tale of Two Cities* expands its opening sentence—"It was the best of times; it was the worst of times"—into a picture of the world of London and Paris in 1775.

Universality may also be sought by suggesting, both physically and psychologically, three distances. Physically, there is the immediate locale of the action, let us say the stock market, New York's Wall Street. Beyond this, affecting it and affected by it, are the Bourse, the Rialto, the oil-producing countries, the economic shiftings and maneuverings of the world. And enfolding this aspect of life are the other concerns of living: traveling, entertaining, spending and consuming, making love, as most persons do. Psychologically, there is, in each person involved, first the individual aspect, a unique human with a combination of characteristics just his own. Beyond these, there are qualities in him common to his group, his profession, his racial and environmental background: a self-made lawyer, Jewish City College alumnus, in a WASP Harvard firm; or a traveling salesman; a Scot. And deeper within him are the fundamental impulsions, the urges and the needs shared by most of mankind.

Minor characters may be less fully depicted; they may be flat, as compared to the major figures, which are shown in the round. Even these may be static or dynamic, that is, unchanged from first to last, or growing in comprehension, in greed, in compassion, or otherwise transformed under the impact of the events and persons that impinge upon them. A specific form of such change in the novel has been labeled the hourglass pattern; this presents two persons, one rising in material or moral value as the other falls, as in *Thaïs*, by Anatole France, in which the courtesan is uplifted by chaste love as the saintly man succumbs to temptation.

The novel has clearly greater scope than the drama. In fact, as

Richard Aldington emphasized: "The excuse for a novel is that one can do any damn thing one pleases." And indeed has done. There are novels that seem to be a succession of episodes, held together like a string of sausages, consummated one after the other in the movement of time. There are others with a tightly knit plot, in which every event comes in its one essential place, until the inevitable close. Some are a series of tales held together in a frame; the best known of these are three. *The Arabian Nights* pictures Scheherazade outwitting the Shah her husband—who, having caught his first wife in an adulterous orgy, swore to marry a virgin every night and have her slain in the morning—by telling him stories that do not end at sleep time, so that he postpones and finally abandons his resolution. Boccaccio's *Decameron* presents seven young ladies and three young gentlemen, withdrawn from Florence because of the 1348 plague, each telling a story on a set theme, each of the ten days of their seclusion. And Chaucer's *Canterbury Tales,* mainly in verse, are told by the pilgrims setting out together from the Tabard Inn in Southwark, on their way to the Canterbury shrine of Thomas à Becket.

Tales are usually brief narratives of happenings. A short story is more carefully woven; its brevity limits it to one of the many appeals of the novel; it may emphasize plot, as the detective story; or local color; or character portrayal; or it may seek to arouse a specific emotion, as the grisly "A Cask of Amontillado" and "The Pit and the Pendulum" of Edgar Allan Poe.

Predecessor of what we today call the novel is the picaresque tale, of the adventures of a rogue, who usually rises in the social scale and marries a lady. Famous among these is the French *Gil Blas* (1715), by Alain René Le Sage, translated by Tobias Smollett and the model for his *Roderick Random* (1749). Henry Fielding's *Tom Jones,* of the same year, is in the picaresque tradition.

The novel occupies the widest range of current prose; in public libraries and on best-sellers lists, books are divided into fiction and nonfiction. It has vague borders: on the north, say, fantasy; on the east, history; on the west, ethics; on the south, journalism. Along the northern border lie the fairy tales, the journeys of Alice in Wonderland and Through the Looking-glass; more recently, the province of Poictesme explored by James Branch Cabell and the shire of the Hobbits surveyed by J. R. Tolkien. A curious combination of fantasy and shuddery Gothic is Mervyn Peake's *Gormenghastly* trilogy of stories.

Nor'-nor'-east lies a region infested by the writers of science fiction, who put forth a modest claim to be historians of the future. They began as far back as Lucian of Samosata, who about 150 A.D. told of interplanetary conflict, and visits to the sun and the moon. Similar visits were pictured by Cyrano de Bergerac in the seventeenth century. Nearer to our time came the more plausible Jules Verne and H. G. Wells. The recent mushrooming of scientifiction has brought many eerie flights of fancy, as in the decade-long *Star Trek* of television, with galactic doom averted by heroic supermen; but also a more sober picture of future life by writers with a sound scientific background, like Arthur C. Clarke and Isaac Asimov.

Toward the east gather the many historical romances, such as Scott's *Ivanhoe*, Dumas' *The Three Musketeers*, with an increasing emphasis on accuracy since Tolstoi's *War and Peace*. In most of these the historical figures serve mainly as a solid background to the imagined central characters. Some, however, pay great attention to the conditions of the time. Mary Renault's novels increase our understanding of ancient Greece. Josephine Tey's *Daughter of Time* challenges the Tudor bias behind Shakespeare's picture of Richard III, and seeks to rehabilitate that tarnished monarch. Across on the west spread the books of moral or social concern, the early *Pilgrim's Progress*, the nineteenth-century *Erewhon*, and other books picturing the evils of our society in contrast with a desired Utopia; or, more recently, gloomy prophecies of the Dystopia, or Kakotopia, in the not too distant future—say, 1984.

Down south along the journalism swamp cluster the books that rise from the current news: Upton Sinclair's *Boston* of the Sacco-Vanzetti trial; Dreiser's *An American Tragedy*, which used transcripts of court records; and the host of scandal-mongering or debunking *romans à clef*, novels scarcely hiding the real persons whose peccadillos or more heinous deeds they lavishly set forth. We are promised—if that be the word—a picture of "the sex-life of Jesus." Oscar Wilde remarked that we used to canonize our heroes, now we vulgarize them. Even our gods. This desire to find feet of clay, a base element, in prominent and esteemed figures, I leave to psychologists to fathom, merely pointing out that to revel in the revelation of a great man's failings bemeans not him but the one that takes joy thereof.

Volumes have been written on the meaning of the word *romance*, but readers today expect a romance to be an adventureful love story, the "Gothic romance" having a sinister aura of perhaps supernatural evil pressing upon the heroine. Realism, on the other hand, is more limited to a faithful presentation of things as they are. Its subdivision, naturalism, has been defined as a slice of life; usually that slice cuts through the viscera, or slightly below.

"Realism" raises the question of truth in fiction. Coleridge made the well-known assertion that the receptor, when he opens a book, grants "a willing suspension of disbelief"; but the author must strive for something less passive. He must, indeed, make his story so vivid that the question of its actuality does not arise during the reading. For ultimately, the quality of a work depends not on its approximation to the life outside the book, but on the consistency with one another of the events within the story, and the appropriateness, in terms of their own nature, of the characters' response. It has thus been said that each work of art fashions its own laws for itself—but they may not be extracted for application to another work.

Receptors, of course, are not bound by general considerations, and many tend to react to what they read, or see on screen, as though the creatures were real. Bells tolled in England when Richardson's Clarissa Harlowe died. Dickens was accosted on the London streets by strangers pleading with him not to let Little Nell succumb, or otherwise trying to influence the next installment of his novels. Motion-picture performers are named instead of the characters they portray: "In that picture, she marries Clark Gable." It is a short step from this emotional confusion to the star-worship of hysterical teenagers, on a road that leads far from the appreciation of a work of art.

Stevenson remarked that, whenever he came upon a passage in fiction that was notoriously untrue, he was sure that it was a direct transcript from life. On the other hand, almost anything can be made credible—that is, accepted within the story's own terms—if it is properly conveyed. For a supreme example of making the impossible "true," look at Aristophanes' account of the building of Cloud-Cuckooland, to separate the gods in the sky from the humans on earth, in his comedy *The Birds*. The birds and the humans in the play take the building for granted, at once arguing about details, and who gets credit for the idea. A clown, or an actor in the Chinese drama, will imperturbably open an imaginary door, and stumble over the nonexistent threshold. There is no question of truth or falsity when truthfulness is not an issue.

Of truth in fiction, there have nonetheless been distinguished four degrees:

The impossible. This is the realm of fairy tales and fantasy. Cervantes here sets his woeful knight Don Quixote. Here Rabelais romps with Gargantua and Pantagruel. Here abide the things that cannot be.

The improbable. This is the playground of the romantic hero, the battlefield of the daredevil secret agent; the happy hunting-ground of most of yesterday's best-sellers, which fed aspiring dreams.

The probable. This is the stamping ground of most best-sellers of our time, from Sinclair Lewis through Hemingway to novels you can list for yourself—the profferings of a dozen "book clubs," works in which you can recognize your neighbors.

The inevitable. This is the world of the dramas and novels whose characters drive to an end determined by their nature, in the face of forces that press upon their days. Here stand the things that must be.

The best-sellers are in the middle range; the best books, at either end. Beauty lies in the extremes.

In whichever category a story may lie, it can be told in various ways. The device of putting the narrative in a series of letters, by one person or several in turn, was used in what is commonly called the first English novel, Samuel Richardson's *Pamela* (1740); it is long out of fashion. A step beyond this is to have a character within the story tell the tale. This of course limits the story to items that character could have experienced, heard, or surmised; but it gives the reader the added challenge of judging the narrator: is he as simple as John Ridd calls himself in that old-time favorite, *Lorna Doone*, or as clever as Jim Hawkins thinks he is, in *Treasure Island?* A few books of this sort seek wider scope by changing the narrator midstream. But by far the most stories are told directly, in the third person, by the author, who may limit himself to what an outside observer can know, but usually assumes an Olympian view, seeing into the minds and motives of the characters, exposing to the receptor impulses and desires usually kept hidden. This revelation is carried to its extreme in the "stream-of-consciousness" technique, best known in the last half-hundred pages of James Joyce's *Ulysses*, as Mrs. Bloom without pause or punctuation spills forth her errant night fancies.

This flow of notions through the mind, which the seventeenth-century metaphysical poet and divine John Donne complained disturbed his prayers, is found in embryo in sixteenth- and seventeenth-century Spanish and Italian writers, as Aretino, in

Diderot's *Rameau's Nephew* (1779), and Carlyle's *French Revolution* (1837). Joyce credits Edouard Dujardin's French *The Laurels Are Felled* (1887) as his source; but the stream was described by philosopher William James and utilized in the novels of his brother Henry. The novels of Dorothy Richardson mark its fullest use, though it is akin to the practice of the surrealists.— Whatever his technique, omniscient narrator, interested bystander, or participant, the author must win the reader with his tale.

A basic distinction between the narrative and the dramatic form is suggested by Susanne Langer, who states that narrative moves in the present; drama, toward something beyond. Persons in the drama, she asserts, are, "consciously or blindly, makers of the future." Great drama deals essentially with commitment (of the characters) and consequence. As against the narrative mode of Memory, it provides the illusion of Destiny.

In recent fiction, however, as in Woolf, Joyce, Kafka, and more, the narrative drive grows weaker. There seems to some extent a "breakdown of narrative"—as a course at the New School is entitled—"as it reflects the loss of faith in history and society." Ortega y Gasset prophesied the "death of the novel"; Vladimir Nabokov declares: "One of the functions of all my novels is to prove that the novel in general does not exist." What is put between the covers of a book today may be far from the linear narrative of yesteryear. Radical fiction, in both novel and drama, exhibits the same movement from old-time values, even from sober significance, as is found in nonrepresentational schools of painting and sculpture.

The novelist Jorge Luis Borges created a world called Tlön, in the language of which there are no nouns. For there—unlike the world of our "erring" fictioneers before the "enlightened" authors of Borges' world—life is not a concurrence of objects in space succeeding one another in time, but a heterogeneous accumulation of fortuitous and independent acts. In such books—as indeed in the plays of Harold Pinter and his like—there is no point to seeking causes or motives of human actions.

While dadaist painters and writers occasionally dropped around and signed their name to a fellow-artist's product, the question of originality is usually seriously raised. Historically, this became important when men began to earn a living by their pens, and copyright was introduced to protect their production. Seneca in the first century declared: "What anyone has said well is mine." On the other hand, the rhetorician Ælian, in the third century, speak-

ing of those that wrote centos (poems of borrowed lines) out of
Homer, said "He spews, they lick it up." Milton in the seventeenth
century stated that one who borrows without improving is a
plagiary. Molière boasted that he took his "goods" where he found
them; Shakespeare without apology appropriated his plots. The
poet Donne was sarcastic, but with the protest of a victim:

> For if one eat my meat, let it be known
> The meat was mine, the excrement is his own.

The great writers have been drawn again and again to the great
themes; more than one would care to list have told the Trojan
stories.

At times, indeed, originality was not desired. Seneca's contemporary Philo of Byblos attributed his *History* to an imaginary
Phoenician. Some thousand years later, the Continent compli-
mented Chaucer as "the great translator." Cervantes apologized
for inventing instead of using the ancient sources; he published
Don Quixote as from the Arabic of Cid Hamet Ben Engeli. Several of the Elizabethans—Gascoigne, Drant, Whetstone; even,
later, Walpole with his *Castle of Otranto* (1764)—called their
works translations from the Italian. The practice of hunting for a
writer's source led Tennyson to cry: "As if no one had heard the
sea moan except Horace!"

Originality lies deeper than subject matter, deeper than form.
Any dauber can hire the great artist's model; any poetaster can
make a sonnet rhyme. "The style is the physiognomy of the mind,"
said Schopenhauer; Buffon: "The style is the man himself." Each
individual presses the subject and the form into his unique mold.
It is in this sense that the quality of a work depends upon its exact
and complete structure, permitting paraphrase only to its own
destruction; it is in this sense, in the measure of the author's personality, that a work is original.

Least bound by rules or conventions, of the literary arts, is the
essay, which ranges wide. It may be best divided into the formal
and the informal. The latter includes what used to be called "the
character," first drawn in the third century B.C. by Theophrastus:
a brief but graphically illustrated picture of human types and failings, most popular in England in the seventeenth century, leading
to the essays of Steele and Addison on Sir Roger de Coverley and
his friends in *The Spectator*, and to the "profiles" of prominent
personalities in today's magazines. Informal essays are subjective,

impressionistic, and often playful, as Lamb's famous discussion of Roast Pig.

Two French writers are noted for their introduction of new forms of the familiar essay. Sainte Beuve, in the mid-nineteenth century, wrote the *causerie,* a "chat" about a writer or book, as though talking casually, yet searchingly, to a friend. Alain in this century developed the shorter *propos,* a "suggestion" of less than a thousand words, in which he takes a nugget of thought and with impeccable logic rounds and polishes it until it shines like burnished gold.

The formal essay is more objective. It ranges from the leader (as the English call it; in America, the editorial) through the book review and the critical essay, which may examine political or social issues, as on the Op-Ed ('opposite the editorial') page of *The New York Times,* on to the lengthier treatise and the learned monograph. As the verb *to essay* shows us, the essay should be regarded as "an attempt"; it is one man's endeavor to please, to inform, to persuade.

Before turning to one specific type of essay, the literary critique, we may linger to note that very few writers have achieved equal mastery of all the literary forms. Samuel Johnson wrote good poetry, one readable novel, as well as several sound essays; but his play was a failure. Oliver Goldsmith is almost unique, having achieved a minor masterpiece in all four literary forms: his poem *The Deserted Village,* his play *She Stoops to Conquer,* his essays *Citizen of the World,* his novel *The Vicar of Wakefield.* David Garrick qualified his praise of Goldsmith: "He wrote like an angel and talked like poor Poll"; Johnson averred: "He adorned whatever he touched." But Goldsmith remains an exception; in the literary as perforce in the scientific field, most workers are specialists.

Most controversial of the various types of essay is the critical discussion of an author or a work. What should the critic seek? Definitions of criticism spread so wide as to be self-contradictory. "Fault-finding" is in the dictionaries. "The distinguishing of beauty," says Elizabeth Barrett Browning. Victor Hugo is blunt: "Is the work good or bad? That's criticism's domain." The best-known notion, which has been called the Goethe-Carlyle-Croce-Spingarn theory, is that the critic should answer three questions: What has the author tried to do? How well has he done it? Was it worth doing?

This prestigious presentation of the critic's concern has itself been subjected to vigorous criticism. The third question has often, in practice, been ignored, for it implies that the critic must set himself up as a judge of values; and especially in these days, when standards are being broken and values denied, a critic that upholds them runs the risk of losing his public. The first two questions have been equally, but more openly, brushed aside. For in the opinion of a large body of writers in the field, in the first place, it is impossible to know an author's intention; in the second place, his aim is irrelevant, the question to ask being not Did he hit the target? but rather What target did he hit? Pope in his *Essay on Criticism* conservatively advises:

> In every work regard the writer's end,
> Since none can compass more than they intend.

This runs quite contrary to the general idea that every great artist has "builded better than he knew"; with the spur of triumphant creation his work soars beyond any conscious plan. André Gide has said:

> Before I explain my book, I want to wait for others to explain it to me. To elucidate it too soon would be to restrict its meaning too soon. For, if we know what we intended to say, we never know whether we have said that alone. One always says more than that.

Thus, basically, the critic is left to his own resources, to look at the work, and to appreciate, estimate, and convey the meaning, mode, and measure of what he has looked upon.

The question of criticism, then, turns rather upon the critic than upon the work. Critics in our time fall roughly into two groups. In France, these are called by Roland Barthes "university" critics and "interpretive" critics; but in England and the United States too many in both groups are teaching for that first label to have distinctive value. Barthes' first group is rather of traditional critics; they are concerned with the work in itself, as literature. The interpretive critics examine and evaluate a work in the light of a particular ideology: existentialism, Marxism, psychoanalysis, phenomenology. Both groups have retreated from the emphasis on an author's biography as explaining his writing, excepting of course the psychoanalytic critics, who hunt in the author's childhood for the wellsprings of his literary preoccupations. This second, interpretive group, Raymond Picard vehemently argues, are often farfetched in seeking to connect a work with their personal ideology, and in any event are turning away from the proper concerns of the literary critic.

What then should we expect of the critic? Hazlitt denounced the ultracrepidarian criticism of William Gifford, who in the *Quarterly Review* of 1818 blasted Keats' poem *Endymion*. (*Ultracrepidarian*, criticism that ventures beyond the critic's range of knowledge. The term is drawn from ancient Greece. A shoemaker found fault with a sandal latchet in a painting of Apelles, favorite artist of Alexander the Great; when Apelles corrected it, the man proceeded to criticize the drawing of the legs, whereupon Apelles said: *Ne sutor ultra crepidam*, "The cobbler should stick to his last.") In recent years, reviewer Heywood Broun protested that he needn't have shoveled coal in a stokehold to write a valid review of O'Neill's *The Hairy Ape*—but it was a ship's engineer who wrote to the director that if the watcher didn't move away in that stoking scene, his backside would be fried to a cinder.

Taking for granted (though the assumption is a strain!) that the critic can express himself clearly, cogently, and persuasively, we may make three main demands. The critic should be informed: he should know literature well, other works of the sort he is surveying; he should know the trends of his time, in such fields as are presented in the work, but also be able to place these in historical perspective. He should be impressionable: open to the new yet not scornful of the old; sensitive to nuances both of language and of feeling; discriminating but not dogmatic. And he should be impartial: ready to consider various points of view; if biased (as who is not?) aware of his own predilections, preferences, and prejudices, to make allowance for them, and of course to make them known to his readers.

Of these qualities, most important is being always open to wonder, to welcome the new with recognition in it of the old— the dual quality of lasting works; being ever eager for what Anatole France deemed the challenge to and the joy of a critic, as it should be to every reader: the adventures of a soul with a masterpiece.

12.

SYMBOLISM AND DISCONTENT

IF WE DEFINE A SYMBOL as something used as a sign of something else, it is obvious that all words are symbols. The word *tree* stands for the object with which our eyes have made us familiar. The words *to* and *from* are signs of direction, precisely as are the arrows where two roads cross.

Symbolism as a literary device depends on the flexibility of language, which ranges through four levels of expression:

1. *Animism:* the belief that every object contains a living spirit. The sea rages, because the sea is a monster.
2. *Metaphor:* identification. One no longer believes in the monster, but likes and uses the figure. The sea rages.
3. *Simile:* comparison. The figure is reduced from identity to analogy: the sea is like a monster.
4. *Reality:* The figure is discarded for the fact: the stormy sea (Homer), the wet sea.

Browning, who requires close attention but often rewards it, has seen the value of the literary use of symbolism:

> Art—wherein man nowise speaks to men,
> Only to mankind—Art may tell a truth
> Obliquely, do the thing shall breed the thought,
> Nor wrong the thought, missing the mediate word.
> So you may paint your picture, twice show truth,
> Beyond mere imagery on the wall—
> So, note by note, bring music from your mind,
> So write a book shall mean beyond the facts,
> Suffice the eye and save the soul besides.

Symbolism as a specific literary school was announced in a manifesto in the French magazine *Figaro* in 1866. It was foreshadowed by Baudelaire, who declared that we walk in a forest of symbols, and Mallarmé, who sought in his poetry to make every line "a plastic image, the expression of a thought, the rouse of a feeling, and the symbol of a philosophy." Despite many followers in England and America, however, the school had no lengthy influence, because its basis was clearly too all-inclusive. Every writer, willy nilly, is a symbolist.

Looking more closely at the naming words, nouns, as symbols, we note that there are basic differences in what they may designate.

1. They may point to things that have objective reality in the world around us: rivers and rolling stones and birds and bicycles.

2. They may point to things that have no objective reality: mermaids; the Sphinx, that monster with a lion's body but a woman's breasts and head; three-headed dogs like Cerberus; Zeus, Proteus, or the Old Man of the Sea, who could take the shape of any living creature.

3. They may, finally, point to things that are in a middle world, of ideas or influences whose reality we cannot prove but only believe or surmise: the soul, beauty, goodness, the will, the deity.

We have already observed how reification slips in, how easy it is for men to shift items from categories 2 or 3 into the realm of objective reality. Indeed, every item I have mentioned in class 2 above was at one time an object of human belief; and old travelers' tales found credence for even stranger marvels, such as the Cyclops, with but one eye and that in his forehead; the blemyae of Ethiopia, men with their faces in their chests; and the Libyan sciapods, who used their feet as sunshades. The ontic urge, to accept things named as things that exist, is especially strong.

A name, which is of course a personal sign, may become a more general symbol, applied to press upon another person the characteristic for which the named individual is noted or notorious. Thus we may call someone a very Hercules, a Shylock, a Daniel come to judgment. A seldom-heard attribution of this sort leads us back to one of the most individualistic English writers, Sir Thomas Urquhart, known to most (if at all) as the translator of Rabelais. The name that Urquhart celebrated was used by James M. Barrie for the title figure of his play *The Admirable Crichton:* a butler who, shipwrecked on a lonely island with the noble family he serves, by virtue of his competence and commanding personality is gradually acknowledged leader; is about to marry his lordship's daughter when a vessel sails into view; by Crichton's decision the signal fire is lighted, and as the rescue ship approaches he becomes again the perfect obsequious butler. Urquhart's *Ekskubalauron* contains his account of an historical person, Sir James Crichton (1560–1582), whom he calls The Admirable Crichton: a model of sixteenth-century chivalry and learning. In Mantua, interrupted by ten tipsy revelers while with his unparalleled mistress, Crichton slays six of them, and is about to pierce the next when a survivor cries "Don't kill the prince!" Crichton lowers his sword and—I pause to quote just the next sentence of this remarkable work:

> The Prince, in the throne of whose judgement the rebellious vapours of tun had installed Nemesis, and caused the irascible faculty shake off the soveraignty of reason, being without himself, and unable to restraine the impetuosity of the wills first motion, runs Crichton through the heart with his own sword, and kills him: in the interim of which lamentable accident, the sweet and beautiful lady (who by this time had slipped herself into a cloth-of-gold petticoat, in the anterior fente whereof was an asteristick pouch, wherein were inchased fifteen several diamonds, representative of the constellation of the primest stars in the sign of Virgo; had enriched a tissue gown and wastcoat of brocado with the precious treasure of her ivory body; and put the foot-stalls of those marble pillars which did support her microcosme, into a paire of incarnation velvet slippers embroidered with purple) being descended to the lower door (which jetting out to the court-wards) where Pomponacio was standing, with the curled tresses of her disheveled hair dangling over her shoulders, by the love-knot of whose naturally guilded filaments were made fast the hearts of many gallant sparks, who from their liberty of ranging after other beauties, were more forcibly curbed by those capillary fetters, than by so many chains of iron; and in the daedalian windings of the crisped pleats whereof, did lye in ambush a whole brigade of Paphian archers, to bring the loftiest martialists to stoop to the shrine of Cupid; and, Arachnalike, now careering, now caracoling it alongst the polygonal plainness of its twisted threads) seaze on the affections of all whose looks should be involved in her locks; and, with a presentation exposing to the beholders all the perfections that ever yet were by the Graces

conferred on the female sex, all the excellencies of Juno, Venus, and Minerva, the other feminean deities, and semi-goddesses of former ages, seeming to be of new revived, and within her compiled, as the compactedst abridgement of all their best endowments, stepped a pace or two into the court (with all the celerity that the intermixed passions of love and indignation was able to prompt her to: during which time, which certainly was very short, because, to the motions of her angelically-composed body, the quantity attending the matter of its constitution was no more obstructive, than were the various exquisite qualities flowing from the form thereof, wherein there was no blemish) the eyes of the prince's thoughts, and those were with him (for the influences of Cupid are like the actions of generation, which are said to be *in instanti*) pryed into, spyed, and surveyed from the top of that sublimely framed head, which culminated her accomplishments, down along the wonderful symmetry of her divinely-proportioned countenance; from the glorious light of two luminaries, Apollo might have borrowed rays to court his Daphne, and Diana her Endymion: even to the rubies of those lips, where two Cupids still were kissing one another for joy of being so near the enjoyment of her two rows of pearles inclosed within them; and from thence through the most graceful objects of all her intermediate parts, to the heavenlike polished prominences of her mellifluent and heroinal breast, whose porphyr streaks (like arches of the ecliptick and coloures, or azimuch and almicantar circle intersecting after) expansed in pretty veinlets (through whose sweet conduits run the delicious streams of Nectar, wherewith were cherished the pretty sucklings of the Cyprian goddesse) smiled on one another to see their courses regulated by the two niple-poles above them elevated, each in their own hemisphere; whose magnetic vertue, by attracting hearts, and sympathy in their refocillation, had a more impowering ascendant over poetic lovers, for furnishing their braines with choise of fancy, than ever had the two tops of Parnassus-hill, when animated or assisted by all the wits of the Pierian muses: then from the snow-white galaxy betwixt those gemel-monts, whose milken paths, like to the plains of Thessaly, do by reflection calefie, to that protuberant and convexe ivory, whose meditullian node, compared with that other, where the ecliptick cuts the equinoxial, did far surpass it in the property whereby the night is brought in competition with the day: whence having past the line, and seeming to depress the former pole to elevate another, the inward prospect of their mind discovered a new America, or land unknown, in whose subterranean and intestine cells were secret mines of greater worth, than those of either Tibar or Peru, for that besides the working in them could not but give delight to the mineralist, their metal was so reciptible for impression, and to the mind so plyable, that alchymists profoundly versed in chymical extractions, and such as knew how to imbue it with syndon, and crown the *magisterum* with the elixir, instead of treasures merchants bring from the Indies, would have educed little worlds more worth than gold and silver.

Having thus hurried to the scene of the fatal fray, the lady "like one of the graces possest with a fury, spoke thus: 'O villains! What have you done?' "

From this longest grammatically structured sentence in our literature, let us turn to life, and look upon the longest-lasting and most widespread example of words as signs that have become potent and actual forces, in the belief that movements in the heavens above influence life on the earth below. Emerson has stated that when men are selfish, astronomy becomes astrology, but Emerson has his history reversed; early man was perforce obsessively self-concerned. He studied the stars to know what would happen in his own life. Which came first, the planets or the gods? The learned astrologers of recent times discern an early science of astrobiology, which applied the mathematical order of the stars to the regulation of agriculture and of human lives in Chaldea and Egypt even before 3000 B.C. They trace the systematization of zodiacal symbols at least as far back as King Sargon I of Babylon, 2637–2582 B.C., who founded the Semitic dynasty of Akkad. The Greek identification of gods and heavenly bodies, called *catasterism*—we still call the planets by the ancient godly names—came earlier than the sixth century B.C. Men saw not only gods but earthly creatures starcast in the sky; the pathway of the months, and of the ages, is marked by the animals that encircle the Zodiac. While etymologists derive the word *zodiac* from Greek *zodion*, 'a small (carved) animal', diminutive of *zoon*, 'animal', the learned astrologers trace the word to Greek *zoe*, 'life', plus *diaklos*, 'wheel' (from *kuklos*, 'circle'), thus identifying it with the Wheel of Life, basic in Eastern beliefs. In the West, a disaster (*dis*, 'away'; *aster*, 'star') occurs when your (lucky) star is away.

Some writers in this field (Waldemar Fenn; Gustav Zollinger; R. M. Gattefossé in *Les Sages écritures*, 1945) maintain that the constellations were the source of the alphabet, Gemini, for instance, suggesting the letter H and the number 8. In his *Dictionary of Symbols*, J. E. Cirlot observes:

Given the importance traditionally attached to the word, it is easy to understand why Man, in every system ever formulated, has always sought to prove the divine power of letters by making them dependent upon mystic and cosmic orders.

The figurations in the heavens were linked with the forces on earth. The four natural elements, and the four human humors, were grouped with the twelve signs of the zodiac, in groups of three:

		begins	begins	begins
Fire	*choleric*	Aries 3/20	Leo 7/23	Sagittarius 11/22
Earth	*melancholic*	Taurus 4/20	Virgo 8/23	Capricorn 12/22
Air	*sanguine*	Gemini 5/20	Libra 9/23	Aquarius 1/20
Water	*phlegmatic*	Cancer 6/21	Scorpio 10/23	Pisces 2/19

These signs mark not only the months, but the ages of the earth, as its course moves through the precession of the equinoxes, completing a cycle of the 26,000 solar years that constitute one Platonic year. Is it by chance or heavenly design that Pisces came in with Christ the Fish? (Latin *pisces*, 'fish'; Greek *ichthys:* the Greek word is an acrostic, its letters being the first letters of the Greek words for Jesus Christ, God's Son, Savior.)

In the Far East, man's destiny is seen shaped by the animals that followed a different route: twelve hurried to pay respects to the dying Buddha (in the fifth century B.C.). The rat rode on the back of the ox, then leapt and thus was first. Their order of arrival is: Rat, Ox, Tiger, Rabbit, Dragon, Snake, Horse, Sheep, Monkey, Rooster, Dog, Boar. Our 1978 is the year of the Horse. A 1976 paperback, *Chinese Astrology* (from the 1969 French) suggests how to balance the Eastern annual prognostications with the monthly calculations of the West.

While the alchemy that led to chemistry took a natural course, dying as the new knowledge replaced the earlier gropings, not only was astrology prior to and for centuries more important than astronomy, but among the general public the belief has not been superseded by the science. The *Encyclopaedia Britannica* calls astrology "for 2,000 years a dominant influence on religion, philosophy and science in Europe." Astronomy became accurate in ancient Egypt mainly as a tool for the priests, who were astrologers to the Pharaohs. Their use of astrology was limited to royal activities; in Greece, however, genethlialogical astrology, the casting of nativities, became available to all citizens, as well as for guiding public events. In Athens, astrologers named a propitious day for beginning the Peloponnesian War (431–404 B.C.) which, alas, belied their prediction by ending with Athens' complete subjection to Sparta, bringing to a close her great period, the glory that was Greece.

In India, where astrology has determined action for over three thousand years—even now, in the many matrimonial advertisements, birthdates and natal signs are requested—the number 108 is sacred (108 beads are on the prayer necklace; Buddha had 108 incarnations before he attained nirvana; the god Shiva taught man the 108 basic postures of the Indian dance) because of the nine subdivisions of the twelve Zodiac signs, 9 times 12 being 108.

In Europe, Charlemagne had his official horoscopist; in the fourteenth century the major universities—as Paris, Padua, Bologna, Florence—had chairs in astrology.

William the Conqueror's astrologer was fortunate; when he set the date for the King's coronation, he forecast a bright future for the land. There followed 850 years of not uninterrupted but on the whole proud English growth. Chaucer tells us that the Wife of Bath's character was determined by her birth at the conjunction of Mars and Venus in Taurus. His *Knight's Tale* has 125 lines of astrological references, with accurate knowledge of judicial and horary astrology. —Yet his *Treatise on the Astrolabe*, for "little Lewis, my son" is a clear and scientific explanation of the instrument and its use.

The translation in 1574 of *The Zodiac of Life*, by Marcellus Palingenius Stellatus, was widely read in Shakespeare's time. Although astrologers were constantly consulted, mingled with the belief were other strains. Shakespeare has Cassius try to persuade Brutus:

> The fault, dear Brutus, is not in our stars
> But in ourselves, that we are underlings.

Ben Jonson probably worked with John Fletcher on the astrological scene in *The Bloody Brother;* the play shows the shifting beliefs of the time: a list of marvels—metallic birds that sing, a mechanical manservant (early robot) and the like—ends with the lines:

> All those new done by the Mathematicks,
> Without which there's no Science, and no Truth.

Thomas Nashe mockingly spoke of the "infallible" naming of days "favorable to clyp and shave haires, to fyshe in rivers, and bathe in baths." Such jibes did not prevent learned men from continuing to consult the stars. Dr. John Dee (1527–1608), Fellow of Trinity College, Cambridge, and sponsor of the first scientific survey of Britain, was renowned for his forecasts; he not only practiced astrology but claimed the guidance, in his predictions, of the Angel Uriel. While Dee was a Fellow at Cambridge, his stage effects for Aristophanes' *Peace* won him fame as a magician; in 1551 he became Astrologer Royal to Queen Mary Tudor; in 1564 he coached Queen Elizabeth in the art. Dr. Simon Forman, who was declared completely ignorant of physics and astronomy by the College of Physicians in 1593, was in 1603 licensed by Cambridge University to practice medicine; he became the most popular astrologer for the gentlemen of the court of Elizabeth and of James I, and especially for the ladies. A number of these, he recorded in his *Diary*, received not only his stellar wisdom but more intimate ministrations. (One of those that succumbed to the astrologer was singled out by historian A. L. Rowse, after reading the *Diary*, as a new candidate for the role of Shakespeare's Dark Lady. That darkness has absorbed many literal researchers.) Ben Jonson's play *Epicoene, or the Silent Woman* refers to the fame of Forman.

In the next century Swift, in a mock almanac, *Predictions for the Ensuing Year*, by "Isaac Bickerstaff," foretold the death of astrologer John Partridge on March 29, 1709; when on March 30 Partridge proclaimed that he was still alive, Swift wrote a *Vindication* to prove the man dead. So great was public interest that Steele assumed the pseudonym Bickerstaff for the author of his paper *The Tatler*. A century later, Horace Walpole spoke of "astrologers and such like cattle"; they continued to thrive, unperturbed. The poet Byron cast his son's horoscope.

Newspapers today, in most parts of the world, print a daily astrological chart with advice, for popular consumption. In this decade, an American college course was given in the curious combined subject of *Astronology*. And when Britain entered the Common Market, Janet Augustin, Doctor of Law, Lecturer for the Inner London Education Authority, and Consultant Astrologer, without royal request but with computer and her permanent mathematics expert—the wizards keep up with the times—set forth a detailed and gloomy prognosis for the land. While a few rulers in the West have maintained an Astrologer Royal, most have regulated their reign on other considerations (whether to happier ends is definitely moot).

Sir John Manolesco, in his *Scientific Astrology*, 1973, refers to himself as "the scientist British Intelligence had to have to counteract Hitler's personal astrologers in W.W.II." In its program, the hit musical *Hair* lists a company astrologer.

Knowing the way to a man's heart, a shrewd cuisinist added to the 1976 Christmas attractions an *Astrological Cookbook*.

Though perhaps merely symbolic for many Jews today, the zodiac is deeply rooted in Hebrew thought. Jewish calendars give the zodiac sign for every month. The wheel of the zodiac year adorns the entrance hall of Yeshiva University in New York, created by the orthodox Jewish community, with its offshoot the Einstein Medical School and hospital. The *Random House Dictionary* states that *mazel tov* in Hebrew means, "literally," 'good luck', but *mazel* is the Hebrew word for 'star', and this expression of best wishes "literally" means: May a good star shine upon your days. It is a frequent remark, in many tongues, that a man was born under a lucky star.

An eager turning to the astrologer came with the flow of handsome young men and hopeful young beauties to Hollywood; they sought a new name that would shine on a theatre marquee, proclaiming the rising star. Whatever one may think of their method, their desire was not unreasonable. The value of a good name may be glimpsed in the career of Hitler, whose (bastard) father changed the family name: it is impossible to think of millions of Germans, erect and with right arm outstretched, shouting in exultation: "Heil Schickelgruber!" Our heroes and our stars turn to the heavenly stars, hoping for names attuned to their hoped-for fortunes. Authors tend to this in their novels. Astrology still thrives on human dreams.

Deeper, and as pervasive—though not availing to brush away credence in the causal stars—has been the belief in heaven (and hell) as the abode of gods and devils fighting for possession of men's bodies and souls. Here too, the word helps bring acceptance of the thing named. The idea became actual; the concept was reified—then deified. The Gospel according to John tells us: "In the beginning was the Word, and the Word was God." It continues, emphasizing the point; I quote the Catholic revised translation, *Imprimatur* 1944:

> He [i.e., the Word] abode, at the beginning of time, with God.
> It was through him that all beings came into being, and without
> him came nothing that has come to be. In him there was life,

and that life was the light of man. And the light shines in darkness, a darkness which was not able to master it.

Words, properly used, bring light to man's understanding.

Some today may find it difficult to grasp the fact that many persons for many years have found truth within this symbol. It was
truth to the great Queen Elizabeth, who, asked her thoughts on
the Sacrament, responded in impromptu verse:

> 'Twas God the Word that spake it;
> He took the Bread and brake it;
> And what the Word did make it,
> That I believe, and take it.

Men have sought a phrase that will clearly mark the difference
between mankind and all other living things. "Man is the only
animal that cooks its food." "Man the tool-maker," "the employer
of utensils." "Man the time-binder." More fundamental than any
of these is "man the word-maker." In a deep sense, this may also
be reversed: the word is the man-maker. We have become what
we are today (the mighty mixture of good and bad) by virtue of
our use of words. Wars may depend upon weapons, but they are
averted or begun by words; nor could today's instruments of
destruction have been fashioned without communication by means
of words. What our descendants shall be hangs upon how we
and they use words. Those ancients were men of discernment,
who saw the Word as God.

Baudelaire has said that the cleverest ruse of the devil is to
persuade us he doesn't exist. The Oxford University chaplain
Ronald Knox, somewhat later, turned the observation: "It was
stupid of modern civilization to have given up believing in the
devil when he is the only explanation of it." But in the western
world—in all the world not counting the Communist countries—
there are more believers than atheists—the man in the middle,
who says we cannot know, we call an agnostic. Even the recently
rebellious, by their very cry "God is dead" imply that there once
was a god living. Among graffiti scrawled on college walls there
has been seen:

> God is Dead.
> —Nietzsche.

—under which, in another hand:

> Nietzsche is dead.
> —God.

God has already managed one resurrection.

There is no question that, in the past several centuries, attention has turned from "the next world" to a greater concern with the affairs of current living. Some (like Rosalind Murray, daughter of the great classical scholar, in her book *The Good Pagan's Failure*) attribute this decline in spiritual values to the Reformation. For the devout Catholic, hope of happiness lay in the eternal hereafter; the early Protestants, particularly the Calvinists, hoped for the rewards of virtue in their current lives. Whatever its cause, the lapse in moral standards may in part account for the surge of new faiths and esoteric remedies, and the wide following of gurus, of the Reverend Moon and other munificent promisers—as those without positive beliefs are susceptible to the appeals of the reasonable-sounding dogmatist and the profferer of world-soothing.

The abandonment of a spiritual foundation in everydaily activity has also produced a widening gap between art and life. In the Middle Ages, the artist was attuned to the Church. In other fields, the worker was also an artist. This association is as old as man. As a note to the exhibit of Assyrian art of the eleventh century B.C. in the British Museum turns it:

> Ancient art was always utilitarian and was present, in varying degrees, in all artifacts, from the proudest of divine statues to the most humble household tool.

Today not only ancient but much contemporary art, incomprehensible to the average citizen, is likely to be stored in a museum. Some thinkers, like Coomaraswamy, remark that the belated recognition of this separation of our values from our actions, of this absence of the heavenly prototype from the earthly manifestation, has produced such bastard and botched attempts to close the gap as pop art, op art, theatre of the absurd, black humor, and other distortions of the lost interrelationship.

A different but corollary view is taken by A. Alvarez, who in *The Penguin Book of English Poetry Since 1945* is called "the most important critic of modern poetry during the fifties and sixties." Alvarez states that, today,

> Art is valuable simply as a means of rejecting the square world. So the poet resigns his responsibilities; he becomes less concerned to create a work than to create a public life; *what he offers is not poetry but instant protest.* Where the pop painter becomes an interior decorator, the pop poet becomes a kind of unacknowledged social worker.

The interconnection of the spiritual and the material worlds has been lost.

Even in the earliest days of man's artistic expression, however, a distinction was recognized. Epics and tragedies dealt with the designs of the gods, abetting or offsetting human actions. But little humor is directed at the gods. And satire is aimed exclusively at humans.

Satire, said Johnson, is "a work in which wickedness or folly is censured." Addison hoped that this could be kept general, promising in *The Spectator* to picture no individual's failings but only those shared by a thousand. Pope laughed at this notion:

> Spare then the person, and expose the vice:
> How sir! not damn the sharper, but the dice?

Satire works in many modes. The *lampoon* is a personal attack; *caricature* draws a distorted likeness; both of these come often with a pictorial *cartoon*. *Sarcasm* is incidental and purely verbal; it is usually blunt and crude. It may be cynical, edged with contempt, or sardonic, with bitter laughter on the brink of angry tears. Swift admitted its venom:

> Like the ever-laughing sage
> In a jest I spend my rage.—
> Though it must be understood
> I would hang them if I could.

Invective is a direct and unremitting attack, which grew into the flytings already discussed, and which is constantly exercised in daily quarrels. *Ridicule* is an attempt to laugh away what one disdains; it is condescending; it seeks to draw the listeners by laughter into a shared condemnation. *Reductio ad absurdum* may be a device in argumentation; in daily dealings it fails to hide a sneer. Being the butt of ridicule afflicts most persons as a major abasement. Voltaire said that he had but one prayer: O Lord, make my enemies ridiculous!

The chief devices employed in extended satire are burlesque and irony. *Burlesque* means more than two men in baggy trousers cracking bawdy jokes, alternating with the strip-tease ecdysiasts of the New York "burlesque house" before Mayor La Guardia shut them down. It consists essentially in a distorted imitation of another work. Low burlesque is a comic treatment of a serious theme, as in the Pyramus and Thisby performance of the bumpkins in *A Midsummer Night's Dream*. *The Beggar's Opera* of John

Gay is a low burlesque of the then-popular Italian opera. Its satire is directed against the vices and excesses of a society the author loved; in contrast with its adaptation, in 1928, by Bertolt Brecht, *The Three-Penny Opera,* which flails at the vices of a society the author wished to overthrow. High burlesque consists in the dignified treatment of a trivial theme; its best example is Pope's *The Rape of the Lock,* based upon an actual incident, Lord Petrie's snipping a lock of Arabella Fermor's hair. It contains such lines as of Arabella (Belinda in the poem) lamenting:

> Oh hadst thou, cruel, been content to seize
> Hairs less in sight, or any hairs but these!

Pope could, of course, turn his satiric pen to more serious purpose, as when he wrote:

> The hungry judges soon the sentence sign,
> And wretches hang that jurymen may dine.

The dramatic burlesque was in full flush of popularity on the American stage at the beginning of this century. In the 1901–1902 season Clyde Fitch had five plays running on Broadway; within a month of their production, three of them were pilloried in burlesques. *Barbara Fritchie* was laughed at in *Barbara Fidgety,* with David Warfield and the comic team of Weber and Fields. The same team, with William Collier and Fay Templeton, turned *The Stubbornness of Geraldine* into *The Stickiness of Gelatine.* And Ethel Barrymore's "Grecian bend" in her first starring role, as the opera singer in *Captain Jinks of the Horse Marines,* was mimicked in *Fiddle-Dee-Dee,* with De Wolfe Hopper leading a cluster of ballet girls, all played by men. A little earlier, Lillian Russell had made her debut in *The Pirates of Penn-Yan,* a burlesque of the Gilbert and Sullivan light opera.

This type of burlesque has continued, occasionally turned to political ends—as in the off-Broadway *MacBird,* which used *Macbeth* to stress overtones of the Kennedy assassination—but more often as a comedy skit in a review. Thus, in the play *Strictly Dishonorable* a man who has persuaded a young woman to come to his room, with intentions told in the play's title, on learning that she is a virgin lets her go unassailed; in the burlesque of this play, when Fanny Brice dressed as Baby Snooks simpers "I'm a voigin," the disgusted lecher ships her off, exclaiming: "Whaddaya tink dis is, Amachoor Night?"

Akin to burlesque is *parody,* which more closely mimics the form of another work, for comic effect or to reveal its weakness. Most of the poems in Lewis Carroll's Alice books are parodies. Wylie Sypher goes so far as to say that any method strictly followed eventually parodies itself. At what point, he asks,

> does Eliot's theory of the impersonality of the poet, his acquaintance with foregoing poetry, become a parody of the poetry of tradition? Answer: at the close of *The Waste Land,* referring to the *Upanishads,* Laforgue, the *Pervigilium Veneris,* Kyd, Nerval, Dante.

A more frequent and more powerful weapon of satire is *irony.* Irony has been explained in supererogatory experteasing technical terms; it consists basically in a double meaning, one sense on the surface, another and usually opposed meaning to be discerned underneath. In dramatic irony, as we have seen, the surface significance is accepted by one or more of the characters involved; the receptor is aware of the deeper meaning. For satiric purposes, five varieties of irony have been distinguished:

Self-disparaging irony is perhaps the earliest, as it is the method employed by Socrates—hence sometimes called *Socratic irony.* With assumed modesty the ironist asks questions, apparently seeking truth but actually leading the respondent to discover his own errors. A modern practitioner was the keen logician Morris Raphael Cohen; when a student, during a discussion of Berkeley and philosophical idealism, inquired: "How do I know that I exist?" Cohen said "Who's asking?"

The *irony of incongruity* sets in juxtaposition such items as call to attention that one of them is out of place, or out of proportion. Thus Pope tells of the belle Belinda's fear lest she "stain her honor or her new brocade," and pictures on her dressing-table

Puffs, Powders, Patches, Bibles, Billets-doux

—changing the alliteration to mark the item unexpected.

The *irony of unconscious self-betrayal* presents a character whose words or actions belie his estimate of himself, as Malvolio in *Twelfth Night,* or Holy Willie in Burns' poem earlier quoted.

The *irony of understatement* speaks casually of significant matters, leaving the receptor to redress the balance, and thus through his own mental activity to take more assured hold of what the author intends as the truth. So Gibbon in *The Decline and Fall of the Roman Empire* tells of (anti-) Pope John XXIII (Baldassaro Cossa, who died in 1419):

Of the three popes, John XXIII was the first victim; he fled and
was brought back a prisoner: the most scandalous charges were
suppressed; the vicar of Christ was accused only of piracy, murder, rape, sodomy, and incest.

The final form of irony is *matter-of-fact statement of the preposterous.* The most notable example of this is Swift's *Modest
Proposal to Relieve the Famine in Ireland,* in which he suggests
that the Irish rear and sell their babies to be served on the English
tables:

> I have been assured by a very knowing American of my acquain-
> tance in London, that a young healthy child, well nursed, is at a
> year old a most delicate, nourishing and wholesome food, whether
> stewed, roasted, baked, or boiled; and I make no doubt that it
> will equally serve in a fricasie or ragoust.

In this ironic device there is a danger: the receptor may react
only—and violently—to the literal level. Although Swift intended
his Modest Proposal as a rebuke to the English, many in Ireland
clamored for his death.

In a more general sense, scholars have spoken of metaphysical
irony, and of romantic irony. *Metaphysical irony* concerns the
contradictions in man's nature and in the universe. On one level,
there is irony in the thought that many, if not most, of a man's
desires are harmful, or fattening, or forbidden. More deeply, there
is the religious antinomy: if God is all-powerful and all-good, how
explain the heavy load of evil that presses upon mankind? *The
Bridge of San Luis Rey* was written by Thornton Wilder to ex-
plore that problem. *Romantic irony* remains on the human level,
noting that love and sadness go arm in arm; that we try to observe
life with detached amusement—Anatole France's formula is irony
and pity—but we become deeply involved. Thomas Mann was led
to declare that the problem of irony is "without exception the
most profound and fascinating in the world."

Irony, like the lampoon and the caricature, may be communi-
cated through nonverbal arts. Thomas Hood's poem "The Song
of the Shirt," picturing the overworked nineteenth-century seam-
stress, had vivid illustration at a London art exhibit of 1974: a
nude (plastic) woman lay across a sewing machine, one breast
partly open with a rat peering out: work the pedal—as the museum guard suggested I do—and the woman moves up and down;
the rat presumably gnaws. Such devices bring irony into the realm
of black humor.

Black humor, although lush in our days, also sent down strong roots in the nineteenth century. Gilbert's *Bab Ballads* aim at amusing, but dwell with levity upon serious things. "The Yarn of the Nancy Bell" presents cannibalism after a shipwreck, with the lone survivor singing:

> Oh I am a cook and a captain bold,
> And the mate of the Nancy brig,
> And a bo'sun tight, and a midshipmite,
> And the crew of the captain's gig.

In another of the ballads, Gentle Alice Brown, the robber's daughter, who had "slain a little baby for the coral on its neck"—but "sins like these one expiates for half-a-crown apiece"—made the mistake of falling in love with an honest, sober, industrious young man; so her father

> Took a life-preserver and he hit him on the head,
> And Mrs. Brown dissected him before she went to bed.

(A Victorian would know that a *life-preserver* was a cane the handle of which was a lead-loaded knob.) Alice repented, and her father

> bestowed her pretty hand
> On a promising young robber, the lieutenant of the band.

At the turn of the century, Harry Graham wrote his *Ruthless Rhymes for Heartless Homes.* Anyone with a heart should read no more than two at a session:

> "There's been an accident," they said.
> "Your servant's cut in half. He's dead."
> "Indeed!" said Mr. Jones. "And please
> Send me the half that's got my keys."
>
> O'er the rugged mountain's brow
> Clara threw the twins she nursed
> And remarked: "I wonder now
> Which will reach the bottom first."

Words have been twisted in various ways, to suit the speaker's purpose. Oldest of the deviations from strict denotation is the propagandist's use of words, selecting terms with pleasant meaning or associations to express his cause, and words with unfavorable implications to describe opposing views. This practice goes as far back as recorded history, and has but grown more widespread with increasing ease of communication. Other misuses of words have more recently grown significant.

Anger has usually led to blunt condemnation, and often to violence, but the literature of "the angry young men" came specifically in 1956, with John Osborne's play *Look Back in Anger*, in sharp revolt against the Noel Coward world. "There's no place for manners in the world I live in," declared the author. "If our writing is bad-mannered, it is because we have had to put our heads down and shove our way to the front." Five years later, he was even more vehement, in a letter "To my fellow-countrymen: There is murder in my brain, and I carry a knife in my heart for every one of you." In 1976 he was still full of sound and fury, his play *Watch It Come Down* as torrential a flow of invective and cruelty as the American *Who's Afraid of Virginia Woolf?*. Allen Ginsberg in America (*Howl*, 1956) and Jean Genet in France (*The Blacks*, 1959)—"saintliness in the perfection of evil"—are others of the angry crew.

Both the propagandists, suave or crude, and the angry young men, however, seek clarity in their utterances; they have a message they wish to put across. Hence John Osborne has called words man's "last link with God.... The verbal breakdown is getting to the point where it is dangerous and nonsensical. I have a great allegiance to words."

Verbal breakdown is the chief form of expression of a major vocabular rebellion in this century. Dada, which heralded "the revolution of the word," and surrealism, which declared that consciousness exists to hide man from himself, and which therefore demanded unconscious, automatic writing, will be glanced at in the final chapter. Their chief recent development has been the theatre of the absurd. This rests upon the premise that life is meaningless, that events occur without motive; therefore writing need show neither purpose nor direction. Arnold P. Hirch, in the Preface to his book on *The Absurd* (1974) states: "I have taken it for granted that for Absurdity to exist, God must be dead." *The New York Times* book reviewer Christopher Lehmann-Haupt declared in 1976 that T. S. Eliot, who died in 1965, is already "very dated" for his belief that aesthetic values depend upon a God in whose mind beauty exists; and many of the new plays make no show of either mind or beauty. Seeking no positive cause, they desiccate the language, sometimes reducing it to silence or simian grunts, as at the close of Ionesco's *The Chairs*. The ab-

surdists look back to their prototype in Alfred Jarry's *Ubu Roi,*
produced in 1896, translated by Gershon Legman as *King Turd.*
This piece was originally a schoolboy's caricature of a disliked
teacher; Jarry picked it up from the boy's brother, and turned it
first into a puppet show for his family's entertainment. The play,
with its mock-science of pataphysics, was seized on and became a
vogue among radical writers; but it remains a silly subsophomoric
romp. Samuel Beckett's *Waiting for Godot,* the most widely shown
and hailed of its successors, is said to represent humanity in quest
of man's unidentified and inexpressive goal. Its two main figures
are stink-footed and lousy-topped. One of them goes offstage to
perform a physiological function; the others, onstage, watch,
applaud, and cry "Encore!" The painter Picasso had more courage;
in his one play, *Desire Caught by the Tail,* he gives stage directions that the character Tart "go to the front, face the audience,
and urinate and syphilize for a full five minutes." (Some critics
feel that's the way Picasso usually treats the receptor.) Beckett's
play has been hailed as the classic of its kind; it is the most widely
known and most frequently revived absurdist drama; but many
tend to agree with a letter to the London *Times* (July 18, 1971)
by Val Gielgud, brother of the actor, John:

> Mr. Hobson [critic of the Sunday *Times*] takes exception to the
> fact—for which, incidentally, he provides no proof—that Sir
> John Gielgud harmed the contemporary theatre by advising Sir
> Alec Guiness and Sir Ralph Richardson not to accept engage-
> ments in *Waiting for Godot.* It may be news to Mr. Hobson
> that quite a number of intelligent people, apart from actors of
> distinction, to this day regard *Waiting for Godot* as a pretentious
> bore . . . and the theatre of Non-Communication as a contradiction
> in terms.

Other absurdist plays have their characters talk incoherent rub-
bish while stuck in garbage cans, or buried to their necks in dirt.
They have, indeed, no desire for clarity, consistence, or continuance. "Things are simple and clear," states Ionesco, "only to
Brechtian boy scouts." And he laughs at "that complicated shal-
low-pate, Jean-Paul Sartre, who makes of his personal passions a
sort of objective truth and wants to impose it on others." Life is
too full of a number of things, too variously undesigned and
unexpected, for dogmatism or didacticism. Propaganda, in a world
without sense or sense of direction, seems to the absurdist truly
absurd.

The discarding of reason and the denial of the value of the

word cannot disguise the fact that these would-be destroyers of
the language are inevitably concerned with words. They are like
the nineteenth-century French diabolists, who pretended to scorn
the average citizen—the justification of the middle class, said
Laforgue, is that out of the dungheap spring roses—but who
nevertheless went out of their way *épater le bourgeois,* to shock
the middle class. Tony Tanner of Cambridge (England) calls his
study of American fiction between 1950 and 1970 *City of Words.*
He takes this title from Jorge Luis Borges, whom he discusses
with Vladimir Nabokov in the chapter "On Lexical Playfields." A
later chapter, on William Burroughs, is "Rub Out the Word"—
yet he reminds us that Burroughs wrote to Allen Ginsberg "What
scared you into time? Into the body? Into shit? I will tell you.
The word." By shit, Tanner suggests that Burroughs meant present society; it seems more likely he had in mind the world of
communes, gurus, and drugs Ginsberg was then frequenting.
Along that path, Bertrand Russell saw even more dire signposts:

> Some have moved to a deliberate discarding of reason, either
> by an act of the will or by the use of drugs and other stimulants.
> This denial of the intellect [as in D. H. Lawrence's "thinking
> with the blood"] led straight to Auschwitz.

The apologists for—I use the word in its technical sense of those
that defend or seek to justify—the abandonment of reason in the
theatre of the absurd naturally claim a valid intention: by com-
bining the most dismal or morbid with the most ridiculous in a
deliberately grotesque caricature, to make us yearn for a world
in which man is not an object of derision. By work itself risible,
they want the people to rise beyond man's meaningless botch to
new significance.

As the angry young men snarl at the world they would destroy,
the absurdists sneer at the world they think is destroying itself.
Their works are often frankly called antidrama, antiart. They are
also antiword, and may soon prove antiaudience. "The best one
can say of most modern creative art," said Oscar Wilde, "is that
it is just a little less vulgar than reality." Modern creative art
seems to have moved farther since his day.

In his *Memoirs,* back in 1771, Beaumarchais traced the pattern:

> Thus it is that all the absurdities in the world have got estab-
> lished: thrust forward through impudence, adopted through gen-
> eral indifference, made credible through repetition, spread by
> enthusiasm—but rendered nil by the first thinking person that
> takes the trouble to examine them.

Raymond Picard brings the analysis to our own time:

> Who would have thought that the atomic age is also the age of
> credulity? Is it because everything, thanks to the progress of sci-
> ence, seems possible, that scientific requirements, or even those of
> simple logical thought, are disappearing from criticism? The
> appeal to clear thinking and coherence has hardly any power
> against the appetite for sensation, against snobbery, against the
> fear of being taken for a Philistine. In any case, it is not by hav-
> ing its absurd aspects exposed that a fashion is suppressed; espe-
> cially not today, when ridicule has lost her salubrious role.—
> If it were again to become a moral weapon, as it was in the 18th
> century, what a massacre there would be!

M. Picard fails to take into account the latent power of ridicule;
it is the fear of seeming ridiculous that keeps the bewildered layman quiet, if not acquiescent, in the face of what critics blatantly
hail.

The vigorous and valid use of satire and other devices persists,
in man's attempt to travel along the corridors of time, peering
through windows of hope and science toward perhaps unattain-
able but at least approachable ideals. Neither the absurdist nor
the angry young man is concerned with beauty. They may function as gadflies on the body politic, as social scavengers, as ethical
remembrancers. But despite the stings and harrowings of those
that mistrust or misuse the word, the legitimate use of words for
proper ends, in the quest of truth and beauty, goes ever on. The
symbol will survive both the sneer and the snarl.

13.
WORDS AT PLAY

WORDS LOOMED SO SIGNIFICANTLY in the life of early man that even when he played with them he took them in earnest. In folklore and fairy tales—which, however fanciful in creatures and events, pattern their morality on human mores—a marriage or a life often hangs upon a riddle. Riddles are the earliest form of wordplay. Several persons were slain by the Sphinx for failing to guess her riddle, before Oedipus by solving it turned her into stone. (She still looks implacable, when you gaze upon her in the desert just outside Cairo.) Her riddle: What goes on four legs in the morning, two in the afternoon, and three at night? Answer: Man, who crawls as a baby, walks erect in his life's midday, and uses a cane in its dusk.

Samson gave the Philistines a riddle at his wedding feast: "Out of the eater came something to eat; out of the strong came something sweet." They could not possibly have guessed this: on his first visit he had slain a lion; on his second he had noticed that bees had hived in its carcass. The wedding guests cajoled Samson's bride into wheedling the answer from him; when they gave it to him, he cried: "If you had not ploughed with my heifer, you would not have found out my riddle!"—and he killed thirty Philistines to give their garments to the wedding guests as his forfeit. They retaliated by burning the bridal house, with the bride and her father inside. This woman was of course not Delilah; Samson ruled as a judge over Israel for twenty years before he took to himself a prostitute in Gaza. We still refer to the Gaza Strip.

The Queen of Sheba and Solomon, as was the custom, matched wits with riddles. One of hers was: What is it that has ten holes; when one is open, nine are closed; when the one closes, the nine are open? Solomon looked at her lovely form, and answered: the body. (The navel closes at birth.) The Queen went back without her lush pubic hair (the forfeit) but with his child inside.

[The name of the Queen of Sheba, Bilqis, has wide ramifications, before her and after. It is related, by way of Aramaic *pilaqta*, 'concubine', to early Avestan *pairika*, 'beautiful women who seduce pious men'. (Bilqis journeyed, the Bible says, to test Solomon's wisdom.) But roundabout, this verbal root moved to Pallas (Greek *pallados*, 'maiden'), an appellation of the virgin goddess Athene. Her statue, the Palladium, in Troy, was surety for the safety of the city; Diomedes and Odysseus bore it off before Troy fell. From the same root came the Persian word *päri*, 'fairy', whence English *peri*. (Note, even here, the shiftings of *l* and *r*.) Gilbert and Sullivan, after three great hits beginning with P— *Pinafore, Pirates of Penzance, Patience*—were troubled for a title to their next play. They hopefully gave it two *p*'s in the subtitle: *Iolanthe; or, The Peer and the Peri*. It did not disappoint them.

[In 1803 the second largest asteroid (minor planet; the asteroids whirl between Mars and Jupiter) was discovered by the German astronomer Heinrich W. M. Olbers; in accord with the godly custom of planetary nomenclature, he called it Pallas. The next year, the English chemist William Hyde Wollaston isolated a white metal from crude platinum; and after the minor planet just discovered he named the new element (46 in the atomic sequence) *palladium*. A generation ago, the name Palladium was often given to a new motion-picture palace (Pallas). Words wander wondrously.]

In each of three widely known works, a riddle is propounded without a given solution. Lewis Carroll has the Mad Hatter ask Alice, at the tea-party in Wonderland: "Why is a raven like a writing-desk?" When Alice says: "I give it up. What's the answer?" the Hatter replies: "I haven't the slightest idea." Jack Point, the melancholy jester in Gilbert and Sullivan's *The Yeomen of the Guard*, asks the Lieutenant of the Tower: "Can you tell me, Sir, why a cook's brain-pan is like an overwound clock?" When the lieutenant brushes him off: "A truce to this fooling!" the jester exclaims: "Just my luck; my best conundrum wasted!" Archie Goodwin, detective Nero Wolfe's leg man, in Rex Stout's *Some Buried Caesar* reverses the question, asking Lily Rowan: "Do you know the difference between a Catholic and a river that runs uphill?"—and comments: "She didn't and I told her and we babbled on." Rex Stout being the least attuned to whimsy, the last of these is the easiest to cap with an answer... When the wind is southerly, I know a hawk from a hernshaw.

In the Philippines, rival princes held riddling contests, in which they might hazard their inheritance; but before turning from the Bible let us note that, though some have lamented its lack of humor, there certainly is no lack of wordplay in the Holy Book. On the Jewish Day of Atonement, the recital of the sins of humankind runs through the alphabet. A number of the Psalms are alphabetical acrostics; the verses of Psalm 119 begin with every letter eight times.—Acrostics, like the classical fixed meters in poetry, were probably intended as mnemonics, to ensure that the verses were repeated exactly as composed. When scripture is holy, it should be remembered and recited verbatim. Mnemosyne, 'Memory', was the mother of the Muses. It is interesting to note that the Greek word for truth, *aletheia*, is from *a*, 'not', and *Lethe*, the River of Forgetfulness: to remember is to know the truth. The English word *alethiology* names that part of logic which deals with truth.

I have already mentioned the pun upon which Jesus established the Catholic Church, and the anagram in Pilate's query "What is truth?" Two further instances may suffice. You probably recall that "It is harder for a rich man to enter the kingdom of heaven than for a camel to go through a needle's eye." Exaggerated? Not at all. For, from its narrow rise and pointed top, the postern gate of the ancient Middle-Eastern walled town was called the Needle's Eye; and it *was* possible for a camel to go through—by kneeling. And you may know the reproach to over-finicking individuals, who "strain out a gnat and swallow a camel." Clear enough, but neater by metathesis in the original Aramaic: 'gnat', *galma;* 'camel', *gamla.*

Acrostics are found in other ancient tongues. The summaries prefixed to the plays of the Roman Plautus are acrostics. Like riddles, however, they have lapsed to purely playful use. Many acrostic verses were written to Elizabeth of England. The first letters of the successive verses appended to *Through the Looking-Glass* spell Alice Pleasance Liddell, the original Wonderland Alice. Some verses also fashion words with the last letters of successive lines; such an arrangement is a *telestich*. Edgar Allan Poe's "A Valentine" is a *cross-acrostic:* the first letter of the first line, second letter of the second line, and so on, spell the name of the woman to whom it was sent. James Branch Cabell prefixed a sonnet to one of his novels; the first letters of its fourteen lines spell "This is nonsense." The making of acrostics was so great a vogue in the late nineteenth century that A. Cyril Pearson in 1884 compiled an *Acrostic Dictionary* of some 40,000 words, an enlarged edition of which was issued in 1901.

A current game variation of acrostics is to make up a description of a person (widely known, or in the immediate group) using that person's initials, for the others to guess who is meant. Thus First Democrat Re-reelected indicates Franklin Delano Roosevelt; Tough Rider, his predecessor Teddy Roosevelt.

Counting-out jingles, used now in children's games, may originally have been used to select victims for human sacrifice, as the Greek youth to the Minotaur. The Aztecs in one year sacrificed some 70,000 to their gods. Another sort of death, the 1665 plague in Derbyshire, England, remembered annually in the village of Eyam, peers through what is now a merry romp:

Ring-a ring o' roses	—	Red spots appear;
A pocket full o' posies	—	Herbal pomanders, preventatives;
Atchoo! Atchoo!	—	Sneezing: the clear onset;
All fall down!	—	Sudden death.

The lapse of serious wordplay—the use for vital ends of riddles, puns, acrostics, counting-out jingles—into entertainment and games, calls for further pondering. It brings to mind some ideas of Gilbert K. Chesterton, who from his conversion of faith grew orthodox, but from his conversion of thought drew paradox (Greek *para*, 'beside', hence 'contrary to'; *doxa*, 'opinion'). In his book *The Defendant*, Chesterton made himself a sort of devil's advocate for unaccepted notions and unexpected associations; and nowhere is he more provocative and cogent than in his essay "A Defence of Nonsense." It begins:

> There are two equal and eternal ways of looking at this twilight world of ours: we may see it as the twilight of evening or the twilight of morning; we may think of anything, down to a fallen acorn, as a descendant or as an ancestor.

and it ends:

> This simple sense of wonder at the shapes of things, and at their exuberant independence of our intellectual standards and our trivial definitions, is the basis of spirituality as it is the basis of nonsense. Nonsense and faith (strange as the conjunction may seem) are the two supreme symbolic assertions of the truth that

to draw out the soul of things with a syllogism is as impossible as to draw out Leviathan with a hook. The well-meaning person who, by merely studying the logical side of things, has decided that "faith is nonsense" does not know how truly he speaks; later it may come back to him in the form that nonsense is faith.

In this conjunction, it seems fit that our best known writer of nonsense, Lewis Carroll, should in his practical hours have been "a singularly serious and conventional don, universally respected, but very much of a pedant and something of a Philistine."

The gradual conversion of serious wordplay into trivial fun and games may be laughed away (as by Chesterton in this essay) with the remark that "mankind in the main has always regarded reason as a bit of a joke." But if we traverse the path in the reverse direction, from amusement to more earnest employment of verbal devices, we may tumble upon a fresh evaluation. For laughter and play were man's earliest exercises in distancing the cruder instincts, in breaking free from the self-tied passions, in attaining a measure of detachment and tolerance in communal living. Even in competitive games—unfortunately disturbed in some periods of organized, professional sports, with greedy gambling, provincial pride, and even politicized international confusion—there was developed an appreciation of a valiant effort on either side, a sense of fair play, a distaste for what the English dismissed with "It isn't cricket," that makes one not entirely despair of the human race. While there is laughter—as while there is poetry—there is hope.

Wordplay may begin with the ABCs. The letters of the alphabet are used for many games. Write them in bold capitals across a sheet of paper. Then see how many four-letter words you can fashion, keeping the letters in their alphabetical order. *Ails* is one. If you arrive at seventy or so, you might try the same thing, starting at *z* and working backwards. *Soda* is one. A group, of course, can try this, to see who has the most in five minutes.

Or take out your Scrabble board, and one tile of each letter. Try to make words, built together as in the game, using just, but all, the twenty-six letters. I made eight sets of the twenty-six (on different occasions) before I stopped; there must be many, but it is frustrating to be balked often at twenty-five. Here is one group; try to set it on the board; this should not be hard, since a repeated letter indicates that the words cross: *dwarf, move, pyx, quick, zany, jobs, plights.* It is much harder to figure one out for yourself.

The alphabet was also used in early forms of cryptography—

another instance of a serious activity being turned to play. It is easy to arrange a secret code that only the one among your friends you wish to correspond with will fathom: agree, say, that in the first word, every letter you write will be three in the alphabet beyond the correct one; in the second word, four beyond; in the third word, five beyond; then repeat this pattern throughout the message. Or any other such pairing only the two of you know. Whatever the pattern, space the letters, not at the end of a word, but in groups of five.

For another code, write the alphabet across a line; over it put the numbers 1 to 26; under it the same numbers, but from 1 at *z* to 26 at *a*. And use the letter with the number under it corresponding to the number above the desired one. This might seem child's play to a professional cryptographer; but it probably saved the life of Jeremiah, who, when the Hebrews were enslaved by the Babylonians, prophesied the ruin of Babylon. He naturally did not dare to name the city; what he proclaimed was the coming doom of Sheshak: *sh* and *k* are the second and twelfth letters from the end of the Hebrew alphabet; second and twelfth from the beginning are *b* and *l*: thus Babylon—as a note to *Jeremiah* 25 in the Bible now explains.

Scrabble is a commercial variety of anagrams; the original game does not have a board or extra-value squares, but permits taking another player's word (displayed before him) if an added letter changes its meaning. Thus *rain* may grow to *train*, to *strain*, *stainer*, *trainers*, *restrains*, *transpires*. We have already seen anagrams and aptagrams, words of letters that can be shifted to form other words; there are also multigrams, the same letters forming several different words. Thus *pears*, *pares*, *reaps*, *spare*, *parse*, *spear*, *rapes*, *prase*, *asper*. *Result* can turn into six other words; *ignored* yields four others; *traces*, seven; *sainted*, three. Marsupial words, with synonyms within them, have also been discussed; but some words hold other words within them in immediate sequence of the letters: *eastern* gives us *east*, *Easter*, *astern*, *aster*, *stern*, *tern*; *ster* and *ter* are olden spellings of *star* and *tar*; old and dialectal *ern*.

The simplest group game in the anagram family is played by taking a fairly long word, such as *valedictory*, to see (within a time limit) who can form the most words using some of its letters. The $64,000 question in a game once on the air was answered— at $8,000 a word—by identifying the following, all the letters of which are in the name Eisenhower: 1. smallest of the mammals. 2. an evening party. 3. a willow whose flexible twigs are used for furniture. 4. short title of a utopian novel. 5. generic term for Greek temple. 6. plural of a wide-mouthed pitcher. 7. a large net for fishing. 8. a frame on which skins are dried, as for parchment. (Answers are at the end of this chapter.)

Various expeditions have traveled to Loch Ness in Scotland, to seek the monster some claim to have seen in the depths of the lake. The British naturalist Sir Peter Scott suggested a technical name for it: *Nessiteras rhombopteryx*. Those trying to snare the monster into actuality were happy to have the support of the noted scientist—until someone figured out that the name is an anagram of "Monster hoax by Sir Peter S."

Aptagrams have been mentioned earlier; some folks have devised a game of seeing who can make the cleverest aptaphrases, such as "Go to the back of the boat," she said sternly. Such expressions are sometimes called Tom Swifties, from Tom Swift, the hero of Edward Stratemeyer's best-selling boys' books of the 1920s.

A favorite group game, a sort of oral anagrams, is Ghosts. In this, one person gives a letter, and each player in turn adds another, aiming to spell a word—but not to end it. More sophisticated players permit adding a letter at either end of those already given.

Buried words may be fun to find, lurking in germinating phrases. There is a spice spelled in the sentence just before this, beginning with the last letter of *lurking*. In the following story, no less than 46 birds lie hidden, waiting for your eyes to release them:

The big stern wheel of the river steamer lingers, and at last begins to revolve; a gleam of light from the paddle, and overhead a wreath of smoke belched from the ravenous maw of the furnace, and the deferred starting is forgotten. Again the waiting crowd, swallowing its late bitterness and smarting, resumes its cheerful march and chatter; voices hum merrily, and the gangways fill with rushing feet. A shout now rends the air as two meagre, belated Swedish-Americans are seen running toward the boat, the taller one traversing with awkward strides the tarpaulin nets and traps of hard-working fishermen without asking let or hindrance; the other one, a small, ardent fellow, puffing away behind, runs with rasher haste down a gully as if in cheering view of lost riches. Meanwhile the boat is stealing away from the wharf and the gang-plank is lifting. An Irishman with matches and pipe rammed into his pocket, his blouse lappet released from his pantaloons, with a face like a saint and a nose like a parsnip, edges from the walnut hatchway to the rail and howls:

"Did I 'ver see the loikes? Tre-le-le-a-a-a-la! Bejaybers I bet on long Racklebones, and a booby prize for the butterball."

Then the tall Swede, being swifter afoot, jumps on the departing gangway, and turning calls to his companion who stands quailing on the edge of the wharf:

"Yump, Yohn, Yump! I tenk you can mek it..en..two.. yumps."

(Hunt them in the foliage of words. They too will be unloosed at the end of the chapter.)

The most widespread game in this general family is undoubtedly the crossword puzzle, first fashioned in 1913, but soon known worldwide, and played in many languages. In World War II, crossword puzzles were used for anti-Nazi messages in code. The game may offer straightforward clues, or tricky ones, which take various forms. There may be:

Buried synonyms: The athlete fir*st ran d*own the beach: *Strand*

Anagrammed synonyms: Tom touched the light with the *palm* of his hand: *Lamp.*

Remainder synonyms: I *regret* that my *name* is not *Maureen:* Subtract the letters in *name* from *Maureen;* what is left makes *rue.*

Puns: Jet flier: *Crow.* Man of the match: *Bridegroom.*

Split words: The rich widow is all for betting: *Dowager,* do wager. Man from Manhattan says he maligns: *Islander,* I slander.

Twisted splits: A backward cad, he is first and last a pain in the neck: *Headache.—a; dac* is *cad* backwards; *he* comes at both ends.

Anagrams: Cloth for striptease: *Tapestries.* Loves to do puzzles: *Solve.*

These are some of the devices to rack the brains of assiduous solvers. And here are two handfuls of brainrackers from one English crossword puzzle (number in parenthesis tells how many letters in the word):

1. Squally rain encountered outside tower (7). *Squally* shows you're to mix up the letters of *rain. Outside:* surround these with a synonym of *encountered.* Desired word is a synonym of *tower.*

2. A sin hotel suffers from a bit of icy weather (9). First three words are an anagram of the answer.

3. The social system that keeps tea in a box (5). Tuck *t* into a synonym of *box* to get the social system.

4. Honest sort of piano (7). This is easy: synonym of *honest*.

5. Pharmacist gets a new tail for his shirt (7). English synonym for a *druggist*. Change the last letter (tail) and get a kind of shirt.

6. Circe gone?—Wrong; she's on duty in the lodge (9). First two words are an anagram for (French) doorkeeper.

7. He meddles with current unit between 3d and 7th of October (8). Word for electric unit, between 3d and 7th letter in the month, gives you one who meddles.

8. All but stabbed the Commanding Officer; face the wall! (6) Drop last letter of synonym of *stabbed;* abbreviation of Commanding Officer. Answer is facing (!) for the wall.

9. One in Paris about to be a thief—one usually does it at night (6). French (feminine) for *one;* put it around what a thief does. The whole word tells what you do before bed.

10. Acquires topless longs (5). Synonym of the wanted word is given first. Guess a synonym of *longs*, and remove the first letter (Thus it is topless—first letter is *y*.)

Have you figured these out? Here they are: 1. minaret 2. hailstone 3. caste 4. upright 5. chemist, chemise 6. concierge 7. tamperer 8. stucco 9. unrobe 10. earns

Anagrams have been perennially popular. Ben Jonson spoke of "a pretty riddling way of wooing, with anagrams." It was said that the preacher of our colonial days, Cotton Mather,

> Took care to guide his flock and feed his lambs
> By words, works, prayers, psalms, alms, and anagrams.

An exceptionally tricky clue gave all the following, for a word of seven letters: Blue and white bird; lowest piano note; large body of water; girl's name; vegetable; exclamation; beverage. You can solve this by seeking seven letters: J.A.C.K.P.O.T.

Many a word can accept a letter at the end, and become a quite different word, as *spat, spate; sin, sink; finis, finish.* More rarely, a word ending in *s* may thus add another *s.* Here are clues for ten such transformations.

Word with s	*Word with double s*
1. troubles	tender touch
2. sons of royalty	their sister
3. strong thick wires	without a taxi
4. slivers of steel, pointed and pricked	unnecessary
5. public conveyance	kiss
6. cannibalistic monsters	the wife of one of them
7. horselike quadrupeds	estimate
8. belonging to a man	evince strong disapproval
9. suppuration	kitty
10. breast supports	alloy of copper

Here are the first words: 1. *cares* 2. *princes* 3. *cables* 4. *needles* 5. *bus* 6. *ogres* 7. *asses* 8. *his* 9. *pus* 10. *bras*

Rhopes (from the Greek word for 'club', from its gradually thickening shape) are another sort of word-building: successive (different) words, each, one letter (or one syllable) longer than the one before. There are even rhopalic verses, each line a foot longer, as Crashaw's "Wishes to His Supposed Mistress";

> Whoe'er she be,
> That not impossible she
> That shall command my heart and me. . . .

Start with an *a*, *i*, or *o*, and see how big a word you can make. More frequently the game is played the other way: each of the following can be reduced a letter at a time, always rearranged to form an actual word, down to a single letter: *drafting, destruction, desperate, transpires, flattering, importance, persevering, decorated, shortness.* (See end of chapter.) There are many more.

Instead of adding a letter, you may of course subtract a letter— or even omit one. The *lipogram*, a word or a passage with a letter deliberately omitted, has a long history, going back at least to the Greek poet Lasus, born in 538 B.C. His pupil Pindar (died 443 B.C.), noted as the creator of the classical three-part form of the ode, playfully in that form wrote verses without using the letter *sigma*. The poet Triphiodorus tried to lighten the Dark Ages with a version of the *Odyssey*, the twenty-four books of which omitted in turn the twenty-four letters of the Greek alphabet, from no *alpha* in book One, to end with no *omega*. In the fifteenth century, a Persian poetaster brought to the great poet Jami some verses he had composed without using the letter *alif*. Jami read the work, pondered a moment, then soberly said: "It would be better if you had left out the other letters too." The many works of the seventeenth-century Spaniard Lope de Vega include five novels, each not using one of the five vowels. Lipogrammatic plays have been produced on the French stage. The eighteenth-century English Addison lists the lipogram among the varieties of false wit. Yet today, on the lawn of an English countryside house of worship, stands a large sign: "CH - - CH ... What's missing?" U R thus invited to the services.

Without going to lipogrammatic extremes, word fanciers have made games by dropping letters from words to form other words. They can play in two fashions: Give clues to the original word and the new word; or explain what is to be dropped, for the company to see how many appropriate words they can write in three minutes. Thus:

DROP the first letter: *flung, larch, event, erase, about*—and so many words beginning with *t* that this can be made a separate quest: *tease, that, taunt, terror.*

SECOND letter out: *plane, drone, fleet, stale, trowel, gloat, friend.*

THIRD letter out: *hand, chain, harm, comma, basted, varnish, mendication.*

FOURTH letter out: *shouts, started, tamper, badge, manage, planted, carat.*

In an 1879 issue of *Vanity Fair* Lewis Carroll—three years after his *The Hunting of the Snark*, but the same year as his *Euclid and His Modern Rivals*—published what he called Doublets, but is more widely known as Bee-line. The game is to travel from one word to another by changing one letter at a time, always having an actual word, in as few moves as you can. Thus you can change *love* into *hate* via *lave* and *have*. From *sin* to *woe* is also a short trip: *son.won.* It takes a bit longer to move from *ship* to *sail;* twice as long from *heat* to *fire*. Among the trips Carroll suggested are: Dip *pen* into *ink*. Make *kettle holder*. Change *tears* into *smile*. Evolve *man* from *ape*. Prove *pity* to be *good.*

Lewis Carroll also said: "With the first seven letters, I can make a word. Can you?" I strove for some time in vain. Then I saw the light. With the first seven letters, *i* makes the word *big-faced*. With *u*, as any caricaturist can demonstrate, *bug-faced*. (Kafka wrote a story, *Metamorphosis*, of a man who turned into an insect.)

A dual variation is Put and Take: given two words, transfer a letter from one to the other, so as to form a related pair. Thus *whoms* and *pleas* becomes *show* and *sample*. Try *bread* and *pot;* *gland* and *round; stoke* and *part; boast* and *hip*. Then devise some to try on submissive friends.

A game that tests powers of observation as well as verbal ingenuity has been drawn from my favorite among Kipling's novels, *Kim*. When Kim is being trained to do secret-service work in India, he is given a brief glance at a table on which are twenty or thirty miscellaneous objects, some very closely alike; he then must write a full description of what he has seen. This Kim Game, while starting with vision, calls for verbal precision in the descriptions—and when the lists of the participants are read aloud, usually leads to considerable oral exercise.

While some games persist, others die—perhaps to be born again. Several years ago "Knock, knock" was heard everywhere. "Who's there!" "Mary." "Mary Who? "Merry Christmas, and try to do better in the New Year." The pattern was so popular that it developed its own burlesque. When, to a twelve-year-old's Knock, I responded "Who's there?" he told me "Boo." "Boo who?" "Stop crying." A hundred and fifty years ago, the game was played with a tapping cane. And always Buff was there. "What says Buff?" And Buff says whatever he can think of to make the company laugh; when one person can no longer keep a straight face, the cane holder recites:

> Buff neither laughs nor smiles
> But looks in your face with a comical grace
> And delivers the staff to you, Sir [or, of course, Ma'am].

And the game may be traced at least to 1611, in which year a glossary defined the verb *buff* as "to break out in laughter."

Except for crossword puzzles, which may be filled in on the train to work, it must be admitted that word games have lapsed in popularity with the last two generations. It is much easier to sit in front of a screen, and watch others working to entertain one, than to exercise one's own body or mind. Radio and especially television have changed the pattern of many lives, turning participants into spectators. Something has of course been gained, but something precious has been lost. This is one of the penalties for what we call progress.

For the more literary, there are verse games. *Bouts rimés* were started in the seventeenth century, when the French poetaster Dulot complained that he had lost three hundred sonnets—then qualified: "Only the rhymes." Rhymes are given, to see who can write the cleverest verses. In Crambo, begun a bit earlier in

England, one player gives a word, for the others to fit with rhyming lines. Samuel Pepys, in his Diary, mentions playing Crambo
to pass the time in a coach. One evening three "top wits," Pope,
Swift, and Gay, stopping at a Berkshire inn, noted the landlord's
pretty daughter, and wrote a Crambo poem of thirteen quatrains,
each with a different rhyme on her name, Molly Mog. Printed in
Mist's Weekly Journal of August 20, 1726, this elicited further
rhymes, one coined by a gentleman incognito who signed himself
Incog. On the sweep of the vogue, the verses were reprinted in
1729 and 1732. Both games were popular in the eighteenth century, at Bath and other resorts.

Today one is more likely to be given a line, or a subject, to
fashion a limerick or a clerihew, forms used almost exclusively
for humorous verse. The limerick, although found earlier, as in
nursery rhyme:

> Hickory dickory dock,
> The mouse ran up the clock
> The clock struck one
> And down he run,
> Hickory dickory dock.

—grew to enormous popularity after Edward Lear's *Book of
Nonsense* in 1846. Lear wrote it for the grandchildren of the Earl
of Derby; but hosts of the jingles today are indeed not for children. Here are just two (innocuous ones), to illustrate the form:

> There was a young lady from Lynn
> Who was so remarkably thin
> That when she essayed
> To drink lemonade
> She slipped through the straw and fell in.

> For beauty I am not a star,
> There are others more handsome by far,
> But my face I don't mind it
> Because I'm behind it:
> It's the fellow in front gets the jar.

Monsignor Ronald Knox, a clergyman with a sense of humor,
once found an unwary newspaper that accepted his hidden-
limerick advertisement: "Evangelical vicar in want of a portable
second-hand font would dispose of the same for a portrait (in
frame) of the Bishop-Elect of Vermont."

The wide popularity of the limerick has led to public contests in every generation since Edward Lear located a nest in an old man's beard. Usually the first four lines are given, contestants to supply the clincher. In a 1907 contest in England, Traylee Cigarettes offered £3 a week for life to the winner. Each entrant had to enclose a coupon showing he'd bought a half-crown's worth of the cigarettes; so successful was the contest that Traylee held another, the prize a freehold completely furnished villa and grounds, a horse and trap, and £2 a week for life. "Professors" at once sprang up, ready for a fee to provide last lines to eager but unselfreliant competitors. Not only in England; when *Liberty* magazine in 1930 held a contest, the University of Miami published a handbook: *How to Write Prize-Winning Limericks*. For its 1951 limerick contest, the *New York Daily News* offered $1,000 as prize.

In 1965 Martin Kaiden, promotion manager of *Business Week*, varied the pattern by supplying the last line, "It isn't how many, it's who." First prize: round trip to Ireland for two, dinner with the Mayor of Limerick, a chance to kiss the Blarney Stone, and $500 spending money. There were 4,200 entries. In 1972, with a short memory, Joseph Papp advertised "The World's Greatest Limerick Contest"—this time for a full limerick, based on *Two Gentlemen of Verona*, then running as a musical based on Shakespeare. The prize: a weekend at the New York Plaza Hotel, with tickets (and limousine) to two of the current Papp productions, and the record album of the *Verona* musical. Here are the winning entries of the last two mentioned contests:

> If it's management men you pursue
> Don't hunt every beast in the zoo;
>   Just look for the signs
>   That say Tigers and Lions:
> It isn't how many, it's who.

> Dear Joe: Yes, it gives me a thrill
> To hear that *Two Gentlemen* still
>   Can give Broadway a hit.
>   No, I don't mind a bit
> If you changed it. Send royalties.
>   —Will.

The *Verona* verses sound as though they were written to justify the strange ways in which Will's play had been altered. But limericks run merrily on.

The clerihew was the casual production of Edmund Clerihew

Bentley, known also as the author of the mystery *Trent's Last Case*. He was seeking to alleviate the boredom of a chemistry lecture, and jotted down:

> Sir Humphrey Davy
> Abominated gravy.
> He lived in the odium
> Of having discovered sodium.

He grew less bored as he went on, through two volumes of cleri-hews. Americans may appreciate his political observation, of the king from whom they exacted their independence; below it, I set a critical "discovery" of the poet:

> George the Third
> Ought never to have occurred.
> One can only wonder
> At so grotesque a blunder.

> How vigilant was Spenser
> As a literary censor!
> He pointed out that there were too few e's
> In Lyly's Euphues.

After my own third lexicographical venturing, I found myself clerihewed to the line:

> Joseph T. Shipley
> Is a candidate for Ripley.
> Believe it or not, it isn't fictionary;
> He's gradually turning into a dictionary.

Other varieties of verse game have been played. The *cento* (Sanskrit *kantha*, 'patched garment') is a poem made up of lines from existing poems. In the Middle Ages, centos were seriously written, mainly on religious subjects, sometimes with all the lines from one poet, as Homer, Virgil, or Horace, sometimes borrowing widely. Many anthologies provide an index of first lines, which may give the browser food for such fancy. In two minutes with the index of *An Anthology of World Poetry*, just now plucked from my shelf, I found:

> I do not ask, for you are fair,
> How long must we two hide the burning gaze;

> Ay me, alas! the beautiful bright hair—
> Albeit the Venice girls get praise . . .
> As the war-trumpet drowns the rustic flute,
> Be still, be still, nor dare:
> This is a fearful thing to bear.

A longer look at poems themselves would bring much better fare. Pope's couplets, and of course Shakespeare's blank verse, are fertile cento fields.

Perhaps more amusing is Cap-a-Verse. Give a line or two of a poem; ask the group to complete a stanza; see who has the cleverest combination. Two lines of Wordsworth were thus converted into a facetious classroom exercise:

> O Cuckoo! Shall I call thee bird?
> Or just a wandering voice?
> State the alternative preferred
> With reasons for your choice.

The American humorist Richard Armour has—and gives—a lot of fun, in his *Punctured Poems,* with culminate couplets, the first line "famous":

> Beauty is truth, truth beauty—that is all
> Of Keats's poem many can recall.

> "A little learning is a dangerous thing,"
> The dropout muttered, leaving school last spring.

There is a Japanese form, the haiku, consisting of three lines of five, seven, and five syllables, that has been as popular in Japan since the thirteenth century—and as often bawdy—as the much younger limerick in English. It may be used, however, to evoke a quiet mood, and is now given, as a game, to American school children. Here are two that suggest the haiku's flavor:

> A fluttering swarm
> Of cherry petals; there comes,
> Driving them, the storm.

> Bright flowers quiver
> Over a mingled murmur:
> Faces in the crowd.

Thus games, begun in earnest, evolved in play, may end in beauty.

This seems an appropriate place to mention a most common form of word ways, the sometimes humorous but more frequently searching folk wisdom set down in brief and pungent expressions. Cervantes remarked that proverbs are short sentences drawn from long experience. This fruit of the people's gathering has other names: *aphorism, apophthegm, gnome, maxim, adage, saw.* Folk sayings are listed by the thousands in special books in many languages; they lie like a sunken fence, a ha-ha, in the path of any word survey. Here is just a sampling, of some that may give recompense to thought, alms to oblivion:

1. It is the grace of lambs to suckle kneeling.
2. One cloud is enough to hide the sun.
3. However far a bird may fly, it takes its tail along.
4. A straight stick is crooked in the water.
5. Every ass loves to hear himself bray.
6. A black hen lays a white egg.
7. He cannot speak well that cannot hold his tongue.
8. If the beard were all, the goat might preach.
9. In every country, the sun rises in the morning.
10. Living well is the best revenge.
11. Many would be cowards if they had courage enough.
12. The higher the ape goes, the more he shows his tail.
13. The sun is never the worse for shining on a dunghill.
14. Who will not be ruled by the rudder must be ruled by the rock.
15. Necessity is the tyrant's plea.
16. It is hard for an empty bag to stand upright.
17. Pull the child out of the water before you punish it.
18. What is past is prologue.
19. Hurt is the price we pay for feeling.
20. Who cuts his own wood warms himself twice.
21. Manners are the happy way of doing things.
22. It is usually easier to suppress criticism than to meet it.
23. Who speaks evil to you will speak evil of you.
24. The learned man knows the rules; the wise man knows the exceptions.
25. Far east is west.
26. The axis of the earth sticks out visibly through the center of every town.
27. We may give advice, but we cannot give conduct.
28. When you have nothing to say, take less than fifteen minutes.
29. Do not fall in love; rise to it!

30.   When Adam slept, Eve from his side arose;
      Strange his first sleep should be his last repose.

Here are some answers:

The words in Eisenhower are: 1. shrew   2. soiree   3. osier
4. Erewhon 5. hieron 6. ewers 7. seine 8. herse.

Here we let fly the buried birds, in order: tern, merlin, eagle,
dove, daw, raven, red start, crow, swallow, bittern, martin, fulmar,
chat, hummer, thrush, wren, grebe, hawk, linnet, kingfisher,
heron, mallard, puffin, thrasher, gull, finch, ostrich, teal, sand-
piper, ousel, petrel, loon, snipe, nuthatch, rail, owl, diver, kestrel,
jay, grackle, boob, butterball, hen, swift, quail, kite.

Here range the rhopes:

a, at, tan, rant, train, rating, darting, drafting
I, it, tie, diet, tired, direct, cordite, doctrine, reduction, introduces,
      destruction
a, at, rat, tear, trade, parted, tapered, repeated, desperate
a, an, ran, rain, train, strain, retains, trainers, restrains, transpires
a, an, ran, rain, grain, rating, granite, integral, faltering, flattering
I, it, tie, rite, inter, retain, certain, reaction, cremation, importance
I, in, gin, ring, grins, resign, serving, severing, reversing, preserv-
      ing, persevering
a, at, ate, tear, trace, create, reacted, decorate, decorated
O, on, ton, torn, thorn, throne, hornets, shortens, shortness

From Chapter 6, the anagrams: Roast Mules turn a somersault.
Just one Roast Mule makes emulators.
Go thou and do likewise.

14.

THOUGHT VERSUS FEELING

HOW SHALL WE most effectively put our thoughts into words? The Elizabethans, and the century after, knew the value of simple terms, Anglo-Saxon monosyllables; but also the wisdom of varying them with lengthier words, which were then being introduced from the classical tongues. Thus Shakespeare could say, in *The Winter's Tale,* "Then comes in the sweet of the year," but also (Macbeth after Duncan's murder):

> No! This my hand will rather
> The multitudinous seas incarnadine,
> Making the green one red.

He knew also the power in punching home an abstraction with a concrete image, as when old Adam in *As You Like It* complains of his lot:

> And unregarded age   in corners thrown.

Milton (as many more) was also efficient in both these ways. In two successive lines of iambic pentameter he uses, first ten words, then three:

> Rocks, caves, lakes, fens, bogs, dens, and shades of death,
> Immutable, immortal, infinite.

And he too could bring an abstraction alive in a vivid phrase:

> Laughter   holding both her sides.

In the next century, however, called the Augustan Age because of its quest of the Roman classical style under Augustus Caesar, with Cicero the chief model, there was a greater emphasis on abstraction and personification, with an accompanying trend away from the monosyllable. Pope mocked the prior practice:

And ten low words oft creep in one dull line.

And Swift in *The Tatler* exclaimed: Monosyllables are the disgrace of our land.

The Romantics broke free of these patterns; but their rebellion ran off in all directions. Some, like Scott, revived old Saxon terms, or like James Macpherson pretended translations, as of the legendary Gaelic poet Ossian; while nonliterary gentlemen erected "ruins" in their gardens, like the freshly viewed ruins of Greek and Roman architecture. In 1810 the Elgin marbles were brought from the Parthenon to England; Byron called the Earl of Elgin a rapacious vandal, but he and others flavored their works with rhapsodies over the isles of Greece, or sought the farther Orient. This practice has continued with the poets of our century. T. S. Eliot, who emphasized tradition, ends *The Waste Land* with Sanskrit. Not only poetic forms but fashions (as of delicate evocation of natural objects) have been drawn from the Far East.

About the middle of the nineteenth century, however, reacting from the looseness of the Romantics, there came a quest for precision, for the exact word to fit the fact and the feeling; what Flaubert called *le mot juste*. Pater said that one should find, "for every lineament of the vision within, the one acceptable word." "The right word in the right place" was offered as a definition of style. To test your own preciseness, to the sentence "He took the proffered cup" add the word *only* in six different places, then see whether you can discern the subtle distinction each different position imparts.

The search for exactitude has continued into our time. T. S. Eliot made the mistake of transferring the ineluctable quest of the writer to an evocation in the receptor, in a frequently quoted prescription:

The only way of expressing emotion in art is by finding an *objective correlative;* in other words, a set of objects, a situation, a chain of events, which shall be the *formula* of that particular emotion; such that when the external facts are given, the emotion is immediately evoked.

Eliot's prominence lent authority to this declaration, but it is roundly wrong. It assumes that there is only one way of rousing a particular emotion, whereas it is the writer's boon that there are many devices, one fortifying another, to deepen the same effect. And it overlooks the fact that the same expression may evoke different responses in different receptors, because of their varying backgrounds and previous verbal association. The far-fetched evening-surgery simile that opens *The Love Song of J. Alfred Prufrock*, one might say the most notorious figure in all T. S. Eliot's verses, is challenged by his fellow-poet-and-critic, C. S. Lewis:

> For twenty years I've tried my level best
> To see if evening—any evening—would suggest
> A patient etherised upon a table.
> —In vain. I simply wasn't able.

While some were thus seeking the holy grail of the inevitable, imperishable phrase, others were equally determined to tear the language to pieces and start over again from scratch. The dadaists devoted themselves to the dissolution of the word. They ripped current expressions apart, to separate the elements of which they are composed, perhaps to revive the basic sense, or to wrest them to new meanings. Such a term as French *société anonyme*, for example, *S.A.*, which at the end of a name is equivalent to English *Ltd.* and American *Inc.*, may be used once more as an anonymous society, such as a cell of Communists or neo-Nazis or guerrillas. The dadaists were followed by the surrealists, who demanded that writing be automatic, without the stultifying influence of the mind. Write expressions on cards, then shuffle them, and deal your product. Put down whatever pops into your head; "as soon as thought intrudes, start over, beginning with an *M*."

I possess a "Language Box," with a different word on each side of 345 cards, and five blank cards for one's own idiosyncrasies. I have just shuffled these, and dealt myself two hands of five cards each. The first, as the words came, reads "warship mercy calendar anchor pudding"—which may be wrung to fancied significance. The second—"paralyze slap stridulate ewe quarter"—I donate to the surrealists. "Why with an M?" said Alice. "Why not?" said the March Hare. In that part of the forest, they were all mad.

Edward Albee says that his plays are "meant to be taken into the unconscious almost directly, without being filtered through the brain cells." Actors and critics have succumbed to the snare. The two stars of Pinter's *No Man's Land* seemed a bit wary. John Gielgud and Ralph Richardson discussed the play in an interview published in *The New York Times* of November 7, 1976, two days before it opened on Broadway. To them it is a "non-story play," with but "suggestions of meaning." Sir John elaborated:

> "There's enough of the conventional theatre in *No Man's Land* for people to expect that there really will be a story—and then they feel rather—swindled when they haven't got a story at the end. . . . This play is very black. If you can't laugh at *No Man's Land,* you can go out feeling very gloomy. I think it's a very black comedy, that's what I think. Of course, they're all horrid people. I wouldn't want to meet them on a dark night, any of them; would you, Ralph?"
> "Jolly right, Johnny," said Ralph.

We are offered plays with lost stories, about people with lost souls.

Brooks Atkinson had earlier gone astray with Samuel Beckett, calling his play "A mystery wrapped in an enigma. *Waiting for Godot* is all feeling. Perhaps that's why it is puzzling and convincing at the same time." Puzzling *and* convincing? Quite a feat! Unfortunately, he neglected to tell of what he was convinced. Macaulay's remark on Samuel Johnson's *Lives of the Poets* seems pertinent: "At the very least, they mean something, a praise to which much of what is called criticism in our time has no pretensions."

Joyce's *Ulysses* is less a novel than an exploration of the possibilities and limits of language; his *Finnegans Wake* overruns those bounds. When Ezra Pound, who had encouraged the earlier book, saw the Finnegan manuscript, he wrote to Joyce: "Unless you have found a new cure for the clap, or evidence of the Second Coming, nothing in the world is worth all this circumambient peripherization."

Occasionally, within Joyce's verbal manipulations and prestidigitations, one can find food for thought. Thus "We may come, touch and go, from atoms to ifs," reminds us of our coming—Adam and Eve—and suggests our exploration in the infinitesimal range of the metaphysical and in the future, which the unleashed atoms have rendered insecure. And Joepeter for Jupiter at once summons and dethrones the gods. But much of the first book, and more of the second, present a guessing game, for which a small band of devoted acolytes seeks and disputes solutions, while the general reader dips in, wets the toes of his curiosity, and retreats to dry ground, in awe or blessed relief, from a veritable maelstrom of intertangled words.

It must not be thought, however, that obscurity of language is the proud monopoly of our own day. Writers have long been urged to be concise, to avoid what Dickens called the Circumlocution Office, to say what they have to say—and stop. Brevity, we are told, is the soul of wit. Yet the Roman poet Horace, the chief classical model of lyric poets since, complained: "I labor to be brief, and grow obscure." More often with the very opposite method, obscurity has had many practitioners in every time. When Browning's book-length poem *Sordello* was published, it was said that the only lines one could understand were the first and the last, and they were both lies. They are:

> Who will, may hear Sordello's story told....
> Who would, has heard Sordello's story told.

George Eliot admitted, however, that "in Browning's best poems he makes us feel that what we took for obscurity in him was superficiality in ourselves." Today it is not earlier writers, but our contemporary poets, whose "obscurity" is often troublesome.

One of the chief reasons for the difficulty felt in reading much current poetry lies in the changed use of the metaphor, where more is meant than meets the eye. The older metaphor had two clearly visible elements, which have been called the tenor and the vehicle: the basic term (say, Richard) and its identification with something in another field (the Lion-hearted). Thus when Hugo speaks of "the fleece of the sinister sheep of the sea," the last word points out for us the rounded waves, with their whitecaps whipped up by the threatening storm. But modern poets often omit the tenor, giving us only the figurative part, for which we must ourselves find the basis. Thus when Valéry begins a poem

> This tranquil roof, where pigeons peck,
> Vibrates between the pines, between the tombs

we must look back to the title, "Marine Cemetery," to figure out that the pigeons are the distant sailboats dipping with the waves of the water.

This is not all. For in the usual metaphor there are several points the two parts have in common. "She's a peach!" You see the pink and cream complexion; almost you touch the soft smoothness, taste the sweet; truly there is ample reason to delight in the figure. But when you read "the skylight of a hypothesis," there is but one point of identification; if you do not find this, the figure fails. And often it does, as with Eliot's etherised patient. "White birches of disaster capped with gold" makes the receptor work hard. And when Theodore Roethke writes "Her quick look, a sidelong pickerel smile," it seems a fishy figure.

Yet there is more. For sometimes the figure is not intended to awaken an image in the reader. It may be purely personal to the poet. Edith Sitwell wrote "With eyes like Mary's when she smiled": asked which of the three (Biblical) Marys she meant, Dame Sitwell replied that she was thinking of a maid the family had when she was a child. Or a figure may be fashioned without any association, purely for pictorial or emotional effect, as when e. e. cummings declares that the moon "shook like a piece of angry candy," or Edith Sitwell looks

> Upon your wood-wild April-soft long hair
> That seems the rising of spring constellations—
> Aldebaran, Procyon, Sirius.

Picture long hair as a seasonal celestial rising; then consider that not one of the three bright stars named is a constellation, and you see some of the problems you face in modern poetry.

Two other forms of metaphor, more fundamental and more permanent, may here be mentioned. An allegory, which ranges from a brief fable to a long poem or novel, is defined as the expression by means of fictional figures of generalizations about human life; it is in form an extended metaphor, the entire work to be translated into meaning for men's daily concerns. As Chesterton observes: "Every great literature has always been allegorical— allegorical of some view of the universe. The *Iliad* is only great because all life is a battle; the *Odyssey* because all life is a journey; the *Book of Job* because all life is a riddle."

"All life" being many things, there may be observed in all literature, of many lands and many times, certain recurrent images that seem to capture a basic aspect of man's relationship with the other forces of the universe. Such a figure is called an archetypal or root metaphor; and to recognize the wide use of one will broaden the receptor's understanding both of the work in which he finds it and of the world. When we read in Blake:

> I give you the end of a golden string,
> Only wind it into a ball;
> It will lead you in at heaven's gate
> Built in Jerusalem's wall.

—we may trace the image in Dante and the Bible; in Plato's "one golden cord" to which we human puppets should cling, for (as Homer tells) Zeus draws all things to him by a golden cord. And—with the spread through more than two millennia—we can find the same figure in Islamic, Hindu, and Chinese contexts. Entwined in this figure is the rosary, the necklace; in the *Bhagavad Gita* we are told of Krishna that "all things are strung on Him like rows of gems on a thread." The thread or cord is spun and cut by the Fates; it is used for rescue by Ariadne and for defiance by Arachne; it is still worn by Parsi and by Jew. The Sanskrit *sutra*, which means a holy maxim, literally means a thread. The sacred cord, as worn by the high caste Hindu, is an external symbol of the Sutratma, the spiritual thread that binds all things. J. E. Cirlot, in his *Dictionary of Symbols* (1962, 1973), points out that the stripes, sashes, bands, and ribbons worn by soldiers and officials, and even the necktie, are emblems of cohesion and binding. Wearing a shirt without a tie signifies that one has (for the time) broken free of the formal ties of the community.

Professor Teufelsdröckh (German, 'Devil's Dung') would have smiled at this, out of Carlyle's *Sartor Resartus* (Latin, 'The Tailor Retailored', 1833); for his main point is that symbols, forms, indeed human institutions, are as clothes: worn for a time, outworn, then changed. This is true of the symbols in most common use: such terms as "Quisling" and "Watergate," scuffed in their crowded days, are soon lost memories. "The Mississippi Bubble," "Teapot Dome," are now seen only in history books. "Achilles' heel" seldom kicks up today in casual conversation. Some basic symbols, however, are longer lasting and more pervasive. Carl Jung states that they are inherited from our remote ancestors and unconsciously present in us all.

Obscurity likewise persists. Basic human drives may be pictured in less fathomable ways. Gertrude Stein, who wrote after studying the utterances of asylumed patients, in her opera *Four Saints in Three Acts* achieved a reversal of the usual mode of writing. An author will normally seek to express an idea, with accordant overtones of patterned sound; Gertrude Stein has written patterns of sound, with merely overtones of accordant sense. Sound, as we have noted, may be the more foreboding the less it is understood.

Obscurity has in every period provoked multiform protests. Coleridge, for example, is pictured in Peacock's *Nightmare Abbey* (1818) as Mr. Flosky, who talks transcendentalism to a young lady, until she interrupts:

"Will you oblige me, Mr. Flosky, by giving me a plain answer to a plain question?" "It is impossible, my dear Miss O'Carroll. I never gave a plain answer to a question in my life. . . . To say that I do not know, would be to say that I am ignorant of some thing; and God forbid that a transcendental metaphysician, who has anticipated cognitions of every thing, and carries the whole system of geometry in his head without ever having looked into Euclid, should fall into so empirical an error as to delcare himself ignorant of any thing: to say that I *do* know would be to pretend to positive and circumstantial knowledge touching present matter of fact, which, when you consider the nature of evidence, and the various lights in which the same thing can be seen—"

"I see, Mr. Flosky, that either you have no information, or you have determined not to impart it." [She has asked if he knows where her boy friend is.]

"My dear Miss O'Carroll, it would have given me great pleasure to have said any thing that would have given you pleasure; but if any living person could make report of having obtained any information on any subject from Ferdinand Flosky, my transcendental reputation would be ruined for ever."

Byron, in *Don Juan,* joined more directly in the charge:

> And Coleridge, too, has lately taken wing,
> Explaining metaphysics to the nation.—
> I wish he would explain his explanation . . .
> And he who understood it would be able
> To add a storey to the Tower of Babel.

More generally, Leigh Hunt estimated such obfuscation: "All this astonishes the galleries; they are persuaded that it must be something fine, because it is so important and so unintelligible, and they clap for the sake of their own reputations." Swinburne is even more blunt, in his verse parody "The Higher Pantheism in a Nutshell":

> Fiddle, we know, is diddle, and diddle, we take it, is dee.

A generation later, W. S. Gilbert found it pertinent to repeat the idea, in *Patience:*

> The meaning doesn't matter if it's only idle chatter
> Of a transcendental kind. . . .
> And every one will say, as you walk your mystic way,
> If this young man expresses himself in terms too deep for me,

Why, what a singularly deep young man this deep young man
    must be!

Today, there seems a crying need for an unaffected spirit to cry
that the Emperor is wearing no clothes!

Harold Pinter, says J. L. Styan, "has been digging over the
territory newly claimed by the absurdists. . . . He practices a new
illogicality, yet one pregnant with the logic of feeling that belongs
to the subtextual world of tragicomedy." Such statements merely
compound the confusion.

It would be a joy, amid the clouded notions that afflict much
talk about modern writing, to find a lass like Austin Dobson's
Phyllida:

> The ladies of St. James's,
> You scarce can understand
> The half of all their speeches,
> Their phrases are so grand;
>
> But Phyllida, my Phyllida,
> Her shy and simple words
> Are clear as after raindrops
> The music of the birds.

A *rara avis* indeed, these difficult days! The very memory seems
archaic.

There is no doubt, because of the limits of one's command of
the language and the different associations different persons
attach to the same words, that some ambiguity will shroud many
statements. Some scholars, like Empson, find this at times an
advantage, and in literature it occasionally well may be. When
Lady Macbeth, told that the King is on his way to her castle,
says "He that's coming Must be provided for," the audience may
hear, beneath the polite remark, the sinister implication. In *Hamlet* Shakespeare wrote:

> In the dead wast and middle of the night

and critics still argue whether he meant *vast, waste, waist,* or indeed all three.

In science and in legal documents, ambiguity is not often advantageous; one should heed the counsel never to be ambiguous
—unintentionally. Fielding in his *Journey from This World to the
Next* puts emphatic words into the mouth of Shakespeare:

Certainly the greatest and most pregnant beauties are ever the plainest and most evidently striking; and when two meanings of a passage can in the least balance our judgment which to prefer, I hold it a matter of unquestionable certainty that neither of them is worth a farthing.

Of course, amphibology is an accepted device in literature; when Macbeth is told that he is safe from harm until Birnam Wood comes to Dunsinane, we wait to learn how the charm will be counteracted.

Life, in the meantime, with the world changing from candle-power and the midnight oil to gas illumination then various forms of electric light, has afforded us no increasing clarity as to our proper purposes and goals or—to those that do envisage man's ultimate harbor—any agreement as to the smoothest avenue of approach to that happy ending. Our skill in making things has found ever more effective tools, especially for speeding up our journeys toward mass slaughter; but our wisdom has not grown proportionately, to guide us in peaceful, humane use of our inventive powers.

The growth of science and technology has, in fact, had three somewhat disturbing, and opposed, effects in the range of the present discussion. It has increased the difficulty of communication, by the introduction of new and troublesome expressions to capture the new and complex inventions and techniques. At the same time, it has multiplied the spread and the influence of communication: more persons around the world may hear and see a single broadcast than have attended every performance of *Hamlet* since Shakespeare first loomed as the ghost onstage. And it has given the average citizen more emphasis in his remark: "I have a right to my opinion." Has he? Not if he overlooks the obligation to seek a proper basis, before expressing an opinion. The only opinion worth holding or hearing is an informed opinion. There is no royal road to geometry. The earlier princeling might neglect his lessons, secure in the fact that there was a whipping-boy to take the punishment for his negligencies or mistakes; but today it is the people themselves that must pay for their ignorant blunders. The public may select a scapegoat, as in the years following the 1929 financial crash it labeled the makeshift shanty-towns of the crowding poor after the President, Hooverville; but the people cannot escape the pain. Our own ignorance tumbles its disasters upon our heads.

Unfortunately, it seems sometimes true that the less one knows, the louder he proclaims his opinions. As the English Prime Minister Harold Macmillan said: "I have never found, in a long experience of politics, that criticism is ever inhibited by ignorance."

Here is a distinction too seldom noted: *ignorance* means 'not knowing something one should reasonably be expected to know'; 'not knowing something one cannot be reasonably expected to know' is *nescience*. A wise man recognizes that his knowledge is like a bonfire burning in the night: the farther it extends its circle of light, the greater (by $2\pi r$) is the spread of the surrounding darkness. Nescience is inevitable, ignorance can be overcome.

Chief among the traps set for the unwary public is what has been called the fallacy of communication: the use of terms to arouse emotion, regardless of their proper sense. "The People's Democratic Republic" today covers more than one despotism. Emerson, at the time of the 1850 Compromise, said: "The word *liberty* in the mouth of Webster is like the word *love* in the mouth of a courtesan." This use of a seemingly factual term to disguise an emotional attitude is a dangerous form of obfuscation. Profundity may be unavoidable, for it resides in the substance; obfuscation is unforgivable, for it lies in the expression. It marks the difference between the pretentious and the profound. Yet specialists in various fields seem often unable to say simple things in uncomplicated phrases. Referring to the trail of Freud, Josephine Tey in *Miss Pym Disposes* declares that "one cannot talk about psychology in anything but jargon, there being no English for most of it." Edward Pessen, Distinguished Professor of History at the City University of New York, stated in a *Times* Op-Ed article:

> Some practitioners of the "new histories" of our era appear to delight in using a "language" incomprehensible not only to students and general readers but to most of their fellow historians as well.

Dr. Howard M. Spiro, after an ironic allowance that simple terms may be carried to an extreme, cautions his colleagues:

> Of course, one can go too far with plain English. I once asked a professor of physiology at Yale to let me examine his belly, and for all the animus he thereafter showed, I might as well have asked in three letters to look at his fundament.
>
> Plain, solid, sensible English is what physicians should learn to write, pewter and not silver, stainless steel and not aluminum. We should write, rewrite and then rewrite again, and then once more, and then again after that.

—Good advice to most writers in any field! I wish I could show you all the versions and variations of this material, before I passed it on to be typed.

Those that have examined successive issues of the Russian Encyclopedia, or the contrasted stories of a conflict in the books of the opposing nations involved, will agree that much school history consists of "rite words in rote order."

Spurred by the reports and recommendations that reach his desk, President John W. Kneller of Brooklyn College prepared an "Instant Jargon Generator." It consists of three columns of nine words each. Select three digits at random, say 2, 8, 3; choose the words thus numbered in the successive columns, and you have "Behavioral Communication Assessment," a resounding title for a jargonade. Gershon Legman has gone further, in his FARK. (Folklore Article Reconstruction Kit) proffering four columns of ten phrases each. Select, say 7, 4, 8, 2: "Based on my own fieldwork in Guatemala/ initiation of basic charismatic subculture development/ recognizes the importance of other disciplines, while taking into account/ the anticipated epistemological repercussions." Legman boasts that the Kit will enable any Folklore Ph.D. who can count up to ten, to create "40,000 new and meaningful, well-balanced, and grammatically acceptable sentences packed with Folklore terms," with more difficult ones for those "bucking for tenure in Anthropology." He offers similar kits in other fields: BARK. for Biophysics; SARK., Sociology; LARK., Linguistics, with more on special demand.

English professors, who should know better, are by no means exempt from earnest jargon; indeed, when they really try they can make their gobbledegoop even more atrocious. Consider this: "The belief that no verse is a discussion of a topic, for example, death, but an epistemological, verbal, event in which the reader's reality is affected has been more than contiguous."

A book devoted to attacking the current "pollution" of language, called on the jacket a "devastating and witty analysis of what is happening to words," may be expected to show in its own writing a high regard for English. Yet Geoffrey Wagner's *On the Wisdom of Words* (1968) seems to approve of the permissive dictionary, *Webster's Third,* and scorns the books on good usage. Professor Wagner is, indeed, so scornful of good usage as to employ verbs that do not agree with their subject. Singular subject, plural verb: "A parody of the machine civilization destroying itself, in Jean Tinguely's self-consuming engine, or as in the 'computers' devised by the British cartoonist Emmett, were long anticipated by

Chaplin in *Modern Times.*" "The effect of continual technological euphemism—since such provide hard words..." (The
Professor, throughout, prefers *such* to *this.*) Plural subject, singular verb: "The inexorable demands of the industrial system, with
its 'mandate' for unbridled competition, commercializes sex and
does so by trading off the ambiguities introduced into love."

A footnote in Wagner's book informs us: "Callipygean is another
euphemism for beautifully buttocked... Still another is pygophiliac." The widely informed Professor is of course aware that
pygophiliac means, rather, '(one) fond of the buttocks'. It is not
the Professor's knowledge of Greek, but his heedlessness of English, that is in question. Among his quotations, Professor Wagner
reminds us of a remark in Jane Austen's *Northanger Abbey:* "I
cannot speak well enough to be unintelligible." It does not follow
that every unintelligible utterance is well spoken. Try this not
unrepresentative statement from Professor Wagner's book: "To
set individual words in a unitary mold at odds with the parts of
speech of which it is composed is the characteristic afflatus of
technological office today, and represents a serious breach of
personality." Perhaps the Professor was so busy running down
others' English that he did not pause to ponder his own.

This should more than suffice of Professor Wagner, but Shakespeare has been so woven into this book, and into my days, that I
am impelled to question two references to his works by the ardent
Professor. Speaking of 'fanny' and 'derriere', he adds: "what a
Shakespearean character forever euphemized as the 'afternoon' of
the body." Later, he speaks of "alphabetical poems, where each
succeeding line begins with the next letter (Shakespeare hiding
an obscenity in one such)." Both Eric Partridge, author of the
standard survey of *Shakespeare's Bawdy,* and the Reference
Librarian of the Folger Shakespeare Library, in Washington, con-
firm my belief that neither of these exists in Shakespeare. Armado's
statement, in *Love's Labor's Lost,* promising to return "in the
posteriors of this day, which the rude multitude call the afternoon," can hardly be twisted to justify the first claim. And Shakespeare wrote no alphabetical poem. Malvolio's identification, in
Twelfth Night, of certain letters of the alphabet as by Olivia's
hand, hardly hides the taboo word, but is neither alphabetical
nor versified. Apparently the Professor, fulminating against language misuse by others, can himself both read and write awry.

Here are three writers in the very field of word ways.

Kenneth Burke in *A Grammar of Motives* (1945) tells that he
has planned a three-volume study of "a pentad of terms as a

generating principle." What is this propelling pentad? "Act, scene, agent, agency, purpose." For years and years before there were courses in journalism, every reporter knew there were five things he must ask, to get a full story: What, Where, Who, How, Why.

Philip Wheelwright, in *The Burning Fountain* (1954) presents a new term, *plurisignation:* when the meaning of a symbol "is a tension between two or more directions of semantic stress"— which means a play on words; specifically, a pun.

Arthur Koestler, in *The Act of Creation* (1964), also presents a new term: *bisociation of matrices:* "a linkage of previously separated fields or forms in a fruitful conjunction." Break through that alliterative f.f.f and you find that he has described—a metaphor. So do the strivings for novelty set a mask over an age-old idea.

Aristotle long ago observed: "Strange words simply puzzle us; ordinary words convey only what we know already; it is from metaphor that we can best get hold of something fresh." And recently I. A. Richards called metaphor "the omnipresent principle of language." But we need no strange words to keep us in touch with timeless thoughts.

In the second century, Tertullian said that Christianity is to be believed because it is absurd. In the twentieth century, Albert Camus declared: "The absurd is the essential concept and the first truth." Whether or not it is the first truth, it may be the last resort of embarrassed politicians. Try to decipher this sentence:

> Cooperation, with due regard to the different levels of economic development, can be developed on the basis of equality and mutual satisfaction of the partners and of reciprocity, permitting, as a whole, an equitable distribution of advantages and obligations of comparable scale, with respect for bilateral and multilateral agreements.

To what did they pledge themselves, the thirty-five heads of sovereign states of our wonderful world, who put their names to this rigmarole in the Helsinki Document of August 1, 1975?

Some writers seem to think that thought is to be avoided. Thus Nobel Prize-winner Saul Bellow warns readers against indulging in the luxury of "deep reading and symbol-mongering, lest they prove guilty of preferring meaning to feeling." Clive Barnes had a similar aberrant moment when he wrote, reviewing Pinter's *Old Times:* "The intensity of the writing makes too much concentration on it almost dangerous." "Too much" is always excessive; but how much is too much? Should we not be always fully alert, ready and eager for the fresh experience that is a new work of art? Dangerous—to whom? To the author, in that consideration might reveal the poverty of his intellect, the niggling scratches of his mind? The only danger to the receptor is disappointment, that the work does not sufficiently challenge the talents he brings to the mutual trans-action, the absorption of the artist's gift into the receptor's spirit. We do not go to a work of art to suck a lollipop, or chew gum.

Clive Barnes moved from his remark about too much concentration to some pretty figures about Pinter's workmanship, such as "Silence falls upon silence like rose petals pretending to be a snow storm." Ted Kalem, writing in *Time* magazine of the same quality in the same play, eschews similes for muted metaphor: "His famous pauses seem to be toothless gaps in the text." It is hard to pin Pinter to specific significance.

It is difficult, at times, to tell whether nonsense is unwitting or intentional. Surely the writer of the following gobbledegoop must have no sense of humor, or else tongue in cheek: "Pronouns are determinants in anaphoric noun phrases, which are themselves nominalizations of parts of the linguistic environment."

While some find it an interesting game to fill a column, or a book, with examples of obfuscatory or befuddled prose, the pompous outpouring of bureaucrap, it may be more fruitful to examine the reasons of those that deliberately render their wording difficult to grasp, so as to extract significance. I recently directed my talk to this end, in a conversation with a noted critic, novelist, and professor of English—whom I will not name, because it is unfair to hear one and judge two, and because it is the general consideration and not the particular man I wish to examine. The arguments are representative of the two points of view.

I asked him why he wrote prose so hard to understand. He replied that life is too complicated for our grasping, too confused for clarity. The artist must present this confusion, the disorder and the anguish of the soul. I responded that art is an act of creation, which implies the formation of cosmos out of chaos. It is the function of the creator, within seeming confusion, to discern and to make visible the order and the form. One can show confusion without confusing, as one can portray a bore (Polonius) without boring.

He then said that routine writing tends to slip into a groove; the expected form leads to a lapse of attention. He therefore shifts the rhythms, uses unexpected phrases and turns of syntax, that demand constant concentration, that catch the mind back from drowsing. I told him that I like to be kept heedful by subtleties of thought and felicities of expression, apt terms and turns of phrases; not to play a guessing game with syntax and semantics. I promised not to fall asleep over Shakespeare, again and again, nor with any book that makes a legitimate, not a spurious riddling claim to my attention. Words that allow one to slip into a groove of habit replacing thought, and words that, per contra, draw attention to themselves, equally divert the proper flow of the work of art.

More brusquely, he said. "That's the way it comes to me, and that's the way I set it down. It's the expression of my personality." I did not reply that his personality *n'intéresse que maman*, but pointed out that most writers weigh what pops into their minds, refining it, seeking to make it more precise, subjecting the spontaneous leap of the spirit to the salutary leaven of thought.

My last word gave him new ammunition. He stated that some works, many works today, aim not at the stimulation of thought but at the quickening of feelings. They need not be understood to be potent. One attempt of modern drama, as of rock music, is actually to "overload," to pound upon the nerves and rouse raw feelings. It seeks catathymia, an anoetic effect, of feeling without thought, approaching the acme of behavior based entirely on the passions.

—And this is indeed the crux of the matter, the fundamental challenge of the destroyers of the word. For all sound rouses feeling. Not just music, not just *Waiting for Godot;* but all sound. The rumble of thunder or distant cannon fire, the whimper of a dog, the rustle of a dress or of wind-stirred leaves, the calls and cries of men: all sounds evoke accordant feelings. Words have an added function: they mean. Words lift man, with sound and feeling, beyond sound and feeling to symbol and sense. And to control. Control of the very feelings that these subversive works seek to arouse. This is indeed why Plato banned poets from his ideal Republic. For—except in incidental accordance, adornment, and byplay—every retreat of words from this man-found and man-only function is a hurtling of language back towards the howl.

Here is the dividing of the ways, the "great divide," on one side of which words flow through verdant pastures of wisdom; on the other, through the canyons and swamps of sheer overpowering passion. Writers have taken their stand on either side. D. H. Lawrence said that he distrusted any decision that did not come from the guts; Disraeli before him stated that man is truly great only when he acts on the spur of passion. Plato, as just indicated, saw that feelings have no place in the council chamber. Fielding spoke of the "fantastic and capricious behavior of the passions." Oscar Wilde smiled at the problem, serenely finding gain where others saw loss: "The advantage of the emotions is that they lead us astray."

It is the current fashion to favor feeling. Yet there is no denying the issue. Thomas Fuller, chaplain to the pleasure-loving King Charles II, pressed home the essential point: "When passion entereth at the fore-gate, wisdom goeth out at the postern."

Words do not merely sound, they speak. We are *homo sapiens* because we are supremely *homo loquens*, speaking man. In art, words are eloquent. In great art, they provide the closest we have come to a reason for our centuries' endeavor. Man's best achievements with his word ways, framing his science, fashioning his art, enabling his wisdom, alone justify his claim to be the highest form of life on what his untamed feelings, his fears and sequent greeds, have made a precarious planet. To preserve it, and us, wisdom must prevail. Wisdom, like most things human, works through words.

SUGGESTED
FURTHER READING

The number in parenthesis indicates the chapter of major relevance. Books sufficiently identified in the text are not repeated here.

Anderson, Donald M., *The Art of Written Forms*, 1909 (7)
Armour, Richard, *On Your Marks*, 1969 (7)
Asimov, Isaac, *Words of Science*, 1959 (4)
———, *Words on the Map*, 1962 (4)

Babcock, C. Merton, ed., *The Ordeal of American English*, 1961 (3)
Barber, Charles, *Linguistic Change in Present-Day English*, 1964 (4)
Barnett, Lincoln, *The Treasure of Our Tongue*, 1965 (2)
Barthes, Roland, *Critical Essays*, 1964 (11)
———, *Writing Degree Zero*, 1967 (11, 14)
Baugh, Albert C., *A History of the English Language*, 1971 (2)
Bayley, Harold, *The Lost Language of Symbolism*, 1912, 1951, (12)
Bentley, Eric, *The Life of the Drama*, 1964 (11)
Black, Max, ed., *The Importance of Language*, 1962 (1, 5)
Bloomfield, Leonard, *Language*, 1933 (5)
Bolinger, Dwight, *Aspects of Language*, 1975 (5)
Borgmann, Dmitri A., *Language on Vacation*, 1965 (13)
Boyd, C. C., *Grammar for Grown-Ups*, 1927 (5)
Brooks, Peter, *The Melodramatic Imagination*, 1976 (11)
Brown, Roland W., *Composition of Scientific Words*, 1954 (4)
Brustein, R., *The Theatre of Revolt*, 1962 (11)
Bryer, P. S., *Purity in Print*, 1968 (9)
Burke, W. J., *The Literature of Slang*, 1939 (8)

Cane, Melville, *Making a Poem*, 1953 (10)
Chafe, Wallace L., *Meaning and the Structure of Language*, 1970, 1975 (5)
Coblentz, Stanton A., *The Poetry Circus*, 1967 (10, 14)
Cohen, Morris Raphael, *A Preface to Logic*, 1944 (10)
———, *Reason and Nature*, 1931 (10)
Collingwood, R. G., *Speculum Mentis*, 1924 (1)
———, *The Principles of Art*, 1955 (10)
Cottle, Basil, *The Plight of English*, 1975 (5)
Cowan, D. A., *Mind Underlines Space-Time*, 1976 (12)

Culler, Jonathan, *Structuralist Poetics*, 1975 (10)
Curme, George O.; Kurath, H., *A Grammar of the English Language*, 1931 (5)
Curry, W. C., *Chaucer and the Medieval Sciences*, 1926, 1960 (12)

Dillard, J. L., *Black English*, 1972 (3)
———, *All-American English*, 1975 (3)
———, *American Talk*, 1976 (3)
Diringer, David, *The Alphabet*, 1948 (7)
Dohan, Mary H., *Our Own Words*, 1975 (2, 3)

Eliade, Mircea, *Occultism, Witchcraft, and Cultural Fashions*, 1975 (12)
Elliott, Robert C., *The Power of Satire*, 1960 (12)
Empson, William, *Seven Types of Ambiguity*, 1949, 1963 (14)
Esslin, M., *The Theatre of the Absurd*, 1962 (12)

Fant, Gunnar, *Speech Sounds and Features*, 1974 (1, 7)
Flood, W. E., *The Origin of Chemical Names*, 1963 (4)
Foster, Bryan, *The Changing English Language*, 1968 (2, 4)
Fowler, Roger, *Understanding Language*, 1974 (5, 14)
Francis, W. Nelson, *The Structure of American English*, 1958 (3)
Franklyn, Julian, *A Dictionary of Rhyming Slang*, 1960 (8)
Fraser, John, *Violence in the Arts*, 1976 (12)
Fryer, Peter, *Mrs. Grundy*, 1963 (9)

Gillette, P. G., *An Uncensored History of Pornography*, 1966 (9)
Gordon, I. A., *The Movement of English Prose*, 1966 (10)
Gowers, Ernest, *The Complete Plain Words*, 1954 (6)
Graves, Robert, *Lars Porsena, or the Future of Swearing*, 1929 (9)
Gray, George B., *Studies in Hebrew Proper Names*, 1896 (3)
Gutke, K. S., *Modern Tragicomedy*, 1966 (11)

Hayakawa, S. I., *Language in Thought and Action*, 1952 (10)
Hook, J. N.; Mathers, E. G., *Modern American Grammar and Usage*, 1956 (5)
Hulbert, James Root, *Dictionaries, English and American*, 1968 (5)
Ihde, Don, *Listening and Voice*, 1976 (7)
Ionesco, Eugene, *Notes and Counter Notes*, 1964 (12)

Jensen, H.; Zirker, Melvin R., *The Satirist's Art*, 1972 (12)
Jespersen, Otto, *Efficiency in Language Change*, 1941 (4)
———, *Essentials of English Grammar*, 1964 (5)
———, *Growth and Structure of the English Language*, 1968 (2)

————, *Logic and Grammar*, 1924 (10)
Johnson, Burgess, *The Lost Art of Profanity*, 1948 (9)
Jones, Louis C., *The Clubs of the Georgian Rakes*, 1942 (9)
Joseph, Sister Miriam, *Shakespeare's Use of the Arts of Language*, 1947 (2)

Kallir, Alfred, *Sign and Design*, 1967 (7, 12)
Kerr, Walter, *How Not to Write a Play*, 1956 (11)
Keyser, Cassius J., *The Meaning of Mathematics*, 1947 (10)
Knelman, Fred H., *1984 and All That*, 1971 (12)
Knuttel, Gerard, *The Letter as a Work of Art*, 1951 (7)
Kökeritz, Helge, *Shakespeare's Pronunciation*, 1953 (7, 9)
Korzybski, Alfred, *Science and Sanity*, 1933 (10)
Krieger, Murray, *Theory of Criticism*, 1975 (11)

Langacker, Ronald W., *Language and Its Structure*, 1968 (5)
Langer, Susanne, *Feeling and Form*, 1953 (10)
————, *Mind*, 1967 (10)
Leech, Geoffrey N., *A Linguistic Guide to English Poetry*, 1969 (10, 14)
————, *Semantics*, 1974 (5)
Legman, Gershon, *The Rationale of the Dirty Joke:* I, 1968; II, 1976 (9)
Levine, Jacob, ed., *Motivation in Humor*, 1969 (12, 13)
Lodge, David, *The Language of Fiction*, 1967 (10, 11)
Lyons, John, *Introduction to Theoretical Linguistics*, 1968 (5)

McCaffrey, Ellen, *Astrology ... in the Western World*, 1942 (12)
Macgregor, Geddes, *A Literary History of the Bible*, 1968 (3)
McKinney, J. P., *The Structure of Modern Thought*, 1971 (1, 5, 14)
McLuhan, Marshall, *The Mechanical Bride*, 1951 (7, 14)
————, *The Gutenberg Galaxy*, 1962 (7, 14)
————, *Understanding Media*, 1973 (7, 12, 14)
Mahood, M. M., *Shakespeare's Word Play*, 1957 (2, 9)
Mander, J., *The Writer and Commitment*, 1961 (12, 14)
Marcus, Stephen, *The Other Victorians*, 1967 (9)
Mathews, Mitford M., *The Beginnings of American English*, 1931 (3)
Mencken, H. L., *The American Language*, 1919, 1936 (3)
————, *Supplements to The American Language*, 1945, 1948 (3)
Menninger, Karl, *Number Words and Number Symbols* (Trans.), 1969 (7)
Monroe, Nellie Eliz., *The Novel and Society*, 1941 (11)
Montagu, Ashley, *The Anatomy of Swearing*, 1967 (9)
Moore, S., *Historical Outlines of English Sounds*, 1951 (1, 2, 7)
Mudd, Kurt P., *Browsing Through Obfuscaland*, 1953 (14)

Nemerov, H. *Poets on Poetry*, 1965 (10)

Newman, Edwin, *Strictly Speaking*, 1974 (5, 14)

———, *A Civil Tongue*, 1976 (5, 14)

Norman, Charles, *Poets on Poetry*, 1962 (10)

Nowottny, Winifred, *The Language Poets Use*, 1962 (10)

Ogden, C. K.; Richards, I. A., *The Meaning of Meaning*, 1923, 1959, (5)

Ogden; Richards; Wood, James, *The Foundations of Aesthetics*, 1925, 1974 (10)

Opie, Iona; Opie, Peter, *The Lore and Language of School Children*, 1959 (8, 13)

Partridge, Eric, *Shakespeare's Bawdy*, 1947, 1968 (9)

———, *Usage and Abusage*, 1947, 1970 (5)

———, *Name Your Child*, 1959, 1968 (3)

———, *Comic Alphabets*, 1961 (7, 13)

———, *You Have a Point There*, 1965 (7)

Pei, Mario, *The Story of the English Language*, 1968 (2)

———, *The World's Chief Languages*, 1946 (1)

Peirce, Charles S., *Essays in the Philosophy of Science*, 1957 (10)

Perrin, Noel, *Dr. Bowdler's Legacy*, 1970 (9)

Peyre, Henri, *The Failure of Criticism*, 1967 (11)

Picard, Raymond, *New Criticism or New Fraud?*, 1965 (11, 12)

Pokorny, Julius, *Indogermanic Etymological Dictionary*, 1969 (4, 5)

Postman, Neil; Weingarten, G.; Moran, T. P., ed., *Language in America*, 1969 (9, 12, 14)

Potter, Simeon, *Language in the Modern World*, 1960 (2, 3)

———, *Changing English*, 1969 (2, 4, 5)

Pyles, Thomas, *Words and Ways of American English*, 1952 (3)

Reichenback, Hans, *From Copernicus to Einstein*, 1942 (12)

Révész, G., *Origins and Prehistory of Language*, 1956 (1)

Roberts, Paul, *Patterns of English*, 1956 (2, 3, 4)

———, *English Syntax*, 1964 (5)

Robinson, Ian, *The Survival of English*, 1975 (2, 4)

Robinson, James Harvey, *The Mind in the Making*, 1921 (5, 10)

Rommetveit, Ragnar, *Words, Meanings, and Messages*, 1968 (5)

Rosner, Joseph, *The Hater's Handbook*, 1965 (9)

Rowse, A. L., *Sex and Society in Shakespeare's Age*, 1975 (9, 12)

Ruby, Lionel, *The Art of Making Sense*, 1954, 1968, (5, 14)

Sagarin, Edward, *The Anatomy of Dirty Words*, 1962 (9)

Savory, Theodore H. *The Language of Science*, 1967 (4, 10)

Schlegel, Friedrich, *Dialogue on Poetry* (Trans.), 1968 (10)

Schumaker, Wayne, *Literature and the Irrational*, 1960, 1966 (12, 14)

Sebeok, Thomas A. ed., *Current Trends in Linguistics*, 1972 (5)

———, *Style in Language*, 1960 (10, 11)

Serjeantson, M. S., *A History of Foreign Words in English*, 1935 (2, 4, 6)

Shannon, Claude E., *A Mathematical Theory of Communication*, 1949 (10, 14)

Sharman, Julian, *A Cursory History of Swearing*, 1884 (9)

Shipley, Joseph T., *Dictionary of Early English*, 1955 (2)

———, *Dictionary of Word Origins*, 1945 (4)

———, Encyclopaedia Britannica, 15th edition, "Word and Letter Games" (13)

———, *Playing with Words*, 1960 (13)

———, *Word Games for Play and Power*, 1962 (13)

———, *Word Play*, 1972 (13)

———, *The Quest for Literature*, 1931 (10, 11, 12, 14)

———, *Trends in Literature*, 1949 (10, 11, 12, 14)

———, ed., Dictionary of World Literary Terms, 1970 (5, 10, 11, 12, 14)

Steiner, George, *After Babel*, 1975 (5)

Stork, F. C.; Widdowson, H. G., *Learning About Linguistics*, 1974 (5)

Strang, Barbara, *A History of the English Language*, 1970 (2)

Styan, J. L., *The Dark Comedy*, 1962, 1968 (11, 12)

Svartengren, S. Hilding, *Intensifying Similes in English*, 1918 (5, 6, 14)

Sypher, Wylie, *Literature and Technology*, 1968 (12, 14)

Thompson, A. R., *The Dry Mock: A Study of Irony in Drama*, 1948 (11, 12)

Thompson, J. A. K., *Irony*, 1926 (12)

Tocqueville, Alexis de, *Democracy in America*, 1835 (3)

Turner, G. W., *Stylistics*, 1973 (5, 10)

Ware, James Redding, *Passing English of the Victorian Era*, 1905, 1973 (3, 8)

Watson, George G., *Literary English Since Shakespeare*, 1970 (3, 10)

Wells, Harry K., *The Failure of Psychoanalysis*, 1963 (10)

Whittemore, K., *From Zero to the Absolute*, 1967 (10)

Wiener, Norbert, *Cybernetics*, 1948 (14)

Wilde, Oscar, *The Decay of Lying; The Critic as Artist*, 1891 (3, 11, 12)

Williams, Joseph M., *The New English*, 1970 (5, 6)

Yaker, H.; Osmond, H; Cheek, E. ed., *The Future of Time*, 1971 (1, 12)

INDEX